Treasury of the True Dharma Eye
Dōgen's *Shōbōgenzō*

Treasury of the True Dharma Eye
Dōgen's *Shōbōgenzō*

Volume VI

The Twelve-Chapter Compilation

An annotated translation
by the Sōtō Zen Text Project

Sōtōshū Shūmuchō
Tokyo

University of Hawai'i Press
Honolulu

© 2023 by Sōtōshū Shūmuchō
The Administrative Headquarters of Sōtō Zen Buddhism
All rights reserved.
Printed in China

Treasury of the True Dharma Eye: Dōgen's *Shōbōgenzō*
Volume VI: The The Twelve-Chapter Compilation

Published in Japan by Sōtōshū Shūmuchō, Tokyo
ISBN: 978-4-911061-00-8

Published for the rest of the world by University of Hawai'i Press, Honolulu

Library of Congress Cataloging-in-Publication Data

Names: Dōgen, 1200–1253, author. | Sōtō Zen Text Project, translator.

Title: Treasury of the true dharma eye : Dōgen's Shōbōgenzō / an
annotated translation by the Sōtō Zen Text Project.

Other titles: Shōbō genzō. English

Description: Honolulu : University of Hawai'i Press, [2024] | Published in
Japan by Sōtōshū Shūmuchō, 2023. | Includes bibliographical
references and index. | Contents: v. 6. The twelve-chapter
compilation

Identifiers: LCCN 2024004760 (print) | LCCN 2024004761 (ebook) | ISBN
9780824899172 (v. 1 ; paperback) | ISBN 9780824899189 (v. 2 ; paperback)
| ISBN 9780824899196 (v. 3 ; paperback) | ISBN 9780824899202 (v. 4 ;
paperback) | ISBN 9780824899219 (v. 5 ; paperback) | ISBN 9780824899226
(v. 6 ; paperback) | ISBN 9780824899233 (v. 7 ; paperback) | ISBN
9780824899240 (v. 8 ; paperback) | ISBN 9780824899257 (paperback) | ISBN
9798880700264 (v. 1 ; pdf) | ISBN 9798880700271 (v. 2 ; pdf) | ISBN
9798880700288 (v. 3 ; pdf) | ISBN 9798880700295 (v. 4 ; pdf) | ISBN
9798880700301 (v. 5 ; pdf) | ISBN 9798880700318 (v. 6 ; pdf) | ISBN
9798880700325 (v. 7 ; pdf) | ISBN 9798880700332 (v. 8 ; pdf)

Subjects: LCSH: Sōtōshū—Doctrines—Early works to 1800.

Classification: LCC BQ9449.D653 E5 2024 (print) | LCC BQ9449.D653 (ebook)
| DDC 294.3/85—dc23/eng/20240318

LC record available at https://lccn.loc.gov/2024004760
LC ebook record available at https://lccn.loc.gov/2024004761

Cover art: Eihei Dōgen Zenji Gyōjōzu scroll, courtesy of Rev. Ōtani Tetsuo
Cover design by Urs App

University of Hawai'i Press books are printed on acid-free paper and meet the
guidelines for permanence and durability of the Council on Library Resources.
Printer-ready copy has been provided by Sōtōshū Shūmuchō

CONTENTS

VOLUME VI

THE TWELVE-CHAPTER COMPILATION

Conventions iii

Abbreviations v

Introduction to the Twelve-Chapter *Shōbōgenzō* 1

T1. The Merit of Leaving Home *Shukke* 出家 3

T2. Receiving the Precepts *Jukai* 受戒 45

T3. The Merit of the Kāṣāya *Kesa kudoku* 袈裟功德 57

T4. Bringing Forth the Mind of Bodhi *Hotsu bodai shin* 發菩提心 .. 111

T5. Offerings to the Buddhas *Kuyō shobutsu* 供養諸佛 131

T6. Refuge in the Treasures of Buddha, Dharma, and Saṃgha
     Kie Buppōsōbō 歸依佛法僧寶 167

T7. Deep Faith in Cause and Effect *Jinshin inga* 深信因果 191

T8. Karma of the Three Times *Sanji gō* 三時業 205

T9. Four Horses *Shime* 四馬 233

T10. The Bhikṣu of the Fourth Dhyāna *Shizen Biku* 四禪比丘 243

T11. One Hundred Eight Gateways to the Illumination of the Dharma
     Ippyakuhachi hōmyō mon 一百八法明門 277

T12. The Eight Understandings of the Great Person
     Hachi dainin gaku 八大人覺 299

Conventions

This publication is an annotated translation, in seven volumes, of one hundred three texts of Dōgen's Japanese *Shōbōgenzō,* plus an additional volume containing an introduction, supplementary notes, appendices, and list of works cited. The translation is based on the edition of the *Shōbōgenzō* published in Kawamura Kōdō 河村孝道, ed., *Dōgen zenji zenshū* 道元禅師全集, vols. 1-2 (Tokyo: Shunjūsha, 1991, 1993), cited herein as DZZ.1 and DZZ.2; volume and page numbers of this edition are noted in braces at the corresponding locations in the translation.

The Japanese text accompanying the translation here follows the punctuation and *kanazukai* of the Kawamura edition; for ease of reference to premodern sources, Kawamura's modern Japanese kanji have been replaced with traditional forms. Also, for ease of reference, the sections into which the texts of the Kawamura edition are divided have been assigned numbers in square brackets by the translators. The translation of Kawamura's longer sections is sometimes broken into separate paragraphs, and transitions to new topics between sections are sometimes marked by a string of asterisks.

Though primarily written in Japanese, the *Shōbōgenzō* includes many passages of Chinese, ranging from long quotations of texts to short phrases inserted into the Japanese sentences. Since this inclusion of Chinese is a prominent linguistic feature of the original texts, the translation seeks to indicate such passages by the use of oblique font. The reader is warned that, given the ubiquity in the Japanese language of expressions adopted from Chinese, the identification of the shorter phrases as Chinese, rather than Japanese, is often rather arbitrary.

Much of the *Shōbōgenzō* is devoted to comment on material in other texts. The translation uses quotation marks to indicate terms and passages on which Dōgen is commenting. Here, again, the reader is warned that the distinction between use and mention can often be difficult to draw.

Sanskrit, Chinese, and Japanese terms appearing in the *Oxford English Dictionary* (3rd edition) are considered to have been adopted into English; other such terms are treated as foreign words and rendered in italics. Romanization of all such terms, whether treated as foreign or English, is given with diacritics.

With some exceptions, Chinese transliterations of Sanskrit terms are rendered as romanized Sanskrit. Indic proper nouns, whether transliterated or translated in the Chinese, are rendered as their presumed originals where possible; the reader is warned that some such reconstructions are unattested and speculative.

The proper noun "Zen" is used in reference to (a) the tradition that Dōgen calls the "buddhas and ancestors," and (b) the Japanese instantiation of that tradition; the Chinese name "Chan" is used in reference to the Chinese instantiation of the tradition.

Romanized readings of the Japanese text given in the notes follow wherever possible the ruby in Kawamura's text; readings not provided by Kawamura are based on *Zengaku daijiten* 禅学大辞典 (1978) and/or Katō Shūkō 加藤宗厚, *Shōbōgenzō yōgo sakuin* 正法眼藏用語索引 (1962).

Citations of T (*Taishō shinshū daizōkyō* 大正新脩大藏經) are from the *SAT Daizōkyō Text Database* (https://21dzk.l.u-tokyo.ac.jp/SAT). Citations of ZZ (*Dainihon zokuzōkyō* 大日本続藏經) are from the *CBETA Hanwen dazangjing* 漢文大藏經 (http://tripitaka.cbeta.org). Citations of KR are from *Kanripo* 漢リポ *Kanseki Repository* (https://www.kanripo.org).

The Kawamura edition provides colophons from several sources, some following the relevant chapter, some in the head notes of the chapter, some in the collation notes (*honbun kōi* 本文校異) for that chapter in the end matter of DZZ.1 and DZZ.2. For the convenience of the reader, this translation collects these colophons (and occasionally others omitted by Kawamura) at the end of each chapter. Colophons without attribution are assumed to have been written by Dōgen.

ABBREVIATIONS

C   Chinese language

DZZ *Dōgen zenji zenshū* 道元禅師全集, Kagamishima Genryū 鏡島元隆 et al., compilers. 7 vols. Tokyo: Shunjūsha, 1988–1993.

ESST *Eihei Shōbōgenzō shūsho taisei* 永平正法眼蔵蒐書大成, Kawamura Kōdō 河村孝道, ed. 27 vols. Tokyo: Taishūkan Shoten, 1974-1982.

J   Japanese language

KR Kanseki Repository (Kanseki Ripo 漢籍リポ). Online: https://www.kanripo.org

M *Dai kanwa jiten* 大漢和辞典, Morohashi Tetsuji 諸橋轍次, ed. 13 vols. (plus 2-vol. supplement). Tokyo: Taishūkan Shoten, 1955-1960.

S   Sanskrit

SCZ *Shōbōgenzō chūkai zensho* 正法眼藏註解全書, Jinbo Nyoten 神保如天 and Andō Bun'ei 安藤文英, eds. 11 vols. Reprint Tokyo: Nihon Bussho Kankōkai, 1956-1957.

SZ *Sōtōshū zensho* 曹洞宗全書. 20 vols. Tokyo: Kōmeisha, 1929-1938.

T *Taishō shinshū daizōkyō* 大正新脩大藏經, Takakusu Junjirō 高楠順次郎 and Watanabe Kaikyoku 渡邊海旭, eds. 100 vols. Tokyo: Daizōkyōkai, 1924–1935.

ZT *Zengaku taikei* 禪學大系. 8 vols. Tokyo: Kokusho Kankōkai, 1952 (orig. publ. 1910-11).

ZTS *Zengaku tenseki sōkan* 禅学典籍叢刊, Yanagida Seizan 柳田聖山 and Shiina Kōyū 椎名宏雄, eds. 12 vols. Kyoto: Rinsen Shoten, 1999-2001.

ZZ *Dainihon zokuzōkyō* 大日本続藏經. 150 vols. Kyoto: Bussho Kankōkai, 1905-1912.

INTRODUCTION TO THE TWELVE-CHAPTER *SHŌBŌGENZŌ*

The *Shōbōgenzō* in twelve chapters (*Jūni kan bon Shōbōgenzō* 十二巻本正法眼藏) is preserved in a manuscript, in three fascicles, owned by Yōkōji 永光寺, the monastery in Ishikawa Prefecture founded by Keizan Jōkin 瑩山紹瑾 (1264–1325). The manuscript, discovered in 1927, represents a copy made in 1446 from a 1420 copy. Only three of the twelve chapters (numbers 3, 9, and 12) have colophons, and only two of these (numbers 3 and 12) are dated.

A version of the twelfth and final chapter of this compilation found in the twenty-eight-text *Himitsu* 秘密 *Shōbōgenzō* collection bears a famous colophon by Dōgen's disciple Ejō 懷奘 stating that the twelve chapters were to be included in a projected one-hundred-chapter *Shōbōgenzō*, but that Dōgen's final illness had forced him to abandon work on that project. Because of this colophon, the works in the twelve-chapter *Shōbōgenzō*, despite their lack of dates, have often been taken as their author's final teachings and, hence, have been the object of much scholarly attention. Since some of these works display religious attitudes seemingly distinct from some chapters of the seventy-five-chapter *Shōbōgenzō*, they have been taken by some interpreters as evidence that Dōgen revised his teachings toward the end of his life.

Except for one chapter (number 11), all the texts in this collection have variant versions in either the sixty-chapter *Shōbōgenzō* or the twenty-eight-text *Himitsu Shōbōgenzō*; since the twelve-chapter *Shōbōgenzō* was unknown in 1812, when the ninety-five-chapter Honzan edition was compiled, it is by these variant versions that they are represented in that compilation. The correspondences are as follows (the *Himitsu* chapters are indicated by fascicle:text):

Twelve chapters	Sixty chapters	*Himitsu* chapters	Honzan chapters
T1	58		86
T2		2:10	94
T3	41		12
T4	34		85
T5	59		87
T6	60		88
T7		1:5	89
T8	8		83
T9	39		85
T10		3:2	90
T11			
T12		3:9	95

TREASURY OF THE TRUE DHARMA EYE
THE TWELVE-CHAPTER COMPILATION
NUMBER 1

The Merit of Leaving Home
Shukke kudoku
出家功德

The Merit of Leaving Home

Shukke kudoku

INTRODUCTION

This first chapter of the twelve-chapter *Shōbōgenzō*, like most in this compilation, is undated but may represent a work of Dōgen's later years. A version of this work is found as number 58 in the sixty-chapter *Shōbōgenzō* compilation and is included in the Honzan edition as number 86. A late manuscript records that, like several other texts of the twelve-chapter compilation, it was copied, presumably by Dōgen's disciple Ejō 懐奘, during the summer retreat of 1255, some three years after its author's death.

In the autumn of 1246, Dōgen composed the "Shukke" 出家 chapter of the *Shōbōgenzō*, a relatively brief work on the theme of going forth from the householder's life into the renunciant Buddhist order. "Shukke kudoku" represents a much-expanded treatment of the same theme. As is common in his late writings, Dōgen here cites many passages from the broader Buddhist literature (as well as several from the Chinese Chan corpus) — passages extolling the extraordinary merit of leaving home and taking the precepts of the bhikṣu or *bhikṣuṇī*. Even those who subsequently break these precepts and fall into the hells are better off for having once gained this good karma that will eventually yield its rewards. All the buddhas and ancestral masters of the Zen lineage, he reminds us, have left home, and those who remain at home can never hope to become a buddha or a Zen ancestor.

正法眼藏第一
Treasury of the True Dharma Eye
Number 1

出家功德
The Merit of Leaving Home

[T1:1] {2:266}

龍樹菩薩言、問曰、若居家戒、得生天上、得菩薩道、亦得涅槃、復何
用出家戒。答曰、雖俱得度、然有難易、居家生業種種事務、若欲專心
道法、家業則廢、若專修家業、道事則廢、不取不捨、能應行法、是名
爲難。若出家、離俗絶諸忿亂、一向專心行道爲易。復次居家、慣鬧多
事多務、結使之根、衆罪之府、是爲甚難。若出家者、譬若有人出在空
野無人之處、而一其心無心無慮。内想既除、外事亦去。如偈説、

Bodhisattva Nāgārjuna said,[1]

*Question: If the precepts of the householder enable one to be born in
the deva realms, gain the bodhisattva path, and attain nirvāṇa, then
what use are the precepts of those who leave home?*

*Answer: Although one can be delivered by both, there is nevertheless
a difference in how difficult or easy this is. The livelihoods of householders involve all kinds of duties. If they wish to concentrate on the
practices of the path, their household business will be neglected; if
they concentrate on their household business, the matters of the path
will be neglected. They should be able to practice the dharma without
either grasping or rejecting anything; this is why we call it "difficult."
Leaving home, distancing oneself from the secular, cutting off anger
and agitation, and concentrating solely on practicing the path is considered "easy." Furthermore, the householder life is disturbed and har-
ried, with many affairs and many duties; it is the root of afflictions, the
seat of transgressions, which makes it very "difficult." Ones who leave
home are like those going forth into a deserted field, who unify their
minds, without either mind or thinking. Internally, their conceptions
are abandoned; externally, their affairs also gone. As the gāthā says,*

---

1   **Bodhisattva Nāgārjuna** (*Ryūju bosatsu* 龍樹菩薩): The first seven sections of the
text here represent direct quotation of the *Dazhidu lun* 大智度論 (T.1509.25:160c28-
161b24), traditionally attributed to the great Indian author Nāgārjuna, regarded as the
fourteenth ancestor of Zen.

[T1:2]

閑坐林樹間、寂然滅衆惡、恬澹得一心、斯樂非天樂、人求富貴利・名衣・好牀褥、斯樂非安穩、求利無厭足、衲衣行乞食、動止心常一、自以智慧眼、觀知諸法實、種種法門中、皆以等觀入、解慧心寂然、三界無能及。以是故知、出家修戒行道、爲甚易。

> Quietly seated in the forest,
> Silently ending a host of evils;
> Tranquilly attaining single-mindedness,
> Its pleasure not the pleasures of heaven.
> People seek wealth, esteem, and benefit,
> Splendid garments and fine bedding.
> The pleasure of those is not tranquility,
> And the search for benefit is insatiable.
> In a patched robe, begging for food,
> Moving or stopping, the mind always unified.
> With the eye of wisdom, by oneself,
> Observing and knowing the truth of the dharmas.
> Among the many dharma gates,
> Entering them all with equanimous insight.
> With the mind of wisdom calm and serene,
> Unequalled in the three realms.[2]

From this, we know that leaving home, cultivating the precepts, and practicing the way are very easy.

[T1:3] {2:267}

復次出家修戒、得無量善律儀、一切具足滿。以是故、白衣等應當出家受具足戒。

Furthermore, by leaving home and cultivating the precepts, one acquires incalculable good restraints, being fully equipped with all of them.[3] Therefore, the white-robed should leave home and receive the full precepts.[4]

[T1:4]

復次佛法中、出家法、第一難修。如閻浮呿提梵志、問舍利弗、於佛法中、何者最難。舍利弗答曰、出家爲難。又問、出家有何等難。答曰、出家內樂爲難。既得內樂、復次何者爲難。修諸善法難。以是故、應出家。

---

2   **three realms** (*sangai* 三界): The threefold world of saṃsāra; see Supplementary Notes, s.v. "Three realms."

3   **good restraints** (*zen ritsugi* 善律儀): Here, probably referring to precepts for the cultivation of good deeds (*shō zenbō kai* 攝善法戒; S. *kuśala-dharma-saṃgrāhaka-śīla*), as opposed to precepts restraining evil deeds (*shō ritsugi kai* 攝律儀戒; *saṃvara-śīla*).

4   **white-robed** (*byakue* 白衣): I.e., the Buddhist laity.

T1. The Merit of Leaving Home *Shukke kudoku* 出家功德　　　7

Furthermore, among the buddha dharmas, the dharma of leaving home is the most difficult to practice. Thus, the brāhmaṇa Jambukhādaka asked Śāriputra, "Among the buddha dharmas, what is the most difficult?"[5]

Śāriputra answered, "Leaving home is difficult."

Again, he asked, "What are the difficulties in leaving home?"

He answered, "In leaving home, inner enjoyment is difficult."[6]

"And once one has attained inner enjoyment, what is still difficult?"

"Cultivating the good dharmas is difficult."

Therefore, one should leave home.

[T1:5]

復次若人出家時、魔王驚愁言、此人諸結使欲薄、必得涅槃、墮僧寶數中。

Furthermore, when people leave home, King Māra is shocked and anguished, saying, "Their afflicted desires are slight; they will surely attain nirvāṇa. They have fallen into the ranks of the saṃgha treasure."

[T1:6]

復次佛法中出家人、雖破戒墮罪、罪畢得解脱、如優鉢羅華比丘尼本生經中説。佛在世時、此比丘尼、得六神通阿羅漢。入貴人舍、常讚出家法、語諸貴人婦女言、姉妹可出家。諸貴婦女言、我等少壯、容色盛美、持戒爲難、或當破戒。比丘尼言、破戒使破、但出家。問言、破戒當墮地獄、云何可破。答言、墮地獄便墮。諸貴婦女、笑之言、地獄受罪、云何可墮。比丘尼言、我自憶念本宿命、時作婬女、著種種衣服、而説舊語。或時著比丘尼衣、以爲戲笑。以是因緣故、迦葉佛時、作比丘尼。自恃貴姓端正、心生憍慢、而破禁戒。破禁戒罪故、墮地獄受種種罪。受畢竟、値釋迦牟尼佛出家、得六神通阿羅漢道。以是故知、出家受戒、雖復破戒、以戒因緣故、得阿羅漢道、若但作惡、無戒因緣、不得道也。我乃昔時、世世墮地獄、從地獄出爲惡人、惡人死還入地獄、都無所得。今以此證知、出家受戒、雖復破戒、以是因緣、可得道果。

Furthermore, in the buddha dharma, those who leave home, even though they break the precepts and commit offenses, attain liberation after the suffering for those offenses has ended, as is taught in the Sūtra of the Prior Lives of the Bhikṣuṇī Utpalavarṇā.[7]

5　**brāhmaṇa Jambukhādaka** (*Enbukadai bonshi* 閻浮呿提梵志): A slightly variant version of this conversation between the ascetic Jambukhādaka and the Buddha's disciple Śāriputra can be found, e.g., in the *Saṃyuktāgama* (*Za ehan jing* 雜阿含經, T.99.2:126a9-14).

6　**inner enjoyment** (*nairaku* 内樂): The *Dazhidu lun* 大智度論 (T.1509.25:161a23-24) here gives "enjoyment of the dharma" (*rakuhō* 樂法).

7　***Sūtra of the Prior Lives of the Bhikṣuṇī Utpalavarṇā*** (*Upparage bikuni honshō kyō* 優鉢羅華比丘尼本生經): No text of this title is extant, but stories of the prior lives of the Buddha's famous disciple Bhikṣuṇī Utpalavarṇā are well known in the tradition. The

At the time of the Buddha, this *bhikṣuṇī* became an arhat with the six spiritual powers.[8] Entering into the residences of the aristocrats, she always praised the dharma of leaving home, saying to the aristocratic women, "Sisters, you should leave home."

The aristocratic women said, "We are young and in our prime, attractive and at the height of our beauty. Keeping the precepts would be hard for us, and we would quite likely break them."

The Bhikṣuṇī said, "If you break the precepts, then you break them. Just leave home."

They asked, "If we break the precepts, we shall fall into the hells. How can you say we can break them?"

She answered, "If you fall into the hells, then you fall into them."

The aristocratic women laughed at this and said, "In the hells, one suffers from one's offenses. How can you say we can fall into them?"

The Bhikṣuṇī said, "I myself recall a former life, when I was a courtesan. I used to dress up in all sorts of costumes and tell old stories. Once, I put on the robes of a bhikṣuṇī as a joke. Due to this cause, at the time of Buddha Kāśyapa, I became a *bhikṣuṇī*.[9] Conceited by my noble pedigree and elegant appearance, my mind gave rise to pride, and I broke the precepts of restraint. Due to the offense of breaking the precepts, I fell into the hells and suffered all sorts of evils. After the suffering was finally over, I met Buddha Śākyamuni, left home, and gained the way of an arhat with the six spiritual powers. Thus, we know that, if one leaves home and receives the precepts, even though one then breaks them, due to the cause of the precepts, one will gain the way of the arhat. But if one simply does evil, without the cause of the precepts, one will not gain the way. Long ago, I fell into the hells in life after life; emerging from the hells, I became an evil person, and when that evil person died, I again entered the hells, without gaining anything at all. Now, from this experience I know that, if one leaves home and receives the precepts, even though one then breaks them, due to the cause of the precepts, one can gain the fruit of the way."

---

following story from the *Dazhidu lun* 大智度論 is also found in the "Shōbōgenzō kesa kudoku" 正法眼藏袈裟功德.

8 **arhat with the six spiritual powers** (*toku roku jinzū arakan* 得六神通阿羅漢): I.e., an arhat who had not only achieved nirvāṇa but had also achieved the six paranormal powers (*jinzū* 神通; S. *abhijñā*) of the advanced contemplative; see Supplementary Notes, s.v. "Spiritual powers."

9 **Buddha Kāśyapa** (*Kashō butsu* 迦葉佛): The sixth of the ancient buddhas, just preceding Buddha Śākyamuni; see Supplementary Notes, s.v. "Seven buddhas."

T1. The Merit of Leaving Home *Shukke kudoku* 出家功徳

[T1:7] {2:268}

復次如佛在祇桓、有一醉婆羅門、來到佛所、求作比丘。佛勅阿難、與剃頭
著法衣。醉酒既醒、驚怪己身忽爲比丘、即便走去。諸比丘問佛、何以聽此
婆羅門、而作比丘。佛言、此婆羅門、無量劫中、初無出家心、今因醉故、
暫發微心、以此因緣故、後出家得道。如是種種因緣、出家之利、功德無
量、以是白衣雖有五戒、不如出家。

> Furthermore, when the Buddha was staying in Jetavana, there was
> a drunken brahman who came to the Buddha seeking to become a
> bhikṣu.[10] The Buddha ordered Ānanda to shave his head and dress him
> in dharma robes.[11] Once he sobered up, he was astonished and appalled
> that he had suddenly become a bhikṣu and immediately ran away. The
> bhikṣus asked the Buddha, "Why did you permit this brahman to be-
> come a bhikṣu?"
>
> The Buddha said, "For innumerable kalpas, this brahman had no
> thought of leaving home. But now, because he became drunk, he brief-
> ly had a slight thought of it. Due to this cause, later he will leave home
> and gain the way."
>
> In various cases like this, the benefit of leaving home is merit immeas-
> urable. Thus, while the white-robed may have the five precepts, they
> are not like leaving home.

[T1:8] {2:270}

世尊すでに醉婆羅門に出家・受戒を聽許し、得道最初の下種とせしめまし
ます。あきらかにしりぬ、むかしよりいまだ出家の功徳なからむ衆生、な
がく、佛果菩提、うべからず。この婆羅門、わづかに醉酒のゆゑに、しば
らく微心をおこして、剃頭・受戒し、比丘となれり。酒醉さめざるあひ
だ、いくばくにあらざれども、この功徳を保護して、得道の善根を増長す
べきむね、これ世尊誠諦の金言なり、如來出世の本懷なり。一切衆生あき
らかに已・今・當のなかに、信受奉行したてまつるべし。まことにそれ發
心・得道、さだめて刹那よりするものなり。この婆羅門、しばらくの出家
の功徳、なほかくのごとし。いかにいはんや、いま人間一生の壽者命者を
めぐらして出家・受戒せん功徳、さらに醉婆羅門よりも劣ならめやは。

The World-Honored One indeed consented to the drunken brahman's
leaving home and receiving the precepts, causing him to plant the first
seeds of gaining the way. Clearly, living beings that have never had the
merit of leaving home will not be able to attain bodhi, the fruit of buddhahood. This brahman, merely because he was drunk, briefly aroused
a slight thought [of leaving home], shaved his head, received the pre-

---

10 **when the Buddha was staying in Jetavana** (*Butsu zai Gion* 佛在祇桓): Dōgen gives
a slightly variant version of this story of the drunken brahman in his "Shōbōgenzō shukke" 正法眼藏出家. "Jetavana" ("the forest of Prince Jeta") was the park and monastery
at Anāthapiṇḍada, near Śrāvastī, where the Buddha often stayed.

11 *Ānanda* (*Anan* 阿難): The Buddha's cousin and personal attendant.

cepts, and became a bhikṣu. Although it was not long before he sobered up, the merit of this was preserved and would increase his good roots for gaining the way. This message is the golden words of truth of the World-Honored One, is the original intention behind the Tathāgata's appearance in the world. Clearly, all living beings should faithfully accept and reverently practice this throughout past, present, and future. Truly, the arousing of the thought [of bodhi] and gaining of the way are something that happens from a *kṣana*.[12] The merit even of the brahman's brief leaving home was like this; needless to say, then, the merit of humans now who would devote their entire lives to leaving home and receiving the precepts — how could it be less than that of the drunken brahman?

[T1:9] {2:271}

轉輪聖王は、八萬歲以上のときにいでて、四洲を統領せり、七寶具足せり。そのとき、この四洲、みな淨土のごとし。輪王の快樂、ことばのつくすべきにあらず。あるいは三千界を統領するもありといふ、金・銀・銅・鐵輪の別ありて、一二三四洲の統領あり、かならず身に十惡なし。この轉輪聖王、かくのごときの快樂にゆたかなれども、かうべにひとすぢの白髮おひぬれば、くらいを太子にゆづりて、わがみ、すみやかに出家し、袈裟を著して、山林にいり、修練し、命終すれば、かならず梵天にむまる。このみづからがかうべの白髮を銀函にいれて、王宮にをさめたり、のちの輪王に相傳す。のちの輪王、また白髮おひぬれば、先王に一如なり。轉輪聖王の、出家ののち、餘命のひさしきこと、いまの人にたくらぶべからず。すでに、輪王八萬上、といふ、その身に三十二相を具せり、いまの人およぶべからず。しかあれども、白髮をみて無常をさとりしれる、白業を修して功德を成就せんがために、かならず出家修道するなり。いまの諸王、轉輪聖王におよぶべからず。いたづらに光陰を貪欲のなかにすごして出家せざるは、來世くやしからん。いはんや小國邊地は、王者の名あれども王者の德なし、貪じてとどまるべからず。出家修道せば、諸天、よろこび、まもるべし、龍神、うやまひ、保護すべし、諸佛の佛眼、あきらかに證明し、隨喜しましまさん。

Wheel-turning sage kings, appearing in the period above age eighty thousand, rule the four continents and are fully endowed with the seven treasures.[13] At that time, the four continents are all like pure lands; and

---

12 **something that happens from a *kṣana*** (*setsuna yori suru mono* 刹那よりするもの): Presumably, meaning "something the cause of which is but a moment." Cf. "Shōbōgenzō Shukke kudoku" 出家功德:

刹那生滅の道理によりて、衆生、發心得道す。

Due to the arising and ceasing of a *kṣaṇa*, living beings bring forth the mind [of bodhi] and gain the way.

13 **Wheel-turning sage kings, appearing in the period above age eighty thousand** (*tenrin jōō wa, hachiman sai ijō no toki ni idete* 轉輪聖王は、八萬歲以上のときにいでて): I.e., *cakravartins*, the ideal Buddhist rulers, who reign during early periods of kalpas, when the human lifespan is eighty thousand years or more. See, e.g., *Abhidharma-kośa* (*Apidamo jushe lun* 阿毘達磨俱舍論, T.1558.29:64b25-27):

T1. The Merit of Leaving Home *Shukke kudoku* 出家功德

the happiness of the wheel-turning kings is beyond words. It is said that there are some who rule over three chiliocosms; they are distinguished by their gold, silver, copper, and iron wheels, their rules extending over one, two, three or four continents, and their persons always free of the ten evils.[14] Although these wheel-turning sage kings enjoy such happiness, once a single white hair appears on their heads, abdicating their positions to a prince, they themselves immediately leave home, don the *kāṣāya*, enter the wilderness, undertake training, and, when their lives end, are invariably reborn into the heaven of Brahmā.[15] They place the white hair from their own heads into a silver box and leave it in the palace, to be handed down to the subsequent wheel-turning king. The subsequent wheel-turning king, when he grows a white hair, does the same as the previous king. After the wheel-turning sage kings leave home, the rest of their lives is very long and cannot be compared with that of people today. It said of them, "Wheel-turning kings, over eighty thousand," and their bodies are endowed with the thirty-two marks; so, people of today could hardly match them.[16] Nevertheless, seeing the white hair, they

---

從此洲人壽無量歲乃至八萬歲有轉輪王生。減八萬時。有情富樂壽量損減。衆惡漸盛。非大人器故無輪王。

During the period when the lifespan of humans on this continent decreases from incalculable years to eighty thousand years, wheel-turning kings are born. In the period below eighty thousand years, the prosperity and lifespan of sentient beings decline, their evils gradually increase, and they are no longer capable of greatness; hence, there are no more wheel-turning kings.

four continents (*shishū* 四洲): The four bodies of land (S. *catur-dvīpa*) surrounding Mt. Sumeru in the geography of a Buddhist world system; see Supplementary Notes, s.v. "Four Continents."

seven treasures (*shippō* 七寶): A standard term (S. *sapta-ratna*) in Buddhist literature for various lists of precious substances; one common version gives gold, silver, beryl, crystal, agate, ruby, and cornelian.

14 **they are distinguished by their gold, silver, copper, and iron wheels** (*kon gon dō tetsurin no betsu arite* 金・銀・銅・鐵輪の別ありて): The four types of *cakravartin*, ranked by the extent of their territories: the gold king rules over all of the four continents surrounding Mount Sumeru; the silver king, over the eastern, western, and southern continents; the copper king, over the eastern and southern; the iron king, over our southern continent of Jambudvīpa.

ten evils (*jūaku* 十惡): S. *daśākuśala*. One standard list: (1) killing, (2) stealing, (3) sexual misconduct, (4) lying, (5) fine talk, (6) slander, (7) treachery, (8) covetousness, (9) anger, and (10) false views. This list is sometimes divided into the three types of karma: body (1-3), speech (4-7), and mind (8-10).

15 **heaven of Brahmā** (*bonten* 梵天): The heaven of the first dhyāna in the realm of form, ruled over by the god Brahmā; see Supplementary Notes, s.v. "Three realms."

16 **"Wheel-turning kings, over eighty thousand"** (*rinnō hachiman jō* 輪王八萬上): From a verse in the *Abhidharma-kośa* (*Apidamo jushe lun* 阿毘達磨倶舍論, T.1558.29:64b21):

DŌGEN'S *SHŌBŌGENZŌ* VOLUME VI

understand impermanence; and practicing the white karma in order to achieve merit, they invariably leave home and train in the way.[17] Kings of today cannot possibly match the wheel-turning sage kings. Those who idly spend their years and months in the midst of desires without leaving home will regret it in the life to come. How much less in a small country and peripheral land, where there are kings in name without the virtues of a king, can they curb their desires. If they were to leave home and train in the way, the devas would rejoice and protect them; the dragon spirits would revere and preserve them, and the buddha eye of the buddhas would clearly verify them and rejoice.

[T1:10] {2:272}

戯女の、むかしは信心にあらず、戯笑のために比丘尼の衣を著せり。おそらくは輕法の罪あるべしといへども、この衣を、その身に著せしちから、二世に佛法にあふ。比丘尼衣とは、袈裟なり。戯笑著袈裟のちからによりて、第二生に、迦葉佛のときにあふたてまつる。出家・受戒し、比丘尼となれり。破戒によりて墮獄受罪すといへども、功徳くちずして、つひに釋迦牟尼佛にあひたてまつり、見佛聞法、發心修習して、ながく三界をはなれて、大阿羅漢となれり。六通・三明を具足せり、かならず無上道なるべし。

The courtesan long ago had no faith but donned the robe of a *bhikṣuṇī* as a joke. Although she may have been guilty of disparaging the dharma, by the power of putting on this robe, she encountered the buddha dharma in a later life. "The robe of a *bhikṣuṇī*" means a *kāṣāya*. By the power of donning a *kāṣāya* as a joke, in a later life, at the time of Buddha Kāśyapa, she encountered him. She left home, received the precepts, and became a *bhikṣuṇī*. Although she may have suffered retribution in hell for breaking the precepts, her merit did not decay, and eventually she encountered Buddha Śākyamuni; seeing the buddha and hearing the dharma, bringing forth the thought [of bodhi] and engaging in the practice, she left the three realms far behind and became a great arhat. Fully endowed with the six powers and three knowledges — without fail, she attained the unsurpassed way.[18]

輪王八萬上、金銀銅鐵輪。

Wheel-turning kings, over eighty thousand;
Their wheels of gold, silver, copper, and iron.

thirty-two marks (*sanjūni sō* 三十二相): The extraordinary physical characteristics ascribed to the bodies of the buddhas and *cakravartins* in Buddhist literature.

17 **white karma** (*byakugō* 白業): I.e., good deeds.

18 **six powers and three knowledges** (*rokutsū sanmyō* 六通・三明): For the former, see above, Note 8; the latter represent three of the six powers: the deva eye, recollection of prior lives, and knowledge of the exhaustion of the contaminants.

T1. The Merit of Leaving Home *Shukke kudoku* 出家功徳

[T1:11]

しかあればすなはち、はじめより一向無上菩提のために、清浄の信心をこらして袈裟を信受せん、その功徳の増長、かの戯女の功徳よりもすみやかならん。いはんやまた、無上菩提のために菩提心をおこし、出家受戒せん、その功徳無量なるべし、人身にあらざれば、この功徳を成就することまれなり。

Thus, if from the very start, solely for the sake of unsurpassed bodhi, with a pure mind firm in its faith, we were to accept the *kaṣāya* in faith, the increase in the merit of that would be faster even than the merit of that courtesan. Not to mention, moreover, that, if, for the sake of unsurpassed bodhi, we were to bring forth the mind of bodhi, leave home, and receive the precepts, the merit of that would be immeasurable. Without a human body, it is rare to achieve this merit.

[T1:12]

西天東土、出家・在家の菩薩・祖師おほしといふとも、龍樹祖師におよばず。酔婆羅門・戯女等の因縁、もはら龍樹祖師、これを挙して、衆生の出家・受戒をすすむ、龍樹祖師、すなはち世尊金口の所記なり。

In Sindh in the West and the Land of the East, while there have been many bodhisattvas and ancestral masters among renunciants and householders, none is the equal of the Ancestral Master Nāgārjuna. The episodes of the drunken brahman, the courtesan, and the like, were raised solely by the Ancestral Master Nāgārjuna to encourage living beings to leave home and receive the precepts. The Ancestral Master Nāgārjuna was predicted by the World-Honored Golden-Mouthed One.[19]

* * * * *

---

19 **predicted by the World-Honored Golden-Mouthed One** (*Seson konku no shoki* 世尊金口の所記): I.e., predicted by the Buddha as a successor in his lineage. The expression *konku shoki* 金口所記 ("predicted by the Golden-Mouthed One") is a fixed phrase, from the Tiantai tradition of the twenty-four Indian successors; see, e.g., *Mohe zhiguan* 摩訶止觀, T.1911.46:1b8:

付法藏人、始迦葉終師子二十三人。末田地與商那同時、則二十四人。諸師皆金口所記。

Of those who transmitted the dharma treasury, beginning with Kāśyapa and ending with Siṃha, there were twenty-three; but Madhyāntika and Śaṇavāsa [shared the succession] in the same generation, so there are twenty-four individuals. These masters were all predicted by the Golden-Mouthed One.

14 DŌGEN'S *SHŌBŌGENZŌ* VOLUME VI

[T1:13] {2:273}

世尊言、南洲有四種最勝、一見佛、二聞法、三出家、四得道。

The World-Honored One said, "The Southern Continent has four things that are the best: (1) seeing the buddha, (2) hearing the dharma, (3) leaving home, and (4) gaining the way."[20]

[T1:14]

あきらかにしるべし、この四種最勝、すなはち北洲にもすぐれ、諸天にもすぐれたり。いまわれら宿善根力にひかれて、最勝の身をえたり。歓喜・随喜して出家・受戒すべきものなり。最勝の善身をいたづらにして、露命を無常の風にまかすることなかれ。出家の生生をかさねて、積功累徳ならん。

We should recognize that these "four things that are the best" are better than in the Northern Continent, better than in the heavens. Now, by the power of our good roots from former lives, we have got the best bodies. Rejoicing in and celebrating this, we should leave home and receive the precepts. Do not waste this best of good bodies and abandon its evanescent life to the winds of impermanence. Piling up life after life of leaving home, we shall *accumulate merit and amass virtue.*[21]

* * * * *

[T1:15]

世尊言、於佛法中、出家果報、不可思議。假使有人、起七寶塔、高至三十三天、所得功德、不如出家。何以故、七寶塔者、貪惡愚人、能破壞故、出家功德、無有壞毀。是故、若教男女、若放奴婢、若聽人民、若自己身、出家入道者、功德無量。

The World-Honored One said,[22]

In the buddha dharma, the rewards of leaving home are inconceivable . . . Even if one were to erect a seven-jeweled stūpa reaching to the

---

20 **The World-Honored One** (*Seson* 世尊): Likely based, not directly on a sūtra, but on the *Lüzong xinxue mingju* 律宗新學名句 by Huaixian 懷顯 (or Weixian 惟顯, dates unknown), at ZZ.105:629b1:

南洲四種別緣、一見佛二聞法三出家四得道。

The Southern Continent has four distinctions: (1) seeing the buddha, (2) hearing the dharma, (3) leaving home, and (4) gaining the way.

21 **accumulate merit and amass virtue** (*shakku ruitoku* 積功累徳): A fixed expression for developing good karma found throughout Buddhist literature, including several times in the *Shōbōgenzō*.

22 **The World-Honored One** (*Seson* 世尊): Quoting two passages from the introduction to the chapter on "The Merit of Leaving Home, Sirīvaddhi" (*Chujia gongde Shilipiti* 出家功德尸利苾提), of the *Damamūka-nidāna-sūtra* (*Xianyu jing* 賢愚經, T.202.4:376b6-7; b11-16; here cited in reverse order).

T1. The Merit of Leaving Home *Shukke kudoku* 出家功德

Heaven of the Thirty-three, the merit gained thereby would not equal that of leaving home.[23] *Why is this? Because, in the case of the seven-jeweled stūpa, the greedy, evil, or stupid person could demolish it; but nothing can destroy the merit of leaving home.*

Therefore,

If one causes a man or a woman to leave home and enter the way, or if one releases a male or female slave to do so, or if one permits the people to do so, or if one does so oneself, the merit is immeasurable.

[T1:16] {2:274}

世尊、あきらかに功徳の量をしろしめして、かくのごとく校量しまします。福増、これをききて、一百二十歳の耆及なれども、しひて出家・受戒し、少年の席末につらなりて修練し、大阿羅漢となれり。

The World-Honored One, knowing clearly the amount of merit, made such a comparison. Sirīvaddhi, upon hearing it, despite being old and decrepit at age one hundred twenty, could not help but leave home and receive the precepts; assigned to the last seats with the youngsters, he undertook training and became a great arhat.[24]

[T1:17]

しるべし、今生の人身は、四大五蘊、因縁和合して、かりになせり、八苦、つねにあり、いはんや刹那刹那に生滅してさらにとどまらず。いはく一弾指のあひだに六十五の刹那生滅すといへども、みづからくらきによりて、いまだしらざるなり。すべて一日一夜があひだに、六十四億九萬九千九百八十の刹那ありて、五蘊生滅すといへども、しらざるなり。あはれむべし、われ生滅すといへども、みづからしらざること。この刹那生滅の量、ただ佛世尊ならびに舍利弗とのみしらせたまふ。餘聖おほかれども、ひとりもしるところにあらざるなり。この刹那生滅の道理によりて、衆生、すなはち善惡の業をつくる、また刹那生滅の道理によりて、衆生、發心・得道す。

We should realize that the human body of the present life has been temporarily formed of the four elements and five aggregates in a coalescence of causes and conditions; it always has the eight kinds of suffering, not to mention that it arises and ceases *kṣaṇa* after *kṣaṇa* without

---

23 **Heaven of the Thirty-three** (*sanjūsan ten* 三十三天): S. *Trāyatriṃśa* (*tōriten* 忉利天); second of the six heavens of the desire realm, located atop Mt. Sumeru, inhabited by thirty-three devas, and ruled by Lord Śakra (*Taishaku Ten* 帝釋天).

24 **Sirīvaddhi** (*Fukuzō* 福増): The old man (transliterated *Shilipiti* 尸利苾提), whose story is told in the chapter of the *Damamūka-nidāna-sūtra* cited in the previous section. His request to join the Buddhist order was rejected by the Buddha's disciple Śāriputra but subsequently accepted by the Buddha. Dōgen refers to this incident in his "Shōbōgenzō shizen biku" 正法眼藏四禪比丘 and quotes the account in the *Damamūka-nidāna-sūtra* in his *Eihei kōroku* 永平廣録 (DZZ.3:244-252, no. 381).

16   DŌGEN'S *SHŌBŌGENZŌ* VOLUME VI

end.[25] That is, although sixty-five *kṣaṇas* arise and cease in a single snap of one's fingers, due to our benightedness, we still do not know it.[26] Altogether, in a single day and night, there are 6,499,980 *kṣaṇas*, in which the five aggregates arise and cease; yet we do not know it.[27] How pitiful that, although we are arising and ceasing, we do not know it. The duration of the arising and ceasing of a *kṣaṇa* is known only by the Buddha, the World-Honored One, and by Śāriputra; there may be many other sages, but not one of them knows this. Due to this principle of the arising and ceasing of a *kṣaṇa*, living beings produce good and evil karma; and due to the arising and ceasing of a *kṣaṇa*, living beings arouse the thought [of bodhi] and gain the way.

[T1:18]

かくのごとく生滅する人身なり、たとひをしむともとどまらじ。むかしより、をしんでとどまれる一人、いまだなし。かくのごとくわれにあらざる人身なりといへども、めぐらして出家・受戒するがごときは、三世の諸佛の所證なる阿耨多羅三藐三菩提、金剛不壞の佛果を證するなり、たれの智人か欣求せざらん。これによりて、過去日月燈明佛の八子、みな四天下を領する王位をすてて出家す。大通智勝佛の十六子、ともに出家せり。大通入定のあひだ、衆のために法華をとく。いまは十方の如來となれり。父王轉輪聖王の所將衆中八萬億人も、十六王子の出家をみて、出家をもとむ。輪王、すなはち聽許す。妙莊嚴王の二子、ならびに父王・夫人、みな出家せり。しるべし、大聖出現のとき、かならず出家するを正法とせりといふことあきらけし。このともがら、おろかにして出家せりといふべからず、

---

25   **four elements and five aggregates** (*shidai goun* 四大五蘊): I.e., the four primary forms of matter (S. *mahābhūta*), earth, water, fire, and wind, of which the physical world is composed; and the five "heaps" (S. *skandha*), form, sensation, perception, formations, and consciousness, into which the psychophysical organism can be analyzed. See Supplementary Notes, s.v. "Four elements and five aggregates."

eight kinds of suffering (*hakku* 八苦): (1) birth, (2) aging, (3) sickness, (4) death, (5) separation from what one loves, (6) association with what one hates, (7) inability to get what we seek, and (8) being contained within the five aggregates.

26   **That is** (*iwaku* いわく): Many manuscript witnesses read here *iwanya* いわんや ("not to mention").

sixty-five *kṣaṇas* (*rokujūgo no setsuna* 六十五の刹那): See, e.g., the *Abhidharma-kośa* (*Apidamo jushe lun* 阿毘達磨倶舎論, T.1558.29:62a22-23):

    對法諸師説、如壯士一疾彈指頃六十五刹那。

    The *ābhidhārmikas* say that for a strong man to snap his fingers once takes sixty-five *kṣaṇas*.

27   **in a single day and night, there are 6,499,980 *kṣaṇas*** (*ichinichi ichiya o furu aida ni, rokujūshioku kyūsen kyūhyaku hachijū no setsuna arite* 一日一夜をふるあひだに、六十四億九萬九千九百八十の刹那ありて): A Japanese rendering of a sentence in the *Mahāvibhāṣā* (*Apidamo da piposha lun* 阿毘達磨大毘婆沙論, T.1545.27:202c7-9). The number *oku* 億 here should be read as 100,000 (S. *śata-sahasra*), not 10,000,000, as is clear from the calculation of a day and a night given by the *Apidamo da piposha lun* 阿毘達磨大毘婆沙論 at T.1545.27:701b8-13.

T1. The Merit of Leaving Home *Shukke kudoku* 出家功德

賢にして出家せりとしらば、ひとしからんことをおもふべし。今釋迦牟尼
佛のときは、羅睺羅・阿難等みな出家し、また千釋の出家あり、二萬釋の
出家あり、勝躅といふべし。はじめ五比丘出家より、をはり須跋陀羅が出
家にいたるまで、歸佛のともがら、すなはち出家す。しるべし、無量の功
德なりといふこと。

Ours is a human body arising and ceasing like this, never stopping despite our reluctance to let it go; from the distant past, there has never been a single person who stopped it by such reluctance. Although in this way it is a human body that is not our own, those who direct it towards leaving home and receiving the precepts will verify the adamantine, indestructible fruit of buddhahood, the *anuttara-samyak-saṃbodhi* verified by the buddhas of the three times. What wise person would not joyfully seek that?

Thus it is that the eight sons of the past Buddha Candrasūryapradīpa all left home, abdicating their positions as kings ruling the four continents under heaven.[28] The sixteen sons of Buddha Mahābhijñā-jñānābhibhū all left home and, while Mahābhijñā was entered into concentration, preached the *Lotus* for the assembly; now, they have become tathāgatas in the ten directions.[29] The eight myriad *koṭis* in the assembly brought by their father the wheel-turning sage king, seeing the sixteen sons leave home, also requested to leave home, and the wheel-turning king granted it. The two sons of King Śubhavyūha, along with their father the king and his wife, all left home.[30]

We should recognize that, at the time of the advent of the Great Sage, it was clear that leaving home was invariably regarded as the true dharma.[31] We should not say that these types left home foolishly; if we recognize that they left home wisely, we should aspire to be like them. At the time of the present Buddha Śākyamuni, Rāhula, Ānanda, and the rest, all left home, while the thousand Śākyas leaving home and the twenty thou-

---

28 **eight sons of the past Buddha Candrasūryapradīpa** (*kako Nichigetsu tōmyō butsu no hasshi* 過去日月燈明佛の八子): Reference to a story recounted in the *Lotus Sūtra* (*Miaofa lianhua jing* 妙法蓮華經, T.262.9:3c17-4b18). (There seems to be no universally accepted Japanese reading for the glyphs 日月 ["sun and moon"] in this Buddha's name: in addition to *nichigetsu*, one finds *nichigachi, jitsugatsu, nichigatsu*, etc.)

29 **sixteen sons of Buddha Mahābhijñā-jñānābhibhū** (*Daitsū chishō butsu no jūrokushi* 大通智勝佛の十六子): Reference to a story recounted in the *Lotus Sūtra* (*Miaofa lianhua jing* 妙法蓮華經, T.262.9:22a18-27b8).

30 **two sons of King Śubhavyūha** (*Myōshōgon ō no nishi* 妙莊嚴王の二子): Reference to a story recounted in the *Lotus Sūtra* (*Miaofa lianhua jing* 妙法蓮華經, T.262.9:59b23-61a4).

31 **advent of the Great Sage** (*Daishō shutsugen* 大聖出現): I.e., the appearance of Buddha Śākyamuni.

18   DŌGEN'S *SHŌBŌGENZŌ* VOLUME VI

sand Śākyas leaving home must be called excellent examples.[32] From the very first leaving home of the five bhikṣus to the last leaving home of Subhadra, those who took refuge in the Buddha left home.[33] We should recognize it was [an act of] incalculable merit.

[T1:19] {2:275}

しかあればすなはち、世人、もし子孫をあはれむことあらば、いそぎ出家せしむべし。父母をあはれむことあらば、出家をすすむべし。かるがゆえに、偈にいはく、

Thus, if people of the world take pity on their children and grandchildren, they should quickly let them leave home; and, if they take pity on their fathers and mothers, they should encourage them to leave home. Therefore, it is said in a gāthā:[34]

[T1:20]

若無過去世、應無過去佛、若無過去佛、無出家受具。

If there were no past time,
There would be no past buddhas;
If there were no past buddhas,
There would be no leaving home and receiving the precepts.

[T1:21]

この偈は、諸佛如來の偈なり。外道の、過去世なし、といふを破するなり。しかあればしるべし、出家受具は、過去諸佛の法なり。われらさいはひに、諸佛の妙法なる出家受具するときにあひながら、むなしく出家・受戒せざらむ、なにのさはりによるとしりがたし。最下品の依身をもて、最上品の功徳を成就せん、閻浮提および三界のなかには、最上品の功徳なるべし。この閻浮の人身いまだ滅せざらんとき、かならず出家受戒すべし。

This gāthā is a gāthā of the buddhas, the tathāgatas. It refutes followers of other paths who deny past time. From this, we know that leaving home and receiving the precepts is the dharma of the buddhas of the past. While

---

32   **Rāhula, Ānanda, and the rest** (*Ragora Anan tō* 羅睺羅・阿難等): I.e., Buddha Śākyamuni's son, his cousin, and his other disciples.

the thousand Śākyas leaving home (*sen Shaku no shukke* 千釋の出家); **the twenty thousand Śākyas leaving home** (*niman Shaku no shukke* 二萬釋の出家): Reference to two accounts found in the *Samantapāsādikā* (*Shanjianlü piposha* 善見律毘婆沙, T.1462.24:790b7-c15).

33   **the five bhikṣus** (*go biku* 五比丘); **Subhadra** (*Shubaddara* 須跋陀羅): I.e., Buddha Śākyamuni's first five disciples and his last convert, inducted into the order just before the Buddha's death.

34   **said in a gāthā** (*ge ni iwaku* 偈にいはく): A slightly variant version of a verse found in the *Mahāvibhāṣā* (*Da piposha lun* 大毘婆沙論, T.1545.27:393b15-16), said in refutation of those who would deny the reality of past and future. Also cited in the "Shōbōgenzō kuyō shobutsu" 正法眼藏供養諸佛.

T1. The Merit of Leaving Home *Shukke kudoku* 出家功德 19

fortunately encountering a time for this leaving home and receiving the precepts that are the wondrous dharma of the buddhas, should we pointlessly fail to leave home and receive the precepts, it would be hard to know just what obstacle was the cause. But, if with this lowest body we achieve the highest merit, it will surely be the highest merit in Jambudvīpa and in the three realms.[35] While this human body in Jambudvīpa has yet to be extinguished, we should certainly leave home and receive the precepts.

* * * * *

[T1:22] {2:276}

古聖云、出家之人、雖破禁戒、猶勝在俗受持戒者。故經偏説、勸人出家、其恩難報。復次勸出家者、即是勸人修尊重業、所得果報、勝琰魔王・輪王・帝釋。故經偏説、勸人出家、其恩難報。勸人受持近事戒等、無如是事、故經不證。

A sage of old has said,[36]

Those who have left home, even if they break the precepts of restraint, are still superior to those who receive and keep the precepts in lay life. Therefore, the sūtras solely say that encouraging someone to leave home is beneficence hard to repay. Moreover, to encourage someone to leave home is to encourage someone to practice acts worthy of respect, the recompense for which surpasses that of King Yama, a wheel-turning king, or Lord Śakra.[37] *Therefore, the sūtras solely say that encouraging someone to leave home is beneficence hard to repay. Encouraging someone to receive the lay precepts is not like this and, therefore, is not attested in the sūtras.*[38]

[T1:23]

しるべし、出家して禁戒を破すといへども、在家にて戒をやぶらざるにはすぐれたり。歸佛、かならず出家・受戒すぐれたるべし。出家をすすむる果報、琰魔王にもすぐれ、輪王にもすぐれ、帝釋にもすぐれたり。たとひ毘舍・首陀羅なれども、出家すれば利利にもすぐるべし。なほ琰魔王にもすぐれ、輪王にもすぐれ、帝釋にもすぐる。在家戒、かくのごとくならず、ゆえに出家すべし。しるべし、世尊の所説、はかるべからざるを。世尊および五百大阿羅漢、ひろくあつめたり。まことにしりぬ、佛法におき

---

35 **Jambudvīpa** (*Enbudai* 閻浮提): I.e., the continent where humans live, south of Mt. Sumeru; see above, Note 13.

36 **A sage of old** (*koshō* 古聖): Quoting the *Mahāvibhāṣā* (*Apidamo da piposha lun* 阿毘達磨大毘婆沙論, T.1545.27:343b29-c5), with slight variation.

37 **King Yama** (*Enma ō* 琰魔王): More often written *Enma* 閻魔; the deva lord of death and king of the hells.

38 **not attested in the sūtras** (*kyō fushō* 經不證): Or, perhaps, "not confirmed by the sūtras"; the *Piposha lun* 毘婆沙論 text (T.1545.27:343c5) reads, "not discussed in the sūtras" (*jing bushuo* 經不説).

て道理あきらかなるべしといふこと。一聖、三明・六通の智慧、なほ近代の凡師のはかるべきにあらず、いはむや五百の聖者をや。近代の凡師らがしらざるところをしり、みざるところをみ、きはめざるところをきはめたりといへども、凡師らがしれるところ、しらざるにあらず。しかあれば、凡師の黒暗愚鈍の説をもて、聖者三明の言に比類することなかれ。婆沙一百二十云、發心出家、尚名聖者、況得忍法。しるべし、發心出家すれば聖者となづくるなり。

We know from this that, even if one breaks the precepts of restraint after leaving home, that is superior to not breaking the precepts as a householder. In taking refuge in the Buddha, leaving home and receiving the precepts is always superior. The recompense for encouraging someone to leave home is superior to that even of King Yama, superior to that even of a wheel-turning king, superior to that even of Lord Śakra. Even if one is a vaiśya or a śūdra, when one leaves home, one will be superior to a kṣatriya; still more, one will even be superior to King Yama, superior to a wheel-turning king, superior to Lord Śakra.[39] The precepts for householders are not like this; therefore, we should leave home.

We should recognize that what is said by the World-Honored One is unfathomable. The World-Honored One and the five hundred great arhats have extensively compiled it.[40] Truly we know that, in the buddha dharma, the principles should be clear. The commoner teachers of recent generations cannot be expected to fathom the wisdom of a single sage possessed of the three knowledges and six spiritual powers, much less that of the five hundred sages. Even if the commoner teachers of recent generations knew what they do not know, saw what they do not see, and mastered what they have not mastered, there would be nothing known to the commoner teachers that they do not know.[41] Therefore, do not

---

39 **vaiśya** (*bisha* 毘舍); **śūdra** (*shudara* 首陀羅); **kṣatriya** (*setsuri* 刹利): Reference to the social classes of India, in which the kṣatriya ("warrior") was ranked above the vaiśya ("farmer/merchant") and śūdra ("worker").

40 **The World-Honored One and the five hundred great arhats have extensively compiled it** (*seson oyobi gohyaku dai arakan, hiroku atsumetari* 世尊および五百大阿羅漢、ひろくあつめたり): Reference to the legend that the *Mahāvibhāṣā*, which Dōgen has just quoted, was compiled at a council of five hundred arhats. The object of the predicate here is unstated and could be taken either as the *Mahāvibhāṣā* or "what it said by the World-Honored One." The point of this somewhat obscure passage would seem to be that the *Mahāvibhāṣā* clarifies the principles [such as the superiority of leaving home] in the otherwise unfathomable teachings of the Buddha.

41 **the commoner teachers of recent generations knew what they do not know** (*kindai no bonshira ga shirazaru tokoro o shiri* 近代の凡師らがしらざるところをしり): A tentative translation of a sentence that could also be read, "Even if they [i.e., the arhats] know what the commoner teachers of recent generations do not know, see what they do not see, and master what they have not mastered, there is nothing known to the commoner teachers that they do not know."

T1. The Merit of Leaving Home *Shukke kudoku* 出家功德 21

compare the ignorant, stupid talk of the commoner teachers to the words of the sages with the three knowledges. In *Vibhāṣā* 120, it is said, "*One who has aroused the aspiration and left home is already called a 'sage'; how much more one who has attained acceptance of the dharma.*"[42] So, we know that when one arouses the aspiration and leaves home, one is called a "sage."

* * * * *

[T1:24] {2:277}

釋迦牟尼佛五百大願のなかの第一百三十七願、我未來成正覺已、或有諸人、於我法中、欲出家者、願無障礙。所謂羸劣・失念・狂亂・憍慢、無有畏懼、癡無智慧、多諸結使、其心散亂、若不爾者、不成正覺。第一百三十八願、我未來成正覺已、若有女人、欲於我法、出家學道、受大戒者、願令成就。若不爾者、不成正覺。第三百十四願、我未來成正覺已、若有衆生、少於善根、於善根中、心生愛樂、我當令其於未來世、在佛法中、出家學道。安止令住梵淨十戒。若不爾者、不成正覺。

Among the five hundred great vows of Buddha Śākyamuni,[43]

Vow one hundred thirty-seven:[44] *In the future, after I have achieved right awakening, if there are those who wish to leave home into my dharma, I vow that they shall have no obstacles — i.e., weakness, loss of mindfulness, confusion, pride, lack of fear, delusion and lack of*

---

42 *Vibhāṣā* 120 (*Basha ippyaku nijū* 婆沙一百二十): Quoting a discussion in fascicle 120 of the *Mahāvibhāṣā* concerning the use of the appellation "noble" (*shō* 聖; S. *ārya*, as opposed to "commoner") in reference to a Buddhist practitioner (*Apidamo da piposha lun* 阿毘達磨大毘婆沙論, T.1545.27:626a19-22):

聖有二種。一世俗。二勝義。得此善根名世俗聖。若入聖道名勝義聖。發心出家尚名聖者。況得忍法。

There are two types of "sage": (1) the mundane and (2) the ultimate. One who attains this good root [of acceptance] is called a mundane sage; if one has entered the noble path [i.e., attained the transmundane path of seeing (*kendō* 見道; S. *darśana-mārga*)], one is called a sage in the ultimate sense. One who has brought forth the mind [of bodhi] and left home is already called a sage; how much more one who has attained [the good root of] acceptance of the dharma.

43 **five hundred great vows of Buddha Śākyamuni** (*Shakamuni butsu gohyaku daigan* 釋迦牟尼佛五百大願): Reference to a set of vows said to have been made by the future Buddha Śākyamuni before his master, Buddha Ratnagarbha (*Hōzō* 寶藏). The vows are best known from the *Karuṇā-puṇḍarīka-sūtra* (*Peihua jing* 悲華經, T.157), but the form of Dōgen's quotation reflects a text known as the *Shijiamouni rulai wubai dayuan jing* 釋迦牟尼如來五百大願經, a work popular in Japan in Dōgen's day but not subsequently transmitted in the Buddhist canon. The text is published in Narita Teikan 成田貞寬, "Kōzanji shozō *Shakamuni nyorai gohyaku daigan kyō* no kenkyū 高山寺所藏「釋迦牟尼如來五百大願經」の研究," *Bukkyō daigaku daigakuin kenkyū kiyō* 佛教大學大學院研究紀要 7 (1979), pp. 1-71.

44 **Vow one hundred thirty-seven** (*dai ippyaku sanjūshichi gan* 第一百三十七願): Narita (1979), p. 30; corresponding to *Peihua jing* 悲華經, T.157.3:208b15-17.

22 DŌGEN'S *SHŌBŌGENZŌ* VOLUME VI

wisdom, many troubles with a mind distracted. If this is not the case, may I not attain right awakening.

Vow one hundred thirty-eight:[45] In the future, after I have achieved right awakening, if there are women who wish to leave home, study the way, and receive the great precepts in my dharma, I vow to enable them to achieve this. If this is not the case, may I not attain right awakening.

Vow three hundred fourteen:[46] In the future, after I have achieved right awakening, if there are living beings who, having few good roots, aspire to good roots, I shall enable them in a future life, to leave home and study the way in the buddha dharma, stabilizing them and enabling them to abide in purity in the ten precepts. If this is not the case, may I not attain right awakening.

[T1:25] {2:278}
しるべし、いま出家する善男子・善女人、みな世尊の往昔の大願力にたすけられて、さはりなく出家・受戒することをえたり。如來すでに誓願して出家せしめまします。あきらかにしりぬ、最尊最上の大功德なりといふことを。

We know from this that all the good sons and good daughters who leave home today, being supported by the power of the great vows of the World-Honored One in the past, are able to leave home and receive the precepts without obstacles. The Tathāgata, having made a vow, enables them to leave home; clearly, we can see that it is the most honored, the supreme great merit.

* * * * *

[T1:26]
佛言、及有依我剃除鬚髮、著袈裟片、不受戒者、供養是人、亦得乃至入無畏城。以是緣故、我如是説。

The Buddha said,[47]

And someone, relying on me, shaves off his beard and hair, and dons the kāṣāya, but does not receive the precepts; one who makes offerings

---

45 **Vow one hundred thirty-eight** (*dai ippyaku sanjūhachi gan* 第一百三十八願): Narita (1979), p. 30; corresponding to *Peihua jing* 悲華經, T.157.3:208b17-18.

46 **Vow three hundred fourteen** (*dai sanbyaku jūshi gan* 第三百十四願): Narita (1979), p. 46; corresponding to *Peihua jing* 悲華經, T.157.3:211b6-9.

47 **The Buddha** (*butsu* 佛): Quoting the *Da fangdeng daji jing* 大方等大集經 (T.397.13:354c20-22).

T1. The Merit of Leaving Home *Shukke kudoku* 出家功德　　　23

to this person will be able even to enter the city of fearlessness.[48] *On account of these conditions, I say this.*

[T1:27]

あきらかにしる、剃除鬚髮して袈裟を著せば、戒をうけずといふとも、これを供養せむ人、無畏城にいらん。

Clearly, we know from this that, if someone shaves off his beard and hair and dons a *kāṣāya*, even though not receiving the precepts, the person who makes offerings to him will enter the city of fearlessness.

[T1:28]

又云、若復有人、爲我出家、不得禁戒、剃除鬚髮、著袈裟片、有以非法惱害此者、乃至破壞三世諸佛法身・報身、乃至盈滿三惡道故。

Again, he said,[49]

If, furthermore, someone leaves home for my sake and, without getting the precepts of restraint, shaves off his beard and hair and dons the kāṣāya, *if someone harms this person on account of his impropriety, it amounts to destroying the dharma bodies and recompense bodies of the buddhas of the three times, amounts to filling up the three evil paths.*[50]

[T1:29] {2:279}

佛言、若有衆生、爲我出家、剃除鬚髮、被服袈裟、設不持戒、彼等悉已爲涅槃印之所印也。若復出家、不持戒者、有以非法、而作惱亂・罵辱・毀呰、以手刀杖打縛斫截、若奪衣鉢、及奪種種資生具者、是人則壞三世諸佛眞實報身、則挑一切人天眼目。是人爲欲隱没諸佛所有正法・三寶種故、令諸天人不得利益、墮地獄故、爲三惡道增長盈滿故。

The Buddha said,[51]

48　**city of fearlessness** (*mui jō* 無畏城): I.e., nirvāṇa.

49　**Again, he said** (*yū un* 又云): Continuing quotation of the passage in the *Da fangdeng daji jing* 大方等大集經 (T.397.13:354c22-24).

50　**if someone harms this person on account of his impropriety** (*u i hihō nōgai shi sha* 有以非法惱害此者): Taking *hihō* 非法 ("non-dharma") here (and in the next section) to refer to the person's failure to take (or keep) the precepts. This phrase is more often read, "if someone improperly harms this person."

filling up the three evil paths (*eiman san akudō* 盈滿三惡道): An unusual expression, perhaps meaning something like, "the three lower realms of saṃsāra (animal, ghost, and the hells) would be filled with such people." See Supplementary Notes, s.v. "Six paths."

51　**The Buddha** (*butsu* 佛): Quoting another passage from the *Da fangdeng daji jing* 大方等大集經 (T.397.13:354a26-b5). In the sūtra, this passage precedes Dōgen's previous two quotations from the text; the order here accords rather with the quotation of the sūtra in the *Fayuan zhulin* 法苑珠林, by Daoshi 道世 (d. 683) (T.2122.53:427a9-16), which may in fact have been Dōgen's actual source.

24 DŌGEN'S *SHŌBŌGENZŌ* VOLUME VI

If there are living beings who leave home for my sake, shave off their beards and hair and clothe themselves in the kāṣāya but do not keep the precepts, they have all already been stamped with the seal of nirvāṇa. If, furthermore, there are those who leave home but do not keep the precepts, anyone who, on account of their impropriety, afflicts them, abuses and humiliates them, disparages them, beats, binds, or cuts them with knife or staff, or seizes their robes and pātra bowls, or seizes their various necessities of daily life — this person will thereby destroy the true recompense body of the buddhas of the three times, will thereby gouge out the eyes of all the humans and devas.[52] For this person wishes to eradicate the true dharma possessed by the buddhas and the seeds of the three treasures; to cause devas and humans to fall into the hells without gaining benefits; and to increase and fill up the three evil paths.

[T1:30]

しるべし、剃髪染衣すれば、たとひ不持戒なれども、無上大涅槃の印のために印せらるるなり。ひと、これを悩乱すれば、三世諸佛の報身を壊するなり、逆罪とおなじかるべし。あきらかにしりぬ、出家の功徳、ただちに三世諸佛にちかしといふことを。

Thus, we know that, when one shaves the head and dyes the robe, even though one does not keep the precepts, one is stamped by the seal of the unsurpassed great nirvāṇa.[53] If someone were to afflict such a person, they would be destroying the recompense bodies of the buddhas of the three times, the same as a heinous offense. Clearly, we know from this that the merit of leaving home is, in itself, close to that of the buddhas of the three times.

* * * * *

[T1:31] {2:280}

佛言、夫出家者、不應起惡、若起惡者、則非出家。出家之人、身口相應。若不相應、則非出家。我棄父母・兄弟・妻子・眷屬・知識、出家修道。正是修集諸善覺時、非是修集不善覺時。善覺者、憐愍一切衆生、猶如赤子。不善覺者、與此相違。

The Buddha said,[54]

---

52 **true recompense body of the buddhas of the three times** (*sanze shobutsu shinjitsu hōjin* 三世諸佛眞實報身): The perfected body attained by all the buddhas, past, present, and future.

53 **shaves the head and dyes the robe** (*teihatsu zen'e* 剃髪染衣): A fixed expression for joining the Buddhist monastic order.

54 **The Buddha** (*butsu* 佛): Quoting the *Nirvāṇa Sūtra* (*Da banniepan jing* 大般涅槃經, T.374.12:498c13-17).

T1. The Merit of Leaving Home *Shukke kudoku* 出家功徳 25

Now, one who leaves home ought not give rise to evil; if one gives rise to evil, that is not leaving home. The physical and verbal acts of a person who leaves home are in accord with each other; if they are not in accord, this is not leaving home. Abandoning father and mother, brothers, wife and child, relatives, and friends, I left home and trained in the way. Truly, this was a time when I cultivated and accumulated virtuous feelings; it was not a time when I cultivated and accumulated nonvirtuous feelings.

"Virtuous feelings" means "compassion for all living beings, as if for an infant"; "nonvirtuous feelings" are the opposite of that.[55]

[T1:32]

それ出家の自性は、憐愍一切衆生、猶如赤子なり。これすなはち不起悪なり、身口相應なり。その儀、すでに出家なるがごときは、その德、いまかくのごとし。

So, the essential nature of leaving home is *"compassion for all living beings, as if for an infant."* This is *"not giving rise to evil"*; it is *"physical and verbal acts in accord."* When the behavior is truly that of leaving home, its virtue is like this now.[56]

* * * * *

[T1:33]

佛言、復次舍利弗、菩薩摩訶薩、若欲出家日、即成阿耨多羅三藐三菩提、即是日轉法輪、轉法輪時、無量阿僧祇衆生、遠塵離垢、於諸法中、得法眼淨、無量阿僧祇衆生、得一切法不受故、諸漏心得解脱、無量阿僧祇衆生、於阿耨多羅三藐三菩提、得不退轉、當學般若波羅蜜。

The Buddha said,[57]

Furthermore, Śāriputra, if bodhisattva-mahāsattvas wish on the very day they leave home to attain anuttara-samyak-saṃbodhi, and on that

---

55 **"Virtuous feelings" means "compassion for all living beings, as if for an infant"** (*zenkaku sha, renmin issai shujō, yūnyo shakushi* 善覺者、憐愍一切衆生、猶如赤子): This sentence does not occur in the sūtra and, though composed in Chinese, would seem to be Dōgen's comment. His definition of "virtuous feelings" (*zenkaku* 善覺) is a fixed phrase for compassion that does appear elsewhere in the *Nirvāṇa Sūtra* (at *Da banniepan jing* 大般涅槃經, T.374.12:474c19-20).

56 **When the behavior is truly that of leaving home, its virtue is like this now** (*sono gi sude ni shukke naru ga gotoki wa, sono toku, ima kaku no gotoshi* その儀すでに出家なるがごときは、その德、いまかくのごとし): Perhaps meaning something like, "When one's behavior is true to the ideal of leaving home, one will have the virtues described here."

57 **The Buddha** (*butsu* 佛): Quoting the *Pañca-viṃśati-sāhasrikā-prajñā-pāramitā-sūtra* (*Mohe bore boluomi jing* 摩訶般若波羅蜜經, T.223.8:220c29-221a6).

26 DŌGEN'S *SHŌBŌGENZŌ* VOLUME VI

very day to turn the dharma wheel, and when they turn the dharma wheel, incalculable asaṃkhyeya of living beings, distancing themselves from the dust and separating themselves from the dirt, in the midst of the dharmas attain clarity of the dharma eye, and incalculable asaṃkhyeya of living beings, by attaining non-appropriation of all dharmas, attain liberation from contaminated mental states, and incalculable asaṃkhyeya of living beings attain non-regression from anuttara-samyak-saṃbodhi, then they should study the prajñā-pāramitā.[58]

[T1:34] {2:281}
いはゆる學般若菩薩とは、祖祖なり。しかあるに、阿耨多羅三藐三菩提は、かならず出家の即日に成熟するなり。しかあれども、三阿僧祇劫に修證し、無量阿僧祇劫に修證するに、有邊・無邊に染汚するにあらず、學人しるべし。

The "bodhisattvas who study prajñā" are ancestor after ancestor. And *anuttara-samyak-saṃbodhi* is invariably brought to maturity on the very day they leave home. Even so, in their practice and verification throughout three *asaṃkheya-kalpas*, in their practice and verification throughout incalculable *asaṃkhyeya-kalpas*, they are not defiled by the extremes of existence and nonexistence.[59] Students should know this.

* * * * *

[T1:35]
佛言、若菩薩摩訶薩、作是思惟、我於何時、當捨國位、出家之日、即成無上正等菩提、還於是日、轉妙法輪、即令無量無數有情、遠塵離垢、生淨法眼、復令無量無數有情、永盡諸漏、心慧解脱、亦令無量無數有情、皆於無上正等菩提、得不退轉。是菩薩摩訶薩、欲成斯事、應學般若波羅蜜。

The Buddha said,[60]

---

58 **attain non-regression from *anuttara-samyak-saṃbodhi*** (*o anokutara sanmyaku sanbodai, toku futaiten* 於阿耨多羅三藐三菩提、得不退轉): I.e., gain a stage (often defined as the seventh ground [*bhūmi*] of the bodhisattva path) beyond which one will surely continue to unsurpassed perfect awakening.

59 **practice and verification throughout three *asaṃkheya-kalpas*** (*san asōgi kō ni shushō shi* 三阿僧祇劫に修證し): Three incalculable æons being the length of time traditionally calculated to complete the bodhisattva path.

they are not defiled by the extremes of existence and nonexistence (*uhen muhen ni zenna suru ni arazu* 有邊・無邊に染汚するにあらず): While this may well be a reference to metaphysical duality of being and nonbeing, the existence or nonexistence in question here might be seen as that of *anuttara-samyak-saṃbodhi* — i.e., throughout their long careers, bodhisattvas do not concern themselves with whether they do or do not have unsurpassed perfect awakening.

60 **The Buddha** (*butsu* 佛): Quoting the *Mahā-prajñā-pāramitā-sūtra* (*Da bore boluomi jing* 大般若波羅蜜經, T.220.5:16b10-16).

T1. The Merit of Leaving Home *Shukke kudoku* 出家功德

If there is a bodhisattva-mahāsattva who thinks,

> *On the very day when at some point I abandon my position as ruler of the country and leave home, I shall attain unsurpassed, perfect bodhi; and again on that day, I shall turn the wheel of the wondrous dharma, thereby enabling incalculable, innumerable sentient beings to distance themselves from the dust and separate themselves from the dirt, and to give rise to the clear dharma eye; and further enabling incalculable, innumerable sentient beings forever to exhaust the contaminants and be liberated in mind and wisdom; and also enabling incalculable, innumerable sentient beings all to attain non-regression from unsurpassed perfect bodhi,*

then this bodhisattva-mahāsattva wishing to accomplish these things ought to study the prajñā-pāramitā.[61]

[T1:36] {2:282}

これすなはち最後身の菩薩として、王宮に降生し、捨國位、成正覺、轉法輪、度衆生の功德を、宣説しましますなり。

This is his proclaiming the merit when, as a bodhisattva in his last body, he descended to birth in the royal palace, abandoned his position as ruler of the country, attained right awakening, turned the dharma wheel, and delivered living beings.[62]

[T1:37]

悉達太子、從車匿邊、索取摩尼雜飾莊嚴七寶把刀、自以右手、執於彼刀、從鞘拔出、即以左手、攬捉紺青優鉢羅色螺髻之髮、右手自持利刀割取、以右手擎、擲置空中。時天帝釋、以希有心、生大歡喜、捧太子髻、不令墮地以天妙衣、承受接取。爾時諸天、以彼勝上天諸供具、而供養之。

Prince Siddhārtha requested from Chandaka his sword, with a hilt of the seven treasures, adorned with maṇi jewels and diverse ornaments.[63] *Taking hold of the sword himself with his right hand and drawing it from its scabbard, with his left hand, he grasped the hair of his conch-shaped topknot, the color of deep blue utpala, and cut it off with the sharp sword held in his own right hand.*[64] *Raising it up in his left hand,*

---

61 **liberated in mind and wisdom** (*shin'e gedatsu* 心慧解脱): I.e., liberated from the hindrances of the afflictions (*bonnō shō* 煩惱障; S. *kleśāvaraṇa*) and from the hindrances to knowledge (*chi shō* 智障; S. *jñeyāvaraṇa*), respectively.

62 **his proclaiming** (*sensetsu shimashimasu* 宣説しまします): The unexpressed subject here is "Buddha Śākyamuni."

63 **Prince Siddhārtha** (*Shidda taishi* 悉達太子): More often read *Shitta* 悉達. Quoting the description of Siddhārtha's leaving home from the *Abhiniṣkramaṇa-sūtra* (*Fo benxingji jing* 佛本行集經, T.190.3:737c3-9).

Chandaka (*Shanoku* 車匿): Siddhārtha's servant, who later became a disciple.

64 *utpala* (*utsupara* 優鉢羅): The blue lotus blossom.

28 DŌGEN'S *SHŌBŌGENZŌ* VOLUME VI

he tossed it into the air. At that time, Deva Lord Śakra, marveling at this and filled with the utmost joy, clasped the prince's hair and, without letting it fall to the ground, received it into a marvelous heavenly robe. Then the devas made offerings to it with the offerings of their most excellent heaven.

[T1:38]

これ釋迦如來、そのかみ太子のとき、夜半に踰城し、日たけてやまにいりて、みづから頭髮を斷じまします。ときに淨居天きたりて、頭髮を剃除したてまつり、袈裟をさづけたてまつれり。これ、かならず如來出世の瑞相なり、諸佛世尊の常法なり。

Here, Tathāgata Śākya, when he was still a prince, fleeing the palace in the middle of the night and entering the mountains as the sun rose, personally cut off his hair. At this time, the Śuddhāvāsa devas went to him, shaved his head and presented him with a *kāṣāya*.[65] This is an auspicious sign whenever a tathāgata appears in the world; it is the constant norm of the buddhas, the world-honored ones.

[T1:39]

三世十方諸佛、みな一佛としても、在家成佛の諸佛ましまさず。過去有佛のゆえに、出家・受戒の功德あり。衆生の得道、かならず出家・受戒によるなり。おほよそ出家・受戒の功德、すなはち諸佛の常法なるがゆえに、その功德、無量なり。聖教のなかに、在家成佛の説あれど、正傳にあらず、女身成佛の説あれど、またこれ正傳にあらず、佛祖正傳するは、出家成佛なり。

Among the buddhas of the three times and ten directions, there are no buddhas, not even a single buddha, who attained buddhahood as householders. Because there are buddhas in the past, there is the merit of leaving home and receiving the precepts. Living beings' gaining of the way depends on their leaving home and receiving the precepts. In sum, it is because the merit of leaving home and receiving the precepts is the constant norm of the buddhas that such merit is incalculable. Although within the sacred teachings there is talk of attaining buddhahood as a householder, this is not the authentic transmission; although there is talk of becoming a buddha in a female body, this too is not the authentic

---

65 **Śuddhāvāsa devas** (*Jōgo ten* 淨居天): Reflecting the story told in the *Fo benxing ji jing* 佛本行集經(T.190.3:737c10ff) immediately following the passage quoted in the previous section — a story that begins,

爾時淨居諸天大衆去於太子。

At this time, the great multitude of the Śuddhāvāsa devas went to the prince.

Śuddhāvāsa, highest of the four heavens of the form realm, is the heaven into which the non-returner is born before entering nirvāṇa.

T1. The Merit of Leaving Home *Shukke kudoku* 出家功德 29

transmission. What the buddhas and ancestors authentically transmit is attaining buddhahood as one who has left home.[66]

* * * * *

[T1:40] {2:283}

第四祖優婆毱多尊者、有長者子、名曰提多迦、來禮尊者、志求出家。尊者曰、汝、身出家、心出家。答曰、我來出家、非爲身心。尊者曰、不爲身心、復誰出家。答曰、夫出家者、無我故。無我我故、即心不生滅、心不生滅、即是常道、諸佛亦常。心無形相、其體亦然。尊者曰、汝當大悟心自通達。宜依佛法僧紹隆聖種。即與出家受具。

[At the time of] the Fourth Ancestor, Venerable Upagupta, there was the son of a rich man by the name of Dhītika who came and paid obeisance to the Venerable, seeking to leave home.[67]

The Venerable said, "Will you leave home with the body or leave home with the mind?"

He replied, "My coming to leave home is not due to the body or the mind."

The Venerable said, "If not due to your body or your mind, then who is leaving home?"

He replied, "It's because leaving home is without me or mine.[68] Because leaving home is without me or mine, the mind does not arise or cease. When the mind does not arise or cease, this is the constant way. The buddhas are also constant. Their minds are without shape; their bodies as well."

---

66 **What the buddhas and ancestors authentically transmit** (*busso shōden suru wa* 佛祖正傳するは): By reference to the "buddhas and ancestors," Dōgen here signals that he will now turn his attention from the broader Buddhist literature to the texts of the Zen tradition.

67 **the Fourth Ancestor, Venerable Upagupta** (*daishi so Ubakikuta sonja* 第四祖優婆毱多尊者): Quoting, with some variation, the *Jingde chuandeng lu* 景德傳燈錄 (T.2076.51:207b28-c5).

Dīthika (*Daitaka* 提多迦): The fifth ancestor in the traditional account of the Zen lineage in India.

68 **"It's because leaving home is without me or mine"** (*fu shukke sha, mugaga ko* 夫出家者、無我我故): Taking *gaga* 我我 here as the equivalent of the more common *gagasho* 我我所 ("I and mine"), as Dōgen himself does below. Kawamura's text agrees with the *Jingde chuandeng lu* 景德傳燈錄 (at T.2076.51:b28-c2), but some other editions read *mugagasho* 無我我所 here. It is also possible to read this phrase as, "It's because those who leave home are without selves."

30 DŌGEN'S *SHŌBŌGENZŌ* VOLUME VI

The Venerable said, "You must have a great awakening, so that your mind personally penetrates it.[69] *It is well that, relying on buddha, dharma, and saṃgha, you perpetuate the sacred lineage."*

Thereupon, he permitted him to leave home and receive the full precepts.

[T1:41]

それ、諸佛の法にあふたてまつりて出家するは、最第一の勝果報なり。その法、すなはち我のためにあらず、我所のためにあらず、身心のためにあらず、身心の出家するにあらず。出家の、我・我所にあらざる道理かくのごとし。我・我所にあらざれば、諸佛の法なるべし、ただこれ諸佛の常法なり。諸佛の常法なるがゆえに、我・我所にあらず、身心にあらざるなり。三界の、かたをひとしくするところにあらず。かくのごとくなるがゆえに、出家、これ最上の法なり。頓にあらず、漸にあらず、常にあらず、無常にあらず、來にあらず、去にあらず、住にあらず、作にあらず、廣にあらず、狹にあらず、大にあらず、小にあらず、無作にあらず。佛法單傳の祖師、かならず出家・受戒せずといふことなし。いまの提多迦、はじめて優婆毱多尊者にあふたてまつりて出家をもとむる道理、かくのごとし。出家受具し、優婆毱多尊者に參じ、つひに第五の祖師となれり。

To encounter the dharma of the buddhas and leave home is the most excellent of karmic recompense. That dharma is not due to me, not due to mine, not due to body or mind; it is not that the body and mind leave home. The principle that leaving home is not [a matter of] me and mine is like this. When it is not me and mine, it must be the dharma of the buddhas; it is just the constant dharma of the buddhas. Because it is the constant dharma of the buddhas, it is not me and mine, it is not body and mind. It is not to be matched shoulder to shoulder with the three realms. Because it is like this, leaving home is the supreme dharma. It is not sudden and is not gradual; it is not permanent and is not impermanent; it is not coming and is not going; it is not stationary and is not active; it is not broad and is not narrow; it is not large and is not small; it is not nonactive.[70] The ancestral masters who uniquely transmitted the buddha dharma never failed to leave home and receive the precepts. Such is the reason why Dhītika here requested to leave home when he first met

---

69 **"You must have a great awakening, so that your mind personally penetrates it"** (*nyo tō daigo shin ji tsūdatsu* 汝當大悟心自通達): A tentative translation of a sentence variously interpreted. Some read the word *tō* 當 not as an imperative but as marking a future tense ("you will have a great awakening"); some take the phrase *shin ji tsūdatsu* 心自通達 not as a reference to Dhītika's understanding but as the object of his awakening ("the mind is naturally penetrating").

70 **it is not stationary and is not active** (*jū ni arazu, sa ni arazu* 住にあらず、作にあらず): Some MS witnesses read here, "it is not stationary and is not moving (*jū ni arazu, gyō ni arazu* 住にあらず、行にあらず) . . . it is not active and is not nonactive (*sa ni arazu, musa ni arazu* 作にあらず、無作にあらず).

T1. The Merit of Leaving Home *Shukke kudoku* 出家功德 31

Venerable Upagupta. Leaving home and receiving the full precepts, he studied under Venerable Upagupta and eventually became the fifth ancestral master.

* * * * *

[T1:42] {2:284}

第十七祖僧伽難提尊者、室羅閥城寶莊嚴王之子也。生而能言、常讚佛事。七歲即厭世樂、以偈告其父母曰、稽首大慈父、和南骨血母、我今欲出家、幸願哀愍故。父母固止之、遂終日不食。乃許其在家出家、號僧伽難提、復命沙門禪利多、爲之師。積十九載、未嘗退倦。尊者每自念言、身居王宮、胡爲出家。一夕天光下屬、見一路坦平、不覺徐行約十里許、至大巖前、有石窟焉、乃燕寂于中。父既失子、即擯禪利多、出國訪尋其子、不知所在。經十年、尊者得法授記已、行化至摩提國。

The Seventeenth Ancestor, Venerable Saṃghanandi, was the son of King Ratnavyūha of Śrāvastī.[71] Able to speak from birth, he constantly praised matters Buddhist. At the age of seven, he grew weary of worldly pleasures and addressed his father and mother with a gāthā that said,

> *Making prostrations to my father of great compassion,*
> *Vandana to the mother of my bones and blood;*
> *I wish now to leave home;*
> *Please grant my wish, for pity's sake.[72]*

His father and mother firmly stopped him, whereupon he did not eat all day, until they permitted him to leave home while remaining at home. They named him Saṃghanandi and had the Śramaṇa Chanliduo serve as his teacher.[73] Throughout nineteen years, he never once slacked off or tired, but the Venerable always thought to himself, "When my body is residing in the royal palace, how can this be leaving home?"

One night a light from the heavens shown down, and he saw a road level and even. Unconsciously, he followed it for about ten miles, until he arrived before a great cliff, with a stone grotto. Within it, he remained in solitary repose. The father, having lost his son, sent away Chanliduo, who left the land in search of the son but could not deter-

---

71 **The Seventeenth Ancestor, Venerable Saṃghanandi** (*dai jūshichi so Sōganandai sonja* 第十七祖僧伽難提尊者): Quoting the *Jingde chuandeng lu* 景德傳燈錄 (T.2076.51:212a25-b8).

Śrāvastī (*Shiraba jō* 室羅閥城): More often transliterated *Shae jō* 舍衛城; capital city of the northern Indian kingdom of Kośala, site of the famous Jetavana park, where the Buddha often stayed. The reconstruction of Saṃghnandi's father's name as Ratnavyūha is uncertain.

72 *Vandana* (*wanan* 和南): Transliteration of the Sanskrit term for "obeisance."

73 **the Śramaṇa Chanliduo** (*shamon Zenrita* 沙門禪利多): A name appearing only in this story for which there is no certain Sanskrit reconstruction.

32 DŌGEN'S *SHŌBŌGENZŌ* VOLUME VI

mine his whereabouts. In the following ten years, after the Venerable had attained the dharma and a conferral of prediction, he went forth and taught throughout Magadha.

[T1:43] {2:285}

在家出家、の稱、このときはじめてきこゆ。ただし宿善のたすくるところ、天光のなかに坦路をえたり。つひに王宮をいでて石窟にいたる、まことに勝躅なり。世樂をいとひ、俗塵をうれふるは、聖者なり、五欲をしたひ、出離をわするるは、凡愚なり。代宗・肅宗、しきりに僧徒にちかづけりといへども、なほ王位をむさぼりて、いまだなげすてず。盧居士は、すでに親を辭して祖となる、出家の功德なり。龐居士は、たからをすてて、ちりをすてず、至愚なりといふべし。盧公の道力と、龐公が稽古と、比類にたらず。あきらかなるは、かならず出家す、くらきは、家にをはる、黑業の因縁なり。

The nomenclature "*leaving home while remaining at home*," is first heard at this time. However, aided by his good karma from former lives, he gained a level road in the light from the heavens. In the end, his leaving the royal palace and going to the stone cave was truly a superlative example. Those who weary of worldly pleasures and are troubled by the dust of the profane world are sages; those who love the five desires and forget about getting free from them are common fools. Although Daizong and Suzong regularly associated with monastics, they were still covetous of their royal status and never renounced it.[74] Layman Lu's having left his parent and become an ancestor was the merit of leaving home.[75] Layman Pang's throwing away his treasure but not throwing off the dust has to be the height of stupidity.[76] Mr. Pang's investigation of the ancients does not bear comparison with Mr. Lu's power of the way. Those who see clearly invariably leave home; those in the dark end up at home, the cause and conditions of black deeds.[77]

* * * * *

---

74 **Daizong and Suzong** (*Daisō Shukusō* 代宗肅宗): Tang-dynasty emperors, reigning 762-779 and 756-762, respectively, both of whom were patrons of Chan Master Nanyang Huizhong 南陽慧忠 (d. 775).

75 **Layman Lu** (*Ro koji* 盧居士): I.e., the Sixth Ancestor, Huineng 慧能, who is said to have abandoned his mother and become a lay postulant in the monastery of the Fifth Ancestor, Hongren. It was in that status that he was recognized as the sixth ancestor, only being ordained as a monk sometime after parting company with Hongren.

76 **Layman Pang** (*Hō koji* 龐居士): Celebrated lay practitioner Pang Yun 龐蘊 (740?-808), who is said to have thrown his wealth into a river but remained in the "dust" of worldly life.

77 **black deeds** (*kokugō* 黑業): I.e., bad karma.

T1. The Merit of Leaving Home *Shukke kudoku* 出家功徳   33

[T1:44]

南嶽懷讓禪師、一日自歎曰、夫出家者、爲無生法、天上・人間、無有勝者。

Chan Master Nanyue Huairang, one day sighed to himself, saying,[78]

Leaving home
Is the unborn dharma;
In the heavens and among humans,
Nothing surpasses it.

[T1:45] {2:286}

いはく、無生法とは、如來の正法なり。このゆえに、天上・人間にすぐれたり。天上といふは、欲界に六天あり、色界に十八天あり、無色界に四種、ともに出家の道におよぶことなし。

The "unborn dharma" here means the true dharma of the tathāgatas. Therefore, it surpasses "in the heavens and among humans." "The heavens" consist in the six heavens of the desire realm, the eighteen heavens of the form realm, and the four kinds in the formless realm; none of them reaches the path of leaving home.

* * * * *

[T1:46]

盤山寶積禪師曰、禪德、可中學道、似地擎山、不知山之孤峻。如石含玉、不知玉之無瑕。若如是者、是名出家。

Chan Master Baoji of Panshan said,[79]

The study of the way is like the earth supporting the mountain without knowing of the mountain's solitary steepness, like the rock containing the gem without knowing of the gem's flawlessness. Such as this is called "leaving home."

---

78   **Chan Master Nanyue Huairang** (*Nangaku Ejō zenji* 南嶽懷讓禪師): 677-744, disciple of the Sixth Ancestor, Huineng 慧能. His words here are found in the *Tiansheng guangdeng lu* 天聖廣燈錄 (ZZ.135:650a2-3), with slight variation:

夫出家者、爲無爲法。
Leaving home
Is the unconditioned dharma.

79   **Chan Master Baoji of Panshan** (*Banzan Hōshaku zenji* 盤山寶積禪師): Dates unknown; a disciple of Mazu Daoyi 馬祖道一 (709-788). His saying occurs at *Jingde chuandeng lu* 景德傳燈錄, T.2076.51:253b20-22.

34   DŌGEN'S *SHŌBŌGENZŌ* VOLUME VI

[T1:47]

佛祖の正法、かならずしも知・不知にかかはれず。出家は佛祖の正法なるがゆえに、その功徳あきらかなり。

The true dharma of the buddhas and ancestors does not necessarily have to do with knowing or not knowing. Because leaving home is the true dharma of the buddhas and ancestors, its merit is clear.

* * * * *

[T1:48]

鎭州臨濟院義玄禪師曰、夫出家者、須辨得平常眞正見解、辨佛・辨魔、辨眞・辨僞、辨凡・辨聖。若如是辨得、名眞出家。若魔佛不辨、正是出一家入一家、喚作造業衆生、未得名爲眞正出家。

Chan Master Yixuan of Linji Cloister in Zhenzhou said,[80]

Those who leave home should be able to discern ordinary and true views, to discern the Buddha and discern Māra, to discern the genuine and discern the fake, to discern the commoner and discern the sage.[81] *If one can discern things like this, it's called truly leaving home; if one doesn't discern Māra and the Buddha, this is actually leaving one home and entering another home. We can call [such people] living beings producing karma; we can't say that they've really left home.*

[T1:49] {2:287}

いはゆる平常眞正見解、といふは、深信因果、深信三寶等なり。辨佛、といふは、ほとけの因中・果上の功徳を、念ずることあきらかなるなり。眞・僞、凡・聖を、あきらかに辨肯するなり。もし魔・佛をあきらめざれば、學道を阻壞し、學道を退轉するなり。魔事を覺知して、その事にしたがはざれば、辨道不退なり。これを、眞正出家の法とす。いたづらに魔事を佛法とおもふものおほし、近世の非なり。學者、はやく魔をしり、佛をあきらめ、修證すべし。

"Ordinary and true views" here means "deep faith in cause and effect," "deep faith in the three treasures," and the like. To "discern the Buddha" means that one's recollection of the merit of the Buddha at the stages of both cause and effect is clear; it means clearly to confirm genuine and fake, commoner and sage. If one is not clear about Māra and the Buddha, one destroys one's study of the way, one turns back from the study of

---

80 **Chan Master Yixuan of Linji Cloister in Zhenzhou** (*Chinshū Rinzaiin Gigen zenji* 鎭州臨濟院義玄禪師): I.e., Linji Yixuan 臨濟義玄 (d. 866). His saying can be found in the *Tiansheng guangdeng lu* 天聖廣燈錄 (ZZ.135:692b9-13); see also *Linji lu* 臨濟錄 (T.1985.47:498a24-27); *Zhengfayanzang* 正法眼藏 (ZZ.118:62b11-14).

81 **should be able to discern ordinary and true views** (*shu bentoku byōjō shinshō kenge* 須辨得平常眞正見解): Or, as is suggested by Dōgen's interpretation in the following section, "should be able to discern with views that are ordinary and true."

T1. The Merit of Leaving Home *Shukke kudoku* 出家功德　　35

the way. When one perceives the doings of Māra and does not go along with them, that is pursuit of the way without regressing. This is what is taken as the dharma of "really leaving home." That there are many who foolishly think that the doings of Māra are the buddha dharma is a failing of recent times. Students should quickly recognize Māra, clarify the Buddha, and pursue practice and verification.

* * * * *

[T1:50]

如來般涅槃時、迦葉菩薩、白佛言、世尊、如來具足知諸根力、定知善星當斷善根、以何因緣、聽其出家。佛言、善男子、我於往昔、初出家時、吾弟難陀、從弟阿難・調達多、子羅睺羅、如是等輩、皆悉隨我出家修道。我若不聽善星出家、其人次當王得紹王位。其力自在、當壞佛法。以是因緣、我便聽其出家修道。善男子、善星比丘若不出家、亦斷善根、於無量世、都無利益。今出家已、雖斷善根、能受持戒、供養恭敬、耆舊・長宿・有德之人、修習初禪乃至四禪、是名善因、能生善法。善法既生、能修習道。既修習道、當得阿耨多羅三藐三菩提。是故我聽善星出家。善男子、若我不聽善星比丘出家受戒、則不得稱我爲如來具足十力。善男子、佛觀衆生具足善法及不善法。是人雖具如是二法、不久能斷一切善根、具不善根。何以故。如是衆生、不親善友、不聽正法、不善思惟、不如法行。以是因緣、能斷善根、具不善根。

> *At the time of the Tathāgata's parinirvāṇa, Bodhisattva Kāśyapa addressed the Buddha, saying, "World-Honored One, the Tathāgata, being fully endowed with the power to know the faculties, surely knew that Sunakṣatra would cut off his good roots; so, for what reason did you permit him to leave home?"*[82]

> *The Buddha said,*

> *Good son, in the past, when I first left home, a group such as my brother Nanda, my cousins Ānanda and Devadatta, my son Rāhula, and so on, all followed me in leaving home and training in the way. If I had not permitted Sunakṣatra to leave home, the man would have succeeded to the throne as the next king and, free to wield his power, would have destroyed the buddha dharma. For this reason, I permitted him to leave home and train in the way.*

> *Good son, even if Bhikṣu Sunakṣatra had not left home, he would still have cut off his good roots and been entirely without benefit*

82　**At the time of the Tathāgata's** *parinirvāṇa* (*nyorai hatsunehan ji* 如來般涅槃時): Quoting the *Nirvāṇa Sūtra* (*Da banniepan jing* 大般涅槃經, T.374.12:562c28-563a18).

Sunakṣatra (*Zensei* 善星): Said in the *Nirvāṇa Sūtra* (T.374.12:560b13ff) to have been Siddhārtha's son, who left home, studied the dharma, and mastered the four dhyānas, only to fall into bad company, develop false views, and eventually become an *icchantika* and descend into the hells.

36 DŌGEN'S *SHŌBŌGENZŌ* VOLUME VI

for incalculable lifetimes. Now, having left home, although he has cut off his good roots, he has been able to receive and keep the precepts, to make offerings to and venerate his elders, honored seniors, and virtuous persons, and to practice the first dhyāna through the fourth dhyāna. These are called good causes, which can produce good practices. When good practices are produced, one can train in the way; when one trains in the way, one attains anuttara-samyak-saṃbodhi. For this reason, I permitted Sunakṣatra to leave home.

Good son, if I had not permitted Bhikṣu Sunakṣatra to leave home and receive the precepts, then I could not be called a tathāgata endowed with the ten powers. Good son, a buddha sees that living beings are endowed with wholesome attributes as well as unwholesome attributes. This person, although endowed with both such attributes, before long would have been capable of cutting off all his wholesome roots and possessing only unwholesome roots. Why? Because living beings like him are not close to wise friends, do not listen to the true dharma, do not consider well, and do not act in accordance with the dharma. For this reason, they are capable of cutting off their wholesome roots and possessing only unwholesome roots.

[T1:51] {2:289}

しるべし、如來世尊、あきらかに衆生の斷善根となるべきをしらせ給ふといへども、善因をさづくるとして、出家をゆるさせ給ふ、大慈大悲なり。斷善根となること、善友にちかづかず、正法をきかず、善思惟せず、如法に行ぜざるによれり。いま學者、必ず善友に親近すべし。善友とは、諸佛まします、ととくなり、罪福あり、とをしふるなり。因果を撥無せざるを善友とし、善知識とす。この人の所説、これ正法なり。この道理を思惟する、善思惟なり。かくのごとく行ずる、如法行なるべし。しかあればすなはち、衆生は、親疏をえらばず、ただ出家・受戒をすすむべし。のちの退・不退をかへりみざれ、修・不修をおそるることなかれ、これまさに釋尊の正法なるべし。

We know from this that it is out of great pity and great compassion that the Tathāgata, the World-Honored One, although knowing clearly that some living beings will cut off their good roots, grants them permission to leave home in order to provide them with good causes. "Cutting off good roots" results from not being close to wise friends, not listening to the true dharma, not considering well, and not acting in accordance with the dharma. Students at present should without fail become close to a wise friend. A "wise friend" is one who explains that there are the buddhas and teaches that there are evils and blessings. One who does not deny cause and effect is considered a good companion, "a wise friend." What this person says is the "true dharma." To consider its truth

T1. The Merit of Leaving Home *Shukke kudoku* 出家功德   37

is "considering well." To act accordingly is "acting in accordance with the dharma." Therefore, regardless of whether living beings are familiar or remote, we should encourage them to leave home and receive the precepts. Do not reflect on whether they will subsequently regress or not regress; do not worry about whether they will practice or not practice. This is indeed the true dharma of Śākya, the Honored One.

* * * * *

[T1:52]

佛告比丘、當知、閻羅王、便作是説、我當何日脱此苦難、於人中生、以得人身、便得出家、剃除鬚髪、著三法衣、出家學道。閻羅王尚作是念、何況汝等、今得人身、得作沙門。是故諸比丘、當念行身口意行、無令有缺。當滅五結、修行五根。如是諸比丘、當作是學。爾時諸比丘、聞佛所説、歡喜奉行。

The Buddha addressed the bhikṣus:[83]

> *You should know that King Yama then made the following statement: "I shall someday slough off these tribulations, be born among humans, and, getting a human body, thereby be able to leave home, shave off my hair and beard, and donning the three dharma robes, leave home and study the way."*[84]

> *If even King Yama could have these thoughts, how much more so all of you, who have now got a human body and been able to become śramaṇas. Therefore, bhikṣus, you should be mindful to practice the practices of body, speech, and mind, without allowing any flaws. You should eradicate the five fetters and cultivate the five faculties.*[85] *In this way, you bhikṣus should study.*

At that time, the bhikṣus, hearing what the Buddha said, rejoiced and put it into practice.

---

83 **The Buddha** (*butsu* 佛): Quoting the *Ekottarāgama* (*Zengyi ahan jing* 增一阿含經, T.125.2:676b20-27).

84 **three dharma robes** (*sanbōe* 三法衣): The three types of garments permitted the bhikṣu: the "assembly robe" (*sōgyari* 僧伽梨; S. *saṃghāṭī*); the "upper robe" (*uttarasō* 欝多羅僧; S. *uttarasaṃghāṭī*); and the "inner robe" (*andae* 安陀會; S. *antarvāsa*). See Supplementary Notes, s.v. "Robe of the Tathāgata."

85 **five fetters** (*goketsu* 五結): A venerable list of spiritual defilements: desire (*ton* 貪), hatred (*i* 恚), pride (*man* 慢), envy (*shitsu* 嫉), and stinginess (*ken* 慳).

five faculties (*gokon* 五根): A standard set of spiritual virtues: faith (*shin* 信), effort (*shōjin* 精進), mindfulness (*nen* 念), concentration (*jō* 定), and wisdom (*e* 慧).

38 DŌGEN'S *SHŌBŌGENZŌ* VOLUME VI

[T1:53] {2:290}

あきらかにしりぬ、たとひ閻羅王なりといへども、人中の生をこひねがふ
こと、かくのごとし。すでにむまれたる人、いそぎ剃除鬚髪し、著三法衣
して、學佛道すべし。これ餘趣にすぐれたる人中の功德なり。しかある
を、人間にむまれながら、いたづらに官途世路を貪求し、むなしく國王・
大臣のつかはしめとして、一生を夢幻にめぐらし、後世は黒闇におもむ
き、いまだたのむところなきは、至愚なり。すでにうけがたき人身をうけ
たるのみにあらず、佛法にあひたてまつれり。いそぎ諸縁を抛捨し、すみ
やかに出家學道すべし。國王・大臣、妻子・眷屬は、ところごとに必ずあ
ふ、佛法は、優曇華のごとくしてあひがたし。おほよそ無常忽ちにいたる
ときは、國王・大臣、親昵・從僕、妻子・珍寶、たすくるなし、ただひと
り黄泉に趣くのみなり。おのれに隨ひゆくは、ただこれ善・惡業等のみな
り。人身を失せんとき、人身を、をしむこころふかかるべし。人身をたも
てるとき、はやく出家すべし、まさにこれ、三世の諸佛の正法なるべし。

We understand clearly from this that even King Yama has such desire
to be born among humans. Those who have already been born as humans should quickly "shave off their hair and beards" and, "donning the
three dharma robes," study the way of the buddhas. This is the virtue of
being human [that makes it] superior to the other destinies. However,
it is the height of stupidity, while born as a human, vainly to covet an
official career or worldly path, pointlessly spending one's life in dreams
and illusions as the agent of a king or great minister, one's next life
headed into darkness, never with anything to rely on. Not only have we
already received the human body, hard to receive; we have been granted
an encounter with the buddha dharma. We should quickly cast aside all
involvements and immediately leave home and study the way. Kings
and great ministers, wives, children, and kinsmen, we will inevitably
encounter everywhere; but the buddha dharma is as difficult to encounter as the *udumbara* blossom.[86] When impermanence suddenly arrives,
kings and great ministers, intimates and servants, wives and children,
our valued possessions will not save us; we will just proceed alone to
the Yellow Springs.[87] All that follows us is just our good and bad karma.
When we are about to lose the human body, we will value it profoundly;
while we still retain the human body, we should quickly leave home.
This indeed is the true dharma of the buddhas of the three times.

---

86 *udumbara* **blossom** (*udonge* 優曇華): Flower of a legendary tree said to bloom only
once every three thousand years.

87 **Yellow Springs** (*kōsen* 黄泉): A pre-Buddhist Chinese term for the netherworld
inhabited by the spirits of the dead.

T1. The Merit of Leaving Home *Shukke kudoku* 出家功德

[T1:54]

その出家行法に、四種あり、いはゆる四依なり。一盡形壽樹下坐、二盡形壽著糞掃衣、三盡形壽乞食、四盡形壽有病服陳棄藥。共行此法、方名出家、方名爲僧。若不行此、不名爲僧、是故名出家行法。

The methods of practice in this leaving home are fourfold, called the "four reliances":[88]

1. Throughout one's life, always to sit beneath trees. 2. Throughout one's life, to wear cast-off rags. 3. Throughout one's life, to beg for food. 4. Throughout one's life, when sick to take stale waste medicine.[89] Only when one practices all these methods is one called one who has left home, one is called a member of the saṃgha. If one does not practice them, one is not called a member of the saṃgha. Therefore, they are called the methods of practice in leaving home.

[T1:55] {2:291}

いま西天東地、佛祖正傳するところ、これ出家行法なり。一生不離叢林なれば、すなはちこの四依の行法、そなはれり。これを、行四依と稱す。これに違して五依を建立せん、しるべし、邪法なり。たれか信受せん、たれか忍聽せん。佛祖正傳するところ、これ正法なり。これによりて、出家する人間、最上最尊の慶幸なり。このゆえに、西天竺國には、すなはち難陀・阿難・調達・阿那律・摩訶男・拔提、ともにこれ師子頬王のむまご、刹利種姓の、もとも尊貴なるなり、はやく出家せり、後代の勝躅なるべし。いま刹利にあらざらんともがら、そのみ、ををしむべからず。王子にあらざらん輩、なにのをしむところかあらん。閻浮提最第一の尊貴より、三界最第一の尊貴に歸するは、すなはち出家なり。自餘の諸小國王・諸離車衆、いたづらにををしむべからざるををしみ、ほこるべからざるにほこり、とどまるべからざるにとどまりて出家せざらん、たれかつたなしとせざらん、たれか至愚なりとせざらん。

At present, in Sindh in the West and the Land of the East, what is directly transmitted by the buddhas and ancestors are these methods of practice in leaving home. When one is "*an entire lifetime without leaving the grove,*" one is equipped with the methods of practice of these four reliances.[90] This is called "practicing the four reliances." Opposing this and setting up five reliances, we should know to be a false dharma.[91]

---

88 **"four reliances"** (*shie* 四依): Quoting the *Dasheng yi zhang* 大乘義章, by Jingying Huiyuan 淨影慧遠 (523-592) (T.1851.44:608b21-25).

89 **stale waste medicine** (*chinki yaku* 陳棄藥): S. *pūti-mukta-bhaiṣajya*; purgative medicine said to be made from the putrid urine and dung of cattle.

90 **"an entire lifetime without leaving the grove"** (*isshō furi sōrin* 一生不離叢林): I.e., spending a lifetime in the monastery; a fixed expression from a saying attributed to Zhaozhou Congshen 趙州從諗 (778-897); see Supplementary Notes, s.v. "For a lifetime not leaving the grove."

91 **five reliances** (*goe* 五依): Likely an allusion to the "five dharmas" (*gohō* 五法)

40 DŌGEN'S *SHŌBŌGENZŌ* VOLUME VI

Who would believe in them? Who would acknowledge them? What is directly transmitted by the buddhas and ancestors — this is the true dharma. Humans who leave home in accordance with this are the highest, the most honored of the blessed.

Therefore, in the Land of Sindhu in the West, Nanda, Ānanda, Devadatta, Aniruddha, Mahānāman, and Bhadrika, all of them the grandchildren of King Siṃhahanu and most honored of the kṣatriya class, were quick to leave home.[92] They are splendid examples for later generations. Those today who are not kṣatriya should not begrudge their status; those who are princes, what would there be to begrudge? To go from being the single most honored in Jambudvīpa to arrive at the single most honored in the three realms — this was their leaving home. Other kings of small countries and the Licchavi, futilely begrudging what one should not begrudge, taking pride in what one should not be proud of, staying where one should not stay, without leaving home — who would not regard them as cowardly?[93] Who would not regard them as utterly stupid?

[T1:56]
羅睺羅尊者は、菩薩の子なり、淨飯王のむまごなり。帝位をゆづらんとす。しかあれども、世尊あながちに出家せしめまします。しるべし、出家の法、最尊なり、と。密行第一の弟子として、いまにいたりて、いまだ涅槃にいりましまさず。衆生の福田として、世間に現住しまします。

Venerable Rāhula was the son of the Bodhisattva and the grandson of King Śuddhodana, who intended to pass on the throne to him.[94] How-

---

recommended by Devadatta, of which there are several lists (e.g., at *Sifen lü* 四分律, T.1428.22:594b2-4):

盡形壽乞食。盡形壽著糞掃衣。盡形壽露坐。盡形壽不食酥鹽。盡形壽不食魚及肉。

Throughout one's life, to beg for food. Throughout one's life, to wear cast off rags. Throughout one's life, to sit outdoors. Throughout one's life, not to eat salt. Throughout one's life, not to eat fish or meat.

92   **Nanda, Ānanda, Devadatta, Aniruddha, Mahānāman, and Bhadrika** (*Nanda Anan Jōdatsu Anaritsu Makanan Batsudai* 難陀・阿難・調達・阿那律・摩訶男・拔提): Nanda was Siddhārtha's younger half-brother; the others were his cousins.

King Siṃhahanu (*Shishikyō ō* 師子頬王): A king of Kapilavastu, the paternal grandfather of Siddhārtha; his son Śuddhodana was Siddhārtha's father.

93   **Licchavi** (*sho Risha shu* 諸離車衆): A kṣatriya clan ruling in Vaiśālī. In his "Shōbōgenzō shizen biku" 正法眼藏四禪比丘, Dōgen tells the story of their sending a debater to challenge the Buddha.

94   **Venerable Rāhula** (*Ragora sonja* 羅睺羅尊者): Prince Siddhārtha's son, who joined the Buddhist order and became known as the disciple foremost in strict practice. He came to be listed among the eighteen arhats, as the one in "profound thought" (*shinshi* 深思). In the *Lotus Sūtra* (*Miaofa lianhua jing* 妙法蓮華經, T.262.9:30a16-b3), the Buddha predicts that he will be reborn under countless buddhas, becoming the eldest son of each.

T1. The Merit of Leaving Home *Shukke kudoku* 出家功徳   41

ever, the World-Honored One urged him to leave home. We know from this that the practice of leaving home is the most honored. As the disciple foremost in exact observance, right down to the present, he has yet to enter nirvāṇa; he exists in the world today as a field of merit for living beings.

[T1:57] {2:292}

西天、傳佛正法眼藏の祖師のなかに、王子の出家せる、しげし。いま震旦の初祖、これ香至王第三皇子なり。王位をおもくせず、正法を傳持せり。出家の最尊なること、あきらかにしりぬべし。これらにならぶるにおよばざる身をもちながら、出家しつべきにおきていそがざらん、いかならん明日をかまつべき。出息入息をまたず、いそぎ出家せん、それかしこかるべし。またしるべし、出家・受戒の師、その恩德、すなはち父母にひとしかるべし。

Among the ancestral masters who transmitted the Buddha's treasury of the true dharma eye in Sindh in the West, there were many princes who left home. And the First Ancestor in Cīnasthāna was the third prince of the king of Xiangzhi.[95] Thinking little of the throne, he received the transmission and kept the true dharma. We can recognize from this that leaving home is the most honored. While having a status that does not come close to ranking with these [Indian princes], in a position to leave home, were we not to make haste to do so, what possible tomorrow could we be waiting for? Immediately to leave home, without waiting for another inhalation or exhalation — that would be wise. And we should realize that the beneficence of the master under whom one leaves home and receives the precepts is equivalent to that of one's father and mother.

[T1:58]

禪苑清規第一云、三世諸佛、皆日出家成道。西天二十八祖、唐土六祖、傳佛心印、盡是沙門。蓋以嚴淨毘尼、方能洪範三界。然則參禪問道、戒律爲先。既非離過防非、何以成佛作祖。

In the *Rules of Purity for the Chan Park*, number 1, it is said,[96]

The buddhas of the three times all speak of leaving home and attaining the way. The twenty-eight ancestors of Sindh in the West and the six ancestors of the Land of Tang who transmitted the seal of the buddha

---

95   **the First Ancestor in Cīnasthāna was the third prince of the king of Xiangzhi** (*Shintan no shoso, kore Kōshi ō daisan kōshi nari* 震旦の初祖、これ香至王第三皇子なり): Reference to Bodhidharma. The Chinese name "Xiangzhi" has tentatively been identified with the ancient south Indian state of Kāñcīpura visited by the Chinese pilgrim Xuanzang.

96   ***Rules of Purity for the Chan Park,*** **number 1** (*Zennen shingi daiichi* 禪苑清規第一): Quoting the opening lines of the text, on "receiving the precepts" (*jukai* 受戒) (*Chanyuan qinggui* 禪苑清規, ZZ.111:877a4-7). Dōgen quotes the same passage in his "Shōbōgenzō shukke" 正法眼藏出家 and "Shōbōgenzō jukai" 正法眼藏受戒.

mind were all śramaṇas. *For it is only by the strict purity of the vinaya that one can be a great model for the three realms. This being the case, in studying Chan and inquiring about the way, the precepts are considered primary. If one has not yet freed oneself from transgressions and warded off impropriety, how could one attain buddhahood or become an ancestor?*

[T1:59]

たとひ澆風の叢林なりとも、なほこれ薝蔔の林なるべし、凡木凡草のおよぶところにあらず、また合水の乳のごとし。乳をもちいんとき、この和水の乳をもちいるべし、餘物をもちいるべからず。

Even a dissolute grove is still a grove of champak, not equaled by common trees and common grasses.[97] Or, again, it is like diluted milk: when we are going to use milk, we had better use this diluted milk and not something else.[98]

[T1:60] {2:293}

しかあればすなはち、三世諸佛皆曰出家成道、の正傳、もともこれ最尊なり。さらに出家せざる三世諸佛おはしまさず。これ、佛佛祖祖正傳の正法眼藏涅槃妙心無上菩提なり。

Thus, the authentic transmission according to which "*the buddhas of the three times all speak of leaving home and attaining the way*" is above all the most honored. There are definitely no buddhas of the three times who did not leave home. This is the treasury of the true dharma eye, the wondrous mind of nirvāṇa, the unsurpassed bodhi, directly transmitted by buddha after buddha and ancestor after ancestor.

正法眼藏出家功德第一
Treasury of the True Dharma Eye
The Merit of Leaving Home
Number One

---

97 **grove of champak** (*senbuku no rin* 薝蔔の林): Champak is an evergreen of the magnolia family, known for its fragrant blossoms. Dōgen plays here with the term *sōrin* 叢林 ("grove") used in reference to the monastic community.

98 **diluted milk** (*gōsui no nyū* 合水の乳): Presumably suggesting that joining even a "diluted" renunciant saṃgha is better than alternative life choices. From a metaphor found in the *Nirvāṇa Sūtra* (T.374.12:421c16-22a14), in which even watered-down teachings of the sūtra are far superior to other texts.

T1. The Merit of Leaving Home *Shukke kudoku* 出家功徳 43

[Chōenji MS:][99]

建長七年乙卯夏安居日

A day of the summer retreat, junior wood year of the rabbit, the seventh year of Kenchō [1255][100]

[Tōunji MS:]

延慶三年八月六日、書寫之

Copied this on the sixth day, eighth month, third year of Engyō [30 August 1310][101]

于時文明十二庚子年三月十七日、於于越州吉祥山永平寺承陽庵書寫之。比丘光周

Copied this in the Jōyō Hermitage, Eihei Monastery, Mount Kichijō, Esshū; seventeenth day, third month, senior metal year of the rat, the twelfth year of Bunmei [26 April 1480]. Bhikṣu Kōshū[102]

---

99 **Chōenji MS** 長圓寺本: Manuscript of the eighty-four-chapter *Shōbōgenzō*, copied 1645 (Shōhō 正保 2) by Kidō Sōe 暉堂宗慧 (d. 1650), second abbot of Chōenji.

100 Presumed to indicate a copy by Ejō.

day of the summer retreat (*ge ango no hi* 夏安居日): Dates of the summer retreat vary; a common practice put it from the fifteenth of the fourth lunar month through the fifteenth of the seventh month; in 1255, this would have corresponded to 22 May through 18 August.

101 Copyist unknown.

102 **Bhikṣu Kōshū** (*biku Kōshū* 比丘光周): Fifteenth abbot of Eiheiji (1434–1492?).

TREASURY OF THE TRUE DHARMA EYE
THE TWELVE-CHAPTER COMPILATION
NUMBER 2

Receiving the Precepts
Jukai

受戒

Receiving the Precepts

Jukai

INTRODUCTION

This second text of the twelve-chapter *Shōbōgenzō* is also found in the twenty-eight-text *Himitsu* collection, where it occurs as number 10 of fascicle 2; in the Honzan edition, it is included as number 94. Like most of the other texts of the twelve-chapter *Shōbōgenzō*, it is undated; nor do the manuscripts preserve colophons on its copying.

This work is less an essay than it is a liturgical text, prescribing the rite through which Dōgen's disciples were to receive what he calls here "the buddha precepts," directly transmitted by the buddhas and ancestors. The sixteen items prescribed here, consisting of the three refuges, the three sets of pure precepts, and the ten grave bodhisattva precepts, are still used in Sōtō Zen ordination ritual today. Though their content is somewhat different, the ritual itself is largely based on the *śrāmaṇera* precept ceremony given in the *Chanyuan qinggui* 禪苑清規, the oldest surviving Zen monastic code and a source for many of Dōgen's own monastic rules and regulations.

正法眼藏第二
Treasury of the True Dharma Eye
Number 2

受戒
Receiving the Precepts

[T2:1] {2:294}

禪苑清規云、三世諸佛、皆曰出家成道。西天二十八祖、唐土六祖、傳佛心印、盡是沙門。蓋以嚴淨毘尼、方能洪範三界。然則參禪問道、戒律爲先。既非離過防非、何以成佛作祖。受戒之法、應備三衣・鉢具並新淨衣物。如無新衣、浣染令淨。入壇受戒、不得借賃衣鉢。一心專注、慎勿異緣。像佛形儀、具佛戒律、得佛受用、此非小事、豈可輕心。若借賃衣鉢、雖登壇受戒、並不得成。若不會受、一生爲無戒之人。濫厠空門、虛受信施。初心入道、法律未諳、師匠不言、陷人於此。今茲苦口、敢望銘心。既受聲聞戒、應受菩薩戒、此入法之漸也。

In the *Rules of Purity for the Chan Park*, it is said,[1]

> The buddhas of the three times all speak of leaving home and attaining the way. The twenty-eight ancestors of Sindh in the West and the six ancestors of the Land of the Tang who transmitted the seal of the buddha mind were all *śramaṇas*. For it is only by maintaining strict purity in accordance with the vinaya that one can be a great model for the three realms. This being the case, in studying Chan and inquiring about the way, the precepts are considered primary. If one has not yet freed oneself from transgressions and warded off impropriety, how could one attain buddhahood or become an ancestor?

> With regard to the procedure for receiving the precepts, one should be prepared with the three robes, *pātra* utensil, and new clean clothing.[2] If one does not have new robes, purify the clothing by washing and dyeing. When entering the platform and receiving the precepts, one may not borrow robes and *pātra*. Concentrate single-mindedly and be

---

1 **Rules of Purity for the Chan Park** (*Zennen shingi* 禪苑清規): Quoting the entirety of the opening section of the text, on "receiving the precepts" (*jukai* 受戒) (*Chanyuan qinggui* 禪苑清規, ZZ.111:877a4-13). This passage is also quoted in full at the opening of the "Shōbōgenzō shukke" 正法眼藏出家 and in part in the "Shōbōgenzō shukke kudoku" 正法眼藏出家功德.

2 **pātra utensil** (*hatsugu* 鉢具): I.e., monk's eating bowl; taking *hatsugu* 鉢具 as synonymous with *hou* 鉢盂 ("*pātra* bowl"). Some readers take it as "*pātra* and seating cloth" (*zagu* 座具), though the subsequent discussion makes no mention of the latter.

*careful to avoid thoughts of extraneous matters. To emulate a buddha's
appearance and deportment, to equip oneself with a buddha's precepts,
to obtain a buddha's benefits — these are not trifling matters; how
could one take them lightly?[3] If one borrows robes and pātra, even
though one mounts the platform and receives the precepts, one will
not actually obtain the precepts. If one does not receive them again,
one will go through one's entire life as a person without the precepts,
mingling improperly with the followers of emptiness and accepting in
vain the donations of the faithful.[4] Beginners who enter the way are
not fully acquainted with the rules. If ordination teachers do not tell
them, they allow people to fall into this error. This is said in earnest,
trusting it will be engraved on the mind. Once one has received the
śrāvaka precepts, one should receive the bodhisattva precepts; this is
the progression for entering the dharma.[5]*

[T2:2] {2:295}

西天東地、佛祖相傳しきたれるところ、かならず入法の最初に受戒あり。
戒をうけざれば、いまだ諸佛の弟子にあらず、祖師の兒孫にあらざるな
り。離過防非を參禪問道とせるがゆえなり。戒律爲先の言、すでにまさし
く正法眼藏なり。成佛作祖、かならず正法眼藏を傳持するによれり。正法
眼藏を正傳する祖師、かならず佛戒を受持するなり。佛戒を受持せざる佛
祖、あるべからざるなり。あるいは如來にしたがひたてまつりてこれを受
持し、あるいは佛弟子にしたがひてこれを受持す、みなこれ命脈稟受せる
ところなり。

In what has been transmitted by the buddhas and ancestors of Sindh in
the West and the Land of the East, at the outset of entering the dharma there
is always the receiving of the precepts. If one has not received the precepts,
one is not yet a disciple of the buddhas, not yet a descendant of the ancestral masters. This is because they take "*freeing oneself from transgression*

---

3 **to obtain a buddha's benefits** (*toku butsu juyū* 得佛受用): The exact sense of the
term *juyū* 受用 here is uncertain. Some readers take it as referring to the buddha's "reward body" (*juyū shin* 受用身; S. *sambhoga-kāya*) that is the product of the bodhisattva's merit; but, in the context here, it would seem more likely a reference to the more
mundane benefits (of alms, prestige, etc.) enjoyed by a buddha.

4 **mingling improperly with the followers of emptiness and accepting in vain the
donations of the faithful** (*ranshi kūmon, kyoju shinse* 濫廁空門、虛受信施): "Followers of emptiness" (*kūmon* 空門) here refers to the monastic order, as followers of the
doctrine of emptiness. Perhaps the unordained are said to "accept in vain" (*kyoju* 虛受)
the alms of the faithful in the sense that donations made to them do not result in the merit
that accrues to gifts to a *bhikṣu*.

5 **śrāvaka precepts** (*shōmon kai* 聲聞戒); **bodhisattva precepts** (*bosatsu kai* 菩薩
戒): I.e., the full precepts (*gusoku kai* 具足戒) of the bhikṣu and *bhikṣuṇī* (in East Asia,
typically 250 rules for the monk and 348 for the nun); and the precepts applicable to both
lay and monastic (in East Asia, typically the ten grave and forty-eight minor rules of the
Brahma's Net Sūtra (*Fanwang jing* 梵網經, T.1484).

T2. The Merit of Leaving Home *Shukke kudoku* 出家功德 49

and warding off impropriety" as "*studying Zen and inquiring about the way.*" The words, "*the precepts are considered primary,*" are quite surely in themselves the treasury of the true dharma eye. "*Attaining buddhahood and becoming an ancestor*" always depend on receiving and keeping the treasury of the true dharma eye. The ancestral masters who receive and keep the treasury of the true dharma eye always receive and keep the buddha precepts. There can be no buddhas or ancestors who do not receive and keep the buddha precepts. Some receive and keep them as followers of the Tathāgata, while some receive and keep them as followers of a disciple of the Buddha; but for all, this is to have received the vital artery.

[T2:3]

いま佛佛祖祖正傳するところの佛戒、ただ嵩嶽曩祖まさしく傳來し、震旦五傳して曹溪高祖にいたれり。青原・南嶽等の正傳、いまにつたはれりといへども、杜撰の長老等、かつてしらざるもあり。もつともあはれむべし。

At present, the buddha precepts directly transmitted by buddha after buddha and ancestor after ancestor are just those correctly transmitted by the Ancient Ancestor of Song Peak and passed down in Cīnasthāna through five generations to the Eminent Ancestor of Caoxi.[6] Although their direct transmission from Qingyuan, Nanyue, and so on, has been passed down to the present, there are some stupid illiterate elders who still do not know it.[7] How utterly pitiful.

[T2:4] {2:296}

いはゆる、應受菩薩戒此入法之漸也、これ、すなはち參禪のしるべきところなり。その應受菩薩戒の儀、ひさしく佛祖の堂奧に參學するもの、かならず正傳す、疏怠のともがらのうるところにあらず。その儀は、かならず祖師を燒香禮拜し、應受菩薩戒を求請するなり。すでに聽許せられて、沐浴清淨にして、新淨の衣服を著し、あるいは衣服を浣染して、華を散じ、香をたき、禮拜恭敬して、その身に著す。あまねく形像を禮拜し、三寶を禮拜し、尊宿を禮拜し、諸障を除去し、身心清淨なることをうべし。その儀、ひさしく佛祖の堂奧に正傳せり。そののち、道場にして、和尚・阿闍梨、まさに受者ををしへて禮拜し、長跪せしめて合掌し、この語をなさしむ、

"*One should receive the bodhisattva precepts; this is the progression for entering the dharma*": this is something students of Zen should know. The procedure for this "*should receive the bodhisattva precepts*" is invariably transmitted directly by those who have long studied within the

6 **Ancient Ancestor of Song Peak** (*Sūgaku nōso* 嵩嶽曩祖): I.e., Bodhidharma, from his residence at the Shaolinsi 少林寺 on Mount Song 嵩山.

Eminent Ancestor of Caoxi (*Sōkei kōso* 曹溪高祖): I.e., the Sixth Ancestor, Huineng 慧能.

7 **Qingyuan, Nanyue** (*Seigen Nangaku* 青原・南嶽): I.e., Qingyuan Xingsi 青原行思 (d. 740) and Nanyue Huairang 南嶽懷讓 (677-744), the two disciples of the Sixth Ancestor from whom the major Chan lineages descended.

halls of the buddhas and ancestors; it is not something got by neglectful types. The procedure always entails burning incense and paying obeisance to the ancestral master and requesting that one "*should receive the bodhisattva precepts.*" Once the request is granted, bathing and purifying oneself, donning new clean robes or washing and dyeing one's robes, scattering blossoms, burning incense, paying obeisance and venerating them, one puts them on. One should make prostrations to all the images, prostrations to the three treasures, prostrations to venerables, remove all hindrances and be pure in body and mind. This procedure has long been directly transmitted in the halls of the buddhas and ancestors. After that, in the practice place, the preceptor and the ācārya duly instruct the ordinand to make prostrations, and, kneeling upright, place palms together and recite the following words:[8]

[T2:5]

歸依佛、歸依法、歸依僧。歸依佛陀兩足中尊、歸依達磨離欲中尊、歸依僧伽諸衆中尊。歸依佛竟、歸依法竟、歸依僧竟。

> "*I take refuge in the buddha; I take refuge in the dharma; I take refuge in the saṃgha.*[9]

> "*I take refuge in the buddha, honored among the two-legged; I take refuge in the dharma, honored among what is free from desire; I take refuge in the saṃgha, honored among assemblies.*

> "*I have taken refuge in the buddha; I have taken refuge in the dharma; I have taken refuge in the saṃgha.*"

[T2:6]

如來至眞無上正等覺、是我大師、我今歸依。從今已後、更不歸依邪魔外道。慈愍故。三説。第三疊慈愍故三遍。

"The Tathāgata, the Arhat, the Unsurpassed Perfectly Awakened One, is my great master, in whom I now take refuge.[10] *Hereafter, I shall not take refuge in evil Māras or other paths. Thanks to his compassion."*

---

8 **preceptor** (*oshō* 和尚); **ācārya** (*ajari* 阿闍梨): Likely indicating the precept master (*kai oshō* 戒和尚) and ritual instructor (*kyōju shi* 教授師), respectively.

9 **"I take refuge in the buddha"** (*kie butsu* 歸依佛): A standard version of the traditional three refuges (*sanki* 三歸; S. *triśaraṇa*). Dōgen is here adapting parts of the account of "receiving the *śramaṇera* precepts" (*shami shoujie wen* 沙彌受戒文) given in the *Chanyuan qinggui* 禪苑清規 (ZZ.111:923ff). At this point in that account (ZZ.111:925a7-10), the ordinand has just completed a repentance ritual, which is then followed by a call for the refuges:

> 善男子、汝既淨治身口意業。次應歸依佛法僧寶。

> Good son, you have now purified the karma of body, speech, and mind. Next, you should take refuge in the treasures of buddha, dharma, and saṃgha.

10 **"The Tathāgata, the Arhat, the Unsurpassed Perfectly Awakened One"** (*Nyorai shishin mujō shōtō gaku* 如來至眞無上正等覺): The first three of the ten epithets (*jūgō*

T2. The Merit of Leaving Home *Shukke kudoku* 出家功徳 51

(Say three times. On the third repetition, say, "Thanks to his compassion," three times.)

[T2:7] {2:297}

善男子、既捨邪歸正、戒已周圓。應受三聚清淨戒。

"Good son, by your having abandoned the false and resorted to the correct, the precepts have been completed.[11] *You should receive the three sets of pure precepts."*[12]

[T2:8]

第一、攝律儀戒。汝從今身至佛身、此戒能持否。答云、能持。三問三答。

"First, the precepts of restraint.[13] *Can you, from your present body until you attain the body of a buddha, keep these precepts or not?"*

Answer: "I can keep them."

(Ask thrice; answer thrice.)

十號) of a buddha: *tathāgata, arhat, samyak-saṃbuddha*. Quoting (with slight variation) the *Chanyuan qinggui* 禪苑清規 at ZZ.111:925a11-12. Passages in parentheses here and below are in the original.

11 **"Good son"** (*zen nanshi* 善男子): The speaker is the preceptor. Variation on *Chanyuan qinggui* 禪苑清規 at ZZ.111:925a13-14:

善男子、既捨邪歸正、戒已周圓。若欲識相護持、應受五戒。

"Good son, by your having abandoned the false and resorted to the correct, the precepts have been completed. If you wish to recognize and keep them, you should receive the five precepts."

"the precepts have been completed" (*kai i shūen* 戒已周圓): I.e., "we have completed the precepts of the three refuges."

12 **"three sets of pure precepts"** (*sanju shōjō kai* 三聚清淨戒): Dōgen here departs from the ritual of the *Chanyuan qinggui* to substitute for that text's five precepts the threefold bodhisattva precepts (*bosatsu kai* 菩薩戒) of the *Fanwang jing* 梵網經 and other Mahāyāna texts.

13 **"precepts of restraint"** (*shō ritsugi kai* 攝律儀戒): I.e., precepts intended to avoid bad karma; S. *saṃvara-śīla*. The pattern of the reverend's call, "Can you keep them?" and the ordinand's response, "I can," mirrors the *Chanyuan qinggui's* 禪苑清規 ritual of receiving the five precepts (ZZ.111:925a16-b3). The set phrase "from your present body until you attain the body of a buddha" (*nyo ju konjin shi busshin* 汝從今身至佛身) does not occur in Zongze's text, but is common elsewhere; see, e.g., its repeated use in the liturgy of the ten grave precepts rite in the *Fanwang jing* 梵網經 (T.1484.24:1020c29-1021a29):

從今身至佛身盡未來際。

From your present body until you attain the body of a buddha, until the end of time.

52 DŌGEN'S *SHŌBŌGENZŌ* VOLUME VI

[T2:9]

第二、攝善法戒。汝從今身至佛身、此戒能持否。答云、能持。三問三答。

> "Second, the precepts of adopting good qualities.[14] Can you, from your present body until you attain the body of a buddha, keep these precepts or not?"

> Answer: "I can keep them."

> (Ask thrice; answer thrice.)

[T2:10]

第三、饒益衆生戒。汝從今身至佛身、此戒能持否。答云、能持。三問三答。

> "Third, the precepts of benefiting living beings.[15] Can you, from your present body until you attain the body of a buddha, keep these precepts or not?"

> Answer: "I can keep them."

> (Ask thrice; answer thrice.)

[T2:11]

上來三聚清淨戒、一一不得犯。汝從今身至佛身、能持否。答云、能持。三問三答。是事如是持。受者、禮三拜、長跪合掌。

> "The above three sets of pure precepts, each and every one, must not be violated.[16] Can you, from your present body until you attain the body of a buddha, keep them or not?"

> Answer: "I can keep them."

> (Ask thrice; answer thrice.)

> "These things should thus be kept."

> (The ordinand makes three prostrations and kneels upright with palms together.)

[T2:12]

善男子、汝既受三聚清淨戒、應受十戒。是乃諸佛菩薩清淨大戒也。

> "Good son, having received the three sets of pure precepts, you should

---

14　**"precepts of adopting good qualities"** (*shō zenbō kai* 攝善法戒); I.e., precepts intended to develop good karma; S. *kuśala-dharma-saṃgrāhaka-śīla*.

15　**"precepts of benefiting living beings"** (*nyōyaku shujō kai* 饒益衆生戒): I.e., precepts intended to guide work for the welfare of others; S. *sattvārtha-kriyā-śīla*.

16　**"The above three sets of pure precepts"** (*jōrai sanju shōjō kai* 上來三聚清淨戒): This section adapts the formula of the *Chanyuan qinggui* 禪苑清規 at ZZ.111:925b3-5, merely substituting its "three sets of pure precepts" for that text's "fivefold pure precepts."

T2. The Merit of Leaving Home *Shukke kudoku* 出家功德　　53

receive the ten precepts.[17] They are the pure major precepts of the buddhas and bodhisattvas."

[T2:13]

第一、不殺生。汝從今身至佛身、此戒能持否。答云、能持。三問三答。

"First, not to kill living beings. Can you, from your present body until you attain the body of a buddha, keep this precept or not?"

Answer: "I can keep it."

(Ask thrice; answer thrice.)

[T2:14] {2:298}

第二、不偸盗。汝從今身至佛身、此戒能持否。答云、能持。三問三答。

"Second, not to steal. Can you, from your present body until you attain the body of a buddha, keep this precept or not?"

Answer: "I can keep it."

(Ask thrice; answer thrice.)

[T2:15]

第三、不貪婬。汝從今身至佛身、此戒能持否。答云、能持。三問三答。

"Third, not to lust. Can you, from your present body until you attain the body of a buddha, keep this precept or not?"

Answer: "I can keep it."

(Ask thrice; answer thrice.)

[T2:16]

第四、不妄語。汝從今身至佛身、此戒能持否。答云、能持。三問三答。

"Fourth, not to lie. Can you, from your present body until you attain the body of a buddha, keep this precept or not?"

Answer: "I can keep it."

(Ask thrice; answer thrice.)

[T2:17]

第五、不酤酒。汝從今身至佛身、此戒能持否。答云、能持。三問三答。

"Fifth, not to deal in alcohol. Can you, from your present body until you attain the body of a buddha, keep this precept or not?"

Answer: "I can keep it."

(Ask thrice; answer thrice.)

17　**"ten precepts"** (*jikkai* 十戒): I.e., the ten grave precepts (*jū jūkai* 十重戒) of the *Fanwang jing* 梵網經 (see, e.g., T.1484.24:1012b1-6). The *Chanyuan qinggui* 禪苑清規 at this point (ZZ.111:925b9-13) gives instead the traditional ten *śramaṇera* precepts.

[T2:18]

第六、不説在家出家菩薩罪過。汝從今身至佛身、此戒能持否。答云、能持。三問三答。

> "Sixth, not to speak of the transgressions of the householder or renunciant bodhisattvas. Can you, from your present body until you attain the body of a buddha, keep this precept or not?"
>
> Answer: "I can keep it."
>
> (Ask thrice; answer thrice.)

[T2:19]

第七、不自讚毀他。汝從今身至佛身、此戒能持否。答云、能持。三問三答。

> "Seventh, not to praise oneself and denigrate others. Can you, from your present body until you attain the body of a buddha, keep this precept or not?"
>
> Answer: "I can keep it."
>
> (Ask thrice; answer thrice.)

[T2:20]

第八、不慳法財。汝從今身至佛身、此戒能持否。答云、能持。三問三答。

> "Eighth, not to be stingy with the dharma or wealth. Can you, from your present body until you attain the body of a buddha, keep this precept or not?"
>
> Answer: "I can keep it."
>
> (Ask thrice; answer thrice.)

[T2:21]

第九、不瞋恚。汝從今身至佛身、此戒能持否。答云、能持。三問三答。

> "Ninth, not to be angry. Can you, from your present body until you attain the body of a buddha, keep this precept or not?"
>
> Answer: "I can keep it."
>
> (Ask thrice; answer thrice.)

[T2:22]

第十、不癡謗三寶。汝從今身至佛身、此戒能持否。答云、能持。三問三答。

> "Tenth, not to disparage the three treasures. Can you, from your present body until you attain the body of a buddha, keep this precept or not?"
>
> Answer: "I can keep it."
>
> (Ask thrice; answer thrice.)

T2. The Merit of Leaving Home *Shukke kudoku* 出家功德 55

[T2:23]
上來十戒、一一不得犯。汝從今身至佛身、能持否。答云、能持。是事如是
持。受者、禮三拜。

> "The above ten precepts, each and every one, must not be violated.[18]
> Can you, from your present body until you attain the body of a buddha,
> keep them or not?"
>
> Answer: "I can keep them."
>
> "These things should thus be kept."
>
> (The ordinand makes three prostrations.)

[T2:24]
上來三歸・三聚清淨戒・十重禁戒、是諸佛之所受持。汝從今身至佛身、此
十六支戒、能持否。答云、能持。三問三答。是事如是持。受者、禮三拜。

> "The above three refuges, three sets of pure precepts, and ten grave
> precepts are received and kept by the buddhas. Can you, from your
> present body until you attain the body of a buddha, keep these sixteen-
> fold precepts or not?"
>
> Answer: "I can keep them."
>
> (Ask thrice; answer thrice.)
>
> "These things should thus be kept."
>
> (The ordinand makes three prostrations.)

[T2:25] {2:299}
次作處世界梵訖云、歸依佛、歸依法、歸依僧。次受者出道場。

> (Next, after performing the "Abiding in the World" chant, say,) "I take
> refuge in the buddha; I take refuge in the dharma; I take refuge in the
> saṃgha."[19]
>
> (Next, the ordinand exits the practice place.)

---

18 **"The above ten precepts"** (*jōrai jikkai* 上來十戒): Paralleling the *Chanyuan qinggui* 禪苑清規, at ZZ.111:925b15-17.

19 **"Abiding in the World" chant** (*sho sekai bon* 處世界梵): Taking *bon* 梵 here as
bonbai 梵唄 ("Sanskrit chant"); some readings take it as *bongyō* 梵行 ("pure practice";
S. *brahmacarya*) and work it into the title, "Purity while Abiding in the World." Dōgen
is here following the *Chanyuan qinggui* 禪苑清規, at ZZ.111:926a18-b1:

> 作梵、闍梨鳴磬云、處世界如虛空、如蓮花不著水、心清淨超於彼。稽首禮無上
> 尊。
>
> (Performing Chant, the *ācārya* sounds the gong and says,)
>
> Abiding in a world like empty space,
> Like the lotus blossom untouched by the water;
> The mind is pure and far beyond it.
> We bow in obeisance to the One Most Honored.

[T2:26]

この受戒の儀、かならず佛祖正傳せり。丹霞天然・藥山高沙彌等、おなじ
く受持しきたれり。比丘戒をうけざる祖師かくのごとくあれども、この佛
祖正傳菩薩戒をうけざる祖師、いまだあらず、必ず受持するなり。

This procedure for receiving the precepts was always directly transmitted by the buddhas and ancestors. Danxia Tianran, Śrāmaṇera Gao
of Yaoshan, and the like, similarly received and kept them.[20] Although
there are such ancestral masters who did not receive the bhikṣu precepts,
there have never been ancestral masters who did not receive these bodhisattva precepts directly transmitted by the buddhas and ancestors. They
invariably received and kept them.

正法眼藏受戒第二
Treasury of the True Dharma Eye
Receiving the Precepts
Number 2

---

20 **Danxia Tianran** (*Tanka Tennen* 丹霞天然): 739-824, disciple of Shitou Xiqian 石
頭希遷, who also studied with Mazu Daoyi 馬祖道一 (709-788). Renowned for his eccentric behavior, he is said to have covered his ears and run away when Shitou sought to
teach him the precepts. (See, e.g., *Jingde chuandeng lu* 景德傳燈錄, T.2076.51:310c-9.)

Śrāmaṇera Gao of Yaoshan (*Yakusan no Kō shami* 藥山の高沙彌): Dates unknown;
a disciple of Yaoshan Weiyan 藥山惟儼 (751-834). He is said to have abandoned his
request for the full bhikṣu precepts when challenged by Yaoshan. (See, e.g., *Jingde
chuandeng lu* 景德傳燈錄, T.2076.51:315c5-27.)

TREASURY OF THE TRUE DHARMA EYE
THE TWELVE-CHAPTER COMPILATION
NUMBER 3

The Merit of the Kāṣāya
Kesa kudoku
袈裟功徳

The Merit of the Kāṣāya

Kesa kudoku

INTRODUCTION

This chapter, one of the longest in the *Shōbōgenzō*, is also found as number 41 in the sixty-chapter compilation, which is reproduced in the ninety-five-chapter Honzan edition as number 12. Unlike most of the texts of the twelve-chapter *Shōbōgenzō*, this work bears a dated colophon, which states that it was presented to the assembly at Kōshōji, on October 17, 1240 — a surprisingly early date for a text in this compilation. An almost identical colophon is found on the "Den'e" 傳衣, a chapter occurring as number 32 in the seventy-five-chapter compilation and included as number 13 in the Honzan edition. A comparison of the two works reveals that our text here represents a reworking of the material in the "Den'e" and suggests that, if the two chapters may share a common origin, they developed in different directions.

正法眼藏第三
Treasury of the True Dharma Eye
Number 3

袈裟功德
The Merit of the Kāṣāya

[T3:1] {2:300}

佛佛祖祖正傳の衣法、まさしく震旦國に正傳することは、嵩嶽の高祖のみなり。高祖は、釋迦牟尼佛より第二十八代の祖なり。西天二十八傳、嫡嫡あひつたはれり、二十八祖、したしく震旦にいたりて初祖たり。震旦國人五傳して、曹溪にいたりて三十三代の祖なり、これを六祖と稱す。第三十三代の祖、大鑑禪師、この衣法を黄梅山にして夜半に正傳し、一生護持、いまなほ曹溪山寶林寺に安置せり。

The direct transmission to the Land of Cīnasthāna of the robe and the dharma directly transmitted by buddha after buddha and ancestor after ancestor was truly done only by the Eminent Ancestor of Song Peak.[1] The Eminent Ancestor was the ancestor in the twenty-eighth generation after Buddha Śākyamuni. Through twenty-eight transmissions, they were handed down in Sindh in the West until the Twenty-eighth Ancestor personally went to Cīnasthāna, where he represents the First Ancestor.[2] After five transmissions through those of the Land of Cīnasthāna, they reached Caoxi, the ancestor in the thirty-third generation, known as the Sixth Ancestor.[3] The ancestor in the thirty-third generation, Chan Master Dajian, received the direct transmission of this robe and dharma in the middle of the night at Mount Huangmei; he guarded them for

---

1 **The direct transmission to the Land of Cīnasthāna** (*Shintan koku ni shōden suru koto* 震旦國に正傳すること): The first three sections here correspond closely to the opening of the "Shōbōgenzō den'e" 正法眼藏傳衣. Dōgen uses here the Chinese transliteration of the Sanskrit term meaning "Land of Chin," a name derived from the Qin 秦 dynasty that first unified China in 221 BCE.

the Eminent Ancestor of Song Peak (*Sūgaku no kōso* 嵩嶽の高祖): I.e., Bodhidharma, from his residence at Shaolinsi 少林寺 on Mount Song 嵩山.

2 **Sindh in the West** (*Saiten* 西天): A term denoting the Indian subcontinent, from the transliteration of S. *Sindhu* as *Tianzhu* 天竺.

3 **Caoxi** (*Sōkei* 曹溪): I.e., the famous Sixth Ancestor, Huineng of Caoxi 曹溪慧能. Mount Caoxi (*Sōkeizan* 曹溪山), in present-day Guangdong, is the site of his temple, the Baolinsi 寶林寺.

60 DŌGEN'S *SHŌBŌGENZŌ* VOLUME VI

his whole life, and even now, it is preserved at the Baolin Monastery at Mount Caoxi.[4]

[T3:2]

諸代の帝王、あひつぎて内裏に奉請し、供養禮拜す。神物護持せるものなり。唐朝中宗・肅宗・代宗、しきりに歸内供養しき。奉請のとき、奉送のとき、ことさら勅使をつかはし、詔をたまふ。代宗皇帝、あるとき、佛衣を曹溪山におくりたてまつる詔にいはく、

Several generations of emperors, in succession, invited it into the inner sanctum of the palace, making offerings and paying obeisance to it, as an object protected by spiritual beings.[5] During the Tang dynasty, the emperors Zhongzong, Suzong, and Daizong frequently recalled it to court and made offerings to it.[6] When requesting it and when returning it, they took special care to dispatch an imperial envoy and hand down an imperial edict. On one occasion, when the Emperor Daizong sent the buddha robe back to Mount Caoxi, his imperial edict said:[7]

[T3:3]

今遣鎮國大將軍劉崇景、頂戴而送。朕爲之國寶。卿可於本寺法安置、令僧衆親承宗旨者、嚴加守護、勿令遺墜。

---

4 **Chan Master Dajian** (*Daikan zenji* 大鑑禪師): Posthumous title of the Sixth Ancestor.

received the direct transmission of this robe and dharma in the middle of the night at Mount Huangmei (*kono ehō o Ōbaisan ni shite yahan ni shōden shi* この衣法を黄梅山にして夜半に正傳し): From the famous account of the secret transmission from the Fifth Ancestor, Hongren 弘忍, to Huineng, in the former's private quarters in his monastery on Mount Huangmei 黄梅山, in Qizhou 蘄州, modern Hubei.

it is preserved at the Baolin Monastery at Mount Caoxi (*Sōkei Hōrinji ni anchi seri* 曹溪寶林寺に安置せり): From the tradition that the robe of Bodhidharma was enshrined at Huineng's monastery and not transmitted to any of his disciples. Though the grammatical subject here is unexpressed, clearly, Dōgen is no longer speaking of "the robe and the dharma" (*ehō* 衣法) but only of "the robe."

5 **protected by spiritual beings** (*shinmotsu goji* 神物護持): A fixed expression for a sacred or awe-inspiring object.

6 **During the Tang dynasty, the emperors Zhongzong, Suzong, and Daizong** (*Tōchō Chūsō Shukusō Daisō* 唐朝中宗・肅宗・代宗): Based on a tradition, found in the *Jingde chuandeng lu* 景德傳燈錄 (T.2076.51:236c25-237a2), that, in the year 760, the Emperor Suzong 肅宗 (r. 756-763) requested that Huineng's robe and begging bowl be installed in the palace and given offerings. In 765, the Emperor Daizong 代宗 (r. 763-780), after a dream in which Huineng requested the return of his robe and bowl, sent them back to Caoxi, with the edict quoted in the next section. The Emperor Zhongzong 中宗 (r. 705-710), though he is said to have honored Huineng, was assassinated in 710, three years before the traditional date of Huineng's death.

7 **buddha robe** (*butsue* 佛衣): A term normally meaning "Buddhist robe," used synonymously with *kāṣāya*; it can also have the sense "the robe of the buddhas (or of Buddha Śākyamuni)."

T3. The Merit of the Kāṣāya *Kesa kudoku* 袈裟功德　　61

We now dispatch Liu Chongjing, Great Defender-General of the State, reverently to accept and escort [the robe].[8] We regard it as a national treasure. Our liege [Liu Chongjing] is to place it for safekeeping in its original monastery and have those of the monks who have personally received the essential import strictly protect it and not allow it to be lost.[9]

[T3:4] {2:301}

まことに無量恆河沙の三千大千世界を統領せんよりも、佛衣現在の小國に、王としてこれを見聞供養したてまつらんは、生死のなかの善生、最勝の生なるべし。　佛化のおよぶところ、　三千界、いづれのところか袈裟なからん。しかありといえども、嫡嫡面授の佛袈裟を正傳せるは、ただひとり嵩嶽の曩祖のみなり、旁出は佛袈裟をさづけられず。二十七祖の旁出、跋陀婆羅菩薩の傳、まさに肇法師におよぶといへども、佛袈裟の正傳なし。震旦の四祖大師、また牛頭山の法融禪師をわたすといへども、佛袈裟を正傳せず。しかあればすなはち、正嫡の相承なしといへども、如來の正法、その功德むなしからず、千古萬古みな利益廣大なり。正嫡相承せらんは、相承なきと、ひとしかるべからず。

Truly, more than ruling over trichiliocosms numerous as the incalculable sands of the Ganges, for a king of a small country where the buddha robe is present, to be able to see and hear of it and to make offerings to it, must be the best birth among good births within birth and death.[10] Wherever the Buddha's teaching reaches, throughout the three chiliocosms, where could there be a place without the *kāṣāya*? Nevertheless, the only one who directly transmitted the buddha *kāṣāya* conferred face-to-face by successor after successor was the Ancient Ancestor of Song Peak; the buddha *kāṣāya* was not conferred on collateral branches. The collateral branch from the Twenty-seventh Ancestor, the transmission to Bodhisattva Bhadrapāla, reached the Dharma Master Zhao, but it lacked the direct transmission of the buddha *kāṣāya*.[11] Again, the Great Master,

---

8　**Liu Chongjing, Great Defender-General of the State** (*chinkoku daishōgun Ryū Sōkei* 鎮國大將軍劉崇景): Biography unknown. The edict is found at *Jingde chuandeng lu* 景德傳燈錄, T.2076.51:236c29-237a2.

9　**those of the monks who have personally received the essential import** (*sōshu shinshō shūshi sha* 僧衆親承宗旨者): Presumably, meaning those of the monastic community initiated into the meaning of the robe.

10　**trichiliocosms** (*sanzen daisen sekai* 三千大千世界): A term used to render the Sanskrit *trisāhasra-mahāsāhasra-lokadhātu* ("three-thousandfold great thousandfold"), equaling one billion Mount Sumeru world systems; a standard measure of the domain of a buddha.

11　**The collateral branch from the Twenty-seventh Ancestor** (*nijūshichi so no bōshutsu* 二十七祖の旁出): From the tradition that Bodhidharma's master, Prajñātāra, also transmitted his dharma to the Bodhisattva Bhadrapāla (*Batuopoluo pusa* 跋陀婆羅菩薩), who subsequently went to China, where he taught the famous Chinese monk Sengzhao 僧肇 (384-414). Dōgen, who also mentions this tradition in his *Eihei kōroku* 永平廣錄

62   DŌGEN'S *SHŌBŌGENZŌ* VOLUME VI

the Fourth Ancestor in Cīnasthāna, while he passed [his dharma] to Chan Master Farong of Mount Niutou, did not directly transmit the buddha *kāṣāya*.[12] Thus, even without inheritance by a direct successor, the merit of the true dharma of the Tathāgata is never fruitless, and its benefits are vast throughout a thousand ages past, ten thousand ages past. But those with the inheritance by direct successor are not equivalent to those without the inheritance.

[T3:5]

しかあればすなはち、人・天、もし袈裟を受持せんは、佛祖相傳の正傳を傳受すべし。印度・震旦、正法・像法のときは、在家なほ袈裟を受持す。いま遠方邊土の澆季には、剃除鬚髪して佛弟子と稱する、袈裟を受持せず、いまだ受持すべきと信ぜず、しらず、あきらめず、かなしむべし。いはんや體・色・量をしらんや、いはんや著用の法をしらんや。

Thus, humans and devas who would receive and keep the *kāṣāya* should receive and keep the direct transmission transmitted among the buddhas and ancestors. In India and Cīnasthāna, during the periods of the true dharma and semblance dharma, even householders received and kept the *kāṣāya*.[13] Now, in this season of decline in a remote peripheral land, it is so sad that those who shave beard and hair and call themselves disciples of the Buddha do not receive and keep the *kāṣāya*, have never

---

(DZZ.4:62, no. 482), shares this with the *Biyan lu* 碧巖錄, case 62 (T.2003.48:194a2-3):

肇乃禮羅什爲師。又參瓦棺寺跋陀婆羅菩薩、從西天二十七祖處。

Sengzhao then paid obeisance to Kumārajīva, and also visited the Bodhisattva Bhadrapāla of the Waguansi, who came from the Twenty-seventh Ancestor in Sindh in the West.

The tradition seems to rest on a conflation of the name Bhadrapāla with Buddhabhadra (*Fotuobatuoluo* 佛陀跋陀羅, 359-429), the famed Indian translator active in China during the time of Sengzhao; it ignores, of course, the century separating the two supposed disciples of Prajñātāra.

12   **the Great Master, the Fourth Ancestor in Cīnasthāna** (*Shintan no shiso daishi* 震旦の四祖大師): I.e., Daoxin 道信 (580–651), who, in addition to transmitting his dharma to the Fifth Ancestor, Hongren 弘忍 (602-675), also transmitted it to Farong 法融 (594-657), regarded as the founder of the "Oxhead" (Niutou 牛頭) lineage, named after his residence on Mount Niutou 牛頭山, in present-day Jiangsu province.

13   **true dharma and semblance dharma** (*shōbō zōhō* 正法・像法): The first two of the three stages in a common reckoning of the degeneration of the dharma: true, semblance, and final dharma (*shō zō mappō* 正像末法). The period of the "true dharma" (*shōbō* 正法) was most often taken as the first thousand years following the *parinirvāṇa* of the Buddha; the "semblance dharma" (*zōhō* 像法), during which there was practice but no longer attainment of awakening, was said to last an additional one thousand years; during the "final dharma" (*mappō* 末法), lasting ten thousand years, there was neither authentic practice nor awakening. Based on the traditional East Asian Buddhist reckoning of the date of Śākyamuni's *parinirvāṇa* as 949 BCE, the final dharma was thought have begun in 1052 CE.

T3. The Merit of the Kāṣāya *Kesa kudoku* 袈裟功徳   63

believed, known, or clarified that they should receive and keep it.[14] How much less do they know its material, color, or dimensions; much less do they know how to wear it.

[T3:6] {2:302}

袈裟は、ふるくより解脱服と稱す。業障・煩悩障・報障等、みな解脱すべきなり。龍、もし一縷をうれば、三熱をまぬかる、牛、もし一角にふるれば、その罪、おのづから消滅す。諸佛成道のとき、かならず袈裟を著す。しるべし、最尊最上の功徳なりといふこと。

The *kāṣāya* has long been called the "vestment of liberation": one is liberated from all hindrances of karma, hindrances of the afflictions, and hindrances of recompense.[15] When dragons obtain but a single thread, they are freed from the three torments; when bulls are touched even by a single corner, their offenses will automatically be extinguished.[16] When

---

14   **season of decline in a remote peripheral land** (*enpō hendo no gyōki* 遠方邊土の澆季): I.e., the age of the final dharma (*mappō* 末法) in Japan. This lament echoes a passage in "Shōbōgenzō den'e" 正法眼藏傳衣, section 12.

15   **"vestment of liberation"** (*gedappuku* 解脱服): This section echoes "Shōbōgenzō den'e" 正法眼藏傳衣, section 13. The "vestment of liberation" is best known from the four-line verse, introduced below, still recited by monks when donning the *kāṣāya*; see Supplementary Notes, s.v. "Robe of the Tathāgata."

hindrances of karma, hindrances of the afflictions, and hindrances of retribution (*gosshō bonnō shō hōshō* 業障・煩悩障・報障): A traditional list of three types of spiritual obstacles (*sanshō* 三障): caused by one's past deeds (S. *karmāvaraṇa*), caused by one's defiled states of mind (S. *kleśāvaraṇa*), and caused by the conditions of one's rebirth (S. *vipākāvaraṇa*).

16   **When dragons obtain but a single thread** (*ryū, moshi ichiru o ureba* 龍、もし一縷をうれば); **when bulls are touched even by a single corner** (*ushi, moshi ikkaku ni furureba* 牛、もし一角にふるれば): Dōgen's Japanese reading of a combination found in the *Fahua wenju ji* 法華文句記, by Zhanran 湛然 (711–782) (T.1719.34:200c7-8):

> 龍得一縷、牛角一觸。
>
> If the dragon obtains a single thread, if the bull is once touched by a corner.

Note that readers disagree on the sense of *kaku* 角 here, taking it either as "corner" (of the *kāṣāya*; more likely in Dōgen's version) or as "horn" (of the bull; perhaps more likely in Zhanran's phrase).

the three torments (*sannetsu* 三熱): From the tradition that dragons are subject to three afflictions: hot winds and sands that burn them, evil winds that expose them, and garuḍa (giant mythical birds) that eat them. The claim (also found in "Shōbōgenzō den'e" 正法眼藏傳衣) that the dragons are liberated from these torments by the *kāṣāya* doubtless reflects the tradition that a thread from the Tathāgata's robe will protect dragons from the garuḍa; see, e.g., *Sāgara-nāga-rāja-paripṛcchā-sūtra* (*Fo shuo hailongwang jing* 佛説海龍王經, T.598.15:151a6-16).

their offenses will automatically be extinguished (*sono tsumi, onozukara shōmetsu su* その罪、おのづから消滅す): Dōgen's source for this claim is uncertain. Though no mention is made there of the bull's "offenses" (*tsumi* 罪) it has been suggested that the claim may reflect a story found in the *Shishi liutie* 釋氏六帖, by the tenth-century author

64 DŌGEN'S *SHŌBŌGENZŌ* VOLUME VI

the buddhas attain the way, they always wear the *kaṣāya*. We should realize that this is the most honored, the highest merit.

[T3:7]

まことに、われら邊地にむまれて末法にあふ、うらむべしといへども、佛佛嫡嫡相承の衣法にあふたてまつる、いくそばくのよろこびとかせん。いづれの家門か、わが正傳のごとく、釋尊の衣法、ともに正傳せる。これにあふたてまつりて、たれか恭敬供養せざらん。たとひ一日に無量恆河沙の身命をすてても、供養したてまつるべし。なほ生生世世の値遇頂戴、供養恭敬を發願すべし。われら、佛生國をへだつること十萬餘里の山海はるかにして通じがたしといへども、宿善のあひもよほすところ、山海に擁塞せられず、邊鄙の愚蒙、きらはるることなし。この正法にあふたてまつり、あくまで日夜に修習す、この袈裟を受持したてまつり、常恆に頂戴護持す。ただ一佛二佛のみもとにして、功德を修せるのみならんや、すでに恆河沙等の諸佛のみもとにして、もろもろの功德を修習せるなるべし。たとひ自己なりといふとも、たふとぶべし、隨喜すべし。祖師傳法の深恩、ねんごろに報謝すべし。畜類なほ恩を報ず、人類いかでか恩をしらざらん。もし恩をしらずば、畜類よりも愚なるべし。

Truly, it is regrettable that we are born in a peripheral land during the final dharma; yet what a joy it is to encounter the robe and dharma inherited by buddha after buddha and successor after successor.[17] What other house has directly transmitted both the robe and the dharma of Śākya, the Honored One, similarly to our direct transmission? Having encountered them, who would not revere and make offerings to them? Even if only for a day, casting aside lives numerous as the incalculable sands of the Ganges, we should make offerings to them; still more, we should vow to encounter and reverently accept them, to make offerings to and revere them, in life after life, through age after age.

It may be hard for us to reach the land of the Buddha's birth, separated as we are from it by more than a hundred thousand miles of mountains and seas; yet, thanks to our good karma from previous lifetimes, we are not constrained by the mountains and seas and are not despised as simpletons from the margins.[18] We encounter the true dharma and te-

---

Yichu 義楚 (see *Giso rokujō* 義楚六帖, ZTS.6B:389a5-6):

異相云、比丘持鉢、有奔牛觸著袈裟。死得爲人、乃至遇佛出家成道。

In the *Yixiang*, it is said that, when a bhikṣu was out begging, a running bull touched against his *kaṣāya*. When it died, it became a human, eventually encountered a buddha, left home, and attained the way.

17   **we are born in a peripheral land during the final dharma** (*warera henji ni mumarete mappō ni au* われら邊地にむまれて末法にあふ): This section echoes "Shōbōgenzō den'e" 正法眼藏傳衣, section 13-15.

18   **hundred thousand miles of mountains and seas** (*jūman yo ri no sengai* 十萬餘里の山海): The Chinese "mile" (*li* 里) varies throughout history but was generally around one-third mile. (At that length, the distance between Varanasi and Kyoto would

T3. The Merit of the Kāṣāya *Kesa kudoku* 袈裟功徳   65

naciously practice it day and night; we reverently receive and keep the *kāṣāya* and forever cherish and protect it. How could we have cultivated merit only under one buddha or two buddhas? We must surely have cultivated all sorts of merit under buddhas equal to the sands of the Ganges. Though it may be of our own doing, we should honor it and rejoice for it.[19] We should sincerely repay the profound beneficence of the transmission of the dharma by the ancestral masters.[20] Even animals repay beneficence; how could humans fail to recognize beneficence?[21] If we fail to recognize beneficence, we must be stupider than animals.

[T3:8] {2:303}

この佛衣佛法の功徳、その傳佛正法の祖師にあらざれば、餘輩いまだあきらめず、しらず。　諸佛のあとを欣求すべくば、まさにこれを欣樂すべし。たとひ百千萬代ののちも、この正傳を正傳とすべし。これ佛法なるべし、證驗まさにあらたならん。水を乳にいるるに相似すべからず、皇太子の、帝位に即位するがごとし。かの合水の乳なりとも、乳をもちいんときは、この乳のほかにさらに乳なからむやは、これをもちいるべし。たとひ水を合せずとも、あぶらをもちいるべからず、うるしをもちいるべからず、さけをもちいるべからず。この正傳も、またかくのごとくならん。たとひ凡師の庸流なりとも、正傳あらんは、用乳のよろしきときなるべし。いはんや佛衣祖祖の正傳は、皇太子の即位のごとくなるなり。俗、なをいはく、先王の法服にあらざれば服せず、佛子いづくんぞ佛衣にあらざらんを著せん。後漢、孝明皇帝、永平十年よりのち、西天・東地に往還する出家・在家、くびすをつぎてたえずといへども、西天にして佛佛祖祖正傳の祖師にあふといはず、如來より面授相承の系譜なし。ただ經・論師にしたがふて、梵本の經教を傳來せるなり。佛法正嫡の祖師にあふ、といはず、佛袈裟相傳の祖師あり、とかたらず。あきらかにしりぬ、佛法の闥奥にいらざりけりといふことを。かくのごときのひと、佛祖正傳の旨、あきらめざるなり。

Apart from the ancestral masters who transmit the true dharma of the buddhas, the merits of this buddha robe and buddha dharma have never been clarified, never known, by other factions.[22] If we are joyfully to seek the traces of the buddhas, we should take delight in this. Even a

---

be roughly 10,000 *li*.)

19　**Though it may be of our own doing** (*tatoi jiko nari to iedomo* たとひ自己なりといへども): The antecedent of "it" here is likely the "merit" (*fukutoku* 福徳) of accepting the robe and studying the dharma.

20　**transmission of the dharma by the ancestral masters** (*soshi denbō* 祖師傳法): The term *soshi* 祖師 ("ancestral master") may refer here specifically to Bodhidharma.

21　**Even animals repay beneficence** (*chikurui nao on o hōzu* 畜類なほ恩を報ず): In "Shōbōgenzō gyōji" 正法眼藏行持, part 2, Dōgen refers to two famous Chinese stories, in which a sparrow and a tortoise express their gratitude for help given them by humans.

22　**the merits of this buddha robe and buddha dharma** (*kono butsue buppō no kudoku* この佛衣佛法の功徳): This section echoes "Shōbōgenzō den'e" 正法眼藏傳衣, sections 16-18.

66   DŌGEN'S *SHŌBŌGENZŌ* VOLUME VI

hundred thousand myriad generations from now, we should take this direct transmission as the direct transmission. It will be the buddha dharma, and the evidence will surely be manifest.[23]

It should not be likened to pouring water into milk; it is like the crown prince assuming the imperial throne. Although it is diluted milk, when we are going to use milk, we should use it if there is no other milk than this; though they are not diluted with water, we should not use oil, should not use lacquer, should not use sake.[24] Direct transmission is also like this: even though they are commoner teachers of a mediocre type, when they have the direct transmission, it is a time when using the milk is acceptable. Needless to say, the direct transmission of buddha after buddha and ancestor after ancestor is more like the crown prince assuming the throne. Even in the secular world it is said, "If they are not the proper raiment of the former kings, they do not wear them."[25] How could a child of the Buddha don what is not the buddha robe?

Ever since the tenth year of Yongping, in the reign of Emperor Xiao Ming of the Later Han, renunciants and householders going back and forth between Sindh in the West and the Land of the East have ceaselessly followed on each other's heels; yet they do not report that, in Sindh in the West, they met an ancestral master of the direct transmission by buddha after buddha and ancestor after ancestor, and they lack a genealogy of inheritance conferred face-to-face from the Tathāgata.[26] They have merely followed sūtra and treatise masters and transmitted the sūtra teachings of the Sanskrit books. They do not say they met the ancestral masters who are direct heirs to the buddha dharma and do not mention the existence of ancestral masters who transmit the buddha *kāṣāya*. It is clear that they have not entered the inner sanctum of the buddha dharma.

---

23   **the evidence will surely be manifest** (*shōken masa ni arata naran* 證驗まさにあらたならん): Taking *arata* あらた here in the sense *arataka* 灼か ("wondrously apparent").

24   **diluted milk** (*gōsui no nyū* 合水の乳): From a metaphor found in the *Nirvāṇa Sūtra* (*Da banniepan jing* 大般涅槃經, T.374.12:421c16-22a14), in which even watered-down teachings of the sūtra are far superior to other texts. A trope also found in the "Shōbōgenzō shukke kudoku" 正法眼藏出家功德.

25   **Even in the secular world it is said** (*zoku nao iwaku* 俗なほいはく): A loose paraphrase of a teaching of the *Xiaojing* 孝經 (Qing dafu 卿大夫, KR.1f0001.004.1a):

非先王之法服不敢服、非先王之法言不敢道、非先王之德行不敢行。

They [i.e., the lords and ministers] dare not wear what are not the robes prescribed by the prior kings; they dare not speak what are not the words prescribed by the prior kings; they dare not engage in what is not the virtuous conduct of the prior kings.

26   **the tenth year of Yongping** (*Eihei jūnen* 永平十年). I.e., 67 CE, the date traditionally given for the introduction of Buddhism to China.

T3. The Merit of the Kāṣāya *Kesa kudoku* 袈裟功德   67

Such people are unclear about the meaning of the direct transmission of the buddhas and ancestors.

[T3:9] {2:304}

釋迦牟尼如來、正法眼藏無上菩提を、摩訶迦葉に附授しましますに、迦葉佛正傳の袈裟、ともに傳授しまします。嫡嫡相承して曹溪山大鑑禪師にいたる、三十三代なり。その體・色・量、親傳せり。それよりのち、青原・南嶽の法孫、したしく傳法しきたり、祖宗の法を搭し、祖宗の法を製す。浣洗の法、および受持の法、その嫡嫡面授の堂奥に參學せざれば、しらざるところなり。

When Tathāgata Śākyamuni bequeathed the treasury of the eye of the true dharma, the unsurpassed bodhi, to Mahākāśyapa, along with it he transmitted the *kāṣāya* directly transmitted by Buddha Kāśyapa.[27] Inherited by successor after successor, it reached Chan Master Dajian of Mount Caoxi, in the thirty-third generation. Its material, color, and dimensions were transmitted firsthand. Thereafter, the dharma descendants of Qingyuan and Nanyue have personally transmitted the dharma, donning the dharma of the ancestors and tailoring the dharma of the ancestors.[28] The procedures for washing it and the procedures for receiving and keeping it cannot be known unless one studies in the inner sanctum of the face-to-face conferral by successor after successor.

[T3:10]

袈裟言有三衣、　　五條衣・七條衣、九條衣等大衣也。上行之流、唯受此三衣、不畜餘衣、唯用三衣、供身事足。若經營作務、大小行來、著五條衣。爲諸善事入衆、著七條衣。教化人天、令其敬信、須著九條等大衣。又在屏處、著五條衣。入衆之時、著七條衣。若入王宮聚落、須著大衣。又復調和煗煥之時、著五條衣。寒冷之時、加著七條衣。寒苦嚴切、加以著大衣。故住一時、正冬入夜、天寒裂竹。如來於彼初夜分時、著五條衣。夜久轉寒、

---

27   **Tathāgata Śākyamuni** (*Shakamuni nyorai* 釋迦牟尼如來): This section echoes "Shōbōgenzō den'e" 正法眼藏傳衣, section 20. The Buddha Kāśyapa was the sixth of the ancient buddhas, just preceding Śākyamuni; see Supplementary Notes, s.v. "Seven buddhas."

28   **dharma descendants of Qingyuan and Nanyue** (*Seigen Nangaku no hōson* 青原・南嶽の法孫): I.e., the members of the lineages descended from the Sixth Ancestor's two prime disciples, Qingyuan Xingsi 青原行思 (d. 740) and Nanyue Huairang 南嶽懷讓 (677-744).

donning the dharma of the ancestors and tailoring the dharma of the ancestors (*soshū no hō o tasshi, soshū no hō o sei su* 祖宗の法を搭し、祖宗の法を製す): An odd remark; the corresponding sentence in the "Shōbōgenzō den'e" 正法眼藏傳衣 gives the less problematic, "donned it [i.e., the *kāṣāya*] in accordance with the dharma of the prior buddhas and tailored it in accordance with the dharma of the prior buddhas" (*senbutsu no hō ni yorite tasshi senbutsu no hō ni yorite sei su* 先佛の法によりて搭し先佛の法によりて製す). The *kāṣāya* in question here cannot, of course, be the legendary robe of Bodhidharma itself, since, as Dōgen himself reports above, section 1, that robe was supposed to have been kept at the Sixth Ancestor's monastery after his death.

68   DŌGEN'S *SHŌBŌGENZŌ* VOLUME VI

加七條衣。於夜後分、天寒轉盛、加以大衣。佛便作念、未來世中、不忍寒
苦諸善男子、以此三衣、足得充身。

Of the kāṣāya, it is said:[29]

*There are three robes: the five-panel robe, the seven-panel robe, and
the great robe of nine panels, and so on.*[30] *Those of superior practice
receive only these three robes and do not accumulate other robes, using only the three robes as sufficient apparel. If one is taking care of
business or working, or is taking trips, long or short, one wears the
five-panel robe. When one joins the assembly for rituals, one wears
the seven-panel robe. When teaching humans and devas, to encourage
their respect and faith, one should wear the great robe of nine panels,
etc. Again, in private quarters, one wears the five-panel robe; in the
assembly, one wears the seven-panel robe. If one enters a royal palace
or village, one should wear the great robe. Again, when it is season-
ably warm, one wears the five-panel robe; when it is cold, one adds
the seven-panel robe; when the cold is bitter and severe, one wears
the great robe on top of that. Once, in the past, on a mid-winter night,
the weather was cold enough to split bamboo.*[31] *During the first part of
that night, the Tathāgata wore the five-panel robe. As the night went on
and it turned colder, he added the seven-panel robe. In the latter part
of the night, when the cold became extreme, he added the great robe.
Thereupon, the Buddha thought, "In some future age, when the cold
cannot be endured, good sons will be able adequately to provide for
themselves with these three robes."*

[T3:11] {2:305}
搭袈裟法

---

29   **Of the *kāṣāya*, it is said** (*kesa gon* 袈裟言): Though run into the following text, this
is a heading provided by Dōgen. Quoting the *Dasheng yi zhang* 大乘義章, by Huiyuan
慧遠 (334-416) (T.1851.44:764c3-17; Dōgen has omitted from his quotation Huiyuan's
explanation that the three robes represent a "middle way" between the extensive ward-
robe of the householder and the shameless nakedness of certain non-Buddhist ascetics.)

30   **There are three robes** (*u san e* 有三衣): The "five-panel robe" (*gojō e* 五條衣) corresponds to the Indian *anataravāsa* (*andae* 安陀衣; "undergarment"); the "seven-panel
robe" (*shichijō e* 七條衣), to the Indian *uttarāsaṃga* (*uttarasō* 欝多羅僧; "upper cloak");
and the "great robe" (*daie* 大衣), to the Indian *saṃghāti* (*sōgyari* 僧伽梨; "assembly
robe").

great robe of nine panels, and so on (*kujōe tō daie* 九條衣等大衣): The suffix *tō* 等
("etc.") here indicates great robes of more than nine panels; as stated below, section 42,
the *saṃghāṭī* robe could have as many as twenty-five panels. See Supplementary Notes,
s.v. "Robe of the Tathāgata."

31   **Once, in the past** (*kojū ichiji* 故住一時): Recalling a precedent recorded in the *Sifen
lü* 四分律 (T.1428.22:856c24-857a3), in which the Buddha permits the wearing of all
three robes in cold weather.

T3. The Merit of the Kāṣāya *Kesa kudoku* 袈裟功德 69

Procedure for donning the kāṣāya.[32]

[T3:12]

偏祖右肩、これ常途の法なり。通兩肩搭の法あり、如來および耆年老宿の儀なり。兩肩を通ず、といふとも、胸臆をあらはすときあり、胸臆をおほふときあり。通兩肩搭は、六十條衣以上の大袈裟のときなり。搭袈裟のとき、兩端ともに左臂肩にかさねかくるなり。前頭は左端のうへにかけて、臂外にたれたり。大袈裟のとき、前頭を左肩より通して、背後にいだし、たれたり。このほか種種の著袈裟の法あり、久參咨問すべし。

Baring the right shoulder is the customary procedure. There is a procedure for wearing it across both shoulders, a manner of the Tathāgata as well as of seniors and elders. Though worn across both shoulders, there are times when the chest is exposed and times when it is covered. Wearing across both shoulders is done when wearing a great *kāṣāya* that is a robe of sixty panels or more.[33] When donning the *kāṣāya*, double it up so that the two ends are together and draped over the left arm and shoulder. Drape the front edge over the left end and let it hang down outside the arm. When using a great *kaṣāya*, pull out the front edge, passing it from the left shoulder behind the back, and let it hang down. Apart from these, there are various other procedures for wearing the *kāṣāya*, so one should seek advice from long-time practitioners.

[T3:13]

梁・陳・隋・唐・宋、あひつたはれて數百歲のあひだ、大小兩乗の學者、おほく講經の業をなげすてて、究竟にあらずとしりて、すすみて佛祖正傳の法を習學せんとするとき、かならず從來の弊衣を脱落して、佛祖正傳の袈裟を受持するなり。まさしくこれ捨邪歸正なり。

During the several hundred years that the Liang, Chen, Sui, Tang, and Song succeeded one another, many students of both the Great and Small Vehicles abandoned the activity of lecturing on the sūtras and, recognizing that this was not the ultimate, went on to study the dharma directly transmitted by the buddhas and ancestors.[34] At this time, they invari-

---

32 **Procedure for donning the kāṣāya** (*takkesa hō* 搭袈裟法): Parts of this section parallel "Shōbōgenzō den'e" 正法眼藏傳衣, section 31.

33 **great kāṣāya that is a robe of sixty panels or more** (*rokujū jō e ijō no dai kesa* 六十條衣以上の大袈裟): As will be discussed below, each panel (*jō* 條) of the *kāṣāya* is made up of several sections (*dankyaku* 壇隔) of cloth; the "great *kāṣāya*" in question here is likely one of fifteen panels with four sections each, or sixty sections total. (See, e.g., *Yugaron gi* 瑜伽論記, by Dullyun 遁倫 [dates unknown], T.1828.42:437a2-4.)

34 **Liang, Chen, Sui, Tang, and Song** (*Ryō Chin Zui Tō Sō* 梁・陳・隋・唐・宋): I.e., the dynasties that ruled in China from the Liang (502-557), when Bodhidharma was supposed to have brought the ancestral lineage to China, until Dōgen's day, during the Song (960-1279). This section echoes the "Shōbōgenzō den'e" 正法眼藏傳衣, section 33.

70   DŌGEN'S *SHŌBŌGENZŌ* VOLUME VI

ably sloughed off their previous tattered robes and received and kept the *kāṣāya* directly transmitted by the buddhas and ancestors. Truly, this was *abandoning the false and taking refuge in the true.*[35]

[T3:14] {2:306}

如來の正法は、西天すなはち法本なり。古今の人師、おほく凡夫の情量・局量の小見をたつ。佛界・衆生界、それ有邊・無邊にあらざるがゆえに、大小乘の教行人理、いまの凡夫の局量にいるべからず。しかあるに、いたづらに西天を本とせず、震旦國にして、あらたに局量の小見を今案して佛法とせる道理、しかあるべからず。

In the true dharma of the Tathāgata, it is Sindh in the West that is the source of the dharma.[36] Many teachers of humans, past and present, have set up small views based on the sentiments and limitations of the common people. Because the realm of the buddhas and the realm of living beings are beyond the extreme of existence and the extreme of non-existence, the teachings, practices, persons, and principles of the Great and Small Vehicles cannot be encompassed by the limited thinking of these common people.[37] Nevertheless, pointlessly denying that Sindh in the West is the source, in the Land of Cīnasthāna, they have newly proposed the small views of their own limited thinking as the buddha dharma — something that just does not make sense.[38]

[T3:15]

しかあればすなはち、いま發心のともがら、袈裟を受持すべくば、正傳の袈裟を受持すべし、今案の新作袈裟を受持すべからず。正傳の袈裟といふは、少林・曹溪正傳しきたれる、如來の嫡嫡相承なり、一代も虧闕なし。その法子法孫の著しきたれる、これ正傳袈裟なり、唐土の新作は正傳にあらず。いま古今に、西天よりきたれる僧徒の所著の袈裟、みな佛祖正傳の袈裟のごとく著せり。一人としても、いま震旦新作の、律學のともがらの所製の袈裟のごとくなるなし。くらきともがら、律學の袈裟を信ず、あきらかなるものは抛却するなり。

Thus, those who bring forth the mind [of bodhi] at present, if they are to receive and keep the *kāsāya*, should receive and keep the *kāsāya* that has been directly transmitted, not some newly constructed *kāsāya* just

---

35 **abandoning the false and taking refuge in the true** (*shaja kishō* 捨邪歸正): A fixed expression found throughout the Chinese Buddhist canon.

36 **the true dharma of the Tathāgata** (*nyorai no shōbō* 如來の正法): The warnings beginning here against Chinese revisions of the *kāsāya* presumably reflect the more detailed criticism found in "Shōbōgenzō den'e" 正法眼藏傳衣, sections 44ff.

37 **teachings, practices, persons, and principles** (*kyō gyō nin ri* 教行人理): A fixed expression, found especially in the texts of Tiantai 天台, for the buddha dharma as a whole.

38 **something that just does not make sense** (*dōri, shika aru bekarazu* 道理、しかあるべからず): Or, perhaps, "something that just is not true."

T3. The Merit of the Kāṣāya *Kesa kudoku* 袈裟功德　　71

recently proposed.[39] "The *kāṣāya* that has been directly transmitted" means the one directly transmitted by Shaolin and Caoxi, the one that has been inherited by successor after successor from the Tathāgata, without the lapse of even a single generation.[40] The one that has been worn by their dharma children and dharma grandchildren — this the *kāṣāya* directly transmitted; the one newly constructed in the Land of the Tang is not the one directly transmitted. Now, the *kāṣāya* worn by the monks, past and present, who have come from Sindh in the West have all been like the *kāṣāya* directly transmitted by the buddhas and ancestors. Not a single one of them had a *kāṣāya* like the ones now newly constructed in Cīnasthāna, built by a bunch of vinaya scholars.[41] Ignorant types believe in the *kāṣāya* of the vinaya scholars; those who understand reject it.

[T3:16]

おほよそ佛佛祖祖相傳の袈裟の功德、あきらかにして信受しやすし。正傳、まさしく相承せり、本樣、まのあたりつたはれり、いまに現在せり。受持、あひ嗣法して、いまにいたる。受持せる祖師、ともにこれ證契傳法の師資なり。

In sum, the merit of the *kāṣāya* transmitted by buddha after buddha and ancestor after ancestor is clear and easy to believe in and accept.[42] Its direct transmission has been exactly inherited; its original form has been handed down before our very eyes and is present even now. Those who receive and keep it have inherited the dharma right down till now. The ancestral masters who received and kept it are all masters and disciples who verify the accord and transmit the dharma.

39　**those who bring forth the mind [of bodhi]** (*hosshin no tomogara* 發心のともがら): I.e., those who aspire to buddhahood and set out on the bodhisattva path; see Supplementary Notes, s.v. "Bring forth the mind." This section echoes "Shōbōgenzō den'e" 正法眼藏傳衣, section 34.

40　**Shaolin and Caoxi** (*Shōrin Sōkei* 少林・曹溪): I.e., the First Ancestor, Bodhidharma, and the Sixth Ancestor, Huineng 慧能.

41　**vinaya scholars** (*ritsugaku* 律學): The criticism here echoes that at "Shōbōgenzō den'e" 正法眼藏傳衣, section 44, where the robe in question is described as "small size" (*shōryō* 小量) — presumably, a reference to the abbreviated *kāṣāya* (*kara* 掛絡).

42　**the merit of the *kāṣāya* transmitted by buddha after buddha and ancestor after ancestor** (*butsubutsu soso sōden no kesa no kudoku* 佛佛祖祖相傳の袈裟の功德): This section echoes "Shōbōgenzō den'e" 正法眼藏傳衣, section 36.

72 DŌGEN'S *SHŌBŌGENZŌ* VOLUME VI

[T3:17]
しかあればすなはち、佛祖正傳の作袈裟の法によりて作法すべし。ひと
りこれ正傳なるがゆえに、凡聖・人天・龍神、みなひさしく證知しきた
れるところなり。この法の流布にむまれあひて、ひとたび袈裟を身體にお
ほひ、利那・須臾も受持せん、すなはちこれ決定成無上菩提の護身符子な
らん。一句・一偈を信心にそめん、長劫光明の種子として、つひに無上菩
提にいたる。一法・一善を身心にそめん、亦復如是なるべし。心念も利那
生滅し、無所住なり、身體も利那生滅し、無所住なりといへども、所修の
功德、かならず熟脱のときあり。袈裟、また作にあらず、無作にあらず、
有所住にあらず、無所住にあらず、唯佛與佛の究竟するところなりといへ
ども、受持する行者、その所得の功德、かならず成就するなり、かならず
究竟するなり。もし宿善なきものは、一生・二生、乃至無量生を經歷すと
いふとも、袈裟をみるべからず、袈裟を著すべからず、袈裟を信受すべか
らず、袈裟をあきらめしるべからず。いま震旦國・日本國をみるに、袈裟
をひとたび身體に著することうるものあり、えざるものあり、貴賤によら
ず、愚智によらず。はかりしりぬ、宿善によれりといふこと。

Thus, we should follow the procedures based on the method of making
a *kāṣāya* directly transmitted by the buddhas and ancestors. Because this
alone is the direct transmission, it is what common people and sages,
humans and devas, dragons and spirits have all long attested to. Having been born where this dharma is widespread, just once to drape the
kāṣāya over our body and receive and keep it even for a *kṣāna* or an instant — this will be a talisman protecting the body that makes us *certain
to achieve unsurpassed bodhi*.[43] A single line or a single gāthā dyed onto
the believing mind serves as a seed bright for long kalpas, eventually
reaching unsurpassed bodhi; a single dharma or a single good deed dyed
onto the body and mind is surely also like this.[44]

Thought arises and ceases in a *kṣāna*, with no abode, and the body
arises and ceases in a *kṣaṇa*, with no abode; nevertheless, the merit we
cultivate inevitably has a time when it ripens and drops.[45] Again, the
kāṣāya is not produced nor unproduced, not with an abode nor without
an abode, something that "*only buddhas with buddhas*" complete; nevertheless, the merit attained by the practitioner who receives and keeps
it will inevitably be achieved, will inevitably be complete.[46] Those who

---

43 **certain to achieve unsurpassed bodhi** (*ketsujō jō mujō bodai* 決定成無上菩提):
Variation on a fixed phrase for the bodhisattva assured of attaining buddhahood. This
section echoes "Shōbōgenzō den'e" 正法眼藏傳衣, sections 37-39.

44 **A single line or a single gāthā** (*ikku ichige* 一句・一偈): A common fixed expression for even a bit of Buddhist scripture.

45 **inevitably has a time when it ripens and drops** (*kanarazu jukudatsu no toki ari*
かならず熟脱のときあり): From the common agricultural metaphor of karma planted,
maturing, and coming to fruition (*shujukudatsu* 種熟脱).

46 **something that "only buddhas with buddhas" complete** (*yui butsu yo butsu no*

T3. The Merit of the Kāṣāya *Kesa kudoku* 袈裟功德

lack good karma from previous lifetimes, although they pass through one life, two lives, up to incalculable lives, will not see the *kāṣāya*, will not wear the *kāṣāya*, will not believe in and accept the *kāṣāya*, will not understand and know the *kāṣāya*. Now, when we look at the Land of Cīnasthāna and the Land of Japan, there are those able once to wear the *kāṣāya* on their bodies and those that are not, not depending on whether their status is high or low, not depending on whether they are stupid or wise; we can understand that it depends on their good karma from former lives.

[T3:18] {2:307}

しかあればすなはち、袈裟を受持せんは、宿善、よろこぶべし、積功累
德、うたがふべからず。いまだえざらんは、ねがふべし、今生いそぎ、そ
の、はじめて下種せんことをいとなむべし。さはりありて受持することえ
ざらんものは、諸佛如來・佛法僧の三寶に、慚愧・懺悔すべし。他國の衆
生、いくばくかねがふらん、わがくにも震旦國のごとく、如來の衣法、ま
さしく正傳親臨せまし、と。おのれがくにに正傳せざること、慚愧ふかか
るらん、かなしむうらみあるらむ。われらなにのさいはひありてか、如來
世尊の衣法正傳せる法に、あふたてまつれる。宿殖般若の大功德力なり。

Thus, those who receive and keep the *kāṣāya* should rejoice at their good karma from former lives and should not doubt that they have *accumulated merit and amassed virtue.*[47] Those who have yet to obtain it should wish for it and, in the present life, immediately endeavor initially to plant the seeds for it. Those who have obstacles and are unable to receive and keep it should feel ashamed and make repentance before the buddhas, the tathāgatas, and the three treasures of buddha, dharma, and saṃgha. How many living beings in other countries must wish, "May the robe and dharma of the Tathāgata actually be directly transmitted to and personally present in our land as it is in the Land of Cīnasthāna." The fact that they have not been directly transmitted to one's land must be deeply shameful, sad, and regrettable. Why are we so blessed to have encountered the dharma that has directly transmitted the robe and dharma of the Tathāgata, the World-Honored One? It is the power of the great merit of prajñā cultivated in former lives.

---

kukyō suru tokoro 唯佛與佛の究竟するところ): Suggestive of a line in the *Lotus Sūtra*; see Supplementary Notes, s.v. "Only buddhas with buddhas can exhaustively investigate the real marks of the dharmas."

47 **accumulated merit and amassed virtue** (*shakku ruitoku* 積功累德): A fixed expression for developing good karma found throughout the Buddhist literature. This section echoes "Shōbōgenzō den'e" 正法眼藏傳衣, sections 39-42.

74 DŌGEN'S *SHŌBŌGENZŌ* VOLUME VI

[T3:19] {2:308}

いま末法惡時世は、おのれが正傳なきをはぢず、他の正傳あるをそねむ。
おもはくは、魔儻ならむ。おのれがいまの所有・所住は、前業にひかれて
眞實にあらず。ただ正傳佛法を歸敬せん、すなはちおのれが學佛の實歸な
るべし。

In the present evil age at the end of the dharma, there are those who
do not feel ashamed that they themselves lack the direct transmission
and who detest the fact that others have the direct transmission; I think
they are the minions of Māra.[48] One's present possessions and abode are
induced by one's past deeds and are not the real truth. Just to take refuge
in and revere the directly transmitted buddha dharma — this will be the
true return of one's study of Buddhism.[49]

[T3:20]

おほよそしるべし、袈裟は、これ諸佛の恭敬歸依しましますところなり、
佛身なり、佛心なり。解脱服と稱し、福田衣と稱し、無相衣と稱し、無上
衣と稱し、忍辱衣と稱し、如來衣と稱し、大慈大悲衣と稱し、勝幡衣と稱
し、阿耨多羅三藐三菩提衣と稱す、まことにかくのごとく受持頂戴すべ
し。かくのごとくなるがゆえに、心にしたがうてあらたむべきにあらず。

In sum, we should realize that the *kāṣāya* is something the buddhas
venerate and take refuge in.[50] It is the buddha body; it is the buddha mind.
It is called the "vestment of liberation," called the "field of merit robe,"
called the "signless robe,"[51] called the "unsurpassed robe," called the "robe
of forbearance," called the "robe of the tathāgata,"[52] called the "robe of
great mercy and great compassion," called the "banner of victory robe,"[53]

---

48 **In the present evil age at the end of the dharma** (*ima mappō akujise* いま末法惡
時世): This section echoes "Shōbōgenzō den'e" 正法眼藏傳衣, section 42.

49 **true return of one's study of Buddhism** (*gakubutsu no jikki* 學佛の實歸): I.e., the
real refuge for those who study Buddhism.

50 **In sum** (*ōyoso* おほよそ): This section echoes "Shōbōgenzō den'e" 正法眼藏傳
衣, section 43.

51 **"vestment of liberation"** (*gedappuku* 解脱服); **"field of merit robe"** (*fukuden e* 福
田衣); **"signless robe"** (*musō e* 無相衣): Expressions likely derived from the "Verse for
Donning the *Kaṣāya*" (see above, Note 15).

52 **"unsurpassed robe"** (*mujō e* 無上依): An unusual name, not encountered elsewhere in the *Shōbōgenzō*.

"robe of forbearance" (*ninniku e* 忍辱衣); **"robe of the tathāgata"** (*nyorai e* 如來衣):
Likely reflecting a verse in the *Lotus Sūtra*; see Supplementary Notes, s.v. "Robe of the
Tathāgata."

53 **"robe of great mercy and great compassion"** (*daiji daihi e* 大慈大悲衣): An
unusual expression, though the expression "robe of compassion" (*jihi e* 慈悲衣) does
occur in a list of terms for the *kaṣāya*, in the *Fozhi biqiu liuwu tu* 佛制比丘六物圖, by
Yuanzhao 元照 (1048–1116); see Supplementary Notes, s.v. "Robe of the Tathāgata."

"banner of victory robe" (*shōban e* 勝幡衣): Another unusual expression, although

T3. The Merit of the Kāṣāya *Kesa kudoku* 袈裟功德　　75

called the "robe of *anuttara-samyak-saṃbodhi*."[54] *We should receive and keep it, and reverently accept it* like this.[55] Because it is like this, we should not alter it as we please.

[T3:21]

その衣財、また絹・布、よろしきにしたがうてもちいる。かならずしも、布は清淨なり、絹は不淨なるにあらず。布をきらふて絹をとる、所見なし、わらふべし。諸佛の常法、かならず糞掃衣を上品とす。

For the robe material, we use either silk or a plant fiber, according to whichever is suitable.[56] It is not necessarily the case that plant fiber is pure and silk is impure; and there is no view that rejects plant fiber in favor of silk, which would be laughable. The constant norm of the buddhas always treats a robe of discarded rags as the highest grade.[57]

[T3:22]

糞掃に十種あり、四種あり。いはゆる、火燒・牛嚼・鼠嚙・死人衣等。五印度人、如此等衣、棄之巷野。事同糞掃、名糞掃衣。行者取之、浣洗縫治、用以供身。そのなかに絹類あり、布類あり。絹・布の見をなげすてて、糞掃を參學すべきなり。糞掃衣は、むかし阿耨達池にして浣洗せしに、龍王、讚歎・雨華・禮拜しき。

There are ten kinds or four kinds of "discarded rags":[58]

---

the *kāṣāya* is identified with the Tathāgata's victory banner in the *Zhiguan fuxing zhuan hongjue* 止觀輔行傳弘決, by Zhanran 湛然 (T.1912.46:185c10), a text Dōgen often cites.

54　**"robe of *anuttara-samyak-saṃbodhi*"** (*anokutara sanmyaku sanbodai e* 阿耨多羅三藐三菩提衣): An expression seemingly of Dōgen's own invention.

55　**receive and keep it, and reverently accept it** (*juji chōdai* 受持頂戴): A common phrase that will be repeated (with some variation) several times below. The second element, *chōdai* 頂戴, is also used for the monk's ritual act of placing the folded *kāṣāya* on the head.

56　**For the robe material** (*sono ezai* その衣財): This section echoes "Shōbōgenzō den'e" 正法眼藏傳衣, section 46.

plant fiber (*fu* 布): The term *fu* 布 can refer to cloth in general or, as in this discussion, to cloth made of plant fiber, as opposed to silk (or wool); the fabric in question can include cotton, linen, hemp, ramie, etc. The issue here is the question of whether silk, the production of which involves the death of the silkworm, is an appropriate fiber for a monk's robe.

57　**discarded rags** (*funzō* 糞掃): Loose rendering of a term, meaning something like "soiled sweepings," used for Sanskrit *pāṃsukūla* ("dung heap"), to designate soiled cloth taken from refuse and used to make the Buddhist robe.

58　**There are ten kinds or four kinds of "discarded rags"** (*funzō ni jisshu ari, shishu ari* 糞掃に十種あり、四種あり): The ten kinds will be listed below, section 61. The four kinds listed in the quotation here are from the *Dasheng yi zhang* 大乘義章 (T.1851.44:764b8-11).

Fire-singed, cow-chewed, mouse-gnawed, and corpse robes. People of the Fivefold India discard such robes in alleys and fields.[59] *Treated the same as something filthy and discarded, they are called "filthy discarded robes." Practitioners collect them, wash and mend them, and use them to provide for their bodies.*

Among them, there are silk types and plant fiber types. Casting aside the view of them as silk or plant fiber, we should study them as discarded rags. Once, when a robe of discarded rags was washed in Lake Anavatapta, the Dragon King praised it, showered it with flowers, and paid obeisance to it.[60]

[T3:23] {2:309}

小乗教師、また化絲の説あり。よところなかるべし、大乗人、わらふべし、いづれか化絲にあらざらん。なんぢ、化をきくみみを信ずとも、化をみる目を疑ふ。

Teachers of the Small Vehicle also have a theory of "transformation thread."[61] It surely lacks any basis and, to people of the Great Vehicle, is laughable. What is not "transformation thread"?[62] You trust the ears that hear of transformation yet doubt the eyes that see transformation.[63]

---

59   **People of the Fivefold India** (*Goindojin* 五印度人): An unusual term for the people of the Indian subcontinent, found in Xuanzang's 玄奘 *Datang xiyuji* 大唐西域記; equivalent to the more common *Gotennin* 五天人 ("people of the Fivefold Sindh"). The *Dasheng yi zhang* 大乗義章 (T.1851.44:764b9) has here "foreigners" (*waiguo zhi ren* 外國之人).

60   **Lake Anavatapta** (*Anokudatchi* 阿耨達池): Seemingly a variant of a story found in the *Ratnakūṭa-sūtra* (*Da baoji jing* 大寶積經, T.310.11:647a11-14), in which it is devas, rather than the dragon, that appreciate the washing of the robe. The lake, imagined to be north of the Himalayas (sometimes identified with Lake Manasarovar, in western Tibet), is said to derive its name ("unheated") from the fact that the dragons residing there are not subject to the hot sands and winds that represent one of their afflictions.

61   **"transformation thread"** (*keshi* 化絲): Likely a reference to the notion that the silk thread of the Buddha's *kāṣāya* does not involve injury because it does not come from the mouth of the silkworm but rather emerges as a "transformation," or "manifestation" (*ke* 化), or from the mouths of "transformation girls" (*kenyo* 化女; presumably, females born spontaneously, rather than from the womb) on another continent. (See *Fayuan zhulin* 法苑珠林, T.2122.53:561a16-23; b22-c8.) This paragraph echoes "Shōbōgenzō den'e" 正法眼藏傳衣, section 47.

62   **What is not "transformation thread"?** (*izure ka keshi ni arazaran* いづれか化絲にあらざらん): Perhaps to be understand as a reminder that, for "people of the Great Vehicle," all things are mere "transformations." The corresponding sentence in the "Shōbōgenzō den'e" 正法眼藏傳衣 reads simply "What is not a transformation?" (*izure ka ke ni arazaru* いづれか化にあらざる).

63   **You trust the ears that hear of transformation** (*nanji, ke o kiku mimi o shinzu* なんぢ、化をきくみみを信ず): Dōgen here addresses the teachers directly, as he often does in his criticisms.

T3. The Merit of the Kāṣāya *Kesa kudoku* 袈裟功徳

[T3:24]

しるべし、糞掃をひろふなかに、絹に相似なる布あらん、布に相似なる絹あらん。土俗萬差にして、造化、はかりがたし、肉眼のよくしるところにあらず。かくのごとくの物をえたらん、絹・布と論ずべからず、糞掃と稱すべし。たとひ人天の、糞掃と生長せるありとも、有情ならじ、糞掃なるべし。たとひ松・菊の、糞掃と生長せるありとも、非情ならじ、糞掃なるべし。糞掃の、絹・布にあらず、金銀・珠玉にあらざる道理を信受するとき、糞掃現成するなり。絹・布の見解、いまだ脱落せざれば、糞掃也未夢見在なり。

We should recognize that, among the discarded rags that are picked up, there may be a plant fiber that resembles silk and silk that resembles a plant fiber.[64] Local practices have myriad variations, and their production is hard to gauge, it not being something readily known by the physical eye. When we get such things, without discussing whether they are silk or plant fiber, we should call them "discarded rags." Even if there were humans or devas that grew into discarded rags, they would not be sentient; they would be discarded rags. And, even if there were pines or chrysanthemums that grew into discarded rags, they would not be insentient; they would be discarded rags. When we believe in the principle that discarded rags are neither silk nor plant fiber, neither gold nor silver, pearls nor jade, then the discarded rags appear. When we have not yet sloughed off the view that they are silk or plant fiber, then we *have not seen the discarded rags even in our dreams.*

[T3:25]

ある僧、かつて古佛にとふ、黄梅夜半の傳衣、これ布なりとやせん、絹なりとやせん。畢竟じて、なにものなりとかせん。古佛いはく、これ布にあらず、これ絹にあらず。しるべし、袈裟は絹・布にあらざる、これ佛道の玄訓なり。

A monk once asked the Old Buddha, "The robe transmitted in the middle of the night at Huangmei — do we take it as a plant fiber, or take it as silk?[65] After all, what do we take it as?"

The Old Buddha said, "It wasn't plant fiber; it wasn't silk."[66]

---

64 **We should recognize** (*shiru beshi* しるべし): This section echoes "Shōbōgenzō den'e" 正法眼藏傳衣, section 47.

65 **A monk once asked the Old Buddha** (*aru sō, katsute kobutsu ni tou* ある僧、かつて古佛にとふ): "Old Buddha" (*kobutsu* 古佛) refers here to the Sixth Ancestor, Huineng, regarding the robe he received from the Fifth Ancestor (as described in section 1, above). The source of this conversation is unknown. This section echoes "Shōbōgenzō den'e" 正法眼藏傳衣, sections 53-55.

66 **"It wasn't plant fiber; it wasn't silk"** (*kore fu ni arazu, kore ken ni arazu* これ布にあらず、これ絹にあらず): Contrary to this saying, Chan authors regularly reported that

78 DŌGEN'S *SHŌBŌGENZŌ* VOLUME VI

We can see here that the fact that the *kāṣāya* is neither silk nor plant fiber is a profound instruction of the way of the buddhas.

[T3:26]

商那和修尊者は、第三の付法藏なり。むまるるときより衣と俱に生ぜり。この衣、すなはち在家のときは俗服なり、出家すれば袈裟となる。また鮮白比丘尼、發願施氎ののち、生生のところ、および中有、かならず衣と俱生せり。今日、釋迦牟尼佛にあふたてまつりて出家するとき、生得の俗衣、すみやかに轉じて袈裟となる、和修尊者におなじ。あきらかにしりぬ、袈裟は、絹・布等にあらざること。いはんや、佛法の功德、よく身心諸法を轉ずること、それかくのごとし。われら出家・受戒のとき、身心依正、すみやかに轉ずる道埋あきらかなれど、愚蒙にしてしらざるのみなり。諸佛の常法、ひとり和修・鮮白に加して、われらに加せざることなきなり。隨分の利益、疑ふべからざるなり。

Venerable Śaṇavāsa was the third in the bequest of the treasury of the dharma.[67] From the time of his birth, he had a robe that was born simultaneously with him. When he was a householder, this robe was a secular garment; when he left home, it became a *kāṣāya*. Again, the Bhikṣuṇī Śuklā, after her vow and donation of robes, in birth after birth, as well as in the intermediate state, was always born together with a robe.[68] Today,

---

the robe of Bodhidharma received by the Sixth Ancestor was made of fine Indian cotton, not of silk as was sometimes mistakenly claimed.

67　**Venerable Śaṇavāsa** (*Shōnawashu sonja* 商那和修尊者): Reference to the legend that the Third Ancestor, Ānanda's disciple Śaṇavāsa, was born wearing a miraculous robe, which enlarged as he grew, became a monk's habit when he left home, and a nine-panel *saṃghāṭī* robe when he took the full precepts. (See, e.g., Xuanzang's 玄奘 *Datang xiyu ji* 大唐西域記, T.2087.51:873b28-c5; *Chuanfa zhengzong ji* 傳法正宗記, T.2078.51:720c20-28.) The reference to Śaṇavāsa here (though not to Śuklā) echoes "Shōbōgenzō den'e" 正法眼藏傳衣, section 56.

68　**Bhikṣuṇī Śuklā** (*Senbyaku bikuni* 鮮白比丘尼): Reference to a legend found in several sources; Dōgen seems to be reflecting here a version found in the *Abhidharma-vibhāṣa-śāstra* (*Apitan piposha lun* 阿毘曇毘婆沙論, T.1546.28:268a1-9):

問曰、何故菩薩中有無衣、白淨比丘尼有衣。答曰、白淨比丘尼施四方僧氎。問曰、菩薩施四方僧衣段、多於白淨比丘尼所施氎縷。答曰、白淨比丘尼施僧氎已、發如是願。使我生生之處、常著衣服。以發願力故、中有生時著衣。入胎出胎、亦常著衣。其身轉大、衣亦隨大。於佛法生信、而後出家、即以此衣作五種衣。懃修方便、得阿羅漢、般涅槃時、即以此衣纏身。

Question: "If the bodhisattas do not have robes in the intermediate state, why did the Bhikṣuṇī Śuklā have a robe?"

Answer: "The Bhikṣuṇī Śuklā donated robes to the monks of the four quarters."

Question: The bodhisattvas have donated more robes to the monks of the four quarters than the robes donated by Bhikṣuṇī Śuklā."

Answer: "After the Bhikṣuṇī Śuklā donated the monks' robes, she made a vow, 'May I in birth after birth always wear a robe.' It is on the strength of this vow that she wore a robe when born in the intermediate state and also always wore a robe when she entered the womb and left the womb. As she grew, the robe also enlarged. When

T3. The Merit of the Kāṣāya *Kesa kudoku* 袈裟功德　79

when she encounters Buddha Śākyamuni and leaves home, the secular clothing she got at birth immediately changes into the *kāṣāya*, just as in the case of Venerable Śaṇavāsa.

Thus, we see that the *kāṣāya* is not silk or plant fiber or the like. Needless to say, the transformation of the dharmas of body and mind by the merit of the buddha dharma is like this. The principle is obvious that, when we leave home and receive the precepts, our bodies and minds, our secondary and primary recompense, are immediately transformed; yet in our ignorance, we simply do not recognize it.[69] It is not the case that the constant norm of the buddhas includes Śaṇavāsa and Śuklā alone and does not include us; we should not doubt that we have our due share of benefit.

[T3:27]

かくのごとくの道理、あきらかに功夫參學すべし。善來得戒の披體の袈裟、かならずしも布にあらず、絹にあらず、佛化難思なり。衣裏の寶珠は、算沙の所能にあらず。

Clearly, we should make concentrated effort and study such a principle. That the *kāṣāya* that drapes the body when one *obtains the precepts with the welcome* is not necessarily either of plant fiber or silk is an instruction of the buddhas difficult to conceive.[70] The precious jewel in the robe is not something that counting sand can get.[71]

---

she developed faith in the buddha dharma and later left home, this robe turned into the five robes [of the *bhikṣuṇī*]. When she zealously practiced, became an arhat, and entered *parinirvāṇa*, her body was wrapped in the robe.

69　**secondary and primary recompense** (*eshō* 依正): A standard Buddhist term for the results of past karma reflected respectively in the circumstances into which one is born and the mental and physical makeup of the person; see Supplementary Notes, s.v. "Secondary and primary recompense."

70　**the *kāṣāya* that drapes the body when one obtains the precepts with the welcome** (*zenrai tokukai no hitai no kesa* 善來得戒の披體の袈裟): Allusion to the tradition that, at the time of Buddha Śākyamuni, disciples were considered to have been inducted into the order by the Buddha's act of welcoming them. There is a common trope in the early Buddhist literature that reads,

佛言、善來比丘、鬚髮自落、袈裟著身。

When the Buddha said, "Welcome, bhikṣu," his beard and hair fell off by themselves, and a *kāṣāya* cloaked his body.

In his "Shōbōgenzō senmen" 正法眼藏洗面 and "Shōbōgenzō shukke" 正法眼藏出家, Dōgen cites this trope in the case of Mahākāśyapa (from *Jingde chuandeng lu* 景德傳燈錄, T.2076.51:206a2-3).

The allusion here echoes "Shōbōgenzō den'e" 正法眼藏傳衣, section 55.

71　**precious jewel in the robe** (*eri no hōju* 衣裏の寶珠): Allusion to the famous parable in the *Lotus Sūtra* of the man who is unaware that his friend had sewn a priceless jewel

80 DŌGEN'S *SHŌBŌGENZŌ* VOLUME VI

[T3:28] {2:310}

諸佛の袈裟の體・色・量の有量・無量、有相・無相、明らめ參學すべし。
西天東地、古往今來の祖師、みな參學正傳せるところなり。祖祖正傳の、
明らかにして疑ふところなきを見聞しながら、いたづらにこの祖師に正傳
せざらんは、その意樂ゆるしがたからん。愚癡のいたり、不信のゆえなる
べし。實をすてて虚をもとめ、本をすてて末をねがふものなり。これ如來
を輕忽したてまつるならん。菩提心をおこさんともがら、かならず祖師の
相傳を傳受すべし。われら、あひがたき佛法にあふたてまつるのみにあら
ず、佛袈裟正傳の法孫として、これを見聞し、學習し、受持することをえ
たり。すなはちこれ、如來をみたてまつるなり、佛説法をきくなり、佛
光明にてらさるるなり、佛受用を受用するなり、佛心を單傳するなり、佛
髓をえたるなり。まのあたり、釋迦牟尼佛の袈裟におほはれたてまつるな
り、釋迦牟尼佛、まのあたりわれに袈裟をさづけましますなり。ほとけに
したがふたてまつりて、この袈裟は、うけたてまつれり。

We should clarify and study what is calculable and incalculable, what
has signs and what lacks signs in the material, color, and dimensions of
the *kāṣāya* of the buddhas.[72] It is something that the ancestral masters
of Sindh in the West and the Land of the East in past and present have
all studied and directly transmitted. It would be hard to condone the
aspirations of those who, even while seeing and hearing that the direct
transmission of ancestor after ancestor is clear, with nothing to doubt,
foolishly did not themselves receive the direct transmission of these ancestral masters. It is the height of stupidity, likely due to lack of faith.
They abandon the truth and seek the false; they abandon the root and
want the branch. It would be dismissive of the Tathāgata.

Those who would give rise to the mind of bodhi should invariable
receive the transmission transmitted by the ancestral masters. Not only
have we encountered the buddha dharma, difficult to meet, but as dharma descendants of the direct transmission of the buddha *kāṣāya*, we
have been able to see and hear of it, to study it, to receive and keep it.
This is to see the Tathāgata, to hear the Buddha preach the dharma, to be

---

into the lining of his robe; see Supplementary Notes, s.v. "Jewel in the robe." The allusion here echoes "Shōbōgenzō den'e" 正法眼藏傳衣, section 56.

counting sand (*sansha* 算沙): Or, perhaps, "sand counters" — i.e., those obsessed with
the details, what we might call "spiritual bean counters"; see Supplementary Notes, s.v.
"Counting sand."

72 **We should clarify and study what is calculable and incalculable, what has signs
and what lacks signs in the material, color, and dimensions of the *kāṣāya* of the
buddhas** (*shobutsu no kesa no tai jiki ryō no uryō muryō usō musō, akirame sangaku su
beshi* 諸佛の袈裟の體・色・量の有量・無量有相無相、明らめ參學すべし): Or, per-
haps, "We should clarify and study whether the material, color, and dimensions of the
kāṣāya of the buddhas are calculable or incalculable, have attributes or lack attributes."
This section echoes "Shōbōgenzō den'e" 正法眼藏傳衣, sections 57-58, which once
seems to have represented the conclusion of that chapter.

T3. The Merit of the Kāṣāya *Kesa kudoku* 袈裟功德 81

illumined by the radiance of the Buddha; to enjoy the enjoyment of the Buddha, uniquely to transmit the mind of the Buddha, to get the marrow of the Buddha. It is personally to be cloaked in the *kāṣāya* of Buddha Śākyamuni; it is Buddha Śākyamuni personally presenting us with the *kāṣāya*. Following the Buddha, we have received this *kāṣāya*.

* * * * *

[T3:29] {2:311}
浣袈裟法

Procedure for washing the kāṣāya.[73]

[T3:30]
袈裟をたたまず、淨桶にいれて、香湯を百沸して、袈裟をひたして、一時ばかりおく。またの法、清き灰水を百沸して、袈裟をひたして、湯のひややかになるをまつ。いまは、よのつねに灰湯をもちいる。灰湯、ここには、あくのゆ、といふ。灰湯さめぬれば、きよくすみたる湯をもて、たびたびこれを浣洗するあひだ、両手にいれてもみあらはず、ふまず。あか、のぞこほり、油、のぞこほるを、期とす。そののち、沈香・栴檀香等を冷水に和して、これをあらふ。そののち、淨竿にかけてほす。よく、ほしてのち、摺襵して、たかく安じて、燒香・散華して、右遶數匝して、禮拜したてまつる。あるいは三拜、あるいは六拜、あるいは九拜して、胡跪合掌して、袈裟を両手にささげて、くちに偈を誦してのち、たちて、如法に著したてまつる。

Without folding the *kāṣāya*, place it in a cleaning bucket; bring perfumed water to a full boil and soak the *kāṣāya* for about two hours. Another method is to bring clean ash water to a full boil, soak the *kāṣāya*, and wait for the water to cool down. At present, it is common practice to use ash water. *Huitang* ("ash water") is called here *akunoyu*.[74] When the ash water has cooled, rinse [the robe] repeatedly in clean clear hot water, without rubbing it between your hands or treading on it. Continue until dirt and grease have been removed. After that, wash it in cold water mixed with aloes incense, sandalwood incense, or the like. After that, hang it on a pure pole to dry.[75] Once it is fully dried, folding it and placing on an elevated place, burn incense, scatter flowers, circumambulate

---

73 **Procedure for washing the kāṣāya** (*kan kesa hō* 浣袈裟法): While the body of the "Shōbōgenzō den'e" 正法眼藏傳衣 lacks a corresponding section on washing, a brief text in Chinese following the colophon (sections 71-73) gives abbreviated instructions for the washing ritual.

74 *Huitang* ("ash water") is called here *akunoyu* (*kaitō, koko ni wa, akunoyu, to iu* 灰湯、ここには、あくのゆ、といふ): Dōgen is here simply giving the Japanese (*kun* 訓) reading of the Chinese term.

75 **pure pole** (*jōkan* 淨竿): A raised horizontal pole used for hanging clothes, etc.

82 DŌGEN'S *SHŌBŌGENZŌ* VOLUME VI

it to the right several times and pay obeisance. Having made three prostrations or six prostrations or nine prostrations, half-kneel with palms together, and, raising the *kāṣāya* with both hands, recite the gāthā aloud.[76] Then stand and don it according to proper procedure.

* * * * *

[T3:31] {2:312}

世尊告大衆言、我往昔在寶藏佛所時、爲大悲菩薩。爾時大悲菩薩摩訶薩、在寶藏佛前、而發願言、世尊、我成佛已、若有衆生入我法中、出家著袈裟者、或犯重戒、或行邪見、若於三寶輕毀不信、集諸重罪比丘・比丘尼・優婆塞・優婆夷、若於一念中、生恭敬心、尊重僧伽梨衣、生恭敬心、尊重世尊或於法僧、世尊、如是衆生、及至一人、不於三乘得受記莂而退轉者、則爲欺誑十方世界、無量無邊阿僧祇等、現在諸佛、必定不成阿耨多羅三藐三菩提。世尊、我成佛已來、諸天龍・鬼神・人及非人、若能於此著袈裟者、恭敬供養、尊重讚歎、其人若得見此袈裟少分、即得不退於三乘中。若有衆生、爲飢渇所逼、若貧窮鬼神、下賤諸人、乃至餓鬼衆生、若得袈裟少分乃至四寸、即得飲食充足、隨其所願、疾得成就。若有衆生、共相違反、起怨賊想、展轉鬭諍、若諸天龍・鬼神・乾闥婆・阿修羅・迦樓羅・緊那羅・摩睺羅伽・狗辨茶・毘舍遮・人及非人、共鬭諍時、念此袈裟、依袈裟力、尋生悲心・柔軟之心・無怨賊心・寂滅之心・調伏善心、還得清淨。有人若在兵甲・鬭訟・斷事之中、持此袈裟少分、至此輩中、爲自護故、供養恭敬尊重、是諸人等、無能侵毀・觸嬈・輕弄、常得勝他、過此諸難。

The World-Honored One addressed the great assembly, saying,[77]

In the past, when I was with Buddha Ratnagarbha, I was Bodhisattva Mahākāruṇā.[78] *At that time, Bodhisattva-mahāsattva Mahākāruṇā made a vow before Buddha Ratnagarbha, saying:*[79]

---

76 **half-kneel with palms together** (*koki gasshō* 胡跪合掌): Literally, "foreign kneel with palms together"; a fixed expression for a position in which one kneels on the right knee, with the left knee raised.

recite the gāthā aloud (*kuchi ni ge o ju shite* くちに偈を誦して): Presumably the gāthā to be recited is the "Verse for Donning the *Kāṣāya*" (see above, Note 15; below, section 54).

77 **The World-Honored One addressed the great assembly** (*seson koku daishu* 世尊告大衆): Though seemingly a quotation from scripture, Dōgen is here providing his own introduction, in Chinese, to the vow he is about to quote.

78 **Buddha Ratnagarbha** (*Hōzō butsu* 寶藏佛): A past buddha who appears in the sūtra quoted here as the teacher of both Buddha Śākyamuni and Buddha Amitābha.

Bodhisattva Mahākāruṇā (*Daihi bosatsu* 大悲菩薩): "Bodhisattva Great Compassion," a sobriquet of Bodhisattva Avalokiteśvara, but here the name of Śākyamuni in a prior life.

79 **Bodhisattva-mahāsattva Mahākāruṇā made a vow before Buddha Ratnagarbha** (*Daihi bosatsu makasatsu, zai Hōzō butsu zen, ni hotsugan* 大悲菩薩摩訶薩、在寶藏佛前、而發願): Quoting the *Mahā-kāruṇā-sūtra* (*Peihua jing* 悲華經) (T.157.3:220a10-b2). A summary version of this passage occurs at "Shōbōgenzō den'e" 正法眼藏傳衣, section 25.

T3. The Merit of the Kāṣāya *Kesa kudoku* 袈裟功德 83

World-Honored One, after I attain buddhahood, if there are living beings who, having entered into my dharma, left home, and donned the *kāṣāya*, violate the major precepts or engage in false views; or if there are bhikṣus, *bhikṣuṇīs*, *upāsakas* or *upāsikās* who, disparaging and lacking faith in the three treasures, accumulate grave offenses; if, for a single moment of thought, they give rise to a reverent mind and honor the *saṃghāti* robe, or give rise to a reverent mind and honor the World-Honored One or the dharma or saṃgha — World-Honored One, should such living beings, even a single one of them, having been unable to receive a prediction in the three vehicles, fall back, then, having deceived incalculable, limitless *asaṃkhyeyas* of present buddhas throughout the realms of the ten directions, I shall certainly not attain *anuttara-samyak-saṃbodhi*.

World-Honored One, after I attain buddhahood, if there are devas or dragons, spirits, humans or non-humans able to venerate, make offerings to, honor, and praise those who wear this *kāṣāya*, if these people can see a small piece of this *kāṣāya*, they will attain non-regression in the three vehicles.

If there are living beings hard pressed by hunger and thirst, living beings such as impoverished spirits, lowly people, and so on down to hungry ghosts, if they obtain a small piece of this *kāṣāya*, even so much as four inches, they will get plenty to eat and drink, and, whatever they wish, they will quickly achieve.

If there are living beings disputing with each other, giving rise to thoughts of enmity and violence and fomenting fights and quarrels, or when devas and dragons, spirits, gandharvas, *asuras*, garuḍas, *kiṃnaras*, *mahoragas*, *kumbhāṇḍas*, piśācīs, humans or non-humans fight and quarrel with each other, if they recall this *kāṣāya*, by the power of the *kāṣāya*, immediately giving rise to a mind of compassion, a mind soft and gentle, a mind without enmity and violence, a mind of quiescence, a good mind well tamed, they will attain purity.[80]

---

80 **devas and dragons, spirits, gandharvas, *asuras*, garuḍas, *kiṃnaras*, mahoragas, kumbhāṇḍas, piśācīs** (*ten ryū kijin kendatsuba ashura karura kinnara magoraga kuhanda bishaja* 天龍・鬼神・乾闥婆・阿修羅・迦樓羅・緊那羅・摩睺羅伽・狗辨茶・毘舍遮): Mythical beings often appearing in Buddhist literature; a standard list of eight such beings, plus *kumbhāṇḍas* (*kuhanda* 狗辨茶; more often written 鳩槃荼), horse-headed demons with huge testicles; and *piśācīs* (*pishaja* 毘舍遮), female fiends. The group of eight (*hachi bu* 八部): devas (*ten* 天): heavenly beings, inhabiting the upper reaches of Mount Sumeru and the celestial realms; *nāgas* (*ryū* 龍): great serpents living in the clouds or bodies of water and associated with rain); spirits (*kijin* 鬼神): here, probably S. *yakṣas* (*yasha* 夜叉), flesh-eating flying demons; gandharvas (*kendatsuba* 乾闥婆): spirit musicians who subsist on scents; *asuras* (*ashura* 阿修羅): demigods, or titans,

84 DŌGEN'S *SHŌBŌGENZŌ* VOLUME VI

If there are people in combat, in arguments, or in disputes, if they go among the parties with a small piece of this kāṣāya and, in order to protect themselves, make offerings to, revere, and respect it, these people will not be violated, harassed, or mocked, and will always triumph over others and avoid these difficulties.

[T3:32]

世尊、若我袈裟、不能成就如是五事聖功德者、則爲欺誑十方世界、無量無邊阿僧祇等現在諸佛、未來不應成就阿耨多羅三藐三菩提作佛事也。没失善法、必定不能破壞外道。

World-Honored One, should my kāṣāya be unable to achieve the sacred merit of these five things, then, having deceived incalculable, limitless, asaṃkhyeyas of present buddhas throughout the realms of the ten directions, in the future I ought not achieve anuttara-samyak-saṃbodhi and perform the works of a buddha; I would have exhausted my good dharmas and certainly be unable to demolish the other paths.[81]

[T3:33] {2:313}

善男子、爾時寶藏如來、申金色右臂、摩大悲菩薩頂讚言、善哉善哉、大丈夫、汝所言者、是大珍寶、是大賢善。汝成阿耨多羅三藐三菩提已。是袈裟服、能成就此五聖功德、作大利益。善男子、爾時大悲菩薩摩訶薩、聞佛讚歎已、心生歡喜、踊躍無量。因佛申此金色之臂、長指合縵、其手柔軟、猶如天衣。摩其頭已、其身即変、狀如童子二十歲人。善男子、彼會大衆、諸天・龍神・乾闥婆・人及非人、叉手恭敬、向大悲菩薩、供養種種華、及至伎樂而供養之。復種種讚歎已、默然而住。

Good sons, at that time, Tathāgata Ratnagarbha extended his golden-hued right arm, rubbed the head of Bodhisattva Mahākāruṇā, and praised him, saying:[82]

Excellent, excellent, great one. What you have said is a rare treasure, is most wise and virtuous. After you attain anuttara-samyak-saṃbodhi, this kāṣāya will achieve these five sacred merits and produce great benefits.

Good sons, at that time, the Bodhisattva-mahāsattva Mahākāruṇā, after hearing the Buddha's praises, leaped with incalculable joy. When the Buddha extended his golden-hued arm, his long fingers joined by

---

who war with the gods; garuḍas (*karura* 迦樓羅): mythical birds that feed on *nāgas*; *kiṃnaras* (*kinnara* 緊那羅): heavenly musicians, sometimes described as part god, part human, part animal; *mahoragas* (*magoraga* 摩睺羅迦): giant python-like snakes.

81 **World-Honored One** (*Seson* 世尊): Continuing the quotation of the *Peihua jing* 悲華經, T.157.3:220b2-6.

82 **Good sons** (*zen nanshi* 善男子): Continuing the quotation of the *Peihua jing* 悲華經, T.157.3:220b6-17.

T3. The Merit of the Kāṣāya *Kesa kudoku* 袈裟功徳 85

silken webbing, his hands were soft and gentle, like celestial robes.[83]
*After it had rubbed his head, [the bodhisattva's] body immediately
changed, becoming like that of a boy of twenty years. Good sons, the
great saṃgha in that assembly — the devas, dragons and spirits, gandharvas, humans and non-humans — with hands folded in veneration,
facing toward Bodhisattva Mahākāruṇā, made offerings of all kinds of
flowers, and also offered him music as well. After repeatedly praising
him in all sorts of ways, they stood silently.*

[T3:34] {2:315}

如來在世より今日にいたるまで、菩薩・聲聞の經・律のなかより、袈裟の
功徳をえらびあぐるとき、かならずこの五聖功徳を、むねとするなり。

From the lifetime of the Tathāgata till today, in the sūtras and vinaya
of the bodhisattvas and *śrāvakas*, whenever the merits of the *kāṣāya* are
brought up, these five sacred merits are taken as essential.[84]

[T3:35]

まことにそれ、袈裟は三世諸佛の佛衣なり。その功徳無量なりといへど
も、釋迦牟尼佛の法のなかにして袈裟をえたらんは、餘佛の法のなかにし
て袈裟をえんにも、すぐれたるべし。ゆえいかんとなれば、釋迦牟尼佛、
むかし因地のとき、大悲菩薩摩訶薩として、寶藏佛のみまへにして、五百
の大願をたてましますとき、ことさらこの袈裟の功徳におきて、かくの
ごとく誓願をおこしまします。その功徳、さらに無量不可思議なるべし。
しかあればすなはち、世尊の皮肉骨髓いまに正傳するといふは、袈裟衣な
り。正法眼藏を正傳する祖師、かならず袈裟を正傳せり。この衣を、傳持
し頂戴する衆生、かならず二、三生のあひだに得道せり。たとひ戲笑のた
め、利益のために身に著せる、かならず得道因縁なり。

Truly, the *kāṣāya* is the buddha robe of the buddhas of the three times,
and its merit is incalculable; yet to get the *kāṣāya* during the dharma
of Buddha Śākyamuni is surely superior to getting the *kāṣāya* during
the dharma of the other buddhas. Why is this? Because, long ago when
Buddha Śākyamuni was at the causal stage, as Bodhisattva-mahāsattva
Mahākāruṇā, when he made the five hundred great vows before Buddha
Ratnagarbha, he specifically made these vows regarding the merits of
this *kāṣāya*.[85] Its merits must surely be incalculable and inconceivable.

---

83   **his long fingers joined by silken webbing** (*chōshi gōman* 長指合縵): Long fingers (*chōshi* 長指) are the third of the thirty-two marks (*sō* 相; S. *lakṣana*) of a buddha;
webbed (*mōman* 網縵) fingers and toes are the fifth of the marks.

84   **sūtras and vinaya of the bodhisattvas and *śrāvakas*** (*bosatsu shōmon no kyōritsu*
菩薩・聲聞の經・律): I.e., the texts of both the Great and Small Vehicles.

these five sacred merits (*kono go shō kudoku* この五聖功徳): I.e., the five vows of
Mahākāruṇā just quoted.

85   **causal stage** (*inji* 因地): I.e., while still a bodhisattva, before he reached the "effect
stage" (*kachi* 果地) of buddhahood.

Thus, the direct transmission even now of the skin, flesh, bones, and marrow of the World-Honored One is the *kāṣāya* robe.[86] The ancestral masters who directly transmitted the treasury of the true dharma eye invariably directly transmitted the *kāṣāya*. Living beings who receive and keep this robe and reverently accept it have invariably attained the way within two or three births. Even when it is worn as a joke or for profit, it is invariably the cause of gaining the way.[87]

[T3:36]

龍樹祖師曰、復次佛法中出家人、雖破戒墮罪、罪畢得解脱、如優鉢羅華比丘尼本生經中説。佛在世時、此比丘尼、得六神通阿羅漢。入貴人舍、常讚出家法、語諸貴人婦女言、姉妹可出家。諸貴婦女言、我等少容色盛美、持戒爲難、或當破戒。比丘尼言、破戒便破、但出家。問言、破戒當墮地獄、云何可破。答言、墮地獄便墮。諸貴婦女、笑之言、地獄受罪、云何可墮。比丘尼言、我自憶念本宿命、時作戲女、著種種衣服、而説舊語。或時著比丘尼衣、以爲戲笑。以是因縁故、迦葉佛時、作比丘尼。時自恃貴姓端正、生憍慢、而破禁戒。破禁戒罪故、墮地獄受種種罪。受畢竟、値釋迦牟尼佛出家、得六神通阿羅漢道。以是故知、出家受戒、雖復破戒、以戒因縁故、得阿羅漢道。若但作惡、無戒因縁、不得道也。我及昔時、世世墮地獄、從地獄出爲惡人。惡人死還入地獄、都無所得。今以此證知、出家受戒、雖復破戒、以是因縁、可得道果。

The Ancestral Master Nāgārjuna said:[88]

Furthermore, in the buddha dharma, those who leave home, even though they break the precepts and commit offenses, attain liberation after the suffering for those offenses has ended, as is taught in the Sūtra of the Prior Lives of the Bhikṣuṇī Utpalavarṇā.[89]

---

five hundred great vows (*gohyaku no daigan* 五百の大願): I.e., the vows appearing in the *Peihua jing* 悲華經, of which the vows on the *kāṣāya* are the last five.

86 **skin, flesh, bones, and marrow** (*hi niku kotsu zui* 皮肉骨髓): An expression occurring very often throughout the *Shōbōgenzō*, in reference to the essence or truth or entirety of something or someone. From the famous story, recorded in the *shinji Shōbōgenzō* 眞字正法眼藏 (DZZ.5:230, case 201), of Bodhidharma's testing of four disciples, to whom he said of each in turn that he (or, in one case, she) had got his skin, flesh, bones, and marrow. See Supplementary Notes, s.v. "Skin, flesh, bones, and marrow."

87 **Even when it is worn as a joke or for profit** (*tatoi keshō no tame, riyaku no tame ni mi ni chaku seru* たとひ戯笑のため、利益のために身に著せる): Introducing the following account of the Bhikṣuṇī Utpalavarṇā.

88 **The Ancestral Master Nāgārjuna** (*Ryūju soshi* 龍樹祖師): Quoting the *Dazhidu lun* 大智度論 (T.1509.25:161a27-b17), a work traditionally attributed to Nāgārjuna. Dōgen also quotes this passage in his "Shōbōgenzō shukke kudoku" 正法眼藏出家功徳.

89 *Sūtra of the Prior Lives of the Bhikṣuṇī Utpalavarṇā* (*Upparage bikuni honshō kyō* 優鉢羅華比丘尼本生經): The Chinese *Youboluohua biqiuni bensheng jing* 優鉢羅華比丘尼本生經 has been reconstructed as Sanskrit *Utpalavarṇā-bhikṣuṇī-jātaka-sūtra*. No text of this title is extant, but stories of the prior lives of the Buddha's famous disciple Bhikṣuṇī Utpalavarṇā (known in Pali texts as Uppalavaṇṇa) are well known in the tradition.

At the time of the Buddha, this *bhikṣuṇī* became an arhat with the six spiritual powers. Entering into the residences of the aristocrats, she always praised the dharma of leaving home, saying to the aristocratic women, "Sisters, you should leave home."

The aristocratic women said, "We are young and in our prime, attractive and at the height of our beauty. Keeping the precepts would be hard for us, and we would quite likely break them."

The Bhikṣuṇī said, "If you break the precepts, then you break them. Just leave home."

They asked, "If we break the precepts, we shall fall into the hells. How can you say we can break them?"

She answered, "If you fall into the hells, then you fall into them."

The aristocratic women laughed at this and said, "In the hells, one suffers from one's offenses. How can you say we can fall into it?"

The Bhikṣuṇī said, "I myself recall a former life, when I was a courtesan. I used to dress up in all sorts of costumes and tell old stories. Once, I put on the robes of a *bhikṣuṇī* as a joke. Due to this cause, at the time of Buddha Kāśyapa, I became a *bhikṣuṇī*. Conceited by my noble pedigree and elegant appearance, I gave rise to pride and broke the precepts of restraint. Due to the offense of breaking the precepts, I fell into the hells and suffered all sorts of pain. After the suffering was finally over, I met Buddha Śākyamuni, left home, and gained the way of an arhat with the six spiritual powers. Thus, we know that, if one leaves home and receives the precepts, even though one then breaks them, due to the cause of the precepts, one will gain the way of the arhat. But if one simply does evil, without the cause of the precepts, one will not gain the way. Long ago, I fell into hell in life after life; emerging from hell, I became an evil person, and when that evil person died, I again entered hell, without gaining anything at all. Now, from this experience I know that, if one leaves home and receives the precepts, even though one then breaks them, due to the cause of the precepts, one can gain the fruit of the way.

[T3:37] {2:317}

この蓮華色、阿羅漢得道の初因、さらに他の功にあらず、ただこれ袈裟を戯笑のためにその身に著せし功徳によりて、いま得道せり。二生、迦葉佛の法にあふたてまつりて比丘尼となれり、三生に、釋迦牟尼佛にあふたてまつりて大阿羅漢となり、三明・六通を具足せり。三明とは、天眼・宿命・漏盡なり。六通とは、神境通・他心通・天眼通・天耳通・宿命通・漏盡通なり。まことにそれ、ただ作惡の人とありしとき、むなしく死して地獄にいる。地獄よりいで、また作惡人となる。戒の因縁あるときは、禁戒を破して地獄におちたりといへども、つひに得道の因縁なり。いま、戯笑のため袈裟を著せる、なほこれ三生に得道す。いはんや無上菩提のために、清淨の信心をおこして袈裟を著せん、その功徳、成就せざらめやは。いかにいはんや、一生のあひだ受持したてまつり、頂戴したてまつらん功徳、まさに廣大無量なるべし。

The first cause of this Utpalavarṇā gaining the way as an arhat was certainly no other merit than just her donning a *kāṣāya* as a joke — the merit by which she has now gained the way. In a second birth, she encountered the dharma of Buddha Kāśyapa and became a *bhikṣuṇī*; in a third life, she encountered Buddha Śākyamuni and became a great arhat, endowed with the three knowledges and six spiritual powers.[90] The "three knowledges" are the deva eye, the knowledge of former lives, and the exhaustion of the contaminants; the "six powers" are the power of magical transformations, the power of the deva eye, the power of the deva ear, the power of knowledge of former lives, and the power of the exhaustion of the contaminants.[91] Truly, when she was simply a person who did evil, she died fruitlessly and entered the hells; only to emerge from the hells and again become an evildoer. When she had the cause and condition of the precepts, although she broke the precepts of restraint and fell into the hells, eventually they became the cause and condition of her gaining the way. Now, even one who dons the *kāṣāya* for a joke gains the way in three births; how much more, then, one who gives rise to a mind of pure faith and dons the *kāṣāya* for the sake of unsurpassed bodhi — how could the merit of that not be achieved? And how much more still must the merit be vast and incalculable of one who receives and keeps it and reverently accepts it throughout a lifetime.

---

90 **endowed with the three knowledges and six spiritual powers** (*sanmyō rokutsū o gusoku seri* 三明・六通を具足せり): The Bhikṣuṇī Utpalavarṇā (*Renge shiki* 蓮華色; *Uhatsurashiki* 優鉢羅色) was known, along with Maudgalyāyana, as the Buddha's disciple preeminent in the *abhijñā* (*jinzū* 神通; "spiritual powers"). In his "Shōbōgenzō sanji gō" 正法眼藏三時業, Dōgen recalls her death at the hands of Devadatta.

91 **"three knowledges"** (*sanmyō* 三明); **"six powers"** (*rokutsū* 六通): See Supplementary Notes, s.v. "Spiritual powers."

T3. The Merit of the Kāṣāya *Kesa kudoku* 袈裟功德

[T3:38]

もし菩提心をおこさん人、いそぎ袈裟を受持頂戴すべし。この好世にあふて佛種をうえざらん、かなしむべし。南洲の人身をうけて、釋迦牟尼佛の法にあふたてまつり、佛法嫡嫡の祖師にむまれあひ、單傳直指の袈裟をうけたてまつりぬべきを、むなしくすごさん、かなしむべし。いま袈裟正傳は、ひとり祖師正傳これ正嫡なり、餘師の、かたを齊しくすべきにあらず。相承なき師にしたがふて袈裟を受持する、なほ功德甚深なり。いはんや嫡嫡面授しきたれる正師に受持せん、まさしき如來の法子法孫ならん。まことに如來の皮肉骨髓を正傳せるなるべし。おほよそ袈裟は、三世十方の諸佛正傳しきたれること、いまだ斷絶せず。十方三世の諸佛菩薩・聲聞緣覺、おなじく護持しきたれるところなり。

Those who would bring forth the mind of bodhi should quickly receive and keep and reverently accept the *kāṣāya*. To encounter this auspicious world and not plant the seed of buddhahood would be lamentable.[92] Having received a human body on the Southern Continent, encountered the dharma of Buddha Śākyamuni, and met in this birth the ancestral masters who are the legitimate successors to the buddha dharma, and then to pass up the *kāṣāya*, uniquely transmitted and directly indicated, that you should have received — this would be lamentable.[93]

In the direct transmission of the *kāṣāya* today, only those in the direct transmission of the ancestral masters are its legitimate successors; it is not the case that other masters could have equal stature. The merit of receiving and keeping a *kāṣāya* under a master without the inheritance is still extremely profound; how much more then to receive and keep it under a true master with the face-to-face conferral from successor after successor — one would be among the true dharma children and dharma grandchildren of the Tathāgata; one would truly have received the direct transmission of the skin, flesh, bones, and marrow of the Tathāgata. In sum, the direct transmission of the *kāṣāya* by the buddhas of the three times and ten directions has never been cut off; it is protected by all the buddhas, bodhisattvas, *śrāvakas*, and *pratyeka-buddhas* of the ten directions and three times.

* * * * *

---

92 **auspicious world** (*kōse* 好世): A term common enough in the Buddhist canon but the only occurrence in the *Shōbōgenzō*; some readers take it to mean "auspicious age."

93 **Southern Continent** (*Nanshū* 南洲): I.e., the continent of Jambudvīpa, south of Mount Sumeru in Buddhist geography; the continent on which buddhas are born. See Supplementary Notes, s.v. "Four Continents."

[T3:39] {2:318}

袈裟をつくるには、麤布を本とす。麤布なきがごときは、細布をもちいる。麤・細の布、ともになきには、絹素をもちいる。絹・布、ともになきがごときは、綾羅等をもちうる、如來の聽許なり。絹布・綾羅等の類、すべてなきくには、如來また皮袈裟を聽許しましす。

In making a *kāṣāya*, a coarse fabric of plant fiber is standard.[94] When there is no coarse plant fiber fabric, a fine fabric of plant fiber is used. When there is neither a coarse nor fine plant fiber fabric, a plain silk is used. When there are neither silk nor plant fiber fabrics, the use of damask, gauze, or the like, is permitted by the Tathāgata. In lands where there are no types of plain silk, damask, gauze, and the like, the Tathāgata permits a skin *kāṣāya*.[95]

[T3:40]

おほよそ袈裟は、そめて青・黄・赤・黒・紫色ならしむべし、いづれも色のなかの壊色ならしむ。如來は、つねに肉色の袈裟を御しましませり、これ袈裟色なり。初祖相傳の佛袈裟は、青黒色なり、西天の屈眴布なり。いま、曹溪山にあり。西天、二十八傳し、震旦、五傳せり。いま曹溪古佛の遺弟、みな佛衣の故實を傳持せり、餘僧のおよばざるところなり。

Generally speaking, the *kāṣāya* should be dyed blue, yellow, red, black, or purple; whichever it is, it is made in a dull shade of the color.[96] The Tathāgata always wore a flesh-colored *kāṣāya*; this is the *kāṣāya* color.[97] The buddha *kāṣāya* transmitted by the First Ancestor was bluish black, of a fine cotton fabric of Sindh in the West.[98] Now kept at Mount Caoxi, it was transmitted twenty-eight times in Sindh in the West and five times in Cīnasthāna. Now, the surviving disciples of the Old Buddha of Caoxi

---

94 **In making a *kāṣāya*** (*kesa o tsukuru ni wa* 袈裟をつくるには): This section echoes "Shōbōgenzō den'e" 正法眼藏傳衣, section 48.

95 **skin *kaṣāya*** (*hi gesa* 皮袈裟): The term *hi* 皮 ("skin") may refer to hide, bark, etc.

96 **the *kāṣāya* should be dyed blue, yellow, red, black, or purple** (*kesa wa, somete sei ō shaku koku shi shoku narashimu beshi* 袈裟は、そめて青・黄・赤・黒・紫色ならしむべし): See *Fanwang jing* 梵網經, T.1484.24:1008b25-26.

dull shade (*ejiki* 壊色): Or "mixed shade"; the term is also used for the *kāṣāya* itself. The term "dull shade robe" (*ejiki e* 壊色衣) is synonymous with "vestment of neutral color" (*kenjiki fuku* 間色服); see Supplementary Notes, s.v. "Robe of the Tathāgata."

97 **the *kāṣāya* color** (*kesa shiki* 袈裟色): I.e., the color indicated by one meaning of the Sanskrit word *kaṣāya* or *kāṣāya*.

98 **The buddha *kāṣāya* transmitted by the First Ancestor** (*shoso sōden no butsu kesa* 初祖相傳の佛袈裟): The description here matches that of the robe left at the stūpa of the Sixth Ancestor, according to the *Song gaoseng zhuan* 宋高僧傳 (T.2061.50:755b20-21):

其塔下葆藏屈眴布欝多羅僧、其色青黒碧縑複袷。

Concealed beneath the stūpa was an *uttarāsaṃga* [robe] of fine cotton fabric, its color bluish black, with a lining of bluish green.

T3. The Merit of the Kāṣāya *Kesa kudoku* 袈裟功徳   91

all transmit and keep the ancient ways of the buddha robe, something other monks cannot match.

[T3:41] {2:319}

おほよそ衣に三種あり。一者糞掃衣、二者毳衣、三者衲衣なり。糞掃は、さきにしめすがごとし。毳衣者、鳥獸細毛、これをなづけて毳とす。行者若無糞掃可得、取此爲衣。衲衣者、朽故破弊、縫衲供身。不著世間好衣。

In general, there are three types of robe.[99] First, the robe of discarded rags; second, the robe of down; third, the robe of patches. The robe of discarded rags is as previously indicated.[100]

The robe of down is made of the fine feathers or fur of birds or animals, which is called "down."[101] Practitioners who cannot get discarded rags take this to make robes. The robe of patches is made of rotted, old, torn, and ruined cloth, sewn together to adorn the body. We do not wear the fine clothes of the worldly.

[T3:42]

具壽鄔波離、謂世尊曰、大德世尊、僧伽胝衣、條數有幾。佛言、有九。何謂爲九。謂、九條・十一條・十三條・十五條・十七條・十九條・二十一條・二十三條・二十五條。其僧伽胝衣、初之三品、其中壇隔、兩長一短、如是應持。次三品、三長一短、後三品、四長一短。過是條外、便成破衲。鄔波離、復白世尊曰、大德世尊、有幾種僧伽胝衣。佛言、有三種、謂上・中・下。上者豎三肘、橫五肘。下者豎二肘半、橫四肘半。二者内名中。鄔波離、白世尊曰、大德世尊、嗢呾羅僧伽衣、條數有幾。佛言、但有七條、壇隔兩長一短。鄔波離、白世尊曰、大德世尊、七條復有幾種。佛言、有其三品、謂上・中・下。上者三五肘、下各減半肘、二内名中。鄔波離、白世尊曰、大德世尊、安呾婆娑衣、條數有幾。佛言、有五條、壇隔一長一短。鄔波離、復白世尊言、安呾婆娑衣、有幾種。佛言、有三、謂上・中・下。上者三五肘、中・下同前、各減半。

Elder Upāli addressed the World-Honored One, saying, "Most Virtuous, World-Honored One, how many panel numbers are there on the saṃghāṭī robe?"[102]

---

99   **three types of robe** (*e ni sanshu* 衣に三種): This section reflects a passage on the four types of *dhūta* ("austerities") in regard to robes found in the *Dasheng yi zhang* 大乘義章 (T.1851.44:764b7-29). In addition to the three types mentioned here, the text lists as the fourth *dhūta* the limitation to three robes, from which Dōgen has already quoted in section 10, above; its passage on the robe of discarded rags was quoted in section 21, above.

100   **The robe of discarded rags is as previously indicated** (*funzō wa, saki ni shimesu ga gotoshi* 糞掃は、さきにしめすがごとし): I.e., in section 21, above.

101   **robe of down** (*sei e* 毳衣): Dōgen here switches (mostly) to Chinese, to quote (with slight variation) the *Dasheng yi zhang* 大乘義章 (T.1851.44:764b26-29). The "down" robe could also refer to fabrics made from fleece.

102   **The Elder Upāli** (*Guju Upari* 具壽鄔波離): Quoting (with some variation) the *Genben shuo yiqie youbu baiyi jiemo* 根本説一切有部百一羯磨, T.1453.24:497a13-27. Upāli (also written 優婆離, etc.) was one of the ten chief disciples of Buddha Śākyamuni.

The Buddha said, "There are nine.[103] What are the nine? Nine panels, eleven panels, thirteen panels, fifteen panels, seventeen panels, nineteen panels, twenty-one panels, twenty-three panels, and twenty-five panels. On the first three classes of *saṃghāṭī* robes, there are two long and one short sections of cloth; they ought to be kept like this.[104] On the next three classes, there are three long and one short; and in the last three classes, there are four long and one short. Anything in excess of these panels, renders the patched robe invalid."

Upāli again spoke to the World-Honored One, saying, "Most Virtuous, World-Honored One, how many types of *saṃghāṭī* robes are there?"

The Buddha said, "There are three types: greater, middling, and lesser. The greater is three cubits in height and five cubits in width; the lesser is two and a half cubits in height and four and a half cubits in width; between these two is called 'middling.'"

Upāli spoke to the World-Honored One, saying, "Most Virtuous, World-Honored One, how many panel numbers are there on the *uttarāsaṃga* robe?"

The Buddha said, "It only has seven panels, with two long and one short sections in each."

Upāli spoke to the World-Honored One, saying, "Most Virtuous, World-Honored One, how many types of seven-panels are there?"

The Buddha said, "There are three classes: greater, middling, and lesser. The greater is three by five cubits; the lesser is a half cubit less in each [dimension]; between these two is called 'middling.'"

Upāli spoke to the World-Honored One, saying, "Most Virtuous, World-Honored One, how many panel numbers are there on the *antarvāsa* robe?"

The Buddha said, "It has five panels, with one long and one short section each."

---

103 **"There are nine"** (*u kyū* 有九): I.e., nine types of *saṃghāṭī*, distinguished by the number of their panels, as listed in the next passage.

104 **On the first three classes of *saṃghāṭī* robes, there are two long and one short sections of cloth** (*sōgyatei e, sho shi sanbon, ki chū dankyaku, ryō chō ittan* 僧伽胝衣、初之三品、其中壇隔、兩長一短): I.e., each panel consists of three sections, two long and one short. This and the following account of the number of long and short sections in the robe panels disagrees with the list given in "Shōbōgenzō den'e" 正法眼藏傳衣, section 21.

they ought to be kept like this (*nyoze ō ji* 如是應持): The sense is uncertain; perhaps, meaning that all three of these robes should have this combination of long and short sections; perhaps, meaning simply that one should keep at least this first class of *saṃghāṭī*.

T3. The Merit of the Kāṣāya *Kesa kudoku* 袈裟功德 93

Upāli again spoke to the World-Honored One, saying, "Most Virtuous, World-Honored One, how many types of antarvāsa robes are there?"

The Buddha said, "There are three: greater, middling, and lesser. The greater is three by five cubits, the middling and lesser are the same as above, each subtracting a half."

[T3:43]

佛言、安呾婆娑、復有二種。何爲二、一者竪二肘、橫五肘。二者竪二肘、橫四肘。僧伽胝者、譯爲重複衣。嗢呾羅僧伽者、譯爲上衣。安呾婆娑者、譯爲內衣、　又云下衣。又云、僧伽梨衣、謂大衣也、亦云入王宮衣、又云説法衣。鬱多羅僧、謂七條衣也、云中衣、　又云入衆衣。安陀會、謂五條衣、云小衣、又云行道衣、作務衣。

The Buddha said, "The antarvāsa also has two types.[105] What two? The first is two cubits in height, five cubits in width; the second is two cubits in height and four cubits in width."

The saṃghāṭī is translated "doubled robe"; the uttarāsaṃga is translated "upper robe"; the antarvāsa is translated "inner robe."[106]

It is also called "under robe."[107] It is also said that the saṃghāṭī robe is called the "great robe," also called the "robe for entering the royal palace," and also called the "robe for preaching the dharma." The uttarāsaṃgha is called the "seven-panel robe," or called the "middle robe," and also called the "robe for entering the assembly." The antarvāsa is called the "five-panel robe," or called the "small robe," and also called the "robe for practicing the way," or the "work robe."

[T3:44] {2:321}

この三衣、かならず護持すべし。又、僧伽胝衣に、六十條の袈裟あり、かならず受持すべし。

These three robes should always be secured and maintained. Also, the *saṃghāṭī* robe has a sixty-panel *kāṣāya*, which should always be received and kept.[108]

---

105 **The Buddha said** (*butsu gon* 佛言): Continuing to quote the *Genben shuo yiqie youbu baiyi jiemo* 根本説一切有部百一羯磨, at T.1453.24:497b1-2.

106 **The *saṃghāṭī* is translated "doubled robe"** (*sōgyatei sha, yaku i jūfuku e* 僧伽胝者、譯爲重複衣): Quoting an interlinear note at *Genben shuo yiqie youbu baiyi jiemo* 根本説一切有部百一羯磨, at T.1453.24:497a27-28. Opinion is divided on the sense of "double" (*jūfuku* 重複) here — some taking it to refer to the fact that the robe is lined; others, that the robe is worn over the *uttarāsaṃga*.

107 **It is also called "under robe"** (*yū un ge e* 又云下衣): Though presented in Chinese as a continuation of the quotation, in fact, this and the remaining sentences in this section do not occur in the extant source.

108 **sixty-panel *kāṣāya*** (*rokujū jō* 六十條): Presumably, reference to the robe of fifteen panels with four sections each, or sixty sections total; see above, Note 33.

[T3:45]

おほよそ、八萬歳より百歳にいたるまで、壽命の増・減にしたがふて、身量の長・短あり。八萬歳と一百歳と、ことなることあり、といふ、また、平等なるべし、といふ。そのなかに、平等なるべし、といふを正傳とせり。佛と人と、身量はるかにことなり、人身ははかりつべし、佛身はつひにはかるべからず。このゆえに、迦葉佛の袈裟、いま釋迦牟尼佛、著しましますに、長にあらず、ひろきにあらず。今釋迦牟尼佛の袈裟、彌勒如來、著しましますに、みじかきにあらず、せばきにあらず。佛身の、長・短にあらざる道理、あきらかに觀見し、決斷し、照了し、警察すべきなり。梵王の、たかく色界にある、その佛頂をみたてまつらず、目連、はるかに光明幡世界にいたる、その佛聲をきはめず。遠・近の見聞ひとし、まことに不可思議なるものなり。如來の一切の功德、みなかくのごとし。この功德を念じたてまつるべし。

In general, the height of the body varies according to the increase or decrease in the lifespan, from eighty thousand years to one hundred years.[109] It is said that eighty thousand years and one hundred years are different and also said that they are equal; of these, that they are equal is considered the correct transmission. Between buddhas and humans, the physical dimensions are vastly different: the human body can be measured, while the body of a buddha ultimately cannot be measured. Therefore, when Buddha Śākyamuni now wears the *kāṣāya* of Buddha Kāśyapa, it is neither long nor wide; and, when Tathāgata Maitreya wears the present *kāṣāya* of Buddha Śākyamuni, it will be neither short nor narrow. The truth that the body of a buddha is neither tall nor short should be clearly scrutinized, determined, illumined, and observed. The Brahmā King, high in the form realm, does not see the Buddha's topknot; Maudgalyāyana, having reached the distant Radiant Banner world, does not reach the limit of the Buddha's voice.[110] That they are seen and heard the same whether from a distance or nearby is truly something

---

109 **from eighty thousand years to one hundred years** (*hachiman sai yori hyaku sai ni itaru made* 八萬歳より百歳にいたるまで): Based on the common Buddhist view that the human lifespan varies in different kalpas or under different buddhas; see, e.g., the *Dīrghāgama* (*Chang ahan jing* 長阿含經, T.1.1:2a4-5).

110 **The Brahmā King** (*Bonnō* 梵王); **Maudgalyāyana** (*Mokuren* 目連): Perhaps reflecting a line in the *Mohe zhiguan* 摩訶止觀, by Zhiyi 智顗 (538-597), commenting on the Buddha's auspicious signs (T.1911.46:6b27-28):

梵天不見其頂。目連不窮其聲。

The Deva Brahmā does not see his topknot; Maudgalyāyana does not reach the limit of his voice.

Both these claims are found in stories in the *Ratnakūṭa-sūtra* (*Da baoji jing* 大寶積經) — the former at T.310.11:54a20ff; the latter at T.310.11:56c10ff. "Radiant Banner" (*Kōmyō ban* 光明幡) is the buddha field of Buddha Radiant King (*Kōmyō ō butsu* 光明王佛), said to lie to the west beyond buddha fields equal to the sands of ninety-nine Ganges Rivers.

T3. The Merit of the Kāṣāya *Kesa kudoku* 袈裟功徳　　95

inconceivable. All the virtues of the Tathāgata are like this. We should bear these virtues in mind.

[T3:46] {2:322}

袈裟を裁縫するに、割截衣あり、揲葉衣あり、攝葉衣あり、縵衣あり、ともにこれ作法なり。その所有にしたがふて受持すべし。佛言、三世佛袈裟、必定却刺。

In cutting and sewing the *kāṣāya*, there is the pieced robe, the bundled leaf robe, the gathered leaf robe, and the plain robe; each of these is a proper method.[111] We should receive and keep whichever of these we have.[112]

The Buddha has said, "The kāṣāya of the buddhas of the three times is invariably backstitched."[113]

[T3:47]

その衣財をえんこと、また清淨を善なりとす。いはゆる糞掃衣を最上清淨とす。三世の諸佛、ともにこれを清淨としまします。そのほか、信心檀那の所施の衣、また清淨なり。あるひは淨財をもて、いちにしてかふ、また清淨なり。作衣の日限ありといへども、いま末法澆季なり、遠方・邊邦なり。信心のもよほすところ、裁縫をえて、受持せんにはしかじ。

In selecting the robe material, again, pure is considered best: the robe of discarded rags is considered the purest.[114] The buddhas of the three

---

111　**pieced robe** (*kassetsu e* 割截衣): A *kāṣāya* made by sewing together separately cut pieces of cloth.

bundled leaf robe (*chōyō e* 揲葉衣): A *kāṣāya* made by attaching pieces of cloth to an underlying fabric.

gathered leaf robe (*shōyō e* 攝葉衣): A *kāṣāya* made by pleating a piece of fabric, without cutting.

plain robe (*man e* 縵衣): A *kāṣāya* made from a single piece of fabric, without panels.

112　**We should receive and keep whichever of these we have** (*sono shotoku ni shitagaute juji su beshi* その所有にしたがふて受持すべし): This sentence could also be interpreted to mean, "We should receive and keep [the type of *kāṣāya*] according to whichever [type of fabric] we have."

113　**The Buddha has said** (*Butsu gon* 佛言): Although presented in Chinese as if a quotation from scripture, no source has been identified. The requirement to back-stitch the *kāṣāya* is, however, found in a number of texts; see, e.g., *Shisong lü* 十誦律, T.1435.23:109b27-29:

淨而却刺。是佛所許如法畜用。直縫所以不得者。以是世人衣法故。以却刺異俗。

[The *kāṣāya* is to be] pure and backstitched; this is the orthodox practice approved by the Buddha. The reason straight stitching is not permitted is that it is the method of lay robes; backstitching distinguishes [the *kāṣāya*] from lay [garments].

114　**In selecting the robe material** (*sono ezai o en koto* その衣財をえんこと): Echoing "Shōbōgenzō den'e" 正法眼藏傳衣, section 65.

96 DŌGEN'S *SHŌBŌGENZŌ* VOLUME VI

times all consider this as pure. In addition, robes [of fabric] given by a *dānapati* of pure faith are also pure; or those purchased in the market-place with pure assets are also pure. Although there are restrictions on the days within which robes are to be made, we are now in a season of decline at the end of the dharma, in a distant quarter and marginal land; so, there is nothing for it but to receive and keep [the *kāṣāya*] cut and sewn where prompted by faith.[115]

[T3:48]
在家の人天なれども、袈裟を受持することは、大乗最極の祕訣なり。いまは、梵王・釋王、ともに袈裟を受持せり、欲・色の勝躅なり、人間には勝計すべからず。在家の菩薩、みなともに受持せり、震旦國には、梁の武帝、隋の煬帝、ともに袈裟を受持せり、代宗・肅宗、ともに袈裟を著し、僧家に參學し、菩薩戒を受持せり。その餘の居士・婦女等の、受袈裟・受佛戒のともがら、古今の勝躅なり。日本國には、聖德太子、袈裟を受持し、法華・勝鬘等の諸經講説のとき、天雨寶華の奇瑞を感得す。それよりこのかた、佛法、わがくにに流通せり。天下の攝籙なりといへども、すなはち人天の導師なり、ほとけのつかひとして、衆生の父母なり。いまわがくに、袈裟の體・色量ともに訛謬せりといへども、袈裟の名字を見聞する、ただこれ聖德太子の御ちからなり。そのとき、邪をくだき正をたてずば、今日、かなしむべし。のちに聖武皇帝、また袈裟を受持し、菩薩戒をうけまします。しかあればすなはち、たとひ帝位なりとも、たとひ臣下なりとも、いそぎ袈裟を受持し、菩薩戒をうくべし。人身の慶幸、これよりもすぐれたるあるべからず。

It is an ultimate arcanum of the Great Vehicle that even householder humans and devas receive and keep the *kāṣāya*. At present, King Brahmā and King Śakra have both received and kept the *kāṣāya* — fine examples in the desire and form [realms]; and among humans, they cannot be counted.[116] Householder bodhisattvas have all received and kept it.

---

115 **there are restrictions on the days within which robes are to be made** (*sa e no nichigen ari* 作衣の日限あり): See, e.g., *Mahāsāṃghika-vinaya* (*Mohe sengqi lü* 摩訶僧祇律, T.1425.22:299a16ff). According to the *Shishi yaolan* 釋氏要覽 (T.2127.54:269a29-b2):

> 準律、大衣服五日成、七條四日成、五條二日成。限日不成、尼犯墮、比丘犯突吉羅罪。

> Following the vinaya, a great robe is done in five days; a seven-panel, in four days; a five-panel, in two days. If not done within the limit of days, for a *bhikṣuṇī*, it is a *prayaścitta* ("expiation") offense, for a bhikṣu, a *duṣkṛta* ("misdeed") offense.

116 **King Brahmā and King Śakra** (*Bonnō Shaku ō* 梵王・釋王): I.e., the devas Brahmā and Indra. This section echoes themes in "Shōbōgenzō den'e" 正法眼藏傳衣, sections 68-69, the final two sections of that text. As noted there, Dōgen may have in mind a passage in the *Fanwang jing* 梵網經 (T.1484.24:1004b7-10) listing those who should receive the precepts:

> 國王王子百官宰相、比丘比丘尼、十八梵天六欲天子、庶民黃門婬男婬女奴婢。八部鬼神金剛神畜生乃至變化人。

T3. The Merit of the Kāṣāya *Kesa kudoku* 袈裟功徳   97

In the Land of Cīnasthāna, the Emperor Wu of the Liang and Emperor Yang of the Sui both received and kept the *kāṣāya*; Daizong and Suzong both wore the *kāṣāya*, practiced with monastics, and received and kept the bodhisattva precepts.[117] Apart from these, laymen and women who received the *kāṣāya* and received the Buddha's precepts are fine examples in past and present.

In the Land of Japan, Prince Shōtoku received and kept the *kāṣāya* and, when he lectured on the sūtras such as the *Lotus* and *Śrīmālā*, was rewarded with the auspicious omen of precious flowers raining from the heavens.[118] From that time on, the buddha dharma spread widely in our land. Even while being regent to all under heaven, he was teacher to humans and devas, and, as an emissary of the Buddha, the father and mother to living beings. In our land, though the material, color, and dimensions of the *kāṣāya* may all have been misunderstood, that we have heard the name "*kāṣāya*" is due only to the power of Prince Shōtoku. We would surely be sad today had he not smashed the false and established the true in his own day. Later, Emperor Shōmu also received and kept the *kāṣāya* and received the bodhisattva precepts.[119] Therefore, whether we are emperors or subjects, we should hasten to receive and keep the *kāṣāya* and receive the bodhisattva precepts. There can be no greater blessing for one in a human body.

Kings, princes, the hundred officials, the prime minister; bhikṣu and *bhikṣunī*; devas of the eighteen heavens of Brahmā and six heavens of the desire realm; commoners, eunuchs, licentious males and females, slaves; the eight classes of demons and spirits, vajra spirits, beasts, and magically transformed beings.

117   **Emperor Wu of the Liang and Emperor Yang of the Sui** (*Ryō no Bu tei, Zui no Yō dai* 梁の武帝、隋の煬帝): Emperor Wu 武 (r. 502-549), a devout Buddhist, said to have taken the precepts, is of course famous in Zen for the story of his interview with Bodhidharma. Emperor Yang 煬 (r. 604-618) is said to have taken the precepts from the Tiantai figure Zhiyi 智顗.

Daizong and Suzong (*Daisō Shukusō* 代宗・肅宗): Tang-dynasty emperors, reigning 762-779 and 756-762, respectively, both of whom were patrons of Chan Master Nanyang Huizhong 南陽慧忠 (d. 775).

118   **Prince Shōtoku** (*Shōtoku taishi* 聖徳太子): Prince regent during Japan's Asuka period, Shōtoku (574-622) was a devout promoter of Buddhism, to whom are traditionally attributed commentaries on the *Lotus*, *Śrīmālādevī*, and *Vimalakīrti Sūtras*.

119   **Emperor Shōmu** (*Shōmu kōtei* 聖武皇帝): Nara-period Emperor Shōmu 聖武 (r. 724-749) was a major patron of Buddhism, who commissioned the great buddha statue at Tōdaiji and established the *kokubunji* 国分寺 system of state-sponsored temples.

[T3:49] {2:323}

有言、在家受持袈裟、一名單縫、二名俗服。乃未用却刺針而縫也。又言、在家趣道場時、具三法衣・楊枝・澡水・食器・坐具、應如比丘修行淨行。

It is said of the kaṣāya received and kept by householders that "one is called 'simply stitched' and a second is called 'secular wear.'"[120] That is, they are not sewn using backstitching. Again, it is said that "when householders proceed to a practice place, they should be equipped with the three dharma robes, the willow pick, washing water, eating utensils, and sitting cloth; they should cultivate pure practice like the bhikṣus."

[T3:50]

古德の相傳、かくのごとし。ただし、いま佛祖單傳しきたれるところ、國王・大臣・居士・士民にさづくる袈裟、みな却刺なり。廬行者、すでに佛袈裟を正傳せり、勝躅なり。

The transmission among the ancient worthies was like this. However, in what has now been uniquely transmitted by the buddhas and ancestors, the kaṣāyas given to kings, ministers, lay practitioners, and commoners are all backstitched. That the Postulant Lu certainly received the direct transmission of the buddha kaṣāya is an excellent example of this.[121]

[T3:51]

おほよそ袈裟は、佛弟子の標幟なり。もし袈裟を受持しをはりなば、毎日に頂戴したてまつるべし。頂上に安じて、合掌してこの偈を誦す、

In general, the kaṣāya is the emblem of a disciple of the Buddha. If we have received and kept a kaṣāya, we should place it on our heads every day. Placing it on our heads, with palms together, we recite this gāthā:[122]

[T3:52]

大哉解脱服、無相福田衣、披奉如來教、廣度諸衆生。

How great the vestment of liberation,
Robe that is a signless field of merit.
Wrapped in the teaching of the Tathāgata,
We deliver living beings everywhere.

---

120 **It is said** (*u gon* 有言): This section, given entirely in Chinese, is part translation and part paraphrase of passages in the *Zhiguan fuxing zhuan hongjue* 止觀輔行傳弘決, T.1912.46:190b4-16.

121 **Postulant Lu** (*Ro anja* 廬行者): I.e., the Sixth Ancestor, Huineng 慧能, who received the backstitched robe of the Buddha while still a layman.

122 **Placing it on our heads** (*chōjō ni anjite* 頂上に安じて): Reference to the practice, still performed today, which Dōgen reports having first witnessed in China (see section 66, below).

this gāthā (*kono ge* この偈): The so-called "Verse for Donning the Kaṣāya"; see above, Note 15.

T3. The Merit of the Kāṣāya *Kesa kudoku* 袈裟功德   99

[T3:53]

しかうしてのち著すべし。袈裟におきては、師想・塔想をなすべし。浣衣
頂戴のときも、この偈を誦するなり。

After that, we should put it on. We should think of it as a teacher, as a stūpa.[123] When placing the washed robe on our heads, as well, we should recite this gāthā.[124]

[T3:54] {2:324}

佛言、剃頭著袈裟、諸佛所加護、一人出家者、天人所供養。

The Buddha said,[125]

When one shaves the head and dons the kāṣāya,
One is protected by the buddhas;
Each one who leaves home,
Receives the offerings of devas and humans.

[T3:55]

あきらかにしりぬ、剃頭著袈裟よりこのかた、一切諸佛に加護せられたて
まつるなり。この諸佛の加護によりて、無上菩提の功德圓滿すべし。この
人をば、天衆・人衆ともに供養するなり。

We see clearly here that, from the time one "*shaves the head and dons the kāṣāya,*" one is protected by all the buddhas. Due to the protection of these buddhas, one will surely perfect the virtues of unsurpassed bodhi. To this person devas and humans make offerings.

---

123 **We should think of it as a teacher, as a stūpa** (*shisō tōsō o nasu beshi* 師想・塔想をなすべし): Perhaps reflecting the *Miaofa lianhua jing wenju* 妙法蓮華經文句, by Zhiyi 智顗 (T.1718.34:10a24); see also the *Ratnakūṭa-sūtra*, in a passage just following that cited in note 60, above (*Da baoji jing* 大寶積經, T.310.11:647a28-b1):

於糞掃衣應生塔想、應生世尊想、應生出世想、應生無我無我所想。如是觀已著
糞掃衣。應如是調伏其心。

One ought to think of the robe of discarded rags as a stūpa, ought to think of it as the World-Honored One, ought to think of it as transmundane, ought to think of it as without me and mine. If one dons the robe of discarded rags after viewing it in this way, one ought thereby to control one's thoughts.

124 **When placing the washed robe on our heads** (*kan e chōdai no toki* 浣衣頂戴のとき): See above, section 29.

125 **The Buddha said** (*butsu gon* 佛言): Quoting lines of a verse found in the *Da fangdeng daji jing* 大方等大集經 (T.397.13:376b15-16).

100 DŌGEN'S *SHŌBŌGENZŌ* VOLUME VI

[T3:56]

世尊告智光比丘言、法衣・體・色・量爲本、得十勝利。一者、能覆其身、
遠離羞恥、具足慚愧、修行善法。二者、遠離寒熱及以蚊蟲・惡獸・毒蟲、
安穩修道。三者、示現沙門出家相貌、見者歡喜、遠離邪心。四者、袈裟即
是人天寶幢之相、尊重敬禮、得生梵天。五者、著袈裟時、生寶幢想、能滅
衆生罪、生諸福德。六者、本制袈裟、染令壞色。離五欲想、不生貪欲。七
者、袈裟是佛淨衣、永斷煩惱、作良福田故。八者、身著袈裟、罪業消除、
十善業道、念念增長。九者、袈裟猶如良田、能善增長菩薩道故。十者、袈
裟猶如甲冑、煩惱毒箭、不能害故。

The World-Honored One addressed the Bhikṣu Jñānaprabha, saying,[126]

The material, color, and dimensions of the dharma robe are fundamental.[127]

It has ten excellent benefits. First, it enables us to cover the body,
avoiding embarrassment and endowing us with a sense of shame, so
that we may cultivate good practices. Second, it keeps off cold and
heat, as well as mosquitos, dangerous beasts, and poisonous snakes,
so that we may practice the way in peace and tranquility. Third, it displays the appearance of the *śramaṇa* who has left home, so that those
who see it take delight and avoid false thoughts. Fourth, the *kāṣāya*
has the mark of a jeweled banner among humans and devas, and those
who honor, value, venerate and pay obeisance to it will attain birth in
the heaven of Brahmā. Fifth, when one wears the *kāṣāya*, one thinks
of it as a jeweled banner, able to eradicate the offenses of living beings
and produce blessings. Sixth, as a basic rule, the *kāṣāya* is dyed a dull
color, which keeps one free from thoughts of desire and does not give
rise to craving. Seventh, the *kāṣāya* is the pure robe of the Buddha,
for it forever cuts off the afflictions and creates a good field of merit.
Eighth, when one wears the *kāṣāya*, evil karma is eliminated, and the
way of the ten virtuous deeds develops moment by moment.[128] Ninth,
the *kāṣāya* is like a good field, for it enables one to develop the bodhisattva path. Tenth, the *kāṣāya* is like armor, for the poison arrows of
the afflictions cannot harm one.

---

126 **The World-Honored One** (*Seson* 世尊): Dōgen here provides an introduction to a
passage of the *Dasheng bensheng xindi guan jing* 大乘本生心地觀經 (T.159.3:313c27-
314a9).

127 **The material, color, and dimensions of the dharma robe are fundamental** (*hōe
tai jiki ryō i hon* 法衣・體・色・量爲本): Following Kawamura's edition; this phrase is
missing in most versions of our text and does seem out of place here; though given as if
the words of the Buddha, it does not in fact occur in the *sūtra*.

128 **way of the ten virtuous deeds** (*jū zengō dō* 十善業道): S. *daśa-kuśala-karma-
patha*. The keeping of the ten virtuous precepts (*jū zen kai* 十善戒) to be followed by
the laity: prohibitions against killing, stealing, sexual misconduct, lies, insults, slander,
flattery, greed, anger, and false views.

T3. The Merit of the Kāṣāya *Kesa kudoku* 袈裟功德 101

[T3:57]

智光當知、以是因緣、三世諸佛、緣覺・聲聞、清淨出家、身著袈裟、三聖
同坐解脫寶床。執智慧劍、破煩惱魔、共入一味諸涅槃界。

> Jñānaprabha, you should know that, for these reasons, the buddhas of
> the three times, *pratyeka-buddhas, śrāvakas*, and pure renunciants are
> clothed with the *kāṣāya*, and the three sages alike sit on the jeweled
> seat of liberation, grasp the sword of wisdom, defeat the Māra of the
> afflictions, and together enter the realms of nirvāṇa of a single flavor.[129]

[T3:58]

爾時世尊、而説偈言、智光比丘應善聽、大福田衣十勝利。　世間衣服增欲
染、如來法服不如是。法服能遮世羞恥、慚愧圓滿生福田。　遠離寒暑及毒
蟲、道心堅固得究竟。示現出家離貪欲、斷除五見正修行。　瞻禮袈裟寶幢
相、恭敬生於梵王福。佛子披衣生塔想、生福滅罪感人天。　肅容致敬眞沙
門、所爲不染諸塵俗。諸佛稱讚爲良田、利樂群生此爲最。　袈裟神力不思
議、能令修植菩提行。道芽增長如春苗、菩提妙果類秋實。　堅固金剛眞甲
冑、煩惱毒箭不能害。我今略讚十勝利、歷劫廣説無有盡。　若有龍身披一
縷、得脫金翅鳥王食。若人渡海持此衣、不怖龍魚諸鬼難。　雷電霹靂天之
怒、披袈裟者無恐畏。白衣若能親捧持、一切惡鬼無能近。　若能發心求出
家、厭離世間修佛道、十方魔宮皆振動、是人速證法王身。

> At that time, the World-Honored One recited a gāthā, saying,[130]
>
> Bhikṣu Jñānaprabha, you should listen well,
> To the ten benefits of the robe, the great field of merit.
> Worldly clothing increases the stain of desire,
> But the dharma garment of the Tathāgata is not like that.
> The dharma garment prevents embarrassment in the world,
> And, with conscience and shame perfected, yields a field of merit.
> Freed from the cold and heat and poisonous snakes,
> The mind of the way is firm and gains the ultimate.
> Displaying the renunciant, free from desires,
> It cuts away the five views and promotes right practice.[131]
> Gazing upon and bowing to the *kāṣāya*, the jeweled banner,
> Those who venerate it are blessed with birth with King Brahmā.

---

129 **Jñānaprabha, you should know** (*Chikō tō chi* 智光當知): Continuing to quote the
passage in the *Dasheng bensheng xindi guan jing* 大乘本生心地觀經 (T.159.3:314a9-12).

three sages (*sanshō* 三聖): Probably a reference to the advanced adepts of the three
vehicles of *śrāvaka, pratyeka-buddha,* and bodhisattva.

130 **At that time** (*ni ji* 爾時): Continuing to quote the passage in the *Dasheng bensheng
xindi guan jing* 大乘本生心地觀經 (T.159.3:314a12-b2).

131 **five views** (*goken* 五見): S. *pañca-dṛṣṭi*. A standard list of five cognitive errors: 1)
reifying views (*shinken* 身見; S. *satkāya-dṛṣṭi*); 2) extreme views (*henken* 邊見; S. *an-
taparigraha-dṛṣṭi*); 3) false views (*jaken* 邪見; S. *mithyā-dṛṣṭi*); 4) attached views (*ken-
shu ken* 見取見; S. *dṛṣṭi-parāmarśa-dṛṣṭi*); 5) views attached to the precepts (*kaigonshu
ken* 戒禁取見; S. *śīla-vrata-parāmarśa-dṛṣṭi*).

When the child of the Buddha dons the robe, thinking of it as a stūpa,
It gives rise to blessings, eradicates offenses, and moves humans
and devas.
The true śramaṇa, solemn and respectful,
Is thereby unstained by the dusts of the world.
Praised by the buddhas as a good field,
The best for the benefit and delight of the living.
Inconceivable, the kāṣāya's spiritual power,
Enabling the cultivation and planting of the practice of bodhi.
Sprouts of the way grow like seedlings in spring;
The wondrous effect of bodhi is akin to the autumn fruit.
The true armor, solid and hard as diamond —
The poison arrows of the afflictions can do no harm.
I have now praised in brief the ten excellent benefits,
Inexhaustible if preached in full for kalpas.
If those with dragon bodies wear but a single thread,
They can escape being food for the king of garuḍas.
If people crossing the sea hold this robe,
They will not fear troubles from dragon, fish, or diverse demons.
When the heavens rage with thunder and lightning,
Those wearing the kāṣāya will have no fear.
If the white-robed can personally keep it with respect,
No evil demons can approach them.
If they can bring forth the mind and seek to leave home,
Rejecting the world and practicing the way of the buddhas,
Demon palaces in the ten directions will all tremble,
And they will quickly realize the body of a dharma king.

[T3:59] {2:327}
この十勝利、ひろく佛道のもろもろの功德を具足せり。長行・偈頌にあら
ゆる功德、あきらかに參學すべし。披閲して速にさしおくことなかれ、句
句にむかひて久參すべし。この勝利は、ただ袈裟の功德なり、行者の猛利
恆修のちからにあらず。佛言、袈裟神力不思議。いたづらに凡夫・賢聖の
はかりしるところにあらず。おほよそ速證法王身のとき、かならず袈裟を
著せり。袈裟を著せざるものの、法王身を證せること、むかしよりいまだ
あらざるところなり。

These ten excellent benefits have broadly endowed us with the various merits of the way of the buddhas. We should clearly study all the merits in the prose and verses. Do not peruse them quickly and set them aside; we should study them long and hard, line by line. These excellent benefits are just the merits of the *kāṣāya*; they are not based on the strength of long, ardent cultivation by the practitioner. The Buddha said, "*Inconceivable, the kāṣāya's spiritual power.*" It is not something to be

T3. The Merit of the Kāṣāya *Kesa kudoku* 袈裟功徳   103

gauged in vain by the common people or the worthies and sages.[132] In general, whenever one "*quickly realizes the body of a dharma king,*" one is always wearing the *kāṣāya*; realization of the body of a dharma king by someone not wearing a *kāṣāya* has never happened from the distant past to the present.

[T3:60]

それ最第一清淨の衣財は、これ糞掃衣なり。その功徳、あまねく大乘・小乘の經・律・論のなかにあきらかなり。廣學咨問すべし。その餘の衣財、またかねあきらむべし。佛佛祖祖、かならずあきらめ、正傳しましますところなり、餘類のおよぶべきにあらず。

The purest robe material is that of the robe of discarded rags. Its virtues are clear in a wide range of sūtras, vinaya, and commentaries of the Great and Small Vehicles. We should make inquiries with those of broad learning. We should also get clear about other robe materials. This is something invariably clarified and directly transmitted by buddha after buddha and ancestor after ancestor; it is not something other types can match.

[T3:61]

中阿含經云、復次諸賢、或有一人、身淨行、口意不淨行、若慧者見、設生恚惱、應當除之。諸賢、或有一人、身不淨行、口意淨行、若慧者見、設生恚惱、應當除之。當云何除。諸賢、猶如阿練若比丘、持糞掃衣、見糞掃中所棄弊衣、或大便汚、或小便・涕唾、及餘不淨之所染汚、見已、左手執之、右手舒張、若非大便・小便・涕唾、及餘不淨之所汚處、又不穿者、便裂取之。如是諸賢、或有一人、身不淨行、口淨行、莫念彼身不淨行。但當念彼口之淨行。若慧者見、設生恚惱、應如是除。

It is said in the Middle-Length Āgama,[133]

Furthermore, worthy ones, suppose there is a person of pure conduct of the body but impure conduct of speech and thought; the wise who feel antipathy upon seeing this ought to get rid of it. Worthy ones, suppose there is a person of impure conduct of the body but pure con-

---

132   **common people or the worthies and sages** (*bonbu kenshō* 凡夫・賢聖): I.e., ordinary people or those on the stages of a Buddhist path.

133   ***Middle-Length Āgama*** (*Chū agon kyō* 中阿含經): Quoting the *Madhyamāgama* at *Zhong ahan jing* 中阿含經, T.26.1:454a15-26, the first two lines of which differ slightly from our version here:

復次、諸賢、或有一人、身淨行、口意淨行。若慧者見、設生恚惱、應當除之。諸賢、或有一人、身不淨行、口淨行。若慧者見、設生恚惱、當云何除。

Furthermore, worthy ones, suppose there is a person of pure conduct of the body and pure conduct of speech and thought; the wise who feel antipathy upon seeing this ought to get rid of it. Worthy ones, suppose there is a person of impure conduct of the body but pure conduct of speech; the wise who feel antipathy upon seeing this, how should they get rid of it?

104 DŌGEN'S *SHŌBŌGENZŌ* VOLUME VI

duct of speech and thought; the wise who feel antipathy upon seeing this ought to get rid of it. How should they get rid of it? Worthy ones, suppose there is an aranya bhikṣu keeping the robe of discarded rags who sees a worn-out robe among discarded rags, soiled by feces or defiled by urine, snot, or other impurities.[134] *Seeing it, he grasps it in his left hand, stretches it out with his right hand, and tears off and takes the parts that are not soiled by feces, urine, snot, or other impurities and have no holes. In this way, worthy ones, there may be a person of impure conduct of the body but pure conduct of speech. Do not think on his impure conduct of the body; only think on his pure practice of speech. The wise who feel antipathy upon seeing this ought to get rid of it like this.*

[T3:62] {2:328}

これ、阿練若比丘の拾糞掃衣の法なり。四種の糞掃あり、十種の糞掃あり。その糞掃をひろふとき、まづ不穿のところをえらびとる。つぎには大便・小便、ひさしくそみて、ふかくして、浣洗すべからざらん、これをとるべからず。浣浄しつべからん、これをとるべきなり。

This is the procedure by which the *aranya* bhikṣu selects the robe of discarded rags. There are four kinds of discarded rags, and there are ten kinds of discarded rags.[135] When picking up these discarded rags, first choose those without holes. Next, do not take those that are unwashable, having been long and deeply stained by feces or urine; we should take the ones that are washable.

[T3:63]

十種糞掃衣

The ten kinds of discarded-rag robes:[136]

[T3:64]

一、牛嚼衣。二、鼠噛衣。三、火燒衣。四、月水衣。五、産婦衣。六、神廟衣。七、塚間衣。八、求願衣。九、王職衣。十、往還衣。

1) the cow-chewed robe.
2) the mouse-gnawed robe.

---

134 ***aranya* bhikṣu** (*arennya biku* 阿練若比丘): A monk living in the forest (S. *aranya*) or other desolate place.

135 **There are four kinds of discarded rags, and there are ten kinds of discarded rags** (*shishu no funzō ari, jisshu no funzō ari* 四種の糞掃あり、十種の糞掃あり): For the four kinds, see above, section 22; the ten kinds are listed just below, section 64.

136 **ten kinds of discarded-rag robes** (*jisshu funzō e* 十種糞掃衣): Listed at *Liuzong xinxue mingju* 律宗新學名句, by Huaixian 懷顯 (or Weixian 惟顯, dates unknown), ZZ.105:656b9-11; from the *Dharmaguptaka-vinaya* (*Sifen lü* 四分律, T.1428.22:850a21-28; see also 1011b25-28). The same list occurs at "Shōbōgenzō den'e" 正法眼藏傳衣, section 66.

T3. The Merit of the Kāṣāya *Kesa kudoku* 袈裟功德

3) the fire-singed robe.
4) the menstrual fluid robe.
5) the childbirth robe.
6) the spirit shrine robe.[137]
7) the burial mound robe.[138]
8) the prayer robe.[139]
9) the royal office robe.[140]
10) the gone and returned robe.[141]

[T3:65] {2:329}

この十種、ひとのすつるところなり、人間のもちいるところにあらず。これをひろふて袈裟の淨財とせり。三世諸佛の、讃歎しましますところ、もちいきたりましますところなり。しかあればすなはち、この糞掃衣は、人・天・龍等のおもくし、擁護するところなり。これをひろふて袈裟をつくるべし、これ最第一の淨財なり、最第一の清淨なり。いま日本國、かくのごとくの糞掃衣なし。たとひ求めんとすともあふべからず、邊地小國悲しむべし。ただ檀那所施の淨財、これをもちいるべし。人天の布施するところの淨財、これをもちいるべし。あるいは淨命よりうるところのものをもて、いちにして貿易せらむ、またこれ袈裟につくりつべし。かくのごときの糞掃、および淨命よりえたるところは、絹にあらず、布にあらず、金・銀・珠・玉・綾・羅・錦・繡等にあらず、ただこれ糞掃衣なり。この糞掃は、弊衣のためにあらず、美服のためにあらず、ただこれ佛法のためなり。これを用著する、すなはち三世の諸佛の皮肉骨髓を正傳せるなり、正法眼藏を正傳せるなり。この功德、さらに人天に問著すべからず、佛祖に參學すべし。

These ten types are what people have thrown away, not something used among humans.[142] They are picked up and regarded as pure material for the *kāṣāya*. They are something praised and used by the buddhas of the three times. Thus, these discarded rag robes are highly valued and protected by humans, devas, dragons, and the like. We should pick them up and make *kāṣāya*; they are the purest material, the purest of all.

At present in the Land of Japan, there are no such discarded rag robes. Even if one searches for them, they are not to be found. How pathet-

---

137　**spirit shrine robe** (*shinbyō e* 神廟衣): Made from cloth left as an offering at a spirit shrine.

138　**burial mound robe** (*chōken e* 塚間衣): Made from a shroud left at a cemetery.

139　**prayer robe** (*gugan e* 求願衣): Made from cloth used as offering to a deity, in support of prayers.

140　**royal office robe** (*ōshoku e* 王職衣): Made from second-hand garments of officials.

141　**gone and returned robe** (*ōgen e* 往還衣): Made from a shroud brought back from the cemetery.

142　**These ten types** (*kono jisshu* この十種): This section, which represents the final passage before the colophon and postscript, echoes themes found in the conclusion to the "Shōbōgenzō den'e" 正法眼藏傳衣, sections 67-70.

106 DŌGEN'S *SHŌBŌGENZŌ* VOLUME VI

ic, this little country in a peripheral place. Just the pure material given by *dānapati* — this we may use; the pure material given by humans and devas — this we may use. Or we may make a *kāṣāya* from what is bought at the market with what is earned by a pure livelihood. Such discarded rags, as well as what is obtained by a pure livelihood, are not silk, not plant fiber, not gold, silver, pearls, gems, damask, gauze, brocade, embroidery, or the like; they are just robes of discarded rags.

These discarded rags are not for the sake of a shabby robe, not for the sake of beautiful dress; they are just for the sake of the buddha dharma. To wear them is itself directly to transmit the skin, flesh, bones, and marrow of the buddhas of the three times, directly to transmit the treasury of the true dharma eye. We should definitely not ask humans and devas about the merit of this; we should study it with the buddhas and ancestors.

正法眼藏袈裟功德第三
Treasury of the True Dharma Eye
The Merit of the Kāṣāya
Number 3

[T3:66]
予、在宋のそのかみ、長連牀に功夫せしとき、齊肩の隣單をみるに、開靜のときごとに、袈裟をささげて頂上に安じて、合掌恭敬し、一偈を默誦す。その偈にいはく、

When I was in the Song, making concentrated effort on the long platform, I observed that, at every breaking of silence, my neighbors seated shoulder to shoulder on the platform would take up the *kāṣāya*, place it on their heads, join their palms in veneration, and silently recite a gāthā.[143] The gāthā said,[144]

---

143 **long platform** (*chōrenjō* 長連牀): The extended daises in the saṃgha hall (*sōdō* 僧堂) on which monks of the great assembly (*daishu* 大衆) sat in meditation, chanted sūtras in prayer services, took their meals, and slept at night. This section echoes "Shōbōgenzō den'e" 正法眼藏傳衣, section 60.

breaking of silence (*kaijō* 開靜): Here, probably the wake-up signal in the saṃgha hall, though the term can also refer to (and is here sometimes taken as) the signal at the end of a meditation session.

my neighbors seated shoulder to shoulder on the platform (*seiken no rintan* 齊肩の隣單): A phrase more often read in the singular: "the neighbor at my shoulder on the next platform."

144 **The gāthā said** (*sono ge ni iwaku* その偈にいはく): Dōgen here repeats the verse given in section 50.

T3. The Merit of the Kāṣāya *Kesa kudoku* 袈裟功德

[T3:67] {2:330}

大哉解脱服、無相福田衣、披奉如來教、廣度諸衆生。

> *How great the vestment of liberation,*
> *Robe that is a signless field of merit.*
> *Wrapped in the teaching of the Tathāgata,*
> *We deliver living beings everywhere.*

[T3:68]

ときに予、未曾見のおもひを生じ、歡喜、みにあまり、感涙、ひそかにおちて衣襟をひたす。その旨趣は、そのかみ阿含經を披閲せしとき、頂戴袈裟の文をみるといへども、その儀則いまだあきらめず。いま、まのあたりみる、歡喜隨喜し、ひそかにおもはく、あはれむべし、郷土にありしとき、をしふる師匠なし、すすむる善友あらず。いくばくか、いたづらにすぐる光陰ををしまざる、かなしまざらめやは。いまの見聞するところ、宿善よろこぶべし。もしいたづらに郷間にあらば、いかでか、まさしく佛衣を相承著用せる僧寶に、隣肩することをえむ、悲喜ひとかたならず、感涙千萬行。

At the time, realizing this was something I had never seen before, I was overcome with joy, and tears of gratitude secretly fell, moistening the lapels of my robe.[145] The point was that, when previously I had perused the *Āgama* sūtras, although I had seen the passage on placing the *kāṣāya* on the head, the rite was still not clear to me.[146] Seeing it now right before my eyes, I rejoiced and was delighted, and thought to myself, "What a pity, that when I was in my native land, I had no master to teach me this, no wise friend to recommend it. How could I not regret, not lament, so many years and months spent in vain? Now, having seen and heard it, I should be happy for the good karma of former lives. Had I futilely remained in my homeland, how could I ever have been shoulder to shoulder with the saṃgha treasure that inherits and wears the robe of the buddha?"[147] My sadness and joy were extraordinary, and my tears of gratitude flowed by the thousands and tens of thousands.

---

145 **At the time** (*toki ni* ときに): This section repeats almost exactly a passage in "Shōbō-genzō den'e" 正法眼藏傳衣, section 60.

146 **passage on placing the *kāṣāya* on the head** (*chōdai kesa no mon* 頂戴袈裟の文): What passage Dōgen is referring to here is unclear.

147 **been shoulder to shoulder with the saṃgha treasure** (*sōbō ni rinken suru* 僧寶に隣肩する): I.e., sit next to members of the saṃgha, who are one of the "three treasures." Dōgen is playing in this sentence with "shoulder" (*ken* 肩).

108 DŌGEN'S *SHŌBŌGENZŌ* VOLUME VI

[T3:69]

ときにひそかに發願す、いかにしてか、われ不肖なりといふとも、佛法の
嫡嗣となり、正法を正傳して、郷土の衆生をあはれむに、佛祖正傳の衣法
を見聞せしめむ。かのときの發願、いまむなしからず、袈裟を受持せる在
家・出家の菩薩おほし、歡喜するところなり。受持袈裟のともがら、かな
らず日夜に頂戴すべし、殊勝景勝の功德なるべし。一句・一偈の見聞は、
若樹若石の見聞、　あまねく九道にかぎらざるべし。袈裟正傳の功德、　わ
づかに一日一夜なりとも、最勝最上なるべし。

At the time, I privately made a vow that, however inadequate I might
be, I would become a legitimate successor to the buddha dharma and,
directly transmitting the true dharma, out of pity for the living beings in
my native land, would let them see and hear of the robe and dharma directly transmitted by the buddhas and ancestors.[148] The vow made at that
time has not been fruitless now, and that there are many bodhisattvas,
both householders and renunciants, who receive and keep the *kāṣāya* is
a matter for rejoicing. Those who receive and keep the *kāṣāya* should
without fail place it on their heads day and night; it will be extraordinari-
ly excellent, exceedingly excellent, merit. Seeing and hearing one line
or one gāthā is seeing and hearing "*whether on trees or on rocks*" everywhere, not only throughout the nine paths.[149] The merit of the direct
transmission of the *kāṣāya*, even if only for one day and one night, is the
most excellent, the supreme.

[T3:70]

大宋嘉定十七年癸未十月中、高麗僧二人ありて、慶元府にきたれり。一人
は智玄となづけ、一人は景雲といふ。この二人、しきりに佛經の義を談ず
といへども、さらに文學士なり。しかあれども、袈裟なし、鉢盂なし、俗
人のごとし。あはれむべし、比丘の形なりといへども、比丘法なし。小國
邊地の、しかあらしむるならむ。日本國の比丘形のともがら、他國にゆか
ぬとき、またかの智玄等にひとしからん。

148　**At the time, I privately made a vow** (*toki ni hisoka ni hotsugan su* ときにひそか
に發願す): This section echoes material found in "Shōbōgenzō den'e" 正法眼藏傳衣,
sections 61-62.

149　**"whether on trees or on rocks"** (*nyaku ju nyaku seki* 若樹若石): Allusion to a well-
known story, found in the *Nirvāṇa Sūtra*, of the "boy of the Himalayas" (Śākyamuni in
a previous life) who wrote a Buddhist teaching on trees and rocks; see Supplementary
Notes. Dōgen's point here seems to be that, whereas one can encounter the Buddhist
teachings everywhere, the merit of transmitting the robe is exceedingly rare.

nine paths (*kudō* 九道): An expression not encountered elsewhere in the *Shōbōgenzō*,
on the meaning of which opinion is divided. Some take it as a secular Chinese reference
to the nine divisions of ancient China; others, as a technical Buddhist reference to the
nine states of existence: i.e., the six paths of rebirth plus the *śrāvaka*, *pratyeka-buddha*,
and bodhisattva (see, e.g., *Lü zong xinxue mingju* 律宗新學名句, ZZ.105:653b13-14).

T3. The Merit of the Kāṣāya *Kesa kudoku* 袈裟功德 109

In the winter of the junior water year of the sheep, seventeenth year of the Jiading era of the Great Song, during the tenth month, there were two monks from Goryeo who came to Qingyuan Prefecture.[150] One was called Jihyeon; the other was Gyeongun.[151] These two, although they spoke constantly of the doctrines of the sūtras of the buddhas, were gentlemen of letters as well. Nevertheless, they had no *kāṣāya* and no *pātra* bowls, like lay people. How pitiful, the fact that they had the appearance of the *bhikṣu* without the dharma of the bhikṣu must be due to their small country in a peripheral land. When those with the appearance of the bhikṣu in the Land of Japan venture to another land, they will be just like Jihyeon, and the like.

[T3:71] {2:331}

釋迦牟尼佛、十二年中、頂戴してさしおきましまさざりき。すでに遠孫なり、これを學すべし。いたづらに名利のために、天を拜し、神を拜し、王を拜し、臣を拜する頂門をめぐらして、佛衣頂戴に回向せん、よろこぶべきなり。

Buddha Śākyamuni placed [the *kāṣāya*] on his head for twelve years, without setting it aside.[152] We are his distant descendants; we should learn from this. We should rejoice in turning this head that, for the sake of fame and profit, has bowed to devas, bowed to gods, bowed to kings, and bowed to ministers, and directing it toward accepting the buddha robe on the head.

---

150 **winter of the junior water year of the sheep, seventeenth year of the Jiading era of the Great Song** (*Daisō Katei jūshichi nen kibi tō* 大宋嘉定十七年癸未冬): I.e., 1223 or 1224 CE. The seventeenth year of the Jiading era corresponds to 1224 in the Gregorian calendar, while the cyclical year of the "tenth stem, eighth branch" (*kibi* 癸未) corresponds to 1223.

Qingyuan Prefecture (*Keigen fu* 慶元府): In present-day Zhejiang, where Dōgen's Tiantong Monastery was located.

151 **Jihyeon** (*Chigen* 智玄); **Gyeongun** (*Keiun* 景雲): Otherwise unknown.

152 **Buddha Śākyamuni placed [the *kāṣāya*] on his head for twelve years** (*Shakamuni butsu, jūni nen chū, chōdai shite* 釋迦牟尼佛、十二年中、頂戴して). Reference to a story, related in "Shōbōgenzō den'e" 正法眼藏傳衣, section 29, of the *saṃghāti* robe that a tree spirit offered to Śākyamuni. As Dōgen says there,

> ときに釋迦牟尼佛、この衣をうけて、頂戴して十二年をふるに、しばらくもおかずといふ。これ阿含經等の説なり。

> Thereupon, Buddha Śākyamuni received the robe, placed it on his head, and spent twelve years without ever setting it aside even for a moment. This is an account in the āgama sūtras.

DŌGEN'S *SHŌBŌGENZŌ* VOLUME VI

[Yōkōji MS:][153]

ときに仁治元年庚子開冬日、在觀音導利興聖寶林寺示衆

*Presented to the assembly at Kannon Dōri Kōshō Hōrin Monastery;
first day of winter, senior metal year of the rat, the first year of Ninji
[17 October 1240]*

[Tōunji MS:]

建長七乙卯夏安居日、令義演書記書寫畢

*A day of the summer retreat, junior wood year of the rabbit, the seventh
year of Kenchō [1255], had Secretary Gien complete the copy*[154]

同七月五日一校了、以御草案爲本

*Completed proofreading, fifth day, seventh month, the same year [8
August 1255], with his draft as the basis*[155]

建治元年丙子五月廿五日書寫了

*Completed copy, twenty-fifth day, fifth month, of the senior fire year of
the rat, the first year of Kenji [20 June 1275 or 8 July 1276]*[156]

于時文明十一己亥年臘月十有三日、於于吉祥山永平寺承陽庵書寫之。
比丘光周

*Copied this in the Jōyō Hermitage, Eihei Monastery, Mount Kichijō;
thirteenth day, month of offerings, junior earth year of the pig, the elev-
enth year of Bunmei [24 January 1480]. Bhikṣu Kōshū*[157]

---

153 **Yōkōji MS** 永光寺本: The complete twelve-chapter *Shōbōgenzō*, in three fascicles, dated 1446.

154 This and the following two colophons are presumed to be by Ejō 懷奘.

day of the summer retreat (*ge ango no hi* 夏安居日): Dates of the summer retreat vary; a common practice put it from the fifteenth of the fourth lunar month through the fifteenth of the seventh month; in 1255, this would have corresponded to 22 May through 18 August.

Gien 義演: Ejō's disciple (d. 1313).

155 **his draft** (*gosōan* 御草案): I.e., Dōgen's draft.

156 **senior fire year of the rat, the first year of Kenji** (*Kenji gannen heishi* 建治元年丙子): The first year of the Kenji era corresponds to 1275 on the Gregorian calendar; the cyclical year *heishi* 丙子 corresponds to 1276.

157 **month of offerings** (*rōgetsu* 臘月): The twelfth lunar month.

Bhikṣu Kōshū (*biku Kōshū* 比丘光周): Fifteenth abbot of Eiheiji (1434–1492?).

TREASURY OF THE TRUE DHARMA EYE
THE TWELVE-CHAPTER COMPILATION
NUMBER 4

Bringing Forth the Mind of Bodhi
Hotsu bodai shin

發菩提心

Bringing Forth the Mind of Bodhi

Hotsu bodai shin

INTRODUCTION

This work, number 4 of the twelve-chapter *Shōbōgenzō*, is also found as number 34 in the sixty-chapter compilation; the latter was incorporated into the ninety-five-chapter Honzan edition as number 85 (or number 70 in the Iwanami reprint). According to a colophon on some late manuscript witnesses reproduced in the Honzan edition, it was composed in the spring of 1244, at Kippōji. This notice is identical with that of another work entitled "Hotsu bodai shin" that is found as number 63 in the seventy-five-chapter compilation (and translated above, in Volume 5). This latter work was included as number 69 in the Honzan *Shōbōgenzō* under the title "Hotsu mujō shin" 發無上心, the title given it in the sixty-chapter compilation, where it occurs as number 53. Although some have taken the two colophons at face value and assumed that both texts were in fact composed on the same day, given that their contents and style are completely different, it seems more likely that the colophon on our text here is a late addition, based on a confusion between the two works, and cannot be used to date this chapter.

Unlike the "Hotsu bodai shin" chapter in the seventy-five-chapter *Shōbōgenzō*, which deals with the metaphysics of the mind of bodhi and its expression in religious acts, the present work emphasizes the bodhisattva's selfless aspiration to liberate all beings from suffering. Relying almost entirely on proof texts from the sūtras and scholastic commentaries, Dōgen here treats the expression *hotsu bodai shin* 發菩提心 in the traditional terms of the bodhisattva's aspiration to achieve the unsurpassed, perfect awakening of a buddha (*bodhi-cittotpāda*). In the process, despite their currency in the Japanese Buddhism of his day (and his own claims elsewhere), he ignores more innovative interpretations of the *bodhi-citta* as an inherent buddha mind, rejects more radical claims that bringing forth this mind is equivalent to the ultimate awakening, and explicitly denies that the ancestral masters of his tradition are to be considered buddhas.

正法眼藏第四
Treasury of the True Dharma Eye
Number 4
發菩提心
Bringing Forth the Mind of Bodhi

[T4:1] {2:332}
おほよそ、心三種あり。

Broadly speaking, there are three types of "mind":[1]

[T4:2]
一者質多心、此方稱慮知心。二者汗栗多心、此方稱草木心。三者矣栗多心、此方稱積聚精要心。

> *First is the mind of citta, called here "the mind of thinking"; second is the mind of hṛdaya, called here "the mind of grasses and trees"; third is the mind of hṛdaya, called here "the mind of accumulated essentials."*

---

1 **Bringing Forth the Mind of Bodhi** (*hotsu bodai shin* 發菩提心): Or "producing the thought of bodhi"; S. *bodhi-cittotpāda*. A standard expression in the literature of the Mahāyāna for the aspiration of the bodhisattva to become a buddha; often abbreviated, as in our text, to the expression "bringing forth the mind (or thought)" (*hosshin* 發心). The rendering of *shin* 心 (S. *citta*) as "mind" (rather than "thought") here represents (a sometimes awkward) attempt at consistency of translation across the various uses of this multivalent term. See Supplementary Notes, s.v. "Bring forth the mind."

three types of "mind" (*shin sanshu* 心三種): The following definitions are borrowed from a passage in the *Mohe zhiguan* 摩訶止觀 (T.1911.46:4a19-24), in which Zhiyi 智顗 (538-597), in a discussion of the *bodhi-citta*, defines three Sanskrit terms rendered by the Chinese *xin* 心 ("mind"):

> 菩提者天竺音也、此方稱道。質多者天竺音、此方言心、即慮知之心也。天竺又稱汚栗馱、此方稱是草木之心也。又稱矣栗馱、此方是積聚精要者爲心也。
>
> *Puti* 菩提 [S. *bodhi*] is the pronunciation of Sindhu; here [in China], it is called *dao* 道 ["way"]. *Zhiduo* 質多 [S. *citta*] is the pronunciation of Sindhu; here, we say *xin* 心 — i.e., the thinking "mind." In Sindhu, there is also the term *wulituo* 汚栗馱 [S. *hṛdaya*], which here is called [*xin* 心 in the sense] the "heart" [or "core"] of grasses and trees. There is also *yilituo* 矣栗馱 [S. *vṛddha* (?)], which here is [*xin* 心 in the sense] the "heart" [or "pith"] of accumulated spiritual essence.

The Sanskrit original of Zhiyi's third term here is uncertain: some scholars have suggested *vṛddha* ("expanded," "developed"), while others take *yilituo* 矣栗馱 simply as an alternative transliteration of *hṛdaya*, here treated as a separate Sanskrit term. These three terms are also introduced in the "Shōbōgenzō shinjin gakudō" 正法眼藏身心學道.

[T4:3]

このなかに、菩提心をおこすこと、かならず慮知心をもちいる。菩提は、天竺の音、ここには、道、といふ。質多、は天竺の音、ここには、慮知心、といふ。この慮知心にあらざれば、菩提心をおこすことあたはず。この慮知を、即菩提心とするにはあらず、この慮知心をもて、菩提心をおこすなり。菩提心をおこす、といふは、おのれいまだわたらざるさきに、一切衆生をわたさん、と發願し、いとなむなり。そのかたち、いやしといふとも、この心をおこせば、すでに一切衆生の導師なり。この心、もとよりあるにあらず、いまあらたに欻起するにあらず、一にあらず、多にあらず、自然にあらず、凝然にあらず、わが身のなかにあるにあらず、わが身は心のなかにあるにあらず。この心は、法界に周遍せるにあらず、前にあらず、後にあらず、あるにあらず、なきにあらず、自性にあらず、他性にあらず、共性にあらず、無因性にあらず。しかあれども、感應道交するところに、發菩提心するなり。諸佛・菩薩の所授にあらず、みづからが所能にあらず。感應道交するに發心する、ゆえに自然にあらず。

Among them, it is always the thinking mind that is used to give rise to the mind of bodhi. "Bodhi" represents the pronunciation of Sindhu; here, it is called "the way."[2] *Citta* represents the pronunciation of Sindhu; here it is called "the thinking mind." If it is not this thinking mind, it cannot give rise to the mind of bodhi. It is not that we take this thinking mind as itself the mind of bodhi; it is by means of this thinking mind that we bring forth the mind of bodhi. To bring forth the mind of bodhi means making a vow and engaging in the effort to deliver all living beings before we ourselves are delivered. Though our status may be lowly, once we bring forth this mind, we are already the teachers of all living beings.

This mind is not something present from the beginning, not something that arises suddenly; it is not one, not many; it is not spontaneous, not fixed; it is not something within our bodies, nor are our bodies within the mind. This mind does not extend throughout the dharma realm; it is not before, not after; it is not existent, not nonexistent; it is not something with its own nature, not something with another's nature, not something with a shared nature, not something with an uncaused nature. Nevertheless, where there is the interaction of feeling and response, the mind of bodhi is brought forth.[3] It is not something bestowed by the buddhas

---

2 **"Bodhi" represents the pronunciation of Sindhu; here, it is called "the way"** (*bodai wa, Tenjiku no on, koko ni wa, dō, to iu* 菩提は、天竺の音、ここには、道、といふ): Amending Kawamura's punctuation. This and the following sentence translate Zhiyi's 智顗 Chinese at *Mohe zhiguan* 摩訶止觀, T.1911.46:4a19-21. The term *dao* 道 ("the way") was often used in Chinese translation for Sanskrit "bodhi."

3 **interaction of feeling and response** (*kannō dōkō* 感應道交): A fixed expression for the communication between a devotee and a deity; the devotee's feeling evokes a response from the deity and vice versa. Dōgen's reliance on the expression here no doubt reflects Zhiyi's use of it to explain bringing forth the mind of bodhi (at *Mohe zhiguan* 摩訶止觀, T.1911.46:4c13-15):

T4. Bringing Forth the Mind of Bodhi *Hotsu bodai shin* 發菩提心

and bodhisattvas, not something we bring about ourselves. The mind is brought forth in the interaction of feeling and response; so, it is not spontaneous.

[T4:4] {2:333}

この發菩提心、おほくは南洲の人身に發心すべきなり。八難處等にも、すこしきはあり、おほからず。菩提心をおこしてのち、三阿僧祇劫、一百大劫、修行す。あるひは無量劫おこなひて、ほとけになる、あるひは無量劫おこなひて、衆生をさきにわたして、みづからはつひにほとけにならず、ただし衆生をわたし、衆生を利益するもあり。菩薩の意樂にしたがふ。おほよそ菩提心とは、いかがして一切衆生をして菩提心をおこさしめ、佛道に引導せましと、ひまなく三業にいとなむなり。いたづらに世間の欲樂をあたふるを、利益衆生とするにはあらず。この發心、この修證、はるかに迷悟の邊表を超越せり。三界に勝出し、一切に拔群せる、なほ聲聞・辟支佛のおよぶところにあらず。

This bringing forth the mind of bodhi occurs mostly among humans of the Southern Continent.[4] There are a few instances under the eight inopportune circumstances but not many.[5] After bringing forth the mind of bodhi, one practices for three *asaṃkhyeya* kalpas and one hundred great kalpas.[6] After practicing for innumerable kalpas, one becomes a buddha; or, after practicing for innumerable kalpas and first delivering living beings, one does not in the end oneself become a buddha: there are those who merely deliver living beings, who merely benefit living beings; it depends on the aspiration of the bodhisattva.

In short, the mind of bodhi means working constantly through the three types of karma at how to cause all living beings to bring forth the mind of bodhi and lead them to the way of the buddhas.[7] Frivolously

---

問、行者自發心他教發心。答、自他共離皆不可。但是感應道交而論發心耳。

Question: Do practitioners bring forth the mind by themselves, or are they caused to bring forth the mind by another?

Answer: It cannot happen apart from self and other together. Only when feeling and response interact can we speak of bringing forth the mind.

4 **Southern Continent** (*nanshū* 南洲): I.e., the continent of Jambudvīpa, south of Mount Sumeru in Buddhist geography. See Supplementary Notes, s.v. "Four Continents."

5 **eight inopportune circumstances** (*hachi nanjo* 八難處): Eight conditions under which it is said to be difficult to encounter Buddhism; S. *aṣṭākṣaṇa*: (1) in hells, (2) as a hungry ghost, (3) as an animal, (4) in heavens of long lives, (5) in the northern continent of Uttarakuru, (6) as deaf or blind, (7) as overly clever, and (8) in the interval between buddhas.

6 **three *asaṃkhyeya* kalpas and one hundred great kalpas** (*san asōgi kō, ippyaku daikō* 三阿僧祇劫、一百大劫): A traditional calculation of the length of the bodhisattva path.

7 **three types of karma** (*sangō* 三業): I.e., actions of body, speech, and thought.

116   DŌGEN'S *SHŌBŌGENZŌ* VOLUME VI

providing them with worldly pleasures is not considered benefiting living beings. This bringing forth the mind, this practice and verification, far transcend the boundaries of delusion and understanding. They surpass the three realms and excel in all ways; they are not something the *śrāvakas* and *pratyeka-buddhas* can reach.[8]

[T4:5] {2:334}

迦葉菩薩、偈をもて釋迦牟尼佛をほめたてまつるにいはく、

Bodhisattva Kāśyapa said in a gāthā praising Buddha Śākyamuni,[9]

[T4:6]

發心畢竟二無別、如是二心先心難。自未得度先度他、是故我禮初發心。初發已爲天人師、勝出聲聞及緣覺。如是發心過三界、是故得名最無上。

Bringing forth the mind and the ultimate — the two are without distinction;
But of these two minds, the former mind is more difficult.[10]
One delivers others before one is delivered oneself;
Therefore, I pay obeisance to the initial bringing forth of the mind.
Once it is brought forth, one is a teacher to devas and humans,
Surpassing the śrāvakas and pratyeka-buddhas.
Bringing forth the mind like this surpasses the three realms;
Therefore, it can be called completely unsurpassed.

[T4:7]

發心とは、はじめて自未得度先度他の心をおこすなり、これを、初發菩提心、といふ。この心をおこすよりのち、さらにそこばくの諸佛にあふたてまつり、供養したてまつるに、見佛聞法し、さらに菩提心をおこす、雪上加霜なり。

"Bringing forth the mind" means to bring forth the mind [that aspires to] "*deliver others before one is delivered oneself.*" This is called "*initially bringing forth the mind of bodhi.*" After bringing forth this mind, in meeting many buddhas and making offerings to them, to see the buddhas, hear their dharma, and further bring forth the mind of bodhi is *adding frost to snow.*[11]

---

8   **They surpass the three realms** (*sangai ni shōshutsu shi* 三界に勝出し): This sentence paraphrases the final lines of the *Nirvāṇa Sūtra* quoted in section 6, below. See Supplementary Notes, s.v. "Three realms."

9   **Bodhisattva Kāśyapa** (*Kashō bosatsu* 迦葉菩薩): Quoting the *Nirvāṇa Sūtra* (*Da banniepan jing* 大般涅槃經, T.374.12:590a21-24).

10   **Bringing forth the mind and the ultimate** (*hosshin hikkyō* 發心畢竟): I.e., the initial aspiration to pursue the bodhisattva path and the culmination of the path in the unsurpassed perfect wisdom of a buddha.

11   **adding frost to snow** (*setsujō kasō* 雪上加霜): A common idiom in Chan texts for adding something superfluous (though Dōgen almost certainly does not mean by it here that repeatedly bringing forth the mind of bodhi is unnecessary).

T4. Bringing Forth the Mind of Bodhi *Hotsu bodai shin* 發菩提心

[T4:8]

いはゆる畢竟とは、佛果菩提なり。阿耨多羅三藐三菩提と初發菩提心と格量せば、劫火・螢火のごとくなるべしといへども、自未得度先度他のこゝろをおこせば、二無別なり。毎自作是念、以何令衆生、得入無上道、速成就佛身。これすなはち如來の壽量なり。ほとけは、發心・修行・證果みなかくのごとし。

"The ultimate" means bodhi, the fruit of buddhahood. When we compare *anuttara-samyak-saṃbodhi* and initially bringing forth the mind of bodhi, while they may be like the fire at the end of a kalpa and a firefly, when we bring forth the mind that "*first delivers others before one is delivered oneself*," "*the two are without distinction.*"

> *I always have this thought:*
> *How can I cause living beings*
> *To enter the unsurpassed path*
> *And quickly achieve a buddha body?*[12]

This is itself the lifespan of a tathāgata: the buddhas' bringing forth the mind, practicing, and verifying the fruit are all like this.[13]

[T4:9] {2:335}

衆生を利益すといふは、衆生をして自未得度先度他のこゝろをおこさしむるなり。自未得度先度他の心をおこせるちからによりて、われ、ほとけにならん、とおもふべからず。たとひ、ほとけになるべき功德熟して圓満すべし、といふとも、なほめぐらして、衆生の成佛得道に回向するなり。

"Benefiting living beings" means causing living beings to bring forth the mind "*first to deliver others before one is delivered oneself.*" Yet we should not think that we will become buddhas on the strength of our causing [beings] to bring forth the mind "*first to deliver others before one is delivered oneself.*" Even though the merit that would enable us to become buddhas may have ripened and become complete, we turn it around and dedicate it to the attaining of buddhahood and gaining of the way by living beings.

---

12 **I always have this thought** (*mai ji sa ze nen* 毎自作是念): Quoting a verse by Buddha Śākyamuni in the *Lotus Sūtra* (*Miaofa lianhua jing* 妙法蓮華經, T.262.9:44a3-4).

13 **lifespan of a tathāgata** (*nyorai no juryō* 如來の壽量): Perhaps recalling the title of Chapter 16 of the *Lotus Sūtra* (*Miaofa lianhua jing* 妙法蓮華經, T.262.9:42a29), in which Śākyamuni reveals the extraordinary length of his lifespan.

118 DŌGEN'S *SHŌBŌGENZŌ* VOLUME VI

[T4:10]

この心、われにあらず、他にあらず、きたるにあらずといへども、この發
心よりのち、大地を擧すれば、みな黄金となり、大海をかけば、たちまち
に甘露となる。これよりのち、土石砂礫をとる、即菩提心を拈來するな
り、水沫泡焔を參ずる、したしく菩提心を擔來するなり。しかあればすな
はち、國城・妻子・七寶・男女・頭目・髓腦・身肉・手足をほどこす、み
な菩提心の鬧聒聒なり、菩提心の活鱍鱍なり。

This mind is not ours, not another's, not coming from elsewhere; yet,
after we bring forth this mind, when we take up the whole earth, it turns
entirely to gold, when we stir up the great oceans, they turn immediately
to ambrosia.[14] Thereafter, to take hold of earth, stones, sand, or pebbles
is itself to take up the mind of bodhi; to study "the water, spray, foam, or
mirage" is to bear the mind of bodhi on your own back.[15] Therefore, to
give away "countries and cities, wives and children, the seven treasures,
males and females, my heads and my eyes, my marrow and my brains,
the flesh of my bodies, my hands and feet" — this is all the noisy hubbub
of the mind of bodhi, the brisk liveliness of the mind of bodhi.[16]

[T4:11]

いまの質多慮知の心、ちかきにあらず、とほきにあらず、みづからにあら
ず、他にあらずといへども、この心をもて、自未得度先度他の道理にめぐ
らすこと不退轉なれば、發菩提心なり。しかあれば、いま一切衆生の、我

---

14 **when we take up the whole earth, it turns entirely to gold** (*daichi o kosureba,
mina ōgon to nari* 大地を擧すれば、みな黄金となり): Perhaps recalling an expression
used in reference to the powers of the advanced bodhisattva, "to churn the Long River
[of the Milky Way] into butter and turn the whole earth into gold" (*kaku Chōga i soraku,
hen daichi i ōgon* 攪長河爲酥酪、變大地爲黄金).

ambrosia (*kanro* 甘露): "Sweet dew"; used to render S. *amṛta*.

15 **"water spray, foam, or mirage"** (*suimatsu hōen* 水沫泡焔): From a verse in the
Lotus Sūtra (*Miaofa lianhua jing* 妙法蓮華經, T.262.9:47b5):

世皆不牢固、如水沫泡焔。

This world is entirely unstable,
Like water spray, foam, or mirage.

16 **"countries and cities"** (*kokujō* 國城): A list based on a passage in the *Lotus Sūtra*,
in which Buddha Śākyamuni speaks of the offerings he made when he was born as kings
in his incalculable former lives (*Miaofa lianhua jing* 妙法蓮華經, T.262.9:34b28-29):

象馬七珍國城妻子奴婢僕從頭目髓腦身肉手足。

Elephants and horses, the seven treasures, countries and cities, wives and children,
male and female servants, my heads and my eyes, my marrow and my brains, the
flesh of my bodies, my hands and feet.

noisy hubbub (*nyōkatsugatsu* 鬧聒聒); **brisk liveliness** (*kappatsupatsu* 活鱍鱍): Two
idioms regularly used in Chan texts to express vigorous activity. The former term is
unusual in Dōgen's writing; for the more common latter term, see Supplementary Notes,
s.v. "Brisk and lively."

T4. Bringing Forth the Mind of Bodhi *Hotsu bodai shin* 發菩提心   119

有と執せる草木・瓦礫・金銀・珍寶をもて菩提心にほどこす、また發菩提心ならざらめや。

The present *citta*, the mind of thinking, is not close by, is not far off, is not our own, is not another's; yet when this mind is turned toward the principle of "*first to deliver others before one is delivered oneself*," without regressing from it, it is the bringing forth of the mind of bodhi. Therefore, when the grass and trees, tiles and pebbles, gold and silver, and precious treasures to which all living beings are attached as their possessions are given over to the mind of bodhi, is this not also bringing forth the mind of bodhi?

[T4:12]

心および諸法、ともに自・他・共・無因にあらざるがゆえに、もし一刹那、この菩提心をおこすより、萬法みな、増上縁となる。おほよそ發心・得道、みな刹那生滅するによるものなり。もし刹那生滅せずは、前刹那の惡、さるべからず、前刹那の惡、いまださらざれば、後刹那の善、いま現生すべからず。この刹那の量は、ただ如來ひとり、あきらかにしらせたまふ。一刹那心能起一語、一刹那語能説一字も、ひとり如來のみなり、餘二乗不能なり。

Because neither the mind nor the dharmas [occur] of themselves, by another, by both, or without cause, after this mind of bodhi has been brought forth for a single *kṣaṇa*, the myriad dharmas all become supporting conditions.[17] More generally, both bringing forth the mind and gaining the way occur according to arising and ceasing in a *kṣaṇa*. If there were not arising and ceasing in a *kṣaṇa*, the evil of the previous *kṣaṇa* would not depart; and if the evil of the previous *kṣaṇa* did not depart, the good of the subsequent *kṣaṇa* would not arise. It is the Tathāgata alone who clearly knows the size of this *kṣaṇa*. "*In one kṣaṇa, his mind can produce a word; in one kṣaṇa, his words can explain a letter*" — this too is only the Tathāgata; the other two vehicles cannot do it.[18]

---

17 [**occur] of themselves, by another, by both, or without cause** (*ji ta gu muin* 自・他・共・無因): A standard list used to deny substantial existence.

kṣaṇa (*setsuna* 刹那): I.e., a "moment," an "instant." Dōgen uses the transliteration of the Sanskrit term, which he will discuss below.

18 **"In one kṣaṇa"** (*issetsuna* 一刹那): From the *Mahāvibhāṣā* (*Apidamo da piposha lun* 阿毘達磨大毘婆沙論, T.1545.27:72b21-24):

問一刹那心能起一語。一刹那語能説一字耶。答佛一刹那心能起一語。一刹那語能説一字。聲聞獨覺一刹那心能起一語。一刹那語不能説一字。

Question: Can the mind produce a word in a single *kṣaṇa* and words express a written term in a single *kṣaṇa*?

Answer: For a buddha, the mind can produce a word in a single *kṣaṇa*, and words can express a written term in a single *kṣaṇa*. For the *śrāvaka* and *pratyeka-buddha*, the mind can produce a word in a single *kṣaṇa*, but words cannot express a written term in a single *kṣaṇa*.

120 DŌGEN'S *SHŌBŌGENZŌ* VOLUME VI

[T4:13] {2:336}

おほよそ壮士の、一弾指のあひだに六十五の刹那ありて、五蘊生滅すれど
も、凡夫、かつて不覺不知なり。怛刹那の量よりは、凡夫もこれをしれ
り。一日一夜をふるあひだに、六十四億九萬九千九百八十の刹那ありて、
五蘊ともに生滅す。しかあれども、凡夫、かつて覺知せず、覺知せざるが
ゆえに、菩提心をおこさず。佛法をしらず、佛法を信ぜざるものは、刹那
生滅の道理を信ぜざるなり。

Generally speaking, during one snap of a strong man's fingers, there
are sixty-five *kṣaṇas*; and though the five aggregates are arising and
ceasing [during this time], the common person never perceives them,
never knows them.[19] Above the duration of a *tat-kṣaṇa*, even the common person can recognize it.[20] In the course of one day and one night,
there are 6,499,980 *kṣaṇas*, during which the five aggregates are all arising and ceasing.[21] Nevertheless, common people never perceive them;
and, because they do not perceive them, they do not bring forth the mind
of bodhi. Those who do not know the buddha dharma, who do not believe in the buddha dharma, do not believe in the principle of the arising
and ceasing of *kṣaṇa*.

[T4:14]

もし如來の正法眼藏涅槃妙心をあきらむるがごときは、かならずこの刹那
生滅の道理を信ずるなり。いまわれら、如來の説教にあふたてまつりて曉
了するににたれども、わづかに怛刹那よりこれをしり、その道理、しかあ
るべしと信受するのみなり。世尊所説の一切の法、明らめしらざること
も、刹那量をしらざるがごとし。學者みだりに貢高することなかれ。極少
をしらざるのみにあらず、極大をも、またしらざるなり。もし如來の道力
によるときは、衆生また三千界をみる。おほよそ本有より中有にいたり、
中有より當本有にいたる、みな一刹那・一刹那にうつりゆくなり。かくの

---

other two vehicles (*yo nijō* 餘二乗): I.e., the *śrāvaka* and *pratyeka-buddha* vehicles.
Following Kawamura's edition; most versions read here the "other sages" (*yo shō* 餘聖).

19   **sixty-five *kṣaṇas*** (*rokujūgo no setsuna* 六十五の刹那): See, e.g., the *Abhidharma-kośa* (*Apidamo jushe lun* 阿毘達磨倶舍論, T.1558.29:62a22-23):

對法諸師説、如壯士一疾彈指頃六十五刹那。

The *ābhidhārmikas* say that for a strong man to snap his fingers once takes sixty-five
kṣaṇas.

20   ***tat-kṣaṇa*** (*tan setsuna* 怛刹那): A unit of time typically defined as 120 *kṣaṇas*. (See,
e.g., *Apidamo jushe lun* 阿毘達磨倶舍論, T.1558.29:62b17; and see the following note
on "one day and one night.")

21   **In the course of one day and one night, there are 6,499,980 *kṣaṇas*** (*ichinichi
ichiya o furu aida ni, rokujūshioku kyūman kyūsen kyūhyaku hachijū no setsuna arite* 一
日一夜をふるあひだに、六十四億九萬九千九百八十の刹那ありて): A Japanese ren-
dering of a sentence in the *Mahāvibhāṣā* (*Apidamo da piposha lun* 阿毘達磨大毘婆沙
論, T.1545.27:202c7-9). The number *oku* 億 here should be read as 100,000 (S. *śata-sahasra*), not 10,000,000, as is clear from the calculation of a day and a night given by the
Apidamo da piposha lun at T.1545.27:701b8-13.

T4. Bringing Forth the Mind of Bodhi *Hotsu bodai shin* 發菩提心

ごとくして、わがこころにあらず、業にひかれて流轉生死すること、一刹那もとどまらざるなり。かくのごとく流轉生死する身心をもて、たちまちに自未得度先度他の菩提心をおこすべきなり。たとひ發菩提心のみちに身心ををしむとも、生・老・病・死して、つひに我有なるべからず。

Those who clearly understand the treasury of the true dharma eye, the wondrous mind of nirvāṇa, necessarily believe in the principle of the arising and ceasing of *kṣaṇa*. Although it appears that, having encountered the teachings of the Tathāgata, we clearly understand [the principle], we only know it from *tat-kṣaṇa* and above, and simply believe that the principle must be true. Our failure to clarify all the dharmas preached by the World-Honored One is like our failure to know the duration of a *kṣaṇa*. Students, do not irresponsibly become arrogant. We not only do not know the extremely small, we also do not know the extremely large; yet, when we rely on the power of the way of the Tathāgata, living beings also see the three chiliocosms.

In sum, our going from this existence to the intermediate state, and from the intermediate state to our next existence, is all movement from *kṣaṇa* to *kṣaṇa*. In this way, without any intention, pulled along by our karma, our flowing through birth and death never pauses for a single *kṣaṇa*. With the body and mind thus flowing through birth and death, we should bring forth the mind of bodhi [that aspires] to "*deliver others before one is delivered oneself.*" Even though we may begrudge the body and mind on the path that brings forth the mind of bodhi, through birth, old age, sickness, and death, they are in the end not our own.

[T4:15] {2:337}

衆生の壽行、生滅してとどまらず、すみやかなること、

On the fact that the lifetime of living beings passes swiftly, arising and ceasing without surcease:

[T4:16]

世尊在世、有一比丘、來詣佛所、頂禮双足、却住一面、白世尊言、衆生壽行、云何速疾生滅。佛言、我能宣説、汝不能知。比丘言、頗有譬喩能顯示不。佛言、有、今爲汝説。譬如四善射夫、各執弓箭、相背攢立、欲射四方、有一捷夫、來語之、日汝等今可一時放箭、我能遍接、倶令不墮。於意云何、此捷疾不。比丘白佛、甚疾、世尊。佛言、彼人捷疾、不及地行夜叉。地行夜叉捷疾、不及空行夜叉。空行夜叉捷疾、不及四天王天捷疾。彼天捷疾、不及日月二輪捷疾。日月二輪捷疾、不及堅行天子捷疾、此是導引日月輪車者。此等諸天、展轉捷疾。壽行生滅、捷疾於彼。刹那流轉、無有暫停。

When the World-Honored One was in the world, there was a bhikṣu who came to the Buddha; prostrating himself at his feet, then standing

123

back to one side, he addressed the World-Honored One, saying, "How swift is the arising and ceasing of the lifetime of living beings?"[22]

The Buddha said, "I can explain it, but you would not understand."

The bhikṣu said, "Is there some example that would show it?"

The Buddha said,

There is, and I shall tell you. Suppose there are four accomplished archers, each holding a bow and arrow, standing together back to back and about to shoot in the four directions. There is a swift fellow who comes to them and says, "You may now all shoot your arrows at the same time, and I can catch them all, without any falling to the ground." What do you think? Is he swift or not?

The bhikṣu said to the Buddha, "Swift indeed, World-Honored One."

The Buddha said,

The speed of that man does not match that of a yakśa that walks on the earth; the speed of a yakśa that walks on the earth does not match that of a yakśa that flies through the sky; the speed of the yakśa that flies through the sky does not match the speed of those in the heavens of the four deva kings; the speed of those devas does not match the speed of the twin wheels of sun and moon; the speed of the twin orbs of sun and moon does not match the speed of the Jianxing Devas, who pull the chariots of the wheels of sun and moon.[23] These devas increase in speed, yet the arising and ceasing of a lifetime are faster than they are. The kṣaṇas flow on, without ever pausing.

[T4:17] {2:338}

われらが壽行、生滅刹那、流轉捷疾なること、かくのごとし。念念のあひだ、行者、この道理をわするることなかれ。この刹那生滅、流轉捷疾にありながら、もし自未得度先度他の一念をおこすごときは、久遠の壽量、たちまちに現在前するなり。三世十方の諸佛、ならびに七佛世尊、および西天二十八祖・東地六祖、乃至傳佛正法眼藏涅槃妙心の祖師、みなともに菩提心を保任せり。いまだ菩提心をおこさざるは、祖師にあらず。

Such is the speed of the flow of the kṣaṇa arising and ceasing. From moment to moment, the practitioner must not forget this principle. Yet,

---

22 **When the World-Honored One was in the world** (*Seson zaise* 世尊在世): Again, quoting the *Mahāvibhāṣā* (*Apidamo da piposha lun* 阿毘達磨大毘婆沙論, T.1545.27:701b21-c4).

23 **Jianxing Devas** (*Kengyō Tenshi* 堅行天子): Deities the names of which do not seem to occur in extant East Asian Buddhist literature outside this passage and for which the original Sanskrit has not been identified. In Indian mythology, the chariot of the sun is typically pulled by seven horses, driven by the charioteer Aruṇa ("Dawn"); that of the moon, by ten horses, driven by Ambara ("Sky").

T4. Bringing Forth the Mind of Bodhi *Hotsu bodai shin* 發菩提心   123

while being at this speed of the flow of the arising and ceasing of *kṣaṇa*, for those who bring forth a single thought of "*delivering others before one is delivered oneself*," a long, long life immediately appears before them. The buddhas of the three times and the ten directions, together with the seven buddhas, the world-honored ones, as well as the twenty-eight ancestors of Sindh in the West and six ancestors of the Land of the East, down to the ancestral masters who have transmitted the Buddha's "treasury of the true dharma eye, the marvelous mind of nirvāṇa" — all have maintained the mind of bodhi. One who has yet to bring forth the mind of bodhi is not an ancestral master.

[T4:18]

禪苑清規一百二十問云。發悟菩提心否。

In the one hundred twenty questions of the *Rules of Purity for the Chan Park*, it is said, "*Have you awakened the mind of bodhi or not?*"[24]

[T4:19]

あきらかにしるべし、佛祖の學道、かならず菩提心を發悟するをさきとせり、といふこと。これすなはち佛祖の常法なり。發悟す、といふは、曉了なり。これ、大覺にはあらず、たとひ十地を頓證せるも、なほこれ菩薩なり。西天二十八祖・唐土六祖等、および諸大祖師は、これ菩薩なり、ほとけにあらず、聲聞・辟支佛等にあらず。いまのよにある參學の輩、菩薩なり、聲聞にあらず、といふこと、あきらめしれるともがら一人もなし。ただみだりに衲僧・衲子と自稱して、その眞實をしらざるによりて、みだりがはしくせり。あはれむべし、澆季、祖道廢せることを。

We can clearly see from this, the fact that the study of the way by the buddhas and ancestors has always given priority to awakening the mind of bodhi. This is the constant norm of the buddhas and ancestors. "To awaken" means "to understand clearly." This is not the great awakening: though one may have suddenly verified the ten stages, one is still a bodhisattva.[25] The twenty-eight ancestors of Sindh in the West and the six ancestors of the Land of Tang, as well as the great ancestral masters —

---

24 **In the one hundred twenty questions of the *Rules of Purity for the Chan Park*** (*Zennen shingi ippyaku nijū mon* 禪苑清規一百二十問): Quoting from the list of questions, at *Chanyuan qinggui* 禪苑清規, ZZ.111:921a14, which begins:

敬佛法僧否。求善知識否。發悟菩提心否。

Have you honored the buddha, dharma, and saṃgha? Have you sought out a wise friend? Have you awakened the mind of bodhi?

25 **This is not the great awakening** (*daikaku ni arazu* 大覺にあらず): I.e., this awakening (*hotsugo* 發悟) is not the unsurpassed perfect awakening of a buddha: one remains a bodhisattva, even if one may have suddenly advanced through the ten stages of the bodhisattva path. The argument here is against the claim, not uncommon in Dōgen's Buddhist world, that bringing forth the mind of bodhi is equivalent to completion of the bodhisattva path.

124 DŌGEN'S *SHŌBŌGENZŌ* VOLUME VI

they are bodhisattvas, not buddhas, not *śrāvakas* or *pratyeka-buddhas*.[26] Among those who study nowadays, there is not a single person who has clearly recognized that they are bodhisattvas, not *śrāvakas*. Arbitrarily calling themselves "patch-robed monks" or "the patch-robed," since they do not know that truth, they are in rank confusion. How deplorable that, in this late season, the way of the ancestors has so declined.

[T4:20] {2:339}

しかあればすなはち、たとひ在家にもあれ、たとひ出家にもあれ、あるひ
は天上にもあれ、あるひは人間にもあれ、苦にありといふとも、樂にあり
といふとも、はやく自未得度先度他の心をおこすべし。衆生界は有邊無邊
にあらざれども、先度一切衆生の心をおこすなり、これすなはち菩提心な
り。

Thus, whether we are a householder or a renunciant, whether in a heaven or among humans, whether in suffering or in bliss, we should quickly bring forth the mind that seeks to "*deliver others before one is delivered oneself.*" Regardless of whether the realm of living beings is limited or limitless, we bring forth the mind that seeks first to deliver all living beings; precisely this is the mind of bodhi.

[T4:21]

一生補處菩薩、まさに閻浮提にくだらんとするとき、覩史多天の諸天のた
めに、最後の教をほどこすにいはく、菩提心是法明門、不斷三寶故。あき
らかにしりぬ、三寶の不斷は、菩提心のちからなりといふことを。菩提心
をおこしてのち、かたく守護し、退轉なかるべし。

When the Bodhisattva, in his final life as heir apparent, was about to descend to Jambudvīpa, in his final teaching to the devas of the Tuṣita Heaven, he said, "*The mind of bodhi is a gateway to the illumination of the dharma because it does not cut off the three treasures.*"[27] It is clear from this that our not cutting off the three treasures is due to the power of the mind of bodhi. After we have brought forth the mind of bodhi, we should firmly protect it and not turn back from it.

26　**they are bodhisattvas, not buddhas, not *śrāvakas* or *pratyeka-buddhas*** (*kore bosatsu nari, hotoke ni arazu, shōmon byakushi butsu tō ni arazu* これ菩薩なり、ほと けにあらず、聲聞・辟支佛等にあらず): A striking claim by an author who elsewhere regularly identifies the ancestors of the Zen lineage as buddhas and locates them beyond the stages of the bodhisattva path.

27　**the Bodhisattva, in his final life as heir apparent** (*isshō fusho bosatsu* 一生補 處菩薩): I.e., the Bodhisattva Jyotipāla (*Gomyō bosatsu* 護明菩薩), who would be reborn in his next life as Siddhārtha and become Buddha Śākyamuni. His words here represent number 82 in the list of 108 "gateways to the illumination of the dharma" (*hōmyōmon* 法明門; S. *dharmāloka-mukha*) given in the *Fo benxing ji jing* 佛本行集 經 (T.190.3:681c27); Dōgen treats the full list in his "Shōbōgenzō ippyakuhachi hōmyō mon" 正法眼藏一百八法明門.

T4. Bringing Forth the Mind of Bodhi *Hotsu bodai shin* 發菩提心   125

[T4:22]

佛言、云何菩薩守護一事。謂、菩提心。菩薩摩訶薩、常勤守護是菩提心、
猶如世人守護一子、亦如瞎者護餘一目、如行曠野守護導者。菩薩守護菩提
心、亦復如是。因護如是菩提心故、得阿耨多羅三藐三菩提。因得阿耨多羅
三藐三菩提故、常・樂・我・淨具足而有、即是無上大般涅槃。是故菩薩守
護一法。

> The Buddha said:[28]
>
> Why does the bodhisattva protect one thing — i.e., the mind of bodhi?
> The *bodhisattva-mahāsattva* always strives to protect the mind of
> bodhi, just as a worldly person protects an only child; or, again, as a
> person blind in one eye protects the other eye; or as a traveler in a vast
> wilderness protects his guide. The bodhisattvas' protection of the mind
> of bodhi is like this. Because they protect the mind of bodhi like this,
> they attain *anuttara-samyak-saṃbodhi*. Because they attain *anuttara-
> samyak-saṃbodhi*, they are endowed with permanence, bliss, self, and
> purity, the unsurpassed great *parinirvāṇa*.[29] Therefore, the bodhisattva
> protects one thing.

[T4:23] {2:340}

菩提心をまぼらんこと、佛語、あきらかにかくのごとし。守護して退轉な
からしむるゆえは、世間の常法にいはく、たとひ生ずれども熟せざるもの
三種あり、いはく魚子・菴羅果・發心菩薩なり。おほよそ退失のものおほ
きがゆえに、われも退失とならんことを、かねてよりおそるるなり。この
ゆえに菩提心を守護するなり。

Such, clearly, are the words of the Buddha on protecting the mind of
bodhi. The reason that we protect it and do not turn back from it is, as is
regularly said in the secular world, "There are three things that are born
but do not reach maturity: *fish eggs, the fruit of the āmra, and the bodhisattva who has brought forth the mind.*"[30] Since there are many who fall

---

28 **The Buddha said** (*Butsu gon* 佛言): Quoting the *Nirvāṇa Sūtra* (*Da banniepan jing*
大般涅槃經, T.374.12:515a29-b6).

29 **permanence, bliss, self, and purity** (*jō raku ga jō* 常・樂・我・淨): The four attributes of nirvāṇa, according to the *Nirvāṇa Sūtra*.

30 **"There are three things that are born but do not reach maturity"** (*tatoi shōzuredo-
mo juku sezaru mono sanshu ari* たとひ生ずれども熟せざるもの三種あり): Reflecting
a notion found in the *Nirvāṇa Sūtra* (*Da banniepan jing* 大般涅槃經, T.374.12:450a7-9):

> 譬如魚母多有胎子成就者少。如菴羅樹花多果少。衆生發心乃有無量。及其成就
> 少不足言。

> Like the mother fish with many eggs in her womb, few of which develop; like the
> *āmra* [i.e., mango] tree with its many flowers and few fruits — living beings who
> bring forth the mind may be incalculable, but those that bring it to realization are so
> few as to be hardly worth mentioning.

The *Dazhidu lun* 大智度論 (T.1509.25:88a10-11) cites the same adage in a verse by
Indra:

126 DŌGEN'S *SHŌBŌGENZŌ* VOLUME VI

back from it, we have long feared that we too might fall back; and for this reason, we protect the mind of bodhi.

[T4:24]

菩薩の初心のとき、菩提心を退轉すること、おほくは正師にあはざるによる。正師にあはざれば正法をきかず、正法をきかざればおそらくは因果を撥無し、解脱を撥無し、三寶を撥無し、三世等の諸法を撥無す。いたづらに現在の五欲に貪著して、前途、菩提の功德を失す。あるひは天魔波旬等、行者をさまたげんがために、佛形に化し、父母・師匠、乃至親族・諸天等のかたちを現じて、きたりちかづきて、菩薩にむかひてこしらへすすめていはく、佛道長遠、久受諸苦、もともうれふべし、しかじ、まづわれ生死を解脱し、のちに衆生をわたさんには。行者、このかたらひをききて、菩提心を退し、菩薩の行を退す。まさにしるべし、かくのごとくの説は、すなはちこれ魔説なり。菩薩、しりてしたがふことなかれ。もはら自未得度先度他の行願を退轉せざるべし。

When, as beginners, bodhisattvas turn back from the mind of bodhi, it is mostly due to their failure to meet a true master. When we do not meet a true master, we do not hear the true dharma; when we do not hear the true dharma, we are likely to deny cause and effect, to deny liberation, to deny the three treasures, to deny all the dharmas of the three times, and the like. Vainly addicted to the five desires in the present, we lose the merit for bodhi on the road ahead. Or the Deva Māra-pāpīyān, and the like, in order to obstruct the practitioner, may assume the appearance of a buddha or appear in the guise of parents, teachers, relatives, devas, and the like; and, drawing near, they will seduce the bodhisattva, saying, "The way to buddhahood is long, with protracted suffering, painful in the extreme.[31] Better first to liberate oneself from birth and death, and then deliver living beings." Hearing such persuasion, the practitioner turns back from the mind of bodhi, turns back from the practice of the bodhisattva. But we should know that such talk is the talk of Māra. Bodhisattvas must recognize this and not go along with it; they should never turn back from their vow *"first to deliver others before one is delivered oneself."*

菩薩發大心、魚子菴樹華、三事因時多、成果時甚少。

The great thoughts of bodhisattvas,
Fish eggs, and *āmra* flowers:
Three things plentiful in origin
But, when it comes to fruition, very scarce.

31   **"The way to buddhahood is long, with protracted suffering"** (*butsudō chōon, ku ju shoku* 佛道長遠、久受諸苦): Variant of a phrase from the *Lotus Sūtra* (*Miaofa lianhua jing* 妙法蓮華經, T.262.9:26a15-17):

若衆生但聞一佛乘者、則不欲見佛不欲親近。便作是念、佛道長遠久受懃苦乃可得成佛。

If living beings only hear of the one buddha vehicle, they will not wish to see the buddha, nor wish to draw near to him. They will think, "The way to buddhahood is long, with protracted suffering, before one attains buddhahood."

T4. Bringing Forth the Mind of Bodhi *Hotsu bodai shin* 發菩提心

[T4:25] {2:341}

自未得度先度他の行願にそむかんがごときは、これ魔説としるべし、外道説としるべし、惡友説としるべし、さらに隨ふことなかれ。

[Talk] that would have us turn back from the vow "*first to deliver others before one is delivered oneself*," we should recognize as the talk of Māra, we should recognize as the talk of other paths, we should recognize as the talk of bad friends. Never go along with it.

[T4:26]

魔有四種。一煩惱魔、二五衆魔、三死魔、四天子魔。煩惱魔者、所謂百八煩惱等、分別八萬四千諸煩惱。五衆魔者、是煩惱和合因縁、得是身四大及四大造色・眼根等色、是名色衆。百八煩惱等諸受和合、名爲受衆。大小無量所有想、分別和合、名爲想衆。因好醜心發、能起貪欲・瞋恚等心、相應・不相應法、名爲行衆。六情・六塵和合故、生六識、是六識分別和合、無量無邊心、是名識衆。死魔者、無常因縁故、破相續五衆壽命、盡離三法識・熱・壽故、名爲死魔。天子魔者、欲界主。深著世樂、用有所得故、生邪見、憎嫉一切賢聖涅槃道法、是名天子魔。魔是天竺語、秦言能奪命者。雖死魔實能奪命、餘者亦能作奪命因縁、亦奪智慧命、是故名殺者。問曰、一五衆魔攝三種魔。何以故別説四。答曰、實是一魔、分別其義故有四。

There are four types of Māra: (1) Māra as mental afflictions; (2) Māra as the five aggregates; (3) Māra as death; and (4) Māra as deva.[32]

Māra as mental afflictions refers to the one hundred eight mental afflictions, further divided into the eighty-four thousand mental afflictions.

Māra as the five aggregates refers to these mental afflictions combining as the causes and conditions that produce this body. The four elements and the forms produced by the four elements — form and eye organ, and the rest — are called "the form aggregate." The combination of the sensations of the hundred eight mental afflictions is called "the sensation aggregate." Our incalculable, large and small perceptions, separate and combined, are called "the perception aggregate." The mental states of craving, anger, and the like, arising from pleasant and unpleasant thoughts, the dharmas associated and not associated [with the mind] are called the "formations aggregate." By the combination of the six sense organs and six sense objects, there arise the six consciousnesses; the incalculable, limitless states of mind of these six consciousnesses, separate and combined, are called "the consciousness aggregate."

Māra as death: because of the causes and conditions of impermanence, the lifespan of the continuing five aggregates is broken down, and the

---

32 **There are four types of Māra** (*Ma u shishu* 魔有四種): Quoting the *Dazhidu lun* 大智度論, T.1509.25:533c21-534a10. The four types are a standard list: respectively, *kleśa-māra*, *skandha-māra*, *mṛtyu-māra*, and *devaputra-māra*.

three factors of consciousness, warmth, and life all depart; therefore, it is called "the Māra of death."

Māra as deva, lord of the realm of desire: because he is deeply attached to worldly pleasures and relies on gaining, he produces false views and detests the way to nirvāṇa of all the worthy sages. This is called "Māra as deva."

"Māra" is a word of Sindhu; in Qin, it means "the one who takes life."[33] Although Māra as death actually takes the life, the others also create the causes and conditions for taking life and take the life of wisdom; therefore, they are called "murderers."

Question: Since the one Māra as the five aggregates includes the other three types, why distinguish them as four? Answer: In reality, they are one Māra; because we distinguish their meanings, we have four.

[T4:27] {2:342}

上來、これ龍樹祖師の施設なり、行者、しりて勤學すべし。いたづらに魔嬈をかうぶりて、菩提心を退轉せざれ、これ守護菩提心なり。

The preceding is the work of the Ancestral Master Nāgārjuna.[34] Practitioners should know it and diligently study it. Do not be foolishly deceived by Māra and turn back from the mind of bodhi — this is protecting the mind of bodhi.

正法眼藏發菩提心第四
Treasury of the True Dharma Eye
Bringing Forth the Mind of Bodhi
Number 4

[Honzan edition:]

爾時寬元二年甲辰二月十四日、在越州吉田縣吉峰精舍示衆
Presented to the assembly at the Yoshimine Vihāra, Yoshida District, Esshū; fourteenth day, second month of the senior wood year of the dragon, the second year of Kangen [24 March 1244][35]

---

33 **in Qin** (*Shin* 秦): I.e., in the Chinese of the Later Qin (Hou Qin 後秦) dynasty (384-417), which ruled North China when Kumārajīva translated the *Dazhidu lun* 大智度論 between the years 402-405. The Sanskrit "*māra*" means "killing" or "killer."

34 **the Ancestral Master Nāgārjuna** (*Ryūju soshi* 龍樹祖師): Traditionally regarded as the author of the *Dazhidu lun* 大智度論 (though the attribution is doubted by modern scholarship).

35 This colophon, presumably by Dōgen, is identical with that of the "Hotsu bodai shin" 發菩提心 chapter that occurs as number 63 in the seventy-five-chapter *Shōbōgenzō*. It first appears on MSS of the late seventeenth century.

T4. Bringing Forth the Mind of Bodhi *Hotsu bodai shin* 發菩提心   129

[Tōunji MS:]

建長七年乙卯四月九日、以御草案書寫之。懷弉

*Copied this from his draft, ninth day, fourth month of the junior wood
year of the rabbit, the seventh year of Kenchō [16 May 1255]. Ejō*[36]

永正七年庚午八月朔日、於于桂林精舍丈室中。七十三歳用兼寫焉

*Copied in the abbot's quarters of Keirin Vihāra; first day, eighth month,
senior metal year of the horse, the seventh year of Eishō [4 September
1510]. Yōken, in his seventy-third year*[37]

---

36   This colophon is also attested by the Rurikōji MS 瑠璃光寺本 (ca. 1491) of the
Shōbōgenzō in eighty-three chapters.

his draft (*gosōan* 御草案): I.e., Dōgen's draft.

37   **Yōken** 用兼: I.e., Kinkō Yōken 金岡用兼 (1437–1513?).

TREASURY OF THE TRUE DHARMA EYE
THE TWELVE-CHAPTER COMPILATION
NUMBER 5

Offerings to the Buddhas
Kuyō shobutsu
供養諸佛

Offerings to the Buddhas

Kuyō shobutsu

INTRODUCTION

This work occurs as the fifth text of the twelve-chapter *Shōbōgenzō*. It corresponds to number 59 in the sixty-chapter compilation, the text reproduced in the Honzan edition as number 87. Like most of the texts of the twelve-chapter compilation, it is undated and lacks a colophon; a colophon on one manuscript witness records that it was copied, presumably by Dōgen's disciple Ejō 懷奘, during the summer retreat of 1255, a time when a number of the twelve-chapter *Shōbōgenzō* texts seem to have been copied.

As its title indicates, the chapter treats the common Buddhist practice of making offerings in veneration of the buddhas. Dōgen divides his treatment of the topic into two roughly equal parts: the first half of the essay treating examples of the offerings made by Buddha Śākyamuni in his prior lives; the second half describing types of offerings, including a lengthy discussion of the construction of the stūpa.

Like some of the other texts of the twelve-chapter *Shōbōgenzō*, the work is noteworthy for its heavy reliance on the standard sources of the Buddhist canon: something like two-thirds of the text consist of direct quotation from sūtras, scholastic commentaries, and monastic codes, with almost no reference to the Zen corpus. Only in the final section does Dōgen refer to his own tradition of the buddhas and ancestors, which alone, he claims, transmits the authentic rules for making offerings.

正法眼藏第五

Treasury of the True Dharma Eye
Number 5

供養諸佛

Offerings to the Buddhas

[T5:1] {2:343}

佛言、若無過去世、應無過去佛、若無過去佛、無出家受具。

The Buddha said,[1]

If there were no past time,
There would be no past buddhas;
If there were no past buddhas,
There would be no leaving home and receiving the precepts.

[T5:2]

あきらかにしるべし、三世にかならず諸佛ましますなり。しばらく過去の
諸佛におきて、そのはじめあり、といふことなかれ、そのはじめなし、と
いふことなかれ。もし始終の有無を邪計せば、さらに佛法の習學にあら
ず。過去の諸佛を供養したてまつり、出家し、隨順したてまつるがごと
き、かならず諸佛となるなり。供佛の功德によりて、作佛するなり。いま
だかつて一佛をも供養したてまつらざる衆生、なにによりてか作佛するこ
とあらん、無因作佛あるべからず。

It should be clearly recognized that the buddhas necessarily live in the
three times. With regard here to buddhas of the past, do not say that they
had a beginning or that they had no beginning. If we falsely reckon that
they did or did not have a beginning or an end, this is surely not the study
of the buddha dharma. Those who have made offerings to the buddhas
of the past, who have left home and followed them, will surely become
buddhas. We become buddhas through the merit of making offerings to
buddhas. How could living beings who have never made offerings to a
single buddha become a buddha? There is no becoming a buddha without cause.

---

1   **The Buddha said** (*butsu gon* 佛言): A slightly variant version of a verse found in
the *Mahāvibhāṣā* (*Da piposha ron* 大毘婆沙論 (T.1545.27:393b15-16). Also cited in the
"Shōbōgenzō shukke kudoku" 正法眼藏出家功德.

134　DŌGEN'S *SHŌBŌGENZŌ* VOLUME VI

[T5:3]

佛本行集經言、佛告目犍連、我念往昔、於無量無邊諸世尊所、種諸善根、
乃至求於阿耨多羅三藐三菩提。目犍連、我念往昔、作轉輪聖王身、値三十
億佛。皆同一號、號釋迦。如來及聲聞衆、尊重承事、恭敬供養、四事具
足、所謂衣服・飮食・臥具・湯藥。時彼諸佛、不與我記、汝當得阿耨多
羅三藐三菩提及世間解・天人師・佛世尊、於未來世、得成正覺。目犍連、我
念往昔、作轉輪聖王身、値八億諸佛。皆同一號、號燃燈。如來及聲聞衆、
尊重恭敬、四事供養、所謂衣服・飮食・臥具・湯藥・幡蓋・華香。時彼諸
佛、不與我記、汝當得阿耨多羅三藐三菩提及世間解・天人師・佛世尊。目
犍連、我念往昔、作轉輪聖王身、値三億諸佛。皆同一號、號弗沙。如來及
聲聞衆、四事供養、皆悉具足。時彼諸佛、不與我記、汝當作佛。

In the *Sūtra of the Collection of the Past Acts of the Buddha*, it is said:[2]

The Buddha addressed Maudgalyāyana, saying:

I remember that, in the past, planting good roots under incalculable,
limitless world-honored ones, I sought *anuttara-samyak-saṃbodhi*.
Maudgalyāyana, I remember that, in the past, assuming the body of a
wheel-turning sage king, I encountered thirty *koṭis* of buddhas, all with
the same name, Śākya.[3] The tathāgatas as well as their *śrāvakas*, I venerated, served, honored, and offered in full the four necessities: robes,
food and drink, bedding, and medicine. At that time, those buddhas did
not give me a prediction, "You shall attain *anuttara-samyak-saṃbodhi*
and, as knower of the world, teacher to devas and humans, world-honored buddha, in a future time, you shall realize true awakening."

Maudgalyāyana, I remember that, in the past, assuming the body of a
wheel-turning sage king, I encountered eight *koṭis* of buddhas, all with
the same name, Randeng.[4] The tathāgatas as well as their *śrāvakas*,
I venerated, served, honored, and offered in full the four necessities:
robes, food and drink, bedding, and medicine; and banners, canopies,
flowers, and incense. At that time, those buddhas did not give me the
prediction, "Attaining *anuttara-samyak-saṃbodhi*, you shall become
knower of the world, teacher of devas and humans, a world-honored
buddha."[5]

2　*Sūtra of the Collection of the Past Acts of the Buddha* (*Butsu hongyō jikkyō* 佛本行
集經): *Fo benxing ji jing* 佛本行集經, T.190.3:655c4-19.

3　**thirty *koṭis* of buddhas** (*sanjū oku butsu* 三十億佛): Taking *oku* 億 here as rendering
S. *koṭi* ("crore"; 10 million); similarly below.

4　**Randeng** (*Nentō* 燃燈): A Chinese translation of "Dīpaṃkara" ("Torch Bearer").

5　**"knower of the world"** (*seken chi* 世間智): This and the following two epithets of a
buddha are from the standard list of ten appearing below, section 5.

T5. Offerings to the Buddhas *Kuyō shobutsu* 供養諸佛 135

Maudgalyāyana, I remember that, in the past, assuming the body of a wheel-turning sage king, I encountered three koṭis of buddhas, all with the same name, Puṣya. To the tathāgatas as well as their śrāvakas, I offered in full all the four necessities. At that time, those buddhas did not give me the prediction, "You shall become a buddha."

[T5:4] {2:345}

このほか、そこばくの諸佛を供養しまします。轉輪聖王身としては、かならず四天下を統領すべし。供養諸佛の具、まことに豊饒なるべし。もし大轉輪王ならば、三千界に王なるべし。そのときの供佛、いまの凡慮、はかるべからず、ほとけ、ときましますとも、解了すること、え難からん。

In addition to these, he made offerings to so many other buddhas. In the body of a wheel-turning sage king, he would necessarily have ruled the four continents under heaven; his provisions for offerings to the buddhas would truly have been abundant.[6] If he was a great wheel-turning king, he would have been king of the three chiliocosms; his offerings to the buddhas at that time cannot be measured by the thinking of common people today, and, even were the Buddha to describe them, they would be hard to understand.[7]

[T5:5]

佛藏經淨見品第八云、佛告舍利弗、我念過去世、求阿耨多羅三藐三菩提、値三十億佛、皆號釋迦牟尼。我時皆作轉輪聖王、盡形供養佛及諸弟子、衣服・飲食・臥具・医藥、爲求阿耨多羅三藐三菩提。而諸佛、不記我、言汝於來世、當得作佛。何以故。我有所得故。舍利弗、我念過去、得値八千佛、皆號定光。時皆作轉輪聖王、盡形供養及諸弟子、衣服・飲食・臥具・医藥、爲求阿耨多羅三藐三菩提。而是諸佛、皆不記我、汝於來世、當得作佛。何以故。我有所得故。舍利弗、我念過世、値六萬佛、皆號光明。我時皆作轉輪聖王、盡形供養及諸弟子、衣服・飲食・臥具・医藥、爲求阿耨多羅三藐三菩提。而是諸佛、亦不記我、汝於來世、當得作佛。何以故。以我有所得故。舍利弗、我念過世、値三億佛、皆號弗沙。我時皆作轉輪聖王、四事供養、皆不記我、以有所得故。舍利弗、我念過世、得値萬八千佛、皆號山王、劫名上八。我皆於此萬八千佛所、剃髮法衣修習阿耨多羅三藐三菩提、皆不記我、以有所得故。舍利弗、我念過世、得値五百佛、皆號華上。我時皆作轉輪聖王、悉以一切、供養諸佛及諸弟子、皆不記我、以有所得故。舍利弗、我念過世、得値五百佛、皆號威德。我悉供養、皆不記我、以有所得故。舍利弗、我念過世、得値二千佛、皆號憍陳如。我時皆作轉輪聖王、悉以一切、供養諸佛、皆不記我、以有所得故。舍利弗、我念過世、値九千佛、皆號迦葉。我以四事、供養諸佛及弟子衆、皆不記我、以有所得故。舍利弗、我念過去、於萬劫中、無有佛出。爾時初五百劫、有九萬辟支

---

6 **four continents under heaven** (*shi tenka* 四天下): The four bodies of land (S. *ca-tur-dvīpa*) surrounding Mt. Sumeru in the geography of Buddhist world systems; see Supplementary Notes, s.v. "Four Continents."

7 **three chiliocosms** (*sanzenkai* 三千界): Abbreviation of *sanzen daisen sekai* 三千大千世界 ("three-thousandfold great thousandfold world system"), equal to one billion Sumeru world systems.

佛。我盡壽、悉皆供養衣服・飲食・臥具・医藥、尊重讚嘆。次五百劫、復以四事、供養八萬四千億諸辟支佛、尊重讚嘆。舍利弗、過是千劫已、無復辟支佛。我時閻浮提死、生梵世中、作大梵王。如是展轉、五百劫中、常生梵世、作大梵王、不生閻浮提。過是五百劫已、下生閻浮提、治化閻浮提、命終生四天王天。於中命終、生忉利天、作釋提桓因。如是展轉、滿五百劫、生閻浮提、滿五百劫、生於梵世、作大梵王。舍利弗、我於九千劫中、但一生閻浮提、九千劫中、但生天上。劫盡燒時、生光音天。世界成已、還生梵世。九千劫中生、都不生人中。舍利弗、是九千劫、無有諸佛・辟支佛、多諸衆生墮在惡道。舍利弗、是萬劫已、有佛出世。號曰普守如來・應供・正遍知・明行足・善逝・世間解・無上士・調御丈夫・天人師・佛世尊。我於爾時、梵世命終、生閻浮提、作轉輪聖王、號曰共天、人壽九萬歲。我盡形壽、以一切樂具、供養彼佛及九十億比丘。於九萬歲、爲求阿耨多羅三藐三菩提。是普守佛、亦不記我、汝於來世、當得作佛。何以故。我於爾時、不能通達諸法實相、貪著計我有所得見。舍利弗、於是劫中、有百佛出世、名號各異。我時皆作轉輪聖王、盡形供養及諸弟子。爲求阿耨多羅三藐三菩提。而是諸佛、亦不記我、汝於來世、當得作佛、以有所得故。舍利弗、我念過世、七百阿僧祇劫中、得值千佛、皆號閻浮檀。我盡形壽、四事供養、亦不記我、以有所得故。舍利弗、我念過世、亦於第七百阿僧祇劫中、得值六百二十萬諸佛、皆號見一切儀。我時皆作轉輪聖王、以一切樂具、盡形供養及諸弟子、亦不記我、以有所得故。舍利弗、我念過世、亦於第七百阿僧祇劫中、得值八十四佛、皆號帝相。我時皆作轉輪聖王、以一切樂具、盡形供養及諸弟子、亦不記我、以有所得故。舍利弗、我念過世、亦於第七百阿僧祇劫中、得值十五佛、皆號日明。我時皆作轉輪聖王、以一切樂具、盡形供養及諸弟子、亦不記我、以有所得故。舍利弗、我念過世、亦於第七百阿僧祇劫中、得值六十二佛、皆號善寂。我時皆作轉輪聖王、以一切樂具、盡形供養、亦不記我、以有所得故。

In the Pure View Chapter, Number 8, of the *Buddha Treasury Sūtra*, it is said,[8]

The Buddha addressed Śāriputra, saying,

I remember that, in the past, seeking anuttara-samyak-sambodhi, I encountered thirty koṭis of buddhas, all named Śākyamuni. At that time, I was always a wheel-turning sage king, who throughout his lives, made offerings to the buddhas and their disciples of robes, food and drink, bedding, and medicine, for the sake of my quest for anuttara-samyak-sambodhi. Yet those buddhas did not give me a prediction, saying, "In the future, you will become a buddha." Why not? Because I was acquisitive.

Śāriputra, I remember that, in the past, I was able to encounter eight thousand buddhas, all named Dingguan.[9] At that time, I was always a

---

8 **Buddha Treasury Sūtra** (*Butsuzō kyō* 佛藏經): *Fozang jing* 佛藏經, T.653.15:797a16-c29.

9 **Dingguan** (*Jōkō* 定光): An alternative translation of "Dīpaṃkara." The names of the buddhas given throughout this passage are sometimes in Chinese translation (as here), sometimes in transliteration (as in "Śākyamuni," just above); since speculation on the

T5. Offerings to the Buddhas *Kuyō shobutsu* 供養諸佛 137

wheel-turning sage king, who throughout his lives, made offerings to them and their disciples of robes, food and drink, bedding, and medicine, for the sake of my quest for *anuttara-samyak-saṃbodhi*. Yet none of those buddhas gave me the prediction, "In the future, you will become a buddha." Why not? Because I was acquisitive.

Śāriputra, I remember that, in the past, I encountered sixty thousand buddhas, all named Guangming.[10] At that time, I was always a wheel-turning sage king, who throughout his lives, made offerings to them and their disciples of robes, food and drink, bedding, and medicine, for the sake of my quest for *anuttara-samyak-saṃbodhi*. Yet none of those buddhas gave me the prediction, "In the future, you will become a buddha." Why not? Because I was acquisitive.

Śāriputra, I remember that, in the past, I encountered three *koṭis* of buddhas, all named Puṣya. At that time, I was always a wheel-turning sage king, who made offerings of the four necessities. Yet none of of them gave me the prediction, because I was acquisitive.

Śāriputra, I remember that, in the past, I was able to encounter eighteen thousand buddhas, all named Shanwang, in a kalpa called Shangba.[11] At the places of all these eighteen thousand buddhas, I shaved my head, donned the robe, and studied *anuttara-samyak-saṃbodhi*. None of them gave me the prediction, because I was acquisitive.

Śāriputra, I remember that, in the past, I was able to encounter five hundred buddhas, all named Huashang.[12] At that time, I was always a wheel-turning sage king, who made offerings of everything to the buddhas and their disciples. None of them gave me the prediction, because I was acquisitive.

Śāriputra, I remember that, in the past, I was able to encounter five hundred buddhas, all named Weide.[13] I made every sort of offering, but none of them gave me a prediction, because I was acquisitive.

Śāriputra, I remember that, in the past, I was able to encounter two thousand buddhas, all named Kauṇḍinya. At that time, I was always a wheel-turning sage king, who made offerings of everything to the

---

original Sanskrit can be problematic, the former will be rendered here in the Chinese reading; the latter, in (possible) Sanskrit reconstruction.

10   **Guangming** (*Kōmyō* 光明): Sanskrit uncertain.

11   **Shanwang** (*San'ō* 山王): Sanskrit uncertain.

Shangba (*Jōhatsu* 上八): Sanskrit uncertain.

12   **Huashang** (*Kejō* 華上): Possibly translating Sanskrit "Padmottara."

13   **Weide** (*Itoku* 威德): Sanskrit uncertain.

buddhas, but none of them gave me a prediction, because I was acquisitive.

Śāriputra, I remember that, in the past, I encountered nine thousand buddhas, all named Kāśyapa. I made offerings of the four necessities to the buddhas and their disciples, but none of them gave me a prediction, because I was acquisitive.

Śāriputra, I remember that, in the past, during ten thousand kalpas, no buddha appeared. At that time, for the first five hundred kalpas, there were ninety thousand *pratyeka-buddhas*. Throughout my lives, making offerings to all of them of robes, food and drink, bedding, and medicine, I venerated and praised them. For the next five hundred kalpas, again making offerings of the four necessities to eighty-four thousand *koṭis* of *pratyeka-buddhas*, I venerated and praised them.

Śāriputra, after those thousand kalpas had passed, there were no more *pratyeka-buddhas*. At that time, I died in Jambudvīpa and was born in the Brahmā world as the Great Brahmā King.[14] In this way, revolving for five hundred kalpas, I was continuously born in the Brahmā world as the Great Brahmā King, and was not born in Jambudvīpa. After these five hundred kalpas had passed, I descended to birth in Jambudvīpa, where I ruled over Jambudvīpa. When my life ended, I was born in the Heavens of the Four Deva Kings.[15] When my life ended there, I was born in the Trāyastriṃśa Heaven, as Śakrodevānām Indra.[16] Revolving in this way, after completing five hundred kalpas, I was born in Jambudvīpa; and, after completing five hundred kalpas there, I was born in the Brahmā world as the Great Brahmā King.

Śāriputra, for nine thousand kalpas, I was born only once in Jambudvīpa; for nine thousand kalpas, I was born only in the heavens. During the kalpa ending fires, I was born in the Heaven of Brilliant Sound.[17] Once the [next] world was formed, I was again born in the Brahmā world. In my births during the nine thousand kalpas, I was never born among humans. Śāriputra, for these nine thousand kalpas, there were no buddhas or *pratyeka-buddhas*, and many living beings fell into the evil paths.

---

14 **Brahmā world** (*Bonse* 梵世): S. *brahma-loka*, the heavens of the first dhyāna in the realm of form (*shikikai* 色界; S. *rūpa-loka*), ruled by the deva king Brahmā.

15 **Heavens of the Four Deva Kings** (*Shitennō ten* 四天王天): Abodes on Mt. Sumeru of the devas guarding the four cardinal directions.

16 **Trāyastriṃśa Heaven** (*Tōri ten* 忉利天): Abode at the top of Mt. Sumeru inhabited by thirty-three devas and ruled by the deva Śakra (or Indra).

17 **Heaven of Brilliant Sound** (*Kōonten* 光音天): Ābhāsvara, highest of the heavens of the second dhyāna, the denizens of which are above the conflagration at the end of a kalpa.

T5. Offerings to the Buddhas *Kuyō shobutsu* 供養諸佛 139

Śāriputra, after the ten thousand kalpas had passed, a buddha appeared in the world. His name was Pushou, a Tathāgata, Worthy of Offerings, Perfectly Knowing, Perfected in Wisdom and Conduct, Well-Gone, Knower of the World, Unsurpassed, Tamer of Persons, Teacher of Devas and Humans, World-Honored Buddha.[18] At that time, when my life in the Brahmā world ended, I was born in Jambudvīpa as a wheel-turning sage king named Gongtian.[19] The lifespan of humans was ninety thousand years. Throughout my lifespan, for those ninety thousand years, I made offerings of all the daily necessities to that buddha, as well as his ninety *koṭis* of bhikṣus, for the sake of my quest for *anuttara-samyak-saṃbodhi*. But that Buddha Pushou did not give me the prediction, "In the future, you shall become a buddha." Why not? At that time, I was unable to penetrate the real marks of the dharmas and was attached to views of self and acquisition.

Śāriputra, during this kalpa, one hunded buddhas appeared in the world, each with a different name. I was always a wheel-turning sage king, who throughout his life made offerings to them and their disciples, for the sake of my quest for *anuttara-samyak-saṃbodhi*. But none of those buddhas gave me a prediction, "In the future, you shall become a buddha," because I was acquisitive.

Śāriputra, I remember that, in the past, during the seven hundredth *asaṃkyeya-kalpa*, I was able to encounter a thousand buddhas, all named Jambūnada. Throughout my lives, I made offerings of the four necessities, but they did not give me a prediction, because I was acquisitive.

Śāriputra, I remember that, in the past, in the seven hundredth *asaṃkhyeya-kalpa*, I was able to encounter six million two hundred thousand buddhas, all named Jianyiqieyi.[20] At that time, I was a wheel-turning sage king, who throughout his lives made donations of all the necessities of daily life to them and their disciples; but they did not give me a prediction, because I was acquisitive.

Śāriputra, I remember that, in the past, again in the seven hundredth *asaṃkhyeya-kalpa*, I was able to encounter eighty-four buddhas, all named Dixiang.[21] At that time, I was always a wheel-turning sage king, who throughout his lives made donations of all the necessities of daily

---

18 **Pushou** (*Fushu* 普守): Sanskrit uncertain. The list, beginning with "tathāgata" (*nyorai* 如來), following this name is the standard set of ten epithets of a buddha.

19 **Gongtian** (*Kuten* 共天): Sanskrit uncertain.

20 **Jianyiqieyi** (*Ken'issaigi* 見一切儀): The sūtra reads 義 for 儀 here; probably Sanskrit "Sarvārthadarśa."

21 **Dixiang** (*Taisō* 帝相): Likely Sanskrit "Indradhvaja."

140 DŌGEN'S *SHŌBŌGENZŌ* VOLUME VI

life to them and their disciples; but they did not give me a prediction, because I was acquisitive.

Śāriputra, I remember that, in the past, again in the seven hundredth asaṃkhyeya-kalpa, I was able to encounter fifteen buddhas, all named Riming.[22] *At that time, I was a wheel-turning sage king, who throughout his lives made donations of all the necessities of daily life to them and their disciples; but they did not give me a prediction, because I was acquisitive.*

Śāriputra, I remember that, in the past, again in the seven hundredth asaṃkhyeya-kalpa, I was able to encounter sixty-two buddhas, all named Shanji.[23] *At that time, I was a wheel-turning sage king, who throughout his lives made donations of all the necessities of daily life to them and their disciples; but they did not give me a prediction, because I was acquisitive.*

[T5:6] {2:348}

如是展轉、乃至見定光佛、乃得無生忍。即記我言、汝於來世、過阿僧祇劫、當得作佛、號釋迦牟尼如來・應供・正遍知・明行足・善逝・世間解・無上士・調御丈夫・天人師・佛世尊。

In this way, I revolved until I met Buddha Dingguang and then attained acceptance of non-arising.[24] *Whereupon, he gave me a prediction, saying, "In the future, after asaṃkhyeya-kalpas have passed, you shall become a buddha named Śākyamuni, a Tathāgata, Worthy of Offerings, Perfectly Knowing, Perfected in Wisdom and Conduct, Well-Gone, Knower of the World, Unsurpassed, Tamer of Persons, Teacher of Devas and Humans, World-Honored Buddha.*

[T5:7] {2:351}

はじめ三十億の釋迦牟尼佛にあいたてまつりて、盡形壽供養よりこのかた、定光如來にあふたてまつらせたまふまで、みなつねに轉輪聖王のみとして、盡形壽供養したてまつりまします。轉輪聖王、おほくは八萬已上なるべし。あるひは九萬歳、八萬歳の壽量、そのあひだの一切樂具の供養なり。定光佛とは、燃燈如來なり。三十億の釋迦牟尼佛にあひたてまつりまします。佛本行集經、ならびに佛藏經の説、おなじ。

---

22 **Riming** (*Nichimyō* 日明): Sanskrit uncertain.

23 **Shanji** (*Zenjaku* 善寂): Sanskrit uncertain.

24 **In this way, I revolved** (*nyoze tenden* 如是展轉): Continuing to quote the *Fozang jing* 佛藏經, at T.653.15:797c29-798a4.

acceptance of non-arising (*mushō nin* 無生忍): S. *anutpattika-dharma-kṣānti*; realization of the emptiness of all dharmas, often said to occur on the seventh stage (S. *bhūmi*) of the bodhisattva path and assure non-regression (*futai* 不退; S. *avaivartika*) from the goal of buddhahood.

T5. Offerings to the Buddhas *Kuyō shobutsu* 供養諸佛   141

After encountering thirty *koṭis* of Śākyamuni Buddhas and making offerings to them throughout his lives until he encountered Tathāgata Dingguang, always taking the body of a wheel-turning sage king, he made offerings throughout his lives. [The lifespans of] wheel-turning sage kings are mostly over eighty thousand. During lifespans of ninety thousand years or eighty thousand years, he made offerings of all the daily necessities. The Buddha Dingguang is Tathāgata Randeng [Dīpaṃkara]. His encountering thirty *koṭis* of Śākyamuni Buddhas is the same in the *Sūtra of the Collection of the Past Acts of the Buddha* and the *Buddha Treasury Sūtra*.

[T5:8] {2:352}
釋迦菩薩、初阿僧企耶、逢事供養七萬五千佛。最初名釋迦牟尼、最後名寶髻。第二阿僧企耶、逢事供養七萬六千佛。最初即寶髻、最後名燃燈。第三阿僧企耶、逢事供養七萬七千佛。最初即燃燈、最後名勝觀。於修相異熟業、九十一劫中、逢事供養六佛。最初即勝觀、最後名迦葉波。

The bodhisattva Śākya,

In the first asaṃkhyeya, encountered, served, and made offerings to seventy-five thousand buddhas.[25] The first was named Śākyamuni; the last was named Baoji.[26] In the second asaṃkhyeya, he encountered, served, and made offerings to seventy-six thousand buddhas. The first was Baoji; the last was named Randeng [Dīpaṃkara]. In the third asaṃkhyeya, he encountered, served, and made offerings to seventy-seven thousand buddhas. The first was Randeng; the last was named Shengguan.[27] During ninety-one kalpas of cultivating the deeds that would ripen as the marks, he encountered, served, and made offerings to six buddhas.[28] The first was Shengguan; the last was named Kāśyapa.

[T5:9]
おほよそ三大阿僧祇劫の供養諸佛、はじめ身命より、國城・妻子・七寶・男女等、さらにをしむところなし、凡慮のおよぶところにあらず。あるひは黄金の粟を白銀の塊にもりみて、あるひは七寶の粟を金銀の塊にもりみて供養したてまつる。あるひは小豆、あるいは水・陸の華、あるひは梅

---

25 **In the first asaṃkhyeya** (*sho asōgiya* 初阿僧企耶): Quoting the *Mahāvibhāṣā* (*Da piposha ron* 大毘婆沙論, T.1545.27:892c5-11). "*Asaṃkhyeya*" here refers to the three "incalculable" kalpas of the Bodhisattva's path to buddhahood.

26 **Baoji** (*Hōkei* 寶髻): S. Ratnaśikhin.

27 **Shengguan** (*Shōkan* 勝觀): S. Vipaśyin; first of the seven buddhas of the past, of which Kāśyapa was the sixth. See Supplementary Notes, s.v. "Seven buddhas."

28   **deeds that would ripen as the marks** (*sō ijuku gō* 相異熟業): I.e., karma that would result in the development of the thirty-two marks (*sō* 相; S. *lakṣana*) of greatness adorning a buddha's body, the final task of the bodhisattva path, said to take one hundred great kalpas.

142 DŌGEN'S *SHŌBŌGENZŌ* VOLUME VI

檀・沈水香等を供養したてまつり、あるひは五茎の青蓮華を、五百の金錢
をもて買取して、燃燈佛を供養したてまつりまします、あるひは鹿皮の
衣、これを供養したてまつる。

In sum, in his offerings to the buddhas over the three great innumerable kalpas, he begrudged nothing whatsoever — beginning with his own bodies and lives, through his countries and cities, wives and children, seven treasures, male and female [servants], and so on — beyond the common person's reckoning.[29] He would make offerings of pieces of gold piled high in silver bowls or the seven treasures piled high in gold and silver bowls.[30] Or he made offerings of small beans, or of the flowers of water and land, or of incense of sandalwood or aloes, and the like; or, buying five blue lotuses with five hundred coins, he made offerings to Buddha Randeng; or he made offerings of a deerskin robe.[31]

---

29 **his own bodies and lives** (*shinmyō* 身命): This and the following in this list of offerings may reflect a passage in the *Lotus Sūtra* (quoted in "Shōbōgenzō hotsu bodai shin" 正法眼藏發菩提心), in which Buddha Śākyamuni speaks of the offerings he made when he was born as kings in his incalculable former lives (*Miaofa lianhua jing* 妙法蓮華經, T.262.9:34b28-29):

象馬七珍國城妻子奴婢僕從頭目髓腦身肉手足。

Elephants and horses, the seven treasures, countries and cities, wives and children, male and female servants, my heads and my eyes, my marrow and my brains, the flesh of my bodies, my hands and feet.

30 **pieces of gold** (*ōgon no zoku* 黃金の粟): Likely reflecting a fixed expression for precious offerings; see, e.g., *Sifen lü* 四分律, T.1428.22:791a8:

金鉢盛滿銀粟。銀鉢盛滿金粟。

Golden bowls piled high with pieces of silver; silver bowls piled high with pieces of gold.

Or *Dazhidu lun* 大智度論, T.1509.25:142c6-8:

八萬四千金鉢盛滿銀粟。銀鉢盛金粟。琉璃鉢盛頗梨粟。頗梨鉢盛琉璃粟。

Eighty-four thousand golden bowls piled high with pieces of silver; silver bowls filled with pieces of gold; *vaiḍūrya* bowls filled with pieces of crystal; crystal bowls filled with pieces of *vaiḍūrya*.

31 **small beans** (*shōzu* 小豆): Reference to the future Śākyamuni's offering of beans to Buddha Vipaśyin; see, e.g., *Fo benxing ji jing* 佛本行集經, T.190.3:670a25-29.

flowers of water and land (*suiriku no hana* 水陸の華): A standard offering; here, perhaps reflecting a list in the *Fo benxing ji jing* 佛本行集經 (T.190.3:733a3-7) that includes sandalwood (*sandan* 旃檀) and aloes (*jinsui* 沈水).

five blue lotuses (*gokyō no shōrenge* 五茎の青蓮華): Allusion to the story of Buddha Śākyamuni in a previous life as the Bodhisattva Māṇava, who offered five flowers to Buddha Dīpaṃkara and received a prediction of his eventual buddhahood; see, e.g., *Fo benxing ji jing* 佛本行集經, T.190.3:666c5ff; *Taizi ruiying benqi jing* 太子瑞應本起經, T.185.3:472c18ff.

deerskin robe (*rokuhi no e* 鹿皮の衣): Allusion to the story that, in a prior life, the future Śākyamuni spread out his deerskin robe and his hair for Buddha Dīpaṃkara to step on; see, e.g., *Fo benxing ji jing* 佛本行集經, T.190.3:667b27ff.

T5. Offerings to the Buddhas *Kuyō shobutsu* 供養諸佛

[T5:10]

おほよそ供佛は、諸佛の要樞にましますべきを供養したてまつるにあらず、いそぎわがいのちの存せる光陰を、むなしくすごさず供養したてまつるなり。たとひ金銀なりとも、ほとけの御ため、なにの益かあらん、たとひ香華なりとも、またほとけの御ため、なにの益かあらん。しかあれども、納受せさせたまふは、衆生をして功徳を増長せしめんための大慈大悲なり。

In sum, in making offering to the buddhas, it is not that we make offerings of what is appropriate to the significant position of the buddhas; it is that we hasten to make offerings while our life lasts, without "passing the years and months in vain."[32] What benefit to the buddhas would gold and silver be? What benefit to the buddhas would incense and flowers be? Nevertheless, their acceptance of them is an act of great compassion and great mercy that enables living beings to increase their merit.

[T5:11] {2:353}

大般涅槃經第二十二云、佛言、善男子、我念過去無量無邊那由他劫、爾時世界、名曰娑婆。有佛世尊、號釋迦牟尼如來・應供・正遍知・明行足・善逝・世間解・無上士・調御丈夫・天人師・佛世尊。爲諸大衆、宣説如是大涅槃經。我於爾時、從善友所轉、聞彼佛當爲大衆説大涅槃。我聞是已、其心歡喜、欲設供養。居貧無物。欲自賣身、薄福不售。即欲還家、路見一人、而便語言、吾欲賣身、若能買不。其人答曰、我家作業、人無堪者。汝設能爲、我當買汝。我即問言、有何作業、人無能堪。其人見答、吾有惡病、良医處藥、應當日服人肉三兩。卿若能以身肉三兩、日日見給、便當與汝金錢五枚。我時聞已、心中歡喜。我復語言、汝與我錢、暇我七日。須我事訖、便還相就。其人見答、七日不可、審能爾者、當許一日。

In the twenty-second roll of the *Nirvāṇa Sūtra*, the Buddha says,[33]

Good sons, I remember that, in the past, incalculable, limitless nayutas of kalpas ago, there was at the time a world called Sahā, where there was a world-honored one named Śākyamuni, a Tathāgata, Worthy of Offerings, Perfectly Knowing, Perfected in Wisdom and Conduct, Well-Gone, Knower of the World, Unsurpassed, Tamer of Persons, Teacher of Devas and Humans, World-Honored Buddha. For the great assemblies, he preached the Great Nirvāṇa Sūtra like this.

At that time, returning from a wise friend's place, I heard that this buddha would preach the Great Nirvāṇa for the great assembly. Upon hearing this, I rejoiced in my heart and wished to prepare offerings. Living in poverty, I had nothing; I was going to sell my own body, but

---

32 **without "passing the years and months in vain"** (*kōin o, munashiku sugosazu* 光陰を、むなしくすごさず): Japanese rendering of a verse that Dōgen will quote below, section 16.

33 ***Nirvāṇa Sūtra*** (*Daihatsu nehan kyō* 大般涅槃經): Quoting the *Da banniepan jing* 大般涅槃經, at T.374.12:497a19-b5.

unfortunately was unable to do so. As I was returning home, I met a person on the road, to whom I said, "I wish to sell my body. Could you buy it?"

The person replied, "No one could endure the work at my house. If you could, I would buy you."

So, I asked him, "What is the work that no one can endure?"

The person replied, "I have a grave illness. A good doctor has prescribed that I take three taels of human flesh daily. If you can provide me with three taels of flesh from your body every day, I'll give you five coins."

Upon hearing this, I rejoiced in my heart and said, "Give me the money and allow me seven days leave. As soon as my affairs are taken care of, I'll come back to you."

The person replied, "Seven days is impossible; if it's necessary, I can allow one day."

[T5:12]

善男子、我於爾時、即取其錢、還至佛所、頭面禮足、盡其所有、而以奉獻。然後、誠心聽受是經。我時闇鈍、雖得聞經、唯能受持一偈文句。如來證涅槃、永斷於生死。若有至心聽、常得無量樂。受是偈已、即便還至彼病人家。善男子、我時雖復日日與三兩肉、以念偈因緣故、不以爲痛。日日不癈、具滿一月。善男子、以是因緣、其病得瘥。我身平復、亦無瘡痍。我時見身具足完具、即發阿耨多羅三藐三菩提心。一偈之力、尚能如是。何況具足受持讀誦。我見此經有如是利、復倍發心、願於未來、得成佛道、字釋迦牟尼佛。善男子、以是一偈因緣力故、令我今日於大衆中、爲諸天人、具足宣説。善男子、以是因緣、是大涅槃、不可思議、成就無量無邊功德。乃是諸佛如來、甚深秘密之藏。

Good sons, at this time, I took the money, went to where the Buddha was, bowed my head at his feet, and presented him with all I had.[34] After that, I listened with sincere mind to this sūtra. At the time, I was dim-witted and, while I heard the sūtra, I was able to receive and keep the words of only one gāthā:

The Tathāgata has verified nirvāṇa,
Forever cutting off birth and death.
If you listen to him with full attention,
You will always have incalculable joy.

After receiving this gāthā, I straightaway returned to the home of the sick man. Good sons, although day after day I gave him three taels of flesh, because I remembered the gāthā, it caused me no pain. Day after day without a break, a full month passed.

---

34 **Good sons** (*zen nanshi* 善男子): Continuing to quote the *Nirvāṇa Sūtra* (*Da pannie-pan jing* 大般涅槃經, T.374.12:497b5-21).

T5. Offerings to the Buddhas *Kuyō shobutsu* 供養諸佛   145

Good sons, as a consequence of this, his illness was cured, and my own body was healed, without any wounds. At that time, upon seeing that my body was fully whole, I brought forth the mind of anuttara-samyak-sambodhi. Such is the power of a single gāthā; how much greater fully to receive and keep, read and recite [the sūtra]. Seeing that this sūtra has such benefits, I doubled my aspiration, vowing that, in the future, I would attain the way of the buddhas and be named Buddha Śākyamuni.

Good sons, it is due to the power of this one gāthā that today I am brought to this great assembly, to preach fully for the sake of devas and humans. Therefore, good sons, this Great Nirvāṇa is inconceivable and achieves incalculable, limitless merits. Thus, it is the treasury of the profound secrets of the buddhas, the tathāgatas.

[T5:13] {2:355}

そのときの賣身の菩薩は、今釋迦牟尼佛の往因なり。他經を會通すれば、初阿僧祇劫の最初、古釋迦牟尼佛を供養したてまつりましますときなり。かのときは、瓦師なり、その名を大光明と稱す。古釋迦牟尼佛ならびに諸弟子に供養するに、三種の供養をもてす、いはゆる、草座・石蜜漿・燃燈なり。そのときの發願にいはく、國土・名號・壽命・弟子、一如今釋迦牟尼佛。

The bodhisattva who sold his body at that time was a past cause of the present Buddha Śākyamuni. If we reconcile this with other scriptures, the beginning of the first *asaṃkhyeya-kalpa* was the time that he made offerings to the ancient Buddha Śākyamuni.[35] At that time, he was a tile-maker, whose name was Da Guangming.[36] In making offerings to the ancient Buddha Śākyamuni and his disciples, he gave three sorts of

---

35 **If we reconcile this with other scriptures** (*takyō o ezū sureba* 他經を會通すれば): Presumably, a reference to the passage in the *Da piposha ron* 大毘婆沙論 (T.1545.27:892c5-6) quoted above, section 8.

36 **At that time, he was a tile-maker, whose name was Da Guangming** (*kano toki wa, gashi nari, sono na o Dai Kōmyō to shōsu* かのときは、瓦師なり、その名を大光明と稱す): Likely based on a passage in the *Dazhidu lun* 大智度論 (T.1509.25:83b15-21) explaining the origin of the disciple Ānanda's name:

釋迦文佛先世作瓦師。名大光明。爾時有佛名釋迦文。弟子名舍利弗目乾連阿難。佛與弟子俱到瓦師舍一宿。爾時瓦師布施草坐燈明石蜜漿三事。供養佛及比丘僧。便發願言。我於當來老病死惱五惡之世作佛。如今佛名釋迦文。我佛弟子名亦如今佛弟子名。

In the past, Buddha Śākyamuni was a tile-maker named Da Guangming. At the time, there was a Buddha named Śākyamuni, with disciples named Śāriputra, Maudgalyāyana, and Ānanda. The Buddha and his disciples lodged together for a night at the place of the tile-maker. At that time, the tile-maker donated three things — grass seats, lamps, and rock sugar syrup. Offering them to the Buddha and the bhikṣu saṃgha, he made a vow, saying, "In the future, in the world of the five evils afflicted by old age, sickness, and death, I shall become a buddha. Like the present buddha,

146 DŌGEN'S *SHŌBŌGENZŌ* VOLUME VI

offerings: grass seats, rock sugar syrup, and lamps. At the time, he made a vow, saying, "*May my land, my name, my lifespan, and my disciples be like those of the present Buddha Śākyamuni.*"

[T5:14] {2:356}

かのときの發願、すでに今日、成就するものなり。しかあればすなはち、ほとけを供養したてまつらんとするに、その身まづし、といふことなかれ、そのいへまづし、といふことなかれ。みづから身をうりて、諸佛を供養したてまつるは、いま大師釋迦尊の正法なり、たれかこれを隨喜・歡喜したてまつらざらん。このなかに、日日に三兩の身肉を割取するぬしにあふ。善知識なりといへども、他人のたふべからざるなり。しかあれども、供佛の深志のたすくるところ、いまの功德あり。いまわれら如來の正法を聽聞する、かの往古の身肉を處分せられたるなるべし。いまの四句の偈は、五枚の金錢にかふるところにあらず。三阿僧祇一百大劫のあひだ、受生・捨生にわするることなく、彼佛是佛のところに證明せられきたりましますところ、まことに不可思議の功德あるべし。遺法の弟子、ふかく頂戴誦持すべし。如來すでに、一偈の力、なほよくかくのごとし、と宣説しします、もともおほきにふかかるべし。

The vow he made at that time is fulfilled today. Therefore, in making offerings to the buddhas, do not say you are poor; do not say your family is poor. To make offerings to the buddhas by selling one's own body is the true dharma of the present Great Master, Śākya, the Honored One: who would not delight and rejoice in it? In this [story], he encounters an employer who cuts three taels of flesh from his body day after day. Even had he been a wise friend, no one else could have endured it.[37] However, helped by his profound determination to make offerings to the Buddha, he has his present merit. Our hearing the true dharma of the Tathāgata now represents that sharing of the flesh of his body in the distant past. The four-line gāthā here is not something to be exchanged for five coins. Over the three *asaṃkyeya* and one hundred great kalpas, even while receiving lives and discarding lives, he never forgot it; attested under this buddha and that buddha, truly it must possess inconceivable merit. Disciples to whom the dharma is bequeathed should recite and retain it with the utmost respect.[38] Since the Tathāgata has declared, "such is the

---

my name shall be Śākyamuni, and my buddha disciples' names shall also be like the names of the disciples of the present buddha."

Dōgen tells this story in his *Eihei kōroku* 永平廣錄 (DZZ.3:120, no. 182) and goes on himself to make a vow to become a buddha named Śākyamuni.

37 **Even had he been a wise friend** (*zen chishiki nari to iedomo* 善知識なりといへども): I.e., "even if the employer had been his teacher."

38 **recite and retain it with the utmost respect** (*chōdai juji* 頂戴誦持): Some MS witnesses have here the more common *chōdai juji* 頂戴受持 ("receive and retain with the utmost respect").

T5. Offerings to the Buddhas *Kuyō shobutsu* 供養諸佛

147

power of a single gāthā," it must have especially great profundity.[39]

[T5:15]

法華經云、若人於塔廟・寶像及画像、以華香・旛蓋、敬心而供養。若使人作樂、擊鼓吹角唄、簫笛・琴・箜篌、琵琶・鐃・銅鈸、如是衆妙音、盡持以供養、或以歡喜心、歌唄頌佛德、乃至一小音、皆已成佛道。若人散亂心、乃至以一華、供養於画像、漸見無數佛。或有人禮拜、或復但合掌、乃至舉一手、或復少低頭、以此供養像、漸見無量佛、自成無上道、廣度無數衆。

In the *Lotus Sūtra*, it is said,[40]

Those who, to stūpa shrines,
To precious statues and painted images,
With reverent thoughts make offerings
Of flowers and incense, banners and canopies;
Those who have others perform music —
Beating on drums and blowing on horns and conches,[41]
Pipes and flutes, playing zithers and harps,
Lutes, gongs, and cymbals,
And all such marvelous sounds as these —
That they bring as offerings;
Or who with joyful minds,
Sing praises of the Buddha's virtues,
Even for a single small sound,
Will all have attained the way of the buddhas.
Those with distracted minds who,
Even with a single flower,
Make offerings to a painted image
Will eventually see innumerable buddhas.
Those who pay obeisance,
Or simply join their palms,
Even raising just a single hand,
Or slightly lowering their heads,
Thereby making offerings to an image,
Will eventually see incalculable buddhas,
Will themselves attain the unsurpassed way,
And everywhere deliver innumerable multitudes.

---

39 **"such is the power of a single gāthā"** (*ichige no chikara, nao yoku kaku no gotoshi* 一偈の力、なほよくかくのごとし): A Japanese translation of the line in the *Nirvāṇa Sūtra* (*Da banniepan jing* 大般涅槃經, T.374.12:497b15-16) quoted above, section 12.

40 ***Lotus Sūtra*** (*Hokke kyō* 法華經): Quoting the *Miaofa lianhua jing* 妙法蓮華經, T.262.9:9a10-22.

41 **horns and conches** (*kakubai* 角唄): Reading *bai* 貝 ("shell") for *bai* 唄 ("chant"), as in the *Sūtra* (T.262.9:9a12).

148　　DŌGEN'S *SHŌBŌGENZŌ* VOLUME VI

[T5:16] {2:357}

これすなはち、三世諸佛の頂顙なり、眼睛なり。見賢思齊の猛利精進すべ
し、いたづらに光陰をわたることなかれ。石頭無際大師云、光陰莫虚度。
かくのごときの功德、みな成佛す。過去・現在・未來、おなじかるべし。さ
らに二あり三あるべからず。供養佛の因によりて、作佛の果を成ずるこ
と、かくのごとし。

This is the crown of the head, the eyes, of the buddhas of the three
times. We should vigorously strive to "*meet someone good and think
to equal him*"; do not pass the years and months in vain.[42] Great Master
Wuji of Shitou said, "*Don't pass the years and months in vain.*"[43] [Those
with] merit like this, all attain buddhahood. It is the same in past, present, and future; there are no second or third ways. Realizing the effect
of becoming a buddha based on the cause of making offerings to the
buddhas is like this.

[T5:17]

龍樹祖師曰、如求佛果、讚歎一偈、稱一南謨、燒一捻香、奉獻一華。如是
小行、必得作佛。

> The Ancestral Master Nāgārjuna said,[44]
>
> *If you seek the fruit of buddhahood, sing one gāthā in praise, chant one
> "namas," burn one pinch of incense, offer one flower.*[45] *By such minor
> acts, we inevitably become buddhas.*

[T5:18] {2:358}

これひとり龍樹祖師菩薩の所説といふとも、歸命したてまつるべし。いか
にいはんや大師釋迦牟尼佛の説を、龍樹祖師、正傳、擧揚しましますとこ

42　**"meet someone good and think to equal him"** (*ken ken shi sei* 見賢思齊): A
common saying, quoted elsewhere in the *Shōbōgenzō*, from the *Lunyu* 論語 4
(KR.1h0005.002.14b):

見賢思齊焉。見不賢而內自省也。

When you meet someone good, think to equal him; when you meet someone not
good, then look within oneself.

43　**Great Master Wuji of Shitou** (*Sekitō Musai daishi* 石頭無際大師): I.e., Shitou
Xiqian 石頭希遷 (700-791), in the final lines of his *Cantong qi* 參同契 (*Jingde chuandeng lu* 景德傳燈錄, T.2076.51:459b20-21):

謹白參玄人、光陰莫虚度。

To those who study the dark, I submit,
Don't pass the years and months in vain.

44　**The Ancestral Master Nāgārjuna** (*Ryūju soshi* 龍樹祖師): Dōgen is here quoting the *Zhiguan fuxing zhuan hongjue* 止觀輔行傳弘決, by Zhanran 湛然 (711-782)
(T.1912.46:252a27-29), which cites a passage of the *Dazhidu lun* 大智度論, traditionally
attributed to Nāgārjuna — most likely, the passage (in fascicle 7) that Dōgen himself will
quote in section 19, below.

45　**chant one "*namas*"** (*shō ichi namo* 稱一南謨): I.e., a salutation to a deity; "hail."

T5. Offerings to the Buddhas *Kuyō shobutsu* 供養諸佛 149

ろなり。われらいま佛道の寶山にのぼり、佛道の寶海にいりて、さいはひ
にたからをとれる、もともよろこぶべし。曠劫の供佛のちからなるべし。
必得作佛、うたがふべからず、決定せるものなり。釋迦牟尼佛の所説、か
くのごとし。

Even if this is something said only by the Bodhisattva, the Ancestral
Master Nāgārjuna, we should take refuge in it; how much more, then,
what was said by the Great Master, Buddha Śākyamuni, that was directly transmitted to and taken up by the Ancestral Master Nāgārjuna. We
should greatly rejoice that, having climbed the treasure mountain of the
way of the buddhas and entered the treasure ocean of the way of the buddhas, we have now fortunately gained the treasure. It must be the power
of offerings to the buddhas over vast kalpas. We should not doubt that
"*we inevitably become buddhas*"; it is something certain. Such is what
Buddha Śākyamuni has preached.

[T5:19]

復次、有小因大果・小緣大報。如求佛道、讚一偈、一稱南無佛、燒一捻
香、必得作佛。何況聞知諸法實相、不生不滅、不不生不不滅、而行因緣
業、亦不失。

> *Again, there are small causes with great effects and small conditions
> with great consequences: in seeking the way of the buddhas, if we sing
> one gāthā, chant "namo-buddhāya" once, burn one pinch of incense,
> we inevitably become buddhas.[46] How much more, then, if, hearing
> that the real marks of the dharmas do not arise or cease, do not not
> arise or not not cease, we still perform the deeds that are the causes and
> conditions, they will not be lost.*

[T5:20]

世尊の所説、かくのごとくあきらかなるを、龍樹祖師、したしく正傳しま
しますなり。誠諦の金言、正傳の相承あり。たとひ龍樹祖師の説なりと
も、餘師の説に比すべからず。世尊の所示を、正傳流布しましますにあふ
ことをえたり、もともよろこぶべし。これらの聖教を、みだりに東土の凡
師の虚説に比量することなかれ。

Such clarity of what the World-Honored One taught was directly transmitted personally by the Ancestral Master Nāgārjuna. The golden words
of truth have an inheritance of direct transmission. While they are said by
the Ancestral Master Nāgārjuna, they should not be compared to what is
said by other masters. We should greatly rejoice that we have been able to
encounter the direct transmission and dissemination of what was taught by
the World-Honored One. Do not recklessly compare these sacred teachings
to the empty theories of the commoner teachers of the Land of the East.

---

46 **Again, there are small causes with great effects** (*fukuji, u shōin daika* 復次、有小因
大果): Quoting (with slight variation) the *Dazhidu lun* 大智度論 (T.1509.25:112c19-22).

150 DŌGEN'S *SHŌBŌGENZŌ* VOLUME VI

[T5:21] {2:359}

龍樹祖師曰、復次諸佛、恭敬法故、供養於法、以法爲師。何以故。三世諸
佛、皆以諸法實相爲師。問曰、何以不自供養身中法、而供養他法。答曰、
隨世間法。如比丘欲供養法寶、不自供養身中法、而供養餘持法・知法・解
法者。佛亦如是。雖身中有法、而供養餘佛法。問曰、如佛不求福德、何以
故供養。答曰、佛從無量阿僧祇劫中、修諸功德、常行諸善。不但求報、敬
功德故、而作供養。

The Ancestral Master Nāgārjuna said,[47]

Furthermore, because the buddhas revere the dharma, they make offerings to the dharma and take the dharma as their teacher. Why is this? The Buddhas of the three times all take the real marks of the dharmas as their teacher.

Question: Why do they not make offerings to the dharma within themselves, but make offerings to the dharma of others?

Answer: They accord with worldly practice. Just as a bhikṣu wishing to make offerings to the dharma treasure does not make offerings to the dharma within himself but makes offerings to another who keeps the dharma, knows the dharma, and understands the dharma, so it is with the buddhas: although they have the dharma within themselves, they make offerings to the dharma of other buddhas.

Question: Since buddhas do not seek merit, why do they make offerings?

Answer: Throughout incalculable asaṃkheya-kalpas, the buddhas cultivate merit, always practicing good deeds. They make offerings, not merely to seek recompense, but because they revere merit.

[T5:22]

如佛在時、有一盲比丘。眼無所見、而以手縫衣。時針衽脱。便言、誰愛
福德、爲我衽針。是時佛、到其所語比丘、我是愛福德人、爲汝衽來。是
比丘、識佛聲、疾起著衣、禮佛足、白佛言、佛功德已滿、云何言愛福德。
佛報言、我雖功德已滿、我深知功德恩・功德果報・功德力。令我於一切衆生
中、得最第一、由此功德、是故我愛。佛爲此比丘、讚功德已、次爲隨意説
法。是比丘、得法眼淨、肉眼更明。

For example, when the Buddha was present, there was a blind bhikṣu.[48] *Though his eyes could not see, he sewed his robes by hand. Once, when the thread slipped out of his needle, he said, "Who loves merit and will thread my needle for me?"*[49]

---

47 **The Ancestral Master Nāgārjuna** (*Ryūju soshi* 龍樹祖師): Again, quoting the *Dazhidu lun* 大智度論 (T.1509.25:128c26-129a6).

48 **For example** (*nyo* 如): Continuing the quotation from the *Dazhidu lun* 大智度論 (T.1509.25:129a6-15).

49 **the thread slipped out of his needle** (*shin jin datsu* 針衽脱): Reading *jin* 衽 ("lapel") as a variant of *jin* 紝 ("thread").

T5. Offerings to the Buddhas *Kuyō shobutsu* 供養諸佛   151

Just at that time, the Buddha arrived at his place and said to the bhikṣu, "I'm a person who loves merit and will thread your needle for you."

Recognizing the Buddha's voice, this bhikṣu immediately stood up, donned his robes, made obeisance at the feet of the Buddha, and addressed the Buddha, saying, "The Buddha's merit is already replete. Why do you say that you love merit?"

The Buddha responded, "While my merit is already replete, I profoundly understand the beneficence of merit, the rewards of merit, the power of merit.[50] That I have attained the prime state among all living beings is due to this merit. For this reason, I love it."

After the buddha had finished praising merit for this bhikṣu, he gave him a spontaneous talk on the dharma. This bhikṣu attained purification of the dharma eye, and his physical eyes also became clear.

[T5:23] {2:360}
この因縁、むかしは先師の室にして夜話をきく。のちには智論の文にむかうてこれを撿挍す。傳法祖師の示誨、あきらかにして遺落せず。この文、智度論第十にあり。諸佛かならず諸法實相を大師としましますこと、あきらけし。釋尊また、諸佛の常法を證しまします。

This episode, I heard long ago in an evening talk in the rooms of my former master.[51] Afterwards, I checked it against the text of the *Zhi lun*.[52] The teachings of the ancestral master who transmitted the dharma are clear, with nothing missing. This passage is in *Zhidu lun* 10. It is clear that the buddhas always take "the real marks of the dharmas" as their great master. Śākya, the Honored One, verifies the constant norm of the buddhas.

[T5:24]
いはゆる諸法實相を大師とする、といふは、佛・法・僧の三寶を供養恭敬したてまつるなり。諸佛は、無量阿僧祇劫、そこばくの功德善根を積集して、さらにその報をもとめず、ただ功德を恭敬して供養しましますなり。佛果菩提のくらいにいたりてなほ小功德を愛し、盲比丘のために衹針しします。佛果の功德をあきらめんとおもはば、いまの因縁、まさしく消息なり。

"To take 'the real marks of the dharmas' as one's great master" means to make offerings and revere the three treasures of buddha, dharma, and saṃgha. Over incalculable *asaṃkheya-kalpas*, the buddhas have accu-

---

50 **beneficence of merit** (*kudoku on* 功德恩): Some versions, both of the source and our text, read here the more likely "causes of merit" (*kudoku in* 功德因).

51 **my former master** (*senshi* 先師): I.e., Dōgen's teacher, Tiantong Rujing 天童如淨 (1162-1227).

52 ***Zhi lun*** (*Chi ron* 智論): I.e., the *Dazhidu lun* 大智度論. Some versions read *Chido ron* 智度論 here.

152 DŌGEN'S *SHŌBŌGENZŌ* VOLUME VI

mulated the good roots of so much merit; without further seeking the recompense for it, they make offerings simply out of reverence for merit. Having reached the stage of bodhi, the fruit of buddhahood, he still loves minor merit and threads the needle for the blind bhikṣu.[53] If we wish to understand clearly the merit of the fruit of buddhahood, the present episode truly conveys its state.

[T5:25] {2:361}

しかあればすなはち、佛果菩提の功德、諸法實相の道理、いまのよにある凡夫の、おもふがごとくにはあらざるなり。いまの凡夫のおもふところは、造惡の、諸法實相ならんとおもふ、有所得のみ、佛果菩提ならんとおもふ。かくのごとくの邪見は、たとひ八萬劫をしるといふとも、いまだ本劫本見、末劫末見をのがれず、いかでか唯佛與佛の究盡しましますところの諸法實相を究盡することあらん。ゆえいかむ、となれば、唯佛與佛の究盡しましますところ、これ諸法實相なるがゆえなり。

Thus, the merit of bodhi, the fruit of buddhahood, and the truth of "the real marks of the dharmas" are not like what common people today think. Common people today think that committing evil could be "the real marks of the dharmas," think that bodhi, the fruit of buddhahood, is precisely something to be acquired.[54] False views like these, though they know eighty thousand kalpas, do not escape *past views of past kalpas, future views of future kalpas*; how could they exhaustively investigate "the real marks of the dharmas" exhaustively investigated by "*only buddhas with buddhas*"?[55] Why is this? Because what is exhaustively investigated by "*only buddhas with buddhas*" is "the real marks of the dharmas."

* * * * *

53 **stage of bodhi, the fruit of buddhahood** (*bukka bodai no kurai* 佛果菩提のくらい): I.e., *anuttara-samyak-saṃbodhi*, the unsurpassed awakening of a buddha.

54 **bodhi, the fruit of buddhahood, is precisely something to be acquired** (*ushotoku nomi, bukka bodai naran* 有所得のみ、佛果菩提ならん): Recalling the warnings against acquisitiveness (*ushotoku* 有所得) in the *Fo benxing ji jing* 佛本行集經 quoted above, section 5.

55 **eighty thousand kalpas** (*hachiman kō* 八萬劫): A standard term for a virtually unlimited period of time.

past views of past kalpas, future views of future kalpas (*hongō honken, matsugō makken* 本劫本見、末劫末見): I.e., the false views of non-Buddhist teachers, often said to be sixty-two in number. Although variously defined, "past views of past kalpas" are typically taken as referring to "eternalist" views (*jōken* 常見) of the past, while "future views of future kalpas" are "annihilationist" views (*danken* 斷見) of the future.

"the real marks of the dharmas" exhaustively investigated by "only buddhas with buddhas" (*yui butsu yo butsu no gūjin shimashimasu tokoro no shohō jissō* 唯佛與佛の究盡しましますところの諸法實相): From a line in the *Lotus Sūtra*; see Supplementary Notes, s.v. "Only buddhas with buddhas can exhaustively investigate the real marks of the dharmas."

T5. Offerings to the Buddhas *Kuyō shobutsu* 供養諸佛

[T5:26]

おほよそ供養に十種あり。いはゆる、一者身供養。二者支提供養。三者現前供養。四者不現前供養。五者自作供養。六者他作供養。七者財物供養。八者勝供養。九者無染供養。十者至處道供養。

Broadly speaking, there are ten types of offering:[56]

1) Offering to the body; 2) offering to a caitya; 3) offering to what is present; 4) offering to what is not present; 5) offering of one's own; 6) offering of another; 7) offering of valuables; 8) superior offering; 9) undefiled offering; 10) offering on the path to the destination.

[T5:27]

このなかの第一の身供養とは、於佛色身、而設供養、名身供養。

On the first of these, "offering to the body":[57]

To make an offering to a buddha's physical body is called "offering to the body."

[T5:28]

第二、供佛靈廟、名支提供養。僧祇律云、有舍利者、名爲塔婆。無舍利者、説爲支提。或云、通名支提。又梵云塔婆、復稱偸婆。此翻方墳、亦言靈廟。阿含言支徵。

On the second:[58]

An offering to a sacred shrine is called "offering to a caitya." In the Mahāsāṃghika Vinaya, it is said, "Where there is a śarīra, it is called a 'stūpa'; where there is no śarīra, it is spoken of as a 'caitya.'"

It is also said, "It is generically called a 'caitya.'"[59] *Again [it is said],*

---

56 **ten types of offering** (*kuyō ni jisshu* 供養に十種): The following discussion of the ten types is drawn from the *Dasheng yi zhang* 大乘義章, by Jingying Huiyuan 淨影慧遠 (523-592) (T.1851.44:742a16-20), which itself cites the *Pusa dichi jing* 菩薩地持經 (T.1581.30:925c4-8). These ten types represent the first of a twofold discussion of offering in the *Dasheng yi zhang* — that of the nature of the offering; the second, on the six types of mind (or thought) with which the offering is to be made, follows below, in section 46.

57 **first of these** (*kono naka no daiichi* このなかの第一): Continuing the citation of the *Dasheng yi zhang* 大乘義章 (T.1851.44:742a21).

58 **second** (*daini* 第二): Continuing the citation of the *Dasheng yi zhang* 大乘義章 (T.1851.44:742a21-24), which cites the *Mahāsāṃghika-vinaya* (*Mohe sengqi lü* 摩訶僧祇律; T.1425.22:498b20-21).

59 **"It is generically called a 'caitya'"** (*tsūmyō shidai* 通名支提): Based on the line in the *Dasheng yi zhang* 大乘義章 (T.1851.44:742a23-24):

地持論中通名支提。

In the *Dichi jing*, it is generically called a "caitya."

(Likely a reference to the *Pusa dichi jing* 菩薩地持經 at T.1581.30:925c9-10.)

154 DŌGEN'S *SHŌBŌGENZŌ* VOLUME VI

"In Sanskrit, it is called '*tapo*,' or '*toupo*,' translated here [i.e., in China] 'square tumulus,' and also 'sacred shrine.'"[60] In the *āgamas*, it is called "*zhizheng*."[61]

[T5:29] {2:362}

あるひは塔婆と稱し、あるひは支提と稱する、おなじきににたれども、南嶽思大禪師の法華懺法にいはく、一心敬禮、十方世界、舍利尊像、支提妙塔、多寶如來、舍身寶塔。

To call it "stūpa" or call it "caitya" appears to be the same; but, in the *Lotus Repentence Ritual* of the Great Chan Master Nanyue Si, it is said,[62]

> Wholehearted adoration
> To the *śarīra* and icons,
> The caityas and wondrous stūpas,
> Throughout worlds in the ten directions;
> To the jeweled stūpa with the whole body
> Of Tathāgata Prabhūtaratna.[63]

---

60   **"In Sanskrit, it is called '*tapo*,' or '*toupo*'"** (*Bon un tōba, fuku shō tōba* 梵云塔婆、復稱偸婆): A sentence from the *Miaofa lianhua jing wenju* 妙法蓮華經文句 by Zhiyi 智顗 (538-597) (T.1718.34:112c20-22). The terms "*tapo*" 塔婆 and "*toupo*" 偸婆 represent Chinese transliterations of the Sanskrit "stūpa" (or, in the latter case, perhaps of a Prakrit "*thūpa*").

61   **In the *āgamas*, it is called "*zhizheng*"** (*Agon gon shichō* 阿含言支徵): Again, from Zhiyi's *Miaofa lianhua jing wenju* 妙法蓮華經文句 (T.1718.34:112c22):

阿含明四支徵。

The *āgamas* explain the four *zhizheng*.

The rather uncommon term *zhizheng* 支徵, seemingly a transliteration of "*caitya*," does not occur in the extant *āgama* texts. Rather, Zhiyi may have had in mind here the *Ayuwang jing* 阿育王經 (T.2043.50:153b07-08):

摩訶迦葉以神力往四支徵、以第一恭敬禮拜供養。

By means of his spiritual powers, Mahākāśyapa visited the four *zhizheng*, where, with the utmost reverence he paid obeisance and made offerings.

A note in this text identifies the four as the sacred sites (usually identified as "the four stūpas" [*shitō* 四塔]) associated with the Buddha's birth, awakening, preaching, and nirvāṇa.

62   **Lotus Repentence Ritual of the Great Chan Master Nanyue Si** (*Nangaku Shi Daizenji no Hokke senbō* 南嶽思大禪師の法華懺法): A repentance ritual text based on the *Lotus Sūtra*, usually thought to be authored by Zhiyi 智顗 (538-597) but here attributed to Zhiyi's teacher, the famed early Tiantai teacher, Nanyue Huisi 南嶽慧思 (515-575). The quotation occurs at *Fahua chanfa* 法華懺法, T.1941.46:952a5-6.

63   **jeweled stūpa with the whole body of Tathāgata Prabhūtaratna** (*Tahō nyorai, shashin hōtō* 多寶如來、舍身寶塔): The stūpa of Prabhūtaratna famously appears in Chapter 11 of the *Lotus Sūtra*. The English "whole body" reflects the Chinese orginal, which reads *quanshen* 全身, rather than the *shashin* 舍身 of Kawamura's MS.

T5. Offerings to the Buddhas *Kuyō shobutsu* 供養諸佛

155

[T5:30]

あきらかに支提と妙塔とは、舍利・尊像と別なるがごとし。

Clearly, "caitya" and "wondrous stūpa," "*śarīra*" and "icon" would seem to be different.

[T5:31]

僧祇律第三十三云、塔法者、佛住拘薩羅國遊行時、有婆羅門耕地。見世尊
行過、持牛杖拄地禮佛。世尊見已、便發微笑。諸比丘白佛、何因緣故笑、
唯願欲聞。便告諸比丘、是婆羅門、今禮二世尊。諸比丘白佛言、何等二
佛。佛告比丘、禮我當其杖下、有迦葉佛塔。諸比丘白佛、願見迦葉佛塔。
佛告比丘、汝從此婆羅門、索土塊扞是地。諸比丘、即便索之。時婆羅門便
與之、得已。爾時世尊、即現出迦葉佛七寶塔、高一由延、面廣半由延。婆
羅門見已、即便白佛言、世尊、我姓迦葉、是我迦葉塔。爾時世尊、即於彼
家、作迦葉佛塔。諸比丘白佛言、世尊、我得授泥土不。佛言、得授。即時
説偈言、眞金百千擔、持用行布施、不如一團泥、敬心治佛塔。

In the *Mahāsāṃghika Vinaya 33*, it is said,[64]

On the procedure for stūpas. The Buddha was residing in the Land of Kośala; while traveling, he came upon a brahman tilling his land.[65] Seeing the Buddha passing by, he plunged his cattle prod into the earth and did obeisance to the Buddha. Seeing this, the World-Honored One smiled. The bhikṣus said to the Buddha, "Why do you smile? We'd like to hear."

He said to the bhikṣus, "This brahman has just now paid obeisance to two World-Honored Ones."

The bhikṣus said to the Buddha, "Which two buddhas?"

The Buddha said to the bhikṣus, "Right beneath his stick when he did obeisance to me there is a stūpa of Buddha Kāśyapa."

The bhikṣus said to the Buddha, "We wish to see the stūpa of Buddha Kāśyapa."

The Buddha said to the bhikṣus, "You should request the land and its earth from this brahman."

The bhikṣus immediately requested them, and the brahman promptly gave them to them. As soon as they had got them, the World-Honored One revealed a stūpa of seven treasures for Buddha Kāśyapa, one yojana in height and a half yojana in width.[66]

---

64 ***Mahāsāṃghika-vinaya*** (*Sōgi ritsu* 僧祇律): Quoting the *Mohe sengqu lü* 摩訶僧祇律, at T.1425.22:497b18-c3.

65 **Land of Kośala** (*Kōsara koku* 拘薩羅國): Kingdom in northeast India; its capital, Śrāvastī, was frequented by the Buddha.

66 **yojana** (*yu* 由): Abbreviation of *yujun* 由旬, a measure of distance, varying greatly depending on the source, but often said to range from seven to nine miles.

156 DŌGEN'S *SHŌBŌGENZŌ* VOLUME VI

As soon as the brahman saw it, he said to the Buddha, "World-Honored One, my family name is Kāśyapa. This is my Kāśyapa stūpa."

At that time the World-Honored One straightaway constructed a stūpa for Kāśyapa at the brahman's house. The bhikṣus said to the Buddha, "World-Honored One, may we donate some mud?"

The Buddha said, "You may."

Thereupon, he recited a gāthā:

> *A hundred thousand piculs of pure gold,*
> *Used to provide a donation,*
> *Are not the equal of one clump of mud,*
> *To build with reverence a buddha's stūpa.*[67]

[T5:32]

爾時世尊、自起迦葉佛塔、下基四方周匝欄楯、圓起二重。方牙四出、上施盤蓋、長表輪相。佛言、作塔法應如是。塔成已、世尊敬過去佛故、便自作禮。諸比丘白佛言、世尊、我得作禮不。佛言、得。即説偈言、人等百千金、持用行布施、不如一善心、恭敬禮佛塔。爾時世人、聞世尊作塔、持香華來、奉世尊。世尊供敬過去佛故、即受香華、持供養塔。諸比丘白佛言、我等得供養不。佛言、得。即説偈言、百千車眞金、持用行布施、不如一善心、華香供養塔。爾時大衆雲集。佛告舍利弗、汝爲諸人説法。佛即説偈言、百千閻浮提、滿中眞金施、不如一法施、隨順令修行。爾時座中有得道者。佛即説偈言、百千世界中、滿中眞金施、不如一法施、隨順見眞諦。爾時婆羅門、不壞信、即於塔前、飯佛及僧。

At that time, the World-Honored One himself erected the stūpa for Buddha Kāśyapa.[68] *It had a square base, surrounded by a railing, with two round stories. Rectangular tusks extended in the four directions, while on top it was provided with a disc covering and a long marker with rings.*[69]

The Buddha said, "The procedure for stūpas should be like this."

After the stūpa was completed, out of reverence for the past buddha, the World-Honored One personally made obeisance to it.[70] *The bhikṣus said to the Buddha, "World-Honored One, may we make obeisance?"*

The Buddha said, "You may."

---

67 **A hundred thousand piculs** (*hyakusen tan* 百千擔): The picul (*dan* 擔) is a unit of weight equal to 100 *jin* 斤 ("catty"); traditionally defined as what could be carried by a shoulder pole, it is often reckoned at 50 (or sometimes 60) kilograms.

68 **the World-Honored One himself erected the stūpa for Buddha Kāśyapa** (*Seson ji ki Kashō butsu tō* 世尊自起迦葉佛塔): Continuing to quote the *Mohe sengqu lü* 摩訶僧祇律, at T.1425.22:497c4-23.

69 **long marker with rings** (*chōhyō rinsō* 長表輪相): Taking *chōhyō* 長表 ("long marker") as referring to the pole at the top of the stūpa.

70 **out of reverence for the past buddha** (*kyō kako butsu ko* 敬過去佛故): Or, perhaps, "Because he revered the buddhas of the past."

T5. Offerings to the Buddhas *Kuyō shobutsu* 供養諸佛

Thereupon, he recited a gāthā:

A hundred thousand in gold from people,
Used to provide a donation,
Are not the equal of one good thought,
In reverent obeisance at a buddha's stūpa.

At that time, the people, hearing that the World-Honored One had built a stūpa, brought incense and flowers, and presented them to the World-Honored One. In order to honor the past buddha, the World-Honored One accepted the incense and flowers, and made offerings to the stūpa. The bhikṣus said to the Buddha, "May we make offerings?"

The Buddha said, "You may."

Thereupon, he recited a gāthā:

A hundred thousand cartloads of pure gold,
Used to provide a donation,
Are not the equal of one good thought,
In offerings of flowers and incense to a stūpa.

At that time, the great assembly gathered like clouds. The Buddha said to Śāriputra, "You should preach the dharma for the people."

The Buddha thereupon recited a gāthā:

A hundred thousand Jambudvīpas,
Filled with donations of purest gold,
Are not the equal of one donation of dharma,
In accordance with which one is brought to practice.

At that time, among the seated were those who gained the way. The Buddha thereupon recited a gāthā:

A hundred thousand worlds,
Filled with donations of purest gold,
Are not the equal of one donation of dharma,
In accordance with which one sees the truth.

At that time, the brahman attained indestructible faith. Immediately in front of the stūpa, he served a meal for the Buddha and the saṃgha.

[T5:33] {2:363}

時波斯匿王、聞世尊造迦葉佛塔、即敕載七百車塼、來詣佛所、頭面禮足、白佛言、世尊、我欲廣作此塔、爲得不。佛言、得。佛告大王、過去世時、迦葉佛、般泥洹時、有王、名吉利。欲作七寶塔、時有臣白王、未來世當有非法人出。當破此塔得重罪。唯願大王當以塼作、金銀覆上。若取金銀者、塔故在得全。王即如臣言、以塼作、金薄覆上。高一由延、面廣半由旬。銅作欄楯、經七年七月七日乃成。作成已、香華供養及比丘僧。波斯匿王白佛言、彼王、福德多有珍寶、我今當作、不及彼王。即便作經七月七日乃成。成已、供養佛・比丘僧。

At this time, King Prasenajit, hearing that the World-Honored One had built a stūpa for Buddha Kāśyapa, ordered seven hundred carts loaded with tiles and came to the place of the Buddha.[71] Prostrating at his feet, he said to the Buddha, "World-Honored One, I wish to enlarge this stūpa. May I do so?"

The Buddha said, "You may."

The Buddha said to the great king, "In ages past, when Buddha Kāśyapa entered parinirvāṇa, there was a king named Jili, who wished to build a stūpa of seven treasures.[72] At that time, a minister said to the king, 'In the future, there will be lawless people who will destroy this stūpa and commit a grave crime. I beseech the Great King to build it with tile covered with gold and silver. Though they may take the gold and silver, the stūpa will remain intact.' The king followed the minister's advice, using tile to build it and covering it with gold leaf. It was one yojana in height and a half yojana in width. The railing was made of copper. It took seven years, seven months, and seven days to complete. After the construction was complete, incense and flowers were offered to the bhikṣu saṃgha."

King Prasenajit said to the Buddha, "That king had abundant merit and precious treasures. What I will now make will not be equal to what that king did."

He thereupon built it, taking seven months and seven days to complete. Once it was completed, he made offerings to the Buddha and the bhikṣu saṃgha.

[T5:34] {2:364}

作塔法者、下基四方、周匝欄楯、圓起二重、方牙四出。上施盤蓋、長表輪相。若言世尊已除貪欲・瞋恚・愚癡、用是塔、爲得越毘尼罪、業報重故。是名塔法。

On the method for constructing the stūpa.[73] The base is square, surrounded by a railing; there are two round stories, with rectangular tusks extending in the four directions. The top is provided with a circular covering, long banners, and wheels.

If one says that the World-Honored One, although having eliminated greed, anger, and delusion, has need of this stūpa, one will have an offense that transgresses the vinaya, for the karmic recompense will be grave.

---

71 **King Prasenajit** (*Hashinoku ō* 波斯匿王): The king of Kośala, a devout patron of the Buddha. Continuing to quote the *Mohe sengqu lü* 摩訶僧祇律, T.1425.22:497c24-498a6.

72 **king named Jili** (*ō myō Kitsuri* 王名吉利): The Sanskrit original is uncertain.

73 **method for constructing the stūpa** (*sa tō hō* 作塔法): Continuing to quote the *Mohe sengqu lü* 摩訶僧祇律, at T.1425.22:498a6-10.

T5. Offerings to the Buddhas *Kuyō shobutsu* 供養諸佛   159

This is called "the method for the stūpa."

[T5:35]

塔事者、起僧伽藍時、先預度好地作塔處。塔不得在南、不得在西、應
在東、應在北。不得僧地侵佛地、佛地不得侵僧地。若塔近死尸林、若
狗食殘、持來污地、應作垣牆。應在西若南作僧房。不得使僧地水流
入佛地、佛地水得流入僧地。塔應在高顯處作。不得在塔院中、浣染曬
衣、著革履、覆頭、覆肩、涕唾地。若作是言、世尊、貪欲・瞋恚・愚
癡已除、用是塔、爲得越毘尼罪、業報重。是名塔事。

On matters of the stūpa.[74] When erecting a saṃghārāma, first survey
in advance a favorable site on which to build the stūpa.[75] The stūpa
must not be located to the south or to the west; it should be in the east
or the north. The saṃgha land must not impinge on the buddha land,
nor the buddha land impinge on the saṃgha land. If the stūpa is near a
charnel field, or a place defiled by dogs bringing food scraps, it should
be fenced off.[76] The saṃgha quarters should be built to the west or
south. Water from the saṃgha land should not be permitted to flow
into the buddha land, but water from the buddha land may flow into the
saṃgha land. The stūpa should be built on a prominent spot. Within
the precincts of the stūpa, one may not wash or dry robes, wear leather
footwear, cover the head, or spit on the ground.

If one says that the World-Honored One, although having eliminated
greed, anger, and delusion, has need of this stūpa, one will have an
offense that transgresses the vinaya, and the karmic recompense will
be grave.

This is called "matters of the stūpa."

[T5:36]

塔龕者、爾時波斯匿王、往詣佛所、頭面禮足、白佛言、世尊、我等爲迦葉
佛作塔、得作龕不。佛言、得。過去世時、迦葉佛、般泥洹後、吉利王、爲
佛起塔。面四面作龕、上作獅子像、種種綵画。前作欄楯、安置華處、龕內
懸幡蓋。若人言世尊、貪欲・瞋恚・愚癡已除、但自莊嚴而受樂者、得越毘
尼罪、業報重。是名塔法。

---

74 **matters of the stūpa** (*tō ji* 塔事): Continuing to quote the *Mohe sengqu lü* 摩訶僧
祇律, at T.1425.22:498a10-18.

75 *saṃghārāma* (*sōgyaran* 僧伽藍): A Buddhist monastery.

76 **The saṃgha land must not impinge on the buddha land** (*futoku sōchi shin butsuji*
不得僧地侵佛地): I.e., the property of the monastic residence must be located separately
from that of the stūpa.

fenced off (*enshō* 垣牆): Following Dōgen's source text; Kawamura's text here (and
below, at *tōin* 塔院) gives *en* (土偏+爰).

160 DŌGEN'S *SHŌBŌGENZŌ* VOLUME VI

On the stūpa shrine.[77] *At that time, King Prasenajit went to the place of the Buddha, made prostrations at his feet, and said, "World-Honored One, in building the stūpa for Buddha Kāśyapa, may we build shrines?"*

The Buddha said, "You may. In the past, after the parinirvāṇa *of Buddha Kāśyapa, King Jili erected a stūpa for the Buddha. On its four sides, he built shrines. At their tops, he placed images of lions and various paintings; at their fronts, he built railings with places for flowers; within the shrines, he hung banners and canopies."*

If a person says that the World-Honored One, although having eliminated greed, anger, and delusion, takes pleasure in his own adornment, one will have an offense that transgresses the vinaya, and the karmic recompense will be grave.

This is called "the method of the stūpa."

[T5:37] {2:367}

あきらかにしりぬ、佛果菩提のうへに、古佛のために塔をたて、これを禮
拜供養したてまつる、これ諸佛の常法なり。かくのごとくの事おほけれ
ど、しばらくこれを擧揚す。佛法は、有部、すぐれたり、そのなか、僧祇
律、もとも根本なり。僧祇律は、法顯、はじめて荊棘をひらきて、西天に
いたり、靈山にのぼれりしついでに、將來するところなり。祖祖正傳しき
たれる法、まさしく有部に相應せり。

It is clear from this that, even after having attained bodhi, the fruit of buddhahood, it is the common practice of the buddhas to build stūpas for the ancient buddhas and pay obeisance and make offerings to them. Instances such as this are many, but, for now, we have brought up this one. The Sarvāstivāda school excels in the buddha dharma, and within it, the *Mahāsāṃghika Vinaya* is the most fundamental.[78] The *Mahāsāṃghika Vinaya* was brought back by Faxian, when he first cleared away the brambles, went to Sindh in the West, and climbed Vulture Peak.[79] The

---

77 **stūpa shrine** (*tō gan* 塔龕): Continuing to quote the *Mohe sengqu lü* 摩訶僧祇律, at T.1425.22:498a18-25. The "shrines" (*gan* 龕) in question are likely niches in the walls of the stūpa base at which offerings can be made.

78 **Sarvāstivāda school** (*U bu* 有部): The Sarvāstivāda (*Setsu issai u bu* 説一切有部) was the representative school of *abhidharma* for Japanese readers like Dōgen — hence, his evaluation of it here. He seems to have thought that the *Mahāsāṃghika-vinaya* was a text of this school, rather than, as its title indicates, of the Mahāsāṃghika school.

79 **Faxian** (*Hokken* 法顯): Famous Buddhist pilgrim (dates unknown) who traveled to India at the turn of the fifth century; he translated the *Mahāsāṃghika-vinaya* with Buddhabhadra in 416.

cleared away the brambles (*keikyoku o hirakite* 荊棘をひらきて): I.e., "overcame difficulties."

climbed Vulture Peak (*Ryōzen ni noborerishi* 靈山にのぼれりし): Faxian's visit to

T5. Offerings to the Buddhas *Kuyō shobutsu* 供養諸佛   161

dharma directly transmitted by ancestor after ancestor exactly conforms to the Sarvāstivāda.

[T5:38] {2:368}

第三現前供養、面對佛身及與支提、而設供養。

On the third,[80]

"Offering to what is present" is to make an offering while facing the body of a buddha or to a caitya.

[T5:39]

第四不現前供養、於不現前佛及支提、廣設供養。謂、現前共不現前、供養佛及支提塔廟、並供不現前佛及支提塔廟。現前供養、得大功德、不現前供養、得太大功德、境寛廣故。共現前・不現前供養者、得最大大功德。

On the fourth,[81]

"Offering to what is not present," is to make offerings broadly to buddhas and caityas that are not present — that is, offerings to buddhas and caityas or stūpas both present and not present, as well as offerings to buddhas and caityas or stūpas not present. Offering to what is present achieves great merit; offering to what is not present achieves still greater great merit, for its scope is vast. One who makes offerings to what is present and not present achieves the greatest of great merit.

[T5:40]

第五自作供養、自身供養佛及支提。

On the fifth,[82]

"Offering of one's own," is to make offerings oneself to a buddha or a caitya.

[T5:41]

第六、他作供養佛及支提。有少財物、不依懈怠、教他施作也。謂、自他供養、彼此同爲。自作供養、得大功德、教他供養、得大大功德、自他供養得最大大功德。

Gṛdhrakūṭa is recorded in his *Record of Buddhist Countries* (*Foguo ji* 佛國記; *Gaoseng Faxian zhuan* 高僧法顯傳, T.2085.51:862c19-863a5).

80 **third** (*daisan* 第三): Returning to the list of the ten types of offerings introduced in section 26, above; quoting here *Dasheng yi zhang* 大乘義章 (T.1851.44:742a25-26).

81 **fourth** (*daishi* 第四): Continuing a slightly variant version of the *Dasheng yi zhang* 大乘義章 (T.1851.44:742a26-b1). Dōgen's version is less clear than his source text, which lists three distinct scenarios: 1) offerings made in the presence of the object of the devotion; 2) offerings in which the object of the devotion is not actually present; and 3) offerings made to objects both present and not present.

82 **fifth** (*daigo* 第五): From *Dasheng yi zhang* 大乘義章 (T.1851.44:742b2-3).

162   DŌGEN'S *SHŌBŌGENZŌ* VOLUME VI

On the sixth,[83]

"Offering by another" to buddhas and caityas. [The case in which] one with few valuables is not remiss in prompting another to perform [the offering]. That is, it is an offering of one's own and the other, that one and this one doing it together. The offering of one's own achieves great merit; the offering of another achieves greater great merit; the offering of one's own and another achieves the greatest great merit.

[T5:42] {2:369}

第七、財物供養佛及支提・塔廟・舍利。謂、財有三種。一資具供養。謂、衣食等。二敬具供養。謂、香華等。三嚴具供養。謂、餘一切寶莊嚴等也。

On the seventh,[84]

"Offering of valuables" to a buddha as well as to a caitya, a stūpa, or śarīra. Valuables are of three types: 1) offering of practical objects: robes, food, and the like; 2) offering of devotional objects: incense, flowers, and the like; 3) offering of decorative objects: all other precious adornments, and the like.

[T5:43]

第八勝供養、勝有三。一專設種種供養。二純淨信心、信佛德重、理合供養。三廻向心。求佛心中而設供養。

On the eighth,[85]

"Superior offering," there are three types of "superior": 1) the various offerings are performed single-mindedly; 2) a mind of pure faith, in which the offering accords with faith in the magnitude of the buddha's merits; 3) a mind of transference, in which the offering is performed with a mind seeking buddhahood.

---

83   **sixth** (*dairoku* 第六): After *Dasheng yi zhang* 大乘義章 (T.1851.44:742b3-6), with slight variation. Dōgen's version here again conflates what are in the original three distinct categories of offering by type of donor: 1) offering by one's self; 2) offering by another; and 3) offering by both.

84   **seventh** (*daishichi* 第七): After *Dasheng yi zhang* 大乘義章 (T.1851.44:742b7-9), with variation.

85   **eighth** (*daihachi* 第八): Based on *Dasheng yi zhang* 大乘義章 (T.1851.44:742b9-13). Here, again, Dōgen's version is less clear than his source. In particular, it misses the point that the first of the three superior minds is that of understanding. Here is the original text:

以殊勝心爲前供養、名勝供養。勝心有三。一專精解心、善解施設種種供養。二純淨信心、信佛德重理合供養。三迴向心、求佛心中而設供養。

When the above offerings are done with a particularly superior mind, they are called "superior offerings." There are three sorts of superior mind: 1) the mind with particularly fine understanding — the various offerings are performed with good understanding; 2) the mind of pure faith — the offering accords with faith in the magnitude of the buddha's merits; 3) the mind of transference — the offering is performed with a mind seeking buddhahood.

T5. Offerings to the Buddhas *Kuyō shobutsu* 供養諸佛

[T5:44]

第九無染供養、無染有二。一心無染。離一切過。二財物無染。離非法過。

On the ninth,[86]

"Undefiled offering," there are two senses of "undefiled": 1) the mind is undefiled, free from all faults; 2) the valuables are undefiled, free from faults in violation of the dharma.

[T5:45]

第十至處道供養、謂、供行順果、名至處道供養。佛果是其所至之處、供養之行、能至彼處、名至處道。至處道供養、或名法供養、或名行供養。就中有三。一者財物供養、爲至處道供養。二隨喜供養、爲至處道供養。三修行供養、爲至處道供養。供養於佛、既有此十供養。於法於僧、類亦同然。謂、供養法者、供養佛所説理教行法、並供養經卷。供養僧者、謂、供養一切三乘聖衆、及其支提、並其形像・塔廟、及凡夫僧。

On the tenth,[87]

"Offering on the path to the destination" — i.e., when the fruit follows from the practice of offering, it is called "offering on the path to the destination." The fruit of buddhahood is the place that is reached; the practice of offering can reach that place — this is called "the path to the destination." "Offering on the path to the destination" is also called "offering of dharma"; is also called "offering of practice."[88] It consists of three kinds: 1) offering of valuables done as an offering on the path to the destination; 2) offering of sympathetic joy done as an offering on the path to the destination; 3) offering of practice done as an offering on the path to the destination.

Offerings to the buddha are of these ten types of offerings; to the dharma and the saṃgha, the types are the same. That is, offerings to dhar-

---

86 **ninth** (*daikyū* 第九): From *Dasheng yi zhang* 大乘義章 (T.1851.44:742b14-15).

87 **tenth** (*daijū* 第十): From *Dasheng yi zhang* 大乘義章 (T.1851.44:742b15-25).

88 **"offering of dharma"** (*hō kuyō* 法供養): I.e., teaching; not to be confused with "offerings to the dharma" (*kuyō hō* 供養法) mentioned below. The *Dasheng yi zhang* 大乘義章 (T.1851.44:742b17-18) identifies this as a usage of the *Vimalakīrti Sūtra*, in which it is discussed in the chapter of this name and defined there (*Weimojie suoshuo jing* 維摩詰所説經, T.475.14:556b19-20) as the sūtras taught by the buddhas.

"offering of practice" (*gyō kuyō* 行供養): The *Dasheng yi zhang* 大乘義章 (T.1851.44:742b18) identifies this as a usage of the *Daśabhūmika-bhāṣya* (*Shidi jing lun* 十地經論, T.1522.26:138b13-15), where it occurs as one of a threefold set of offerings:

一切供養者有三種供養。一者利養供養、謂衣服臥具等。二者恭敬供養、謂香花幡蓋等。三者行供養、謂修行信戒行等。

"All offerings" includes three types of offering: 1) offering of support — robes, bedding, and the like; 2) offering of reverence — incense, flowers, banners, canopies, and the like; 3) offering of practice — practice, faith, observance of precepts, and the like.

164 DŌGEN'S *SHŌBŌGENZŌ* VOLUME VI

ma are offerings to the principles and practices preached by the buddha, as well as offerings to the sūtra scrolls. Offerings to the saṃgha means offerings to all the sages of the three vehicles, as well as their caityas, together with their images and stūpas, as well as to the commoner monks.

[T5:46] {2:370}

次、供養心有六種。一福田無上心。生福田中最勝。二恩德無上心。一切善樂、依三寶出生。三生一切衆生最勝心。四如優曇鉢華難遇心。五三千大千世界殊獨一心。六一切世間出世間具足依義心。謂、如來具足世間出世間法、能與衆生爲依止處、名具足依義。以此六心、雖是少物、供養三寶、能獲無量無邊功德。何況其多。

Next,

There are six kinds of thoughts with which to make offerings.[89] (1) The thought that they [i.e., the buddhas or the three treasures] are the unsurpassed fields of merit: among the fields of merit, they produce the best. (2) The thought that they provide unsurpassed blessings; all felicity arises based on the three treasures. (3) The thought that they produce the best among living beings. (4) The thought that they are as difficult to encounter as the *udumbara* blossom. (5) The thought that they are unique in the trichiliocosm. (6) The thought that they are fully endowed with reliable teachings in both the mundane and transmundane realms: the tathāgatas are fully endowed with the dharmas of the mundane and transmundane realms, which provide living beings with a place on which to rely; this is called "fully endowed with reliable teachings." If we make even a few offerings to the three treasures with these six thoughts, we acquire incalculable, limitless merit; how much more, then, if we make many offerings.

[T5:47] {2:371}

かくのごとくの供養、かならず誠心に修設すべし。諸佛、かならず修しきたりましますところなり。その因緣、あまねく經・律にあきらかなれども、なほ佛祖、まのあたり正傳しきたりまします。執事服勞の日月、すなはち供養の時節なり。形像・舍利を安置し、供養禮拜し、塔廟をたて、支提をたつる儀則、ひとり佛祖の屋裡に正傳せり、佛祖の兒孫にあらざれば正傳せず。またもし如法に正傳せざれば、法儀、相違す、法儀、相違するがごときは、供養、まことならず、供養、まことならざれば、功德、おろそかなり。かならず如法供養の法、ならひ正傳すべし。令韜禪師は、曹溪

---

89 **There are six kinds of thoughts with which to make offerings** (*kuyō shin u rokushu* 供養心有六種): Proceeding here to the second discussion of offering in Huiyuan's *Dasheng yi zhang* 大乘義章 (T.1851.44:742b26-c3), that of the thought regarding the objects of the offering that should accompany the act. Huiyuan again cites as his source the *Pusa dichi jing* 菩薩地持經 (T.1581.30:925b26-c3), which identifies the list as pure thoughts of the bodhisattva regarding the Tathāgata (while Huiyuan himself includes the three treasures as objects of both his thoughts and his offerings).

T5. Offerings to the Buddhas *Kuyō shobutsu* 供養諸佛　165

の塔頭に陪侍して、年月をおくり、盧行者は、晝夜にやすまず碓米供衆す
る、みな供養の如法なり。これその少分なり、しげくあぐるにいとまあら
ず。かくのごとく供養すべきなり。

We should always perform such offerings with a sincere mind. This is what the buddhas have always practiced. Accounts of them are apparent throughout the sūtras and vinaya; but the buddhas and ancestors have also directly transmitted them to us: their days and months of serving and laboring are the times when they are making offerings. The rules for installing images and *śarīra*, for making offerings and paying obeisance, for erecting stūpas and erecting caityas — these have been directly transmitted solely within the house of the buddhas and ancestors; to those not descendants of the buddhas and ancestors, they are not directly transmitted. Furthermore, if they are not directly transmitted in accordance with the dharma, the procedures will be at variance [with the rules]; and when the procedures vary, the offerings will not be authentic; when the offerings are not authentic, their merit will be negligible. We should study and directly transmit the procedures for making offerings in accordance with the dharma.

Chan Master Lingtao spent years serving at the stūpa of Caoxi; the practitioner Lu pounded rice for the assembly day and night without rest — both were offerings made in accordance with the dharma.[90] They are but a small bit; there is no time to give more. We should make offerings like this.

正法眼藏供養諸佛第五
Treasury of the True Dharma Eye
Offerings to the Buddhas
Number 5

90　**Chan Master Lingtao** (*Reitō zenji* 令韜禪師): I.e., Caoxi Lingtao 曹溪令韜 (671-759), a disciple of the Sixth Ancestor, Huineng 慧能; he became head of Huineng's stūpa following his master's death. (See *Jingde chuandeng lu* 景德傳燈錄, T.2076.51:244a1-2.)

practitioner Lu (*Ro anja* 盧行者): Reference to Huineng's service as a layman in the granary of the Fifth Ancestor's monastery at Dongshan 東山.

166 DŌGEN'S *SHŌBŌGENZŌ* VOLUME VI

[Chōenji MS:][91]

建長七年夏安居日
A day of the summer retreat, seventh year of Kenchō [1255][92]

[Tōunji MS:]

弘安第二己卯六月廿三日、在永平寺衆寮書寫之
Copied this in the common quarter of Eihei Monastery; twenty-third day, sixth month of the junior earth year of the rabbit, the second year of Kōan [2 August 1279][93]

于時文明十二庚子年卯月廿日、於于越之吉祥山永平寺承陽庵書寫之。
比丘光周
Copied this in the Jōyō Hermitage, Eihei Monastery, Mount Kichijō, Esshū; twentieth day, month of deutzia blossoms, senior metal year of the rat, the twelfth year of Bunmei [29 May 1480]. Bhikṣu Kōshū[94]

---

91 **Chōenji MS** 長圓寺本: Manuscript of the eighty-four-chapter *Shōbōgenzō* copied 1645 (Shōhō 正保 2) by Kidō Sōe 暉堂宗慧 (d. 1650), second abbot of Chōenji.

92 Presumed to indicate a copy by Ejō.

day of the summer retreat (*ge ango no hi* 夏安居日): Dates of the summer retreat vary; a common practice put it from the fifteenth of the fourth lunar month through the fifteenth of the seventh month; in 1255, this would have corresponded to 22 May through 18 August.

93 Copyist unknown; perhaps Ejō 懷奘 or his disciple Giun 義雲 (1253–1333).

94 **month of deutzia blossoms** (*bōgetsu* 卯月): The fourth lunar month (*uzuki* 卯月).

Bhikṣu Kōshū (*biku Kōshū* 光周): Fifteenth abbot of Eiheiji (1434–1492?).

TREASURY OF THE TRUE DHARMA EYE
THE TWELVE-CHAPTER COMPILATION
NUMBER 6

Refuge in the Treasures of Buddha, Dharma, and Saṃgha
Kie buppōsōbō

歸依佛法僧寶

Refuge in the Treasures of Buddha, Dharma, and Saṃgha

Kie buppōsōbō

INTRODUCTION

This work, also known as *Kie sanbō* 歸依三寶 ("Refuge in the Three Treasures") represents number 88 in the Honzan edition and number 60 in the sixty-chapter compilation. It is undated but bears a colophon, perhaps by Dōgen's disciple Ejō, reporting that it was copied from Dōgen's own first draft during the summer retreat of 1257.

As its title indicates, the work celebrates the venerable Buddhist practice, found everywhere throughout the tradition, of formally declaring one's allegiance to the religion by going for refuge to its founder, its teachings, and its religious order. Quoting passages from the sūtras and scholastic treatises, Dōgen defines and describes the practice and goes on to relate examples of the miraculous power of taking refuge to overcome karma — the deva saved from rebirth as a pig, the dragons promised freedom from their past evil deeds, the god Śakra released from the womb of a donkey, the rabbit whose recitation of the refuge summoned the gods to its rescue. The essay ends with a reminder that all Buddhist practice always begins with refuge in and obeisance to the three treasures, without which it cannot be considered Buddhist practice.

正法眼藏第六

Treasury of the True Dharma Eye
Number 6

歸依佛法僧寶

Refuge in the Treasures of
Buddha, Dharma, and Saṃgha

[T6:1] {2:372}

禪苑清規曰、敬佛法僧否。〈一百二十問第一〉

In the Rules of Purity for the Chan Park, *it is said, "Do you venerate the buddha, dharma, and saṃgha or not?"[1]* (The first of the one hundred twenty questions.)

[T6:2]

明らかにしりぬ、西天東土、佛祖正傳する處は、恭敬佛法僧なり。歸依せ
ざれば恭敬せず、恭敬せざれば歸依すべからず。この歸依佛法僧の功德、
必ず感應道交するとき成就するなり。たとひ天上・人間・地獄・鬼畜なり
といへども、感應道交すれば、必ず歸依したてまつるなり。すでに歸依し
たてまつるがごときは、生生世世、在在處處に增長し、必ず積功累德し、
阿耨多羅三藐三菩提を成就するなり。おのづから惡友にひかれ、魔障にあ
ふて、しばらく斷善根となり、一闡提となれども、つひには續善根し、そ
の功德增長するなり。歸依三寶の功德、つひに不朽なり。

Clearly, what is transmitted by the buddhas and ancestors of Sindh in the West and the Land of the East is veneration of the buddha, dharma, and saṃgha. If we do not take refuge in them, we do not venerate them; if we do not venerate them, we would not take refuge in them. The merit of taking refuge in the buddha, dharma, and saṃgha is invariably achieved when feeling and response interact.[2] Whether they be devas, humans, hell beings, ghosts, or beasts, when feeling and response interact, they invariably take refuge.[3] Those who have taken refuge grow in life after

---

1   **Rules of Purity for the Chan Park** (*Zennen shingi* 禪苑清規): *Chanyuan qinggui* 禪苑清規, ZZ.63:545b15. The parenthetical remark is in Dōgen's text, in reference to a set of questions in the *Chanyuan qinggui*.

2   **feeling and response interact** (*kannō dōkō* 感應道交): A fixed expression for the communication between a devotee and a deity; the devotee's feeling evokes a response from the deity and vice versa.

3   **devas, humans, hell beings, ghosts, or beasts** (*tenjō ningen jigoku kichiku* 天上・

170 DŌGEN'S *SHŌBŌGENZŌ* VOLUME VI

life, in age after age, wherever they are in place after place, invariably accumulating merit and amassing virtue, and achieving *anuttara-samyak-sambodhi*. Even if, tempted by evil friends or encountering demonic obstructions, their good roots are temporarily severed, and they become *icchantika*, eventually they will continue their good roots, and their merit will grow.[4] The merit of refuge in the three treasures never decays.

[T6:3]

その歸依三寶とは、まさに淨信をもはらして、あるひは如來現在世にもあれ、あるひは如來滅後にもあれ、合掌し低頭して、口にとなへていはく、

"Refuge in the three treasures" means, with pure faith alone, regardless of whether it be during the Tathāgata's lifetime or after his extinction, to join the palms, bow the head, and recite:

[T6:4] {2:373}

我某甲、今身より佛身にいたるまで、歸依佛、歸依法、歸依僧。

歸依佛兩足尊、歸依法離欲尊、歸依僧衆中尊。

歸依佛竟、歸依法竟、歸依僧竟。

I, so and so, from my present body until I reach the body of a buddha,

Take refuge in the Buddha; take refuge in the dharma; take refuge in the samgha.[5]

I take refuge the Buddha, honored among the two-legged; I take refuge in the dharma, honored as free from desire; I take refuge in the samgha, honored among assemblies.

I have taken refuge in the Buddha; I have taken refuge in the dharma; I have taken refuge in the samgha.

[T6:5]

はるかに佛果菩提をこころざして、かくのごとく僧那を始發するなり。しかあればすなはち、身心いまも刹那刹那に生滅すといへども、法身かならず長養して、菩提を成就するなり。

Setting one's sights on distant bodhi, the fruit of buddhahood, we thus initiate the *samnāha*.[6] Thus, though body and mind arise and disap-

---

人間・地獄・鬼畜): I.e., sentient beings in the five destinies (*dō* 道; S. *gati*) of rebirth in samsāra; see Supplementary Notes, s.v. "Six paths."

4 *icchantika* (*issendai* 一闡提): Those whose good roots have been cut off, such that they cannot achieve awakening.

5 **Take refuge in the Buddha** (*kie butsu* 歸依佛): A chant, versions of which are widespread throughout the Buddhist world. See, e.g., *Chanyuan qinggui* 禪苑清規, ZZ.63:547b8-10.

6 *samnāha* (*sōna* 僧那): "To gird oneself," "to put on armor"; used in reference to the bodhisattva's vow to attain supreme bodhi.

T6. Refuge in the Three Treasures *Kie buppōsōbō* 歸依佛法僧寶 171

pear in *kṣāna* after *kṣāna*, the dharma body will inevitably mature and achieve bodhi.[7]

[T6:6]

いはゆる歸依とは、歸は、歸投なり、依は、依伏なり、このゆえに歸依といふ。歸投の相は、たとへば子の父に歸するがごとし。依伏は、たとへば民の王に依するがごとし。いはゆる救濟の言なり。佛は、これ大師なるがゆえに歸依す、法は、良藥なるがゆえに歸依す、僧は勝友なるがゆえに歸依す。

In the term "*kie*" ["to take refuge"], "*ki*" means "*kitō*" ["to resort and submit to"]; "*e*" means "*ebuku*" ["to rely on and prostrate oneself"].[8] Therefore, we say "to take refuge." The mark of "resorting and submitting to" is like the child resorting to the father; "relying on and prostrating oneself" is like the subjects relying on their king. That is, it is a term for aid and rescue.[9] Because the Buddha is a great teacher, we take refuge in him; because the dharma is the good medicine, we take refuge in it; because the saṃgha are the best friends, we take refuge in them.

[T6:7]

問、何故、偏歸此三。答、以此三種畢竟歸處、能令衆生出離生死、證大菩提故歸。

Question: Why do we take refuge solely in these three?[10]

---

7 *kṣāna* (*setsuna* 利那): A "moment."

8 **In the term "*kie*"** (*iwayuru kie to wa* いはゆる歸依とは): Giving a definition of the compound Japanese expression used to translate the Sanskrit *śaraṇa* ("refuge," "protection"). This section seems based on the *Dasheng yi zhang* 大乗義章 of Huiyuan 慧遠 (523-592) (T.1851.44:654a8-9), a text Dōgen will quote in the following section:

言三歸者。歸投依伏。故曰歸依。歸投之相如子歸父。依伏之義如民依王如。性依勇。歸依不同隨境説三。所謂歸佛歸法歸僧。依佛為師。故曰歸佛。憑法為藥。故稱歸法。依僧為友。故名歸僧。

"The three refuges." To resort and submit to, to rely on and prostrate oneself; therefore, they are called "refuges." The mark of "resorting and submitting to" is like the child resorting to the father; the sense of "relying on and prostrating oneself" is like the subjects relying on the king, like the timid relying on the brave [reading *qie* 怯 for *xing* 性]. . . . We depend on the Buddha as our teacher; therefore, we say, "I take refuge in the Buddha." We rely on the dharma as our medicine; therefore, we chant, "I take refuge in the dharma." We depend on the saṃgha as our friends; therefore, we say, "I take refuge in the saṃgha."

9 **That is, it is a term for aid and rescue** (*iwayuru gusai no gon nari* いはゆる救濟の言なり): Reflecting a definition of "refuge" (*kie* 歸依) in the *Abhidharma-kośa* (*Apidamo jushe lun* 阿毘達磨倶舍論, T.1558.29:76c18).

10 **Question** (*mon* 問): Lines from the *Dasheng yi zhang* 大乗義章 (T.1851.44:654a12-14) that follow immediately after the definition of the three refuges given in section 6, above.

172 DŌGEN'S *SHŌBŌGENZŌ* VOLUME VI

Answer: We take refuge in them because these three are the ultimate places of refuge, enabling living beings to escape birth and death and realize great bodhi.

[T6:8]

此三、畢竟不可思議功德なり。佛、西天には佛陀耶と稱す、震旦には覺と翻ず、無上正等覺なり。法は、西天には達磨と稱す、また曇無と稱す、梵音の不同なり、震旦には法と翻ず。一切の善・惡・無記の法、ともに法と稱すといへども、いま三寶のなかの歸依する處の法は、軌則の法なり。僧は西天には僧伽と稱す、震旦には和合衆と翻ず。かくのごとく稱讚しきたれり。

These three are ultimately [possessed of] inconceivable merit.[11] In Sindh in the West, "buddha" is called "*butsudaya*"; in Cīnasthāna, it is translated "awakening" — the unsurpassed, perfect awakening.[12] In Sindh in the West, "dharma" is called "*daruma*," also called "*donmu*," the Indic pronunciation varying; in Cīnasthāna, it is translated "law."[13]

---

11   **These three are ultimately [possessed of] inconceivable merit** (*shi san, hikkyō fukashigi kudoku nari* 此三、畢竟不可思議功德なり): This section reflects a passage in the *Dasheng yi zhang* 大乘義章 (T.1851.44:654a16-b4) on the meaning of the terms for the three objects of refuge. The first line here may reflect the statement at *Dasheng yi zhang* 大乘義章 (T.1851.44:654b12-13):

三寶如是。具不可思議六神通力。故説爲寶。

The three treasures are like this: they are possessed of the inconceivable six spiritual powers; therefore, they are called "treasures."

12   **In Sindh in the West, "buddha" is called "*butsudaya*"** (*butsu, Saiten ni wa butsudaya to shōsu* 佛、西天には佛陀耶と稱す): The Japanese pronunciation *butsudaya* transliterates Sanskrit *buddhāya*, the dative form of *buddha* in the invocation *namo buddhāya* (*namu butsudaya* 南無佛陀耶; "homage to the Buddha"). The *Dasheng yi zhang* 大乘義章 (T.1851.44:654a17) has here simply the less problematic *fotuo* 佛陀 (Japanese *butsuda*; "buddha").

in Cīnasthāna, it is translated "awakening" (*Shintan ni wa kaku to honzu* 震旦には覺と翻ず): "Cīnasthāna" (*Shintan* 震旦) is a Sanskrit name for China ("Land of the Qin"). The Japanese *kaku* 覺 most often renders Sanskrit *bodhi* ("awakening"); presumably, Dōgen wants us to understand here "awakened one — one with unsurpassed, perfect awakening" (*mujō shōtō kaku* 無上正等覺). In fact, the *Dasheng yi zhang* 大乘義章 (T.1851.44:654a17) here has *juezhe* 覺者 (J. *kakusha*; "awakened one").

13   **In Sindh in the West, "dharma" is called "*daruma*," also called "*donmu*," the Indic pronunciation varying** (*hō wa, Saiten ni wa daruma to shōsu, mata donmu to shōsu, bonnon no fudō nari* 法は、西天には達磨と稱す、また曇無と稱す、梵音の不同なり): Dōgen seems to be saying here that the variant transliterations of the Sanskrit "dharma" represent two different Indic originals, though his source for such a claim is by no means clear. On the contrary, the *Dasheng yi zhang* 大乘義章 (T.1851.44:654a27-28), on which he has been relying here, seems to say quite the opposite:

所言法者、外國正音名爲達摩、亦名曇無。本是一音傳之別耳。此翻名法。

"Dharma" in foreign pronunciation is "*damo*," or "*tanwu*"; originally these are the same pronunciation, differing in their transmission. They are translated as "law."

T6. Refuge in the Three Treasures *Kie buppōsōbō* 歸依佛法僧寶 173

Although all phenomena, good, evil, and neutral, are called "dharmas," the "dharma" of the three treasures in which we take refuge is the "dharma" of rules and regulations. In Sindh in the West, "saṃgha" is called "*sōgya*"; in Cīnasthāna, it is translated "harmonious assembly." In this way, have they been praised.

[T6:9] {2:374}
住持三寶

形像・塔廟佛寶。黄紙・朱軸所傳法寶。剃髮・染衣・戒法・儀相僧寶。

The three treasures as maintained:[14] *The buddha treasure as images and stūpas; the dharma treasure as transmitted on yellow paper and vermilion spindle; the saṃgha treasure as the tonsure, dyed robes, precepts, and rituals.*[15]

[T6:10]
化儀三寶

釋迦牟尼世尊佛寶。所轉法輪・流布聖教法寶。阿若憍陳如等五人僧寶。

The three treasures as teaching:[16] *The buddha treasure as Śākyamuni, the World-Honored One; the dharma treasure as the dharma wheel turned and sacred teachings disseminated; the saṃgha as Ājñā-ta-kauṇḍinya and the rest of the five.*[17]

---

14 **The three treasures as maintained** (*jūji sanbō* 住持三寶): I.e., the three treasures understood as the sacred objects and practices of the Buddhist community. The set of four types of the three treasures given here and in the following three sections seems to be based on the *Lüzong xinxue mingju* 律宗新學名句 by Huaixian 懷顯 (or Weixian 惟顯, dates unknown), ZZ.105:623a14-b3. For a variant version, see *Sifen lü xingshichao zichiji* 四分律行鈔資持記, by Yuanzhao 元照 (1048-1116) (T.1805.40:280a13-15). This fourfold treatment of the three treasures is rather different from the threefold division of the three treasures given in Dōgen's *Kyōju kaimon* 教授戒文, used as the basis for the Sōtō Zen ordination ritual; see *Busso shōden bosatsu kai kyōju kaimon* 佛祖正傳菩薩戒教授戒文, DZZ.6:212-214.

15 **yellow paper and vermilion spindle** (*ōshi shujiku* 黄紙・朱軸): I.e., the paper and roller of a scroll of scripture.

16 **The three treasures as teaching** (*kegi sanbō* 化儀三寶): I.e., the three treasures understood as the elements of the Buddha's historical mission.

17 **Ājñāta-kauṇḍinya and the rest of the five** (*Anyakyōjinnyo tō gonin* 阿若憍陳如等五人): I.e., the first five disciples of Buddha Śākyamuni.

[T6:11]

理體三寶

五分法身名爲佛寶。滅理無爲名爲法寶。學無學功德名爲僧寶。

The three treasures as essence of principle:[18] *The fivefold dharma body is called "the buddha treasure"; the principle of cessation, the unconditioned, is called "the dharma treasure"; the merit of student and non-student is called "the saṃgha treasure."*[19]

[T6:12]

一體三寶

證理大覺名爲佛寶。清淨離染名爲法寶。至理和合無擁無滯、名爲僧寶。

The three treasures as single essence:[20] *The great awakening that verifies the principle is called "the buddha treasure"; purity, free from defilement, is called "the dharma treasure"; harmony with the ultimate principle, without obstacles and without impediments, is called "the saṃgha treasure."*

[T6:13]

かくのごとくの三寶に歸依したてまつるなり。もし薄福少德の衆生は、三寶の名字、なほききたてまつらざるなり、いかにいはんや、歸依したてまつることえむや。

We take refuge in such three treasures. Living beings of meager blessings and few virtues have never even heard the term "three treasures," how much less, then, could they take refuge in them.[21]

---

18 **The three treasures as essence of principle** (*ritai sanbō* 理體三寶): I.e., the three treasures understood from a higher doctrinal perspective.

19 **fivefold dharma body** (*gobun hosshin* 五分法身): The ultimate body of the buddha as possessed of five virtues: ethics (*kai* 戒), concentration (*jō* 定), wisdom (*e* 慧), liberation (*gedatsu* 解脱), and knowledge of liberation (*gedatsu chiken* 解脱知見).

principle of cessation, the unconditioned (*metsuri mui* 滅理無爲): I.e., the third sacred truth of the cessation of suffering, the unconditioned state of nirvāṇa.

student and non-student (*gaku mugaku* 學無學): I.e., those still on the Buddhist path and those who have completed it; S. *śaikṣa* and *aśaikṣa*, respectively.

20 **The three treasures as single essence** (*ittai sanbō* 一體三寶): I.e., the three treasures as unified spiritual state.

21 **Living beings of meager blessings and few virtues** (*hakufuku shōtoku no shujō* 薄福少德の衆生): Likely a variant of *hakutoku shōfuku nin* 薄德少福人 ("people of meager virtues and few blessings"), from a line in the *Lotus Sūtra* (*Miaofa lianhua jing* 妙法蓮華經, T.262.9:8b15) describing those for whom the Buddha must use expedient means (*hōben* 方便; S. *upāya*) to convey his teachings.

T6. Refuge in the Three Treasures *Kie buppōsōbō* 歸依佛法僧寶

[T6:14]

法華經曰、是諸罪衆生、以惡業因縁、過阿僧祇劫、不聞三寶名。

In the *Lotus Sūtra*, it is said,[22]

These evil living beings,
Because of their bad deeds,
Through *asaṃkheya-kalpas*,
Do not hear the name "three treasures."

[T6:15]

法華經は、諸佛如來一大事の因縁なり。大師釋尊所説の諸經のなかには、法華經これ大王なり、大師なり。餘經・餘法は、みなこれ法華經の臣民なり、眷属なり。法華經の中の所説、これまことなり。餘經中の所説、みな方便を帶せり、ほとけの本意にあらず。餘經中の説をきたして、法華に比校したてまつらん、これ逆なるべし。法華の功徳力をかうぶらざれば、餘經あるべからず。餘經は、みな法華に歸投したてまつらんことをまつなり。この法華經のなかに、いまの説、ましまず。しるべし、三寶の功徳、まさに最尊なり、最上なりといふことを。

The *Lotus Sūtra* is the reason for "the one great matter" of the buddhas, the tathāgatas.[23] Among the sūtras preached by Great Master Śākyamuni, the *Lotus Sūtra* is the great king, the great master. The other sūtras, the other teachings, are all the subjects, the retinue, of the *Lotus Sūtra*. Whatever is taught in the *Lotus Sūtra*, is true. What is taught in the other sūtras, always includes expedient devices, not the original intention of the Buddha. To bring the teachings of other sūtras to validate the *Lotus* would be to have it backwards. Were they not covered by the power of the merit of the *Lotus*, the other sūtras would simply not exist. The other sūtras depend on taking shelter under the *Lotus*. In this *Lotus Sūtra*, we find the present teaching. We should recognize that the merit of the three treasures is truly the most esteemed, the supreme.

---

22 **Lotus Sūtra** (*Hokke kyō* 法華經): *Miaofa lianhua jing* 妙法蓮華經, T.262.9:43c14-15.

23 **the reason for "the one great matter" of the buddhas, the tathāgatas** (*shobutsu nyorai ichi daiji no innen* 諸佛如來一大事の因縁): From the famous phrase in the *Lotus Sūtra* (*Miaofa lianhua jing* 妙法蓮華經, T.262.9:7a21-22), in which Buddha Śākyamuni reveals that the buddhas come into this world only to lead beings to buddhahood; see Supplementary Notes, s.v. "Buddhas, the world-honored ones, appear in the world for the reason of one great matter."

176 DŌGEN'S *SHŌBŌGENZŌ* VOLUME VI

[T6:16] {2:375}

世尊言、衆人怖所逼、多歸依諸山・園苑及叢林・孤樹・制多等。此歸依非勝、此歸依非尊。不因此歸依、能解脱衆苦。諸有歸依佛、及歸依法・僧、於四聖諦中、恒以慧觀察、知苦、知苦集、知永超衆苦、　知八支聖道。此歸依最勝、此歸依最尊。必因此歸依、能解脱衆苦。

> The World-Honored One said,[24]
>
> The people, fearing oppression,
> Often take refuge in the mountains,
> In parks and forests,
> Under lone trees, at caityas, and the like.
> These refuges are of no efficacy;
> These refuges are of no worth.
> Not by means of these refuges
> Can one be liberated from sufferings.
> Beings who take refuge in the buddha
> And refuge in the dharma and the saṃgha,
> Within the four sacred truths,
> Constantly observing them with wisdom,
> Know suffering; know the cause of suffering;
> Know the permanent transcendence of suffering;
> Know the sacred eightfold path
> [That leads to tranquil nirvāṇa].[25]
> This refuge is the most excellent;
> This refuge is the most exalted.
> Invariably by means of this refuge,
> Can one be liberated from sufferings.

[T6:17]

世尊、明らかに一切衆生のためにしめしまします。衆生、いたづらに所逼をおそれて、山神・鬼神等に歸依し、あるひは外道の制多に歸依することなかれ。かれはその歸依によりて衆苦を解脱することなし。おほよそ外道の邪教にしたがうて、牛戒・鹿戒・羅刹戒・鬼戒・瘂戒・聾戒・狗戒・雞戒・雉戒、以灰塗身、長髮爲相、以羊祠時、先咒後殺、四月事火、七日服風、百千億華、供養諸天、諸所欲願、因此成就。如是等法、能爲解脱因者、無有是處。智者所不讚、唐苦無善報。

The World-Honored One has clearly explained this for all living beings: living beings, fearing oppression, ought not take refuge in mountain gods, spirits, and the like, or take refuge in the caityas of other paths.

24　**The World-Honored One** (*Seson* 世尊): Quoting a verse attributed to the Buddha in the *Abihidharma-kośa* (*Apidamo jushe lun* 阿毘達磨倶舍論, T.1558.29:76c19-29).

25　[**That leads to tranquil nirvāṇa**] (*shu annon nehan* 趣安隱涅槃): The translation supplies this line, missing in the Kawamura edition, from the *Apidamo jushe lun* 阿毘達磨倶舍論, T.1558.29:76c27.

T6. Refuge in the Three Treasures *Kie buppōsōbō* 歸依佛法僧寶 177

By such refuges, they will not transcend sufferings. In general, following the false teachings of the other paths, [there are:][26]

The cow discipline, deer discipline, rākṣasa discipline, spirit discipline, mute discipline, deaf discipline, dog discipline, chicken discipline, pheasant discipline; [there are those who] smear their bodies with ashes and grow their hair long; sacrifice goats, first reciting spells and then slaughtering them; worship fire for four months or live on wind for seven days; make offerings to the devas of hundreds of thousands of koṭis of flowers, [thinking that] by this their wishes will be fulfilled. It cannot be the case that practices such as these could be the cause of liberation. They are not praised by the wise; they are suffering in vain, without reward.

[T6:18] {2:376}
かくのごとくなるがゆえに、いたづらに邪道に歸せざらんこと、あきらかに甄究すべし。たとひこれらの戒にことなる法なりとも、その道理、もし孤樹・制多等の道理に符合せらば、歸依することなかれ。人身うることかたし、佛法あふことまれなり。いたづらに鬼神の眷属として一生をわたり、むなしく邪見の流類として多生をすごさん、悲むべし。はやく佛・法・僧三寶に歸依したてまつりて、衆苦を解脱するのみにあらず、菩提を成就すべし。

Such being the case, we should clearly ascertain that we are not to take refuge in false paths. Even when they are teachings different from these disciplines, if their principles match the principle of the "lone trees, caityas, and the like," do not take refuge in them.[27] To obtain a human body is hard; to encounter the buddha dharma is rare. It would be deplorable to spend our one life foolishly in the entourage of demons or pass through many lives in vain as a follower of false views. Quickly taking refuge in the buddha, dharma, and saṃgha, we should not only be liberated from sufferings but achieve bodhi.

---

26   **false teachings of the other paths** (*gedō no jakyō* 外道の邪教): The following disciplines represent practices attributed to non-Buddhist Indian ascetics. Dōgen's passage here combines two canonical sources: the first six practices (through the "deaf discipline") are found in the *Dazhidu lun* 大智度論 (T.1509.25:226a17); the remaining practices and summary comment appear in the *Nirvāṇa Sūtra* (*Da banniepan jing* 大般涅槃經, T.374.12:462a17-21). The final sentence of the passage is again taken from the *Dazhidu lun* 大智度論 (T.1509.25:226a17-18).

27   **"lone trees, caityas, and the like"** (*koju seita tō no dōri* 孤樹・制多等の道理): I.e., the worthless refuges rejected by the Buddha in section 16, above.

178 DŌGEN'S *SHŌBŌGENZŌ* VOLUME VI

[T6:19]

希有經曰、教化四天下及六欲天、皆得四果、不如一人受三歸功德。

In the *Sūtra of the Wondrous*, it is said,[28]

To convert beings of the four continents under heaven, as well as in the six heavens of the desire realm, so that they all attain the fourth fruit, is not equal to the merit of a single person receiving the three refuges.[29]

[T6:20]

四天下とは、東・西・南・北洲なり。そのなかに、北洲は、三乗の化、いたらざる處、かしこの一切衆生を教化して、阿羅漢となさん、まことに、はなはだ希有なり、とすべし。たとひその益ありとも、一人ををしへて三歸をうけしめん功德には、およぶべからず。また六天は、得道の衆生まれなり、とする處なり。かれをして四果をえしむとも、一人の受三歸の功德の、おほく、ふかきに及ぶべからず。

The "four continents under heaven" refers to the continents of east, west, south and north.[30] Among them, the northern continent is a place to which the teaching of the three vehicles does not extend; we must take it as exceedingly rare indeed to seek to convert all the living beings there and make them arhats. Though there may be benefit in that, it does not equal the merit of teaching and causing a single person to receive the three refuges. Again, the six heavens are places where there are few living beings that gain the way. Though one might cause them to attain the fourth fruit, it would not equal the amount and the depth of the merit of a single person receiving the three refuges.

---

28 **Sūtra of the Wondrous** (*Keu kyō* 希有經): I.e., the *Xiyou jiaoliang gongde jing* 希有校量功德經 (T.690), attributed to Jñānagupta. In fact, Dōgen's quotation here is from a passage in the *Fahua xuanyi shiqian* 法華玄義釋籤 by Zhanran 湛然 (711–782) (T.1717.33:884a8-9), which cites the sūtra.

29 **fourth fruit** (*shika* 四果): I.e., the status of the arhat, last of the four stages on the *śrāvaka* path to nirvāṇa.

30 **"four continents under heaven"** (*shi tenge* 四天下): I.e., the continents surrounding the central Mount Sumeru in Buddhist cosmology. Jambudvīpa, the continent we inhabit, is in the south; the northern continent, Uttarakuru, is considered the most pleasant of the four, where beings live for a thousand years, food is available without effort, and life is beatific. Lacking as they do the experience of suffering, beings in Uttarakuru are unlikely candidates for conversion to Buddhism. See Supplementary Notes, s.v. "Four Continents." Similarly, the devas in the six heavens, though they are sometimes depicted converting to Buddhism, have little motivation in their long, pleasurable lives, to seek nirvāṇa.

T6. Refuge in the Three Treasures *Kie buppōsōbō* 歸依佛法僧寶 179

[T6:21] {2:377}

增一阿含經曰、有切利天子、五衰相現、當生猪中。愁憂之聲、聞於天帝。天帝聞之、喚來告曰、汝可歸依三寶。即時如教、便免生猪。佛説偈言、諸有歸依佛、不墜三惡道、盡漏處人天、便當至涅槃。受三歸已、生長者家、還得出家、成於無學。

It is said in the *Incremental by One Āgama*,[31]

There was a deva in the Trāyastriṃśa on whom appeared the five signs of decline; he was about to be reborn as a pig.[32] His cries of despair were heard by the Deva Lord. Hearing them, the Deva Lord summoned him and said, "You should take refuge in the three treasures."

He forthwith did as instructed and thereby escaped rebirth as a pig.

The Buddha recited a gāthā:
All who take refuge in the Buddha
Will not fall into the three evil paths;
Exhausting their afflictions in lives as humans and devas,
They soon arrive at nirvāṇa.[33]

After receiving the refuges, he was born in the house of a wealthy man, was able to leave home, and become a non-student.[34]

[T6:22]

おほよそ歸依三寶の功德、はかりはかるべきにあらず、無量無邊なり。

In sum, the merit of taking refuge in the three treasures cannot be calculated; it is incalculable and limitless.

---

31   ***Incremental by One Āgama*** (*Zōichi* [also read *zōitsu*] *agongyō* 增一阿含經): I.e., the *Ekottarāgama*. In fact, Dōgen's source here is not this sūtra collection but the passage immediately following that quoted above from the *Fahua xuanyi shiqian* 法華玄義釋籤 (T.1717.33:884a9-14), which summarizes a story told in the *Zengyi ahan jing* 增一阿含經 at T.125.2:677b28-678a14.

32   **Trāyastriṃśa** (*Tōri* 忉利): A heaven at the top of Mt. Sumeru inhabited by thirty-three devas and ruled by the deva Śakra (or Indra), referred to here as the "Deva Lord" (*Tentai* 天帝).

five signs of decline (*gosuisō* 五衰相): Indications that a deva's life is coming to an end. The *Abhidharma-kośa* (*Apidamo jushe lun* 阿毘達磨倶舍論, T.1558.29:56b29-c8) gives both minor and major sets of five, the latter of which lists (1) clothing becomes soiled, (2) headdress flowers wither, (3) armpits become sweaty, (4) body smells foul, and (5) situation no longer enjoyable.

33   **three evil paths** (*san akudō* 三惡道): I.e., existence as an animal, hungry ghost, or hell being; see Supplementary Notes, s.v. "Six paths."

34   **non-student** (*mugaku* 無學): S. *aśaikṣa*; the stage of the arhat, who has completed Buddhist training.

180 DŌGEN'S *SHŌBŌGENZŌ* VOLUME VI

[T6:23]

世尊在世に、二十六億の餓龍、ともに佛所に詣し、みなことごとくあめの
ごとくなみだをふらして、まうしてまうさく、

When the World-Honored One was in the world, twenty-six *koṭis* of
hungry dragons came to the Buddha, and all of them, shedding tears like
rain, said to him,[35]

[T6:24]

唯願哀愍、救濟於我。大悲世尊、我等憶念過去世時、於佛法中、雖得出
家、備造如是種種惡業。以惡業故、經無量劫身、在三惡道。亦以餘報故、
生在龍中、受極大苦。佛告諸龍、汝等今當盡受三歸、一心修善。以此縁
故、於賢劫中、値最後佛。名曰楼至。於彼佛世、罪得除滅。時諸龍等聞是
語已、皆悉至心、盡其形壽、各受三歸。

*"We beg you to have pity and rescue us.[36] O great compassionate
World-Honored One, when we recall ages past, although we were able
to leave home in the buddha dharma, we committed all manner of evil
deeds. Because of these evil deeds, our bodies have passed innumerable kalpas in the three evil paths. And further, because of additional
recompense, we have been born as dragons, experiencing extreme suffering."*

*The Buddha addressed the dragons, "You should all now receive the
three refuges and single-mindedly practice good. As a consequence of
this, during the Worthy Kalpa, you will meet the last buddha, whose
name is Rudita. In the age of that buddha, your offenses will be eliminated."[37]*

*At that time, upon hearing these words, the dragons all with utmost
sincerity, accepted the three refuges for the rest of their lives.*

[T6:25] {2:378}

ほとけみづから諸龍を救濟しましますに、餘法なし、餘術なし、ただ三歸
をさづけまします。過去世に出家せしとき、かつて三歸をうけたりといへ
ども、業報によりて餓龍となれるとき、餘法の、これをすくふべきなし。
このゆえに、三歸をさづけまします。しるべし、三歸の功徳、それ最尊最

---

35 **When the World-Honored One was in the world** (*Seson zaise ni* 世尊在世に):
Dōgen begins here, in Japanese, a story from the *Da fangdeng daiji jing* 大方等大集經
(T.397.13:291b21-22), the Chinese text of which he will quote in the next section.

36 **"We beg you to have pity"** (*yui gan aimin* 唯願哀愍): Dōgen here quotes the story
he introduced in the preceding section. His version combines two passages in the *Da
fangdeng daiji jing* 大方等大集經: the dragons' speech (at T.397.13:291b22-26), and the
Buddha's response (at T.397.13:292a7-10).

37 **Rudita** (*Rōshi* 楼至): The last of the one thousand buddhas of our present, Worthy
Kalpa (*kengō* 賢劫; S. *bhadra-kalpa*). His name is sometimes reconstructed as Ruci or
Rucita; but he is elsewhere identified as "Buddha Weeping" (*Tiku fo* 啼哭佛) (see, e.g.,
Jizang's 吉藏 *Fahua yishu* 法華義疏, T.1721.34:629a7-8).

T6. Refuge in the Three Treasures *Kie buppōsōbō* 歸依佛法僧寶 181

上、甚深不可思議なりといふこと。世尊、すでに證明しまします、衆生、
まさに信受すべし。十方の諸佛の名號を稱念せしめましまさず、ただ三歸
をさづけましまず。佛意の甚深なる、たれかこれを測量せん。いまの衆
生、いたづらに各各の一佛の名號を稱念せんよりは、すみやかに三歸をう
けたてまつるべし、愚闇にして、大功德をむなしくすることなかれ。

In rescuing the dragons, the Buddha himself had no other method, no
other technique; he simply gave them the three refuges. When they left
home in the past, they may have received the three refuges; yet when, as
recompense for their deeds, they had become hungry dragons, no other
methods could rescue them. Therefore, he gave them the three refuges.
We should recognize that the merit of the three refuges is the most ex-
alted, the supreme, most profound, inconceivable. Since the World-Honored One bears witness to them, living beings should believe in and accept them. Without having them recite the names of the buddhas of the
ten directions, he just gave them the three refuges. The Buddha's intention is most profound; who can fathom it? Rather than reciting in vain
the names of the buddhas one by one, living beings nowadays should
quickly receive the three refuges. Do not stupidly squander their great
merit.

[T6:26] {2:379}

爾時衆中、有盲龍女。口中膿爛、滿諸雜蟲、狀如屎尿、乃至穢惡、猶若婦
人根中不淨、腺臭難看。種種噉食、膿血流出、一切身分、常有蚊虻・諸惡
毒蠅之所唼食、身體臭處、難可見聞。爾時世尊、以大悲心、見彼龍婦眼盲
困苦如是、問言、妹何緣故得此惡身、於過去世、曾爲何業。龍婦答言、世
尊、我今此身、衆苦逼迫、無暫時停、設復欲言、而不能說。我念過去三
十六億、於百千年、惡龍中受如是苦、乃至日夜刹那不停。爲我往昔九十
一劫、於毘婆尸佛法中、作比丘尼、思念欲事、過於醉人。雖復出家、不能
如法、於伽藍内、敷施床褥、數數犯於非梵行事、以快欲心、生大樂受。或
貪求他物、多受信施。以如是故、於九十一劫、常不得受天人之身、恒三惡
道、受諸燒煮。佛又問言、若如是者、此中劫盡、妹何處生。龍婦答言、我
以過去業力因緣、生餘世界、彼劫盡時、惡業風吹、還來生此。時彼龍婦、
說此語已、作如是言、大悲世尊、願救濟我、願救濟我。爾時世尊、以手掬
水、告龍女言、此水名爲瞋陀留脂藥和。我今誠實發言語汝。我於往昔、爲
救鴿故、棄捨身命、終不疑念起慳借心。此言若實、令汝惡患、悉皆除瘥。
時佛世尊、以口含水、灑彼盲龍婦女之身、一切惡患臭處、皆瘥。既得瘥
已、作如是說言、我今於佛乞受三歸。是時世尊、即爲龍女、授三歸依。

At that time, there was in the assembly a blind dragon woman.[38] *Her
mouth was swollen and inflamed, filled with insects, as if it were ex-
crement and urine, so filthy and foul, it was as unclean as the inside of
a woman's organ, rank-smelling and unbearably ugly, chewed up and*

---

38 **At that time, there was in the assembly a blind dragon woman** (*ni ji shuchū, u
mō ryūnyo* 爾時衆中、有盲龍女): Quoting a story from the *Da fangdeng daiji jing* 大
方等大集經 (T.397.13:292a10-b7) that follows immediately after the passage quoted in
section 24, above.

oozing with pus and blood. All over her body, mosquitos, horseflies, and various poisonous flies were constantly nibbling at her, and the stench of her body was unbearable.

At that time, the World-Honored One seeing, with a mind of great compassion, that the dragon woman was blind and suffering like this, asked her, "Sister, how did you acquire this awful body? What deeds did you commit in the past?"

The dragon woman said, "World-Honored One, this present body of mine suffers such unceasing torments that I cannot describe them. I remember that, of the past thirty-six koṭis [of years], for a hundred thousand years, I have experienced such suffering in [the body of] an evil dragon, day and night without a moment's relief. Ninety-one kalpas ago, during the dharma of Buddha Vipaśyin, I was a bhikṣuṇī, with thoughts more lustful than a drunken man.[39] Although I had left home, I was unable to live in accordance with the dharma. Laying out a mattress in the saṃghārāma, I repeatedly engaged in impure acts, with a mind delighting in lust and enjoying sensations of great pleasure.[40] Or I craved others' possessions and accepted many donations of the faithful. Because of this, for ninety-one kalpas, I never received the body of a deva or human but only burned in the three evil paths."

The Buddha again asked her, "In that case, where will my sister be born when this kalpa is exhausted?"

The dragon woman replied, "By the power of my past karma, I shall be born in another world, and, when that kalpa is exhausted, the winds of my evil karma will blow me back to be born here."

Then, when the dragon woman had finished these words, she said, "Great compassionate World-Honored One, save me! Save me!"

At that time, the World-Honored One, scooping up some water with his hands, said to the dragon woman, "This water is called 'cintāruci medicinal compound.'[41] Now, I shall tell you something in all truth. In the past, I gave up my life to rescue a pigeon, never having doubts or feeling reluctant. If these words are true, your afflictions will all be healed."

39　**Buddha Vipaśyin** (*Bibashi butsu* 毘婆尸佛): I.e., the first of the seven buddhas of the past, said to have lived in the Adornment æon (*shōgon kō* 莊嚴劫; S. *vyūha-kalpa*), preceding ours; see Supplementary Notes, s.v. "Seven buddhas."

40　*saṃghārāma* (*garan* 伽藍): Buddhist monastery.

41　**"'*cintāruci* medicinal compound'"** (*shindarushi yakuwa* 瞋陀留脂藥和): The name of this medicine does not seem to occur elsewhere in the Buddhist canon; its Sanskrit original has tentatively been reconstructed as *cintāruci* ("wish-fulfilling"), perhaps the "wish-fulfilling water" (*nyoi sui* 如意水) found elsewhere in the literature.

T6. Refuge in the Three Treasures *Kie buppōsōbō* 歸依佛法僧寶　　183

Then the Buddha, the World-Honored One, taking the water in his mouth, sprayed it on the body of the blind dragon woman; and all the afflictions and foul-smelling places were healed. Once they were healed, she spoke thus, "Now, I beg to receive from the Buddha the three refuges."

Thereupon, the World-Honored One promptly administered the three refuges to the dragon woman.

[T6:27] {2:381}

この龍女、むかしは毘婆尸佛の法のなかに、比丘尼となれり。禁戒を破すといふとも、佛法の通塞を見聞すべし。いまは、まのあたり釋迦牟尼佛にあひたてまつりて、三歸を乞受す。ほとけより三歸をうけたてまつる、厚殖善根といふべし。見佛の功德、必ず三歸によれり。われら盲龍にあらず、畜身にあらざれども、如來をみたてまつらず、ほとけにしたがひたてまつりて三歸をうけず、見佛、はるかなり、はぢつべし。世尊みづから、三歸をさづけましします。しるべし、三歸の功德、それ甚深無量なりといふこと。天帝釋の、野干を拜して三歸をうけし、みな三歸の功德、甚深なるによりてなり。

This dragon woman had become a *bhikṣuṇī* long ago, during the dharma of Buddha Vipaśyin. Though she may have broken the precepts, she must have seen and heard about the passage and obstruction of the buddha dharma.[42] Now, meeting Buddha Śākyamuni face-to-face, she begs to receive the three refuges. Her receiving the three refuges from the Buddha should be called "*thickly planting good roots*"; the merit of her seeing the Buddha inevitably depended on the three refuges.[43]

Although we are not blind dragons nor inhabit animal bodies, we do not see the Tathāgata nor receive the three refuges from him. We should be ashamed that our seeing the Buddha is still far off. The World-Honored One himself administered the three refuges. We should realize that the merit of the three refuges is most profound, incalculable. That Deva Lord Śakra made obeisance to a fox and received the three refuges is entirely because the merit of the three refuges is most profound.[44]

42　**passage and obstruction of the buddha dharma** (*buppō no tsūsoku* 佛法の通塞): I.e., what is and is not in accord with Buddhism, or "how things work" in Buddhism. The compound term *tsūsoku* 通塞 is a common expression indicating that a road or way is "open or blocked"; often carrying the idiomatic sense of affairs "going smoothly or not."

43　**"thickly planting good roots"** (*kōjiki zengon* 厚殖善根): A fixed expression for creating much good karma. "The three refuges" here may refer to those she received from Buddha Śākyamuni, but the following clause suggests that it was the refuges she took under Buddha Vipaśyin that planted the roots of her eventually seeing Buddha Śākyamuni.

44　**Deva Lord Śakra** (*Ten Taishaku* 天帝釋): Dōgen here introduces the theme of the story he will relate in section 33, below.

184 DŌGEN'S *SHŌBŌGENZŌ* VOLUME VI

[T6:28]

佛在迦毘羅衛尼拘陀林時、釋摩男來至佛所、作如是言、云何名爲優婆塞
也。佛即爲説、若有善男子・善女人、諸根完具、受三歸依、是即名爲優婆
塞也。釋摩男言、世尊、云何名爲一分優婆塞。佛言、摩男、若受三歸、及
受一戒、是名一分優婆塞。

> *When the Buddha was staying in the nyagroda grove in Kapilavastu, Śākya Mahānāma came to the Buddha and spoke thus, "What is an upāsaka?"*[45]

> *The Buddha said to him, "If a good son or good daughter with sense organs intact has received the refuges, he or she is called an 'upāsaka.'"*

> *Śākya Mahānāma said, "World-Honored One, what is a one-part upāsaka?"*[46]

> *The Buddha said, "Mahānāma, if one has received the three refuges as well as one of the precepts, he or she is called a 'one-part upāsaka.'"*

[T6:29] {2:382}

佛弟子となること、かならず三歸による。いづれの戒をうくるも、かなら
ず三歸をうけて、そののち諸戒をうくるなり。しかあれば即ち、三歸によ
りて得戒あるなり。

Becoming a disciple of the Buddha always depends on the three refuges. Regardless of which precepts one receives, one always receives the three refuges and then receives the precepts. Therefore, taking the precepts depends on having taken the three refuges.

[T6:30]

法句經云、昔有天帝、自知命終生於驢中、愁憂不已、曰、救苦厄者、唯佛
世尊。便至佛所、稽首伏地、歸依於佛。未起之間、其命便終、生於驢胎。
母驢輞斷、破陶家坏器。器主打之、遂傷其胎、還入天帝身中。佛言、殞命
之際、歸依三寶、罪對已畢。天帝聞之得初果。

---

45 **When the Buddha was staying in the *nyagroda* grove in Kapilavastu** (*Butsu zai Kabirae nikuda rin ji* 佛在迦毘羅衛尼拘陀林時): Quoting (with slight variation) the *Nirvāṇa Sūtra* (*Da banniepan jing* 大般涅槃經, T.374.12:568b9-14; T.375.12:815a16-21). The *nyagroda* is the banyan, or Indian fig, tree; Kapilavastu was the capital of the kingdom ruled by the Śākya clan.

Śākya Mahānāma (*Shaku Manan* 釋摩男): A lay relative of the Buddha, not to be confused with the Mahānāma listed among the Buddha's first five disciples.

"upāsaka" (*ubasoku* 優婆塞): A Buddhist layman; though here the text uses the term in reference to both male and female, the latter is usually known as *upāsikā* (*ubai* 優婆夷).

46 **"one-part *upāsaka*"** (*ichibun ubasoku* 一分優婆塞): I.e., an *upāsaka* who has taken one of the five precepts. One who has taken two precepts is called *shōbun* 少分 ("few parts"); one who has taken three or four precepts is called *tabun* 多分 ("many parts"); one who has taken all five is called *manbun* 滿分 ("all parts"). See, e.g., *Yupose jie jing* 優婆塞戒經, T.1488.24:1049a21-26.

T6. Refuge in the Three Treasures *Kie buppōsōbō* 歸依佛法僧寶 185

It is said in the Dharma Verse Sūtra,[47]

Long ago, Deva Lord Śakra, knowing that his life was ending and he would be reborn in a donkey, was in ceaseless despair, saying, "Only the Buddha, the World-Honored One, can rescue me from this pain and distress."

Thereupon, he went to the Buddha, prostrated himself and lay on the ground, taking refuge in the Buddha. Before he could stand up, his life ended, and he was reborn in the womb of a donkey. The bridle on the mother donkey snapped, and she broke the unfired pots in a potter's house. The potter hit her, injuring her womb, and Deva Lord Śakra returned to his original body.

The Buddha said, "Just as you died, you took refuge in the three treasures, and the recompense for your offenses was finished."

Upon hearing this, Deva Lord Śakra attained the first fruit.[48]

[T6:31] {2:383}

おほよそ世間の苦厄をすくふこと、佛世尊には、しかず。このゆえに、天帝、いそぎ世尊のみもとに詣す。伏地のあひだに命終し、驢胎に生ず。歸佛の功德により、驢母の轡やぶれて、陶家の坏器を破す。器主、これをうつ。驢母の身、いたみて、託胎の驢、やぶれぬ。即ち天帝の身に、かへりいる。佛説をききて、初果をうる、歸依三寶の功德力なり。

In general, nothing is the equal of the Buddha, the World-Honored One, in saving us from the agonies of this world. Therefore, Deva Lord Śakra hurried to visit the place of the World-Honored One. While he was prostrating himself, his life ended, and he was born in the womb of a donkey. By the merit of his having taken refuge in the Buddha, the mother donkey's bridle broke, and she smashed the earthenware utensils in a potter's house. The potter struck her, injuring her, and the donkey in her womb was destroyed. Whereupon, he returned to his body as Deva Lord Śakra. That, upon hearing the words of the Buddha, he attained the first fruit was [due to] the power of the merit of having taken refuge in the three treasures.

---

47 **Dharma Verse Sūtra** (*Hokku kyō* 法句經): I.e., the *Dharmapāda*; in fact, Dōgen's version of this story is taken from the *Zhiguan fuxing zhuan hongjue* 止觀輔行傳弘決 by Zhanran 湛然 (T.1912.46:259c21-27), which summarizes a story found in the *Faju piyu jing* 法句譬喩經 (T.211.4:475b19-c8).

48 **first fruit** (*shoka* 初果): I.e., the state of "stream-entrant" (*yoru* 預流; S. *srotāpanna*), first of the four fruits on the *śrāvaka* path to nirvāṇa.

[T6:32]

しかあれば即ち、世間の苦厄、すみやかにはなれて、無上菩提を證得せぬ
こと、必ず歸依三寳のちからなるべし。おほよそ三歸のちから、三惡道を
はなるるのみにあらず、天帝釋の身に還入す。天上の果報をうるのみにあ
らず、須陀洹の聖者となる。まことに三寳の功德海、無量無邊にましますり。
なり。世尊在世は、人天、この慶幸あり。いま如來滅後、後五百歲のと
き、人天いかがせん。しかあれども、如來の形像・舍利等、なほ世間に現
住しまします。これに歸依したてまつるに、また、かみのごとくの功德を
うるなり。

Thus, it is invariably the power of taking refuge in the three treasures
that quickly frees one from the agonies of this world and enables one to
verify unsurpassed bodhi.[49] In sum, the power of the three refuges not
only distanced him from the three evil paths but returned him to the body
of Deva Lord Śakra; he not only acquired the recompense of [birth in]
heaven but became a sage of the *srotāpanna* [fruit]. Truly the ocean of
the three treasures is incalculable and limitless. While the World-Honored One was in the world, humans and devas enjoyed this blessing;
now, in "*the latter five hundred years following the extinction of the
Tathāgata*," what are humans and devas to do?[50] Yet images, relics, and
the like, of the Tathāgata still remain in the world. When we take refuge
in them, we also acquire merit like that above.

[T6:33]

未曾有經曰、佛言、憶念過去無數劫時、毘摩大國徙陀山中、有一野干。
而爲師子所逐、欲食。奔走墮井、不能得出。經於三日、開心分死、而説
偈言、禍哉、今日苦所逼、便當没命於丘井、一切萬物皆無常、恨不以身飴
師子、南無歸依十方佛、表知我心淨無己。時天帝釋聞佛名、肅然毛豎、念
古佛、自惟孤露無導師、耽著五欲自沈没。即與諸天八萬衆、飛下詣井欲問
詰。乃見野干在井底、兩手攀土不得出。天帝復自思念言、聖人應念無方
術。我今雖見野干形、斯必菩薩非凡器。仁者向説非凡言、願爲諸天説法
要。於時野干仰答曰、汝爲天帝無教訓、法師在下自處上、都不修敬問法
要。法水清淨能濟人、云何欲得自貢高。天帝聞是大慚愧、給侍諸天愕然
笑。天王降趾大無利。天帝即時告諸天、慎勿以此懷驚怖、是我頑蔽、德不
稱、必當因是聞法要。即爲垂下天寳衣、接取野干出於上。諸天爲設甘露
食。野干得食生活望。非意禍中致斯福。心懷踴躍、慶無量。野干、爲天帝
及諸天廣説法要。

49　**enables one to verify unsurpassed bodhi** (*mujō bodai o shōtoku senu* 無上菩提を
證得せぬ): Adopting the reading *shōtoku seshimuru* 證得せしむる found in other MSS.

50　**"the latter five hundred years following the extinction of the Tathāgata"** (*nyorai metsu go, go gohyaku sai* 如來滅後、後五百歲): A fixed expression for the final,
degenerate age of the dharma of Buddha Śākyamuni, as used especially in the *Lotus
Sūtra* (see, e.g., *Miaofa lianhua jing* 妙法蓮華經, T.262.9:54b29).

T6. Refuge in the Three Treasures *Kie buppōsōbō* 歸依佛法僧寶 187

In the *Sūtra of the Unprecedented*, it is said:[51]

The Buddha said,

> I remember that, innumerable kalpas in the past, there was a fox on Mount Sītā, in the great country of Bhīmā.[52] It was chased by a lion that wanted to eat it. While fleeing, it fell into a well, from which it could not get out. After three days, recognizing that death was certain, it recited a gāthā:
>
>> O woe this day, afflicted by pain,
>> I shall lose my life in an empty well.
>> All the myriad things being impermanent,
>> I regret not feeding my body to the lion.
>> I take refuge in the buddhas of the ten directions;
>> Know that my mind is pure and selfless.
>
> Then, Deva Lord Śakra, hearing the names of the buddhas,
> Awestruck, with hair on end, recalled the ancient buddhas.[53]
> And thought to himself, "I'm alone, without guide;
> Drowning in thrall to the five desires."
> So, with a throng of eighty thousand devas,
> He flew down to the well to question [the fox].
> Then, seeing the fox at the bottom of the well,
> Its two paws clawing the earth to no avail,
> Śakra again pondered and said,
> "The sage must think he's without any means.
> While now I see the body of a fox,
> Surely this is a bodhisattva, no common vessel.
> Benevolent one, your speech before was not common words.
> Please preach the gist of the dharma to the devas."
> At that time, the fox looked up and replied,
> "As Deva Lord Śakra, you lack proper learning:
> While the dharma master is below, you place yourself above,
> Asking for the gist of the dharma while showing no respect.
> The water of the dharma is pure and salvific;

---

51 ***Sūtra of the Unprecedented*** (*Mizōu kyō* 未曾有經): Again, Dōgen is quoting from Zhanran's *Zhiguan fuxing zhuan hongjue* 止觀輔行傳弘決 (T.1912.46:272a25-b17), which itself cites the sūtra; the relevant passage in the latter text occurs at *Weicengyou yinyuan jing* 未曾有因緣經, T.754.17:576c21-577a28.

52 **Mount Sītā, in the great country of Bhīmā** (*Bima daikoku Shidasan* 毘摩大國徙陀山): The Sanskrit reconstructions for these place names are uncertain; they do not seem to occur outside the context of this story.

53 **Then, Deva Lord** Śakra, hearing the names of the buddhas (*ji Ten Taishaku mon butsumyō* 時天帝釋聞佛名): Though the fox's verse has ended here, Dōgen, like his source, continues the narrative in couplets of seven characters each.

How can you assume such an arrogant stance?"
When Śakra heard this, he was very ashamed.
And the devas in attendance laughed in surprise,
"The deva king descended and gained nothing by it."
Then Deva Lord Śakra admonished the devas,
"Please do not be surprised at this;
I was stubborn and failed to express my virtue,
But surely by this we shall hear the dharma gist."
Then he lowered his heavenly jeweled robe,
And the fox took hold and was pulled out.
The devas set out an ambrosia feast,
And, having eaten, the fox gained the will to live.
Blessed with such fortune in the midst of disaster,
His mind leapt with a joy incalculable.

The fox then extensively preached the essentials of the dharma for the
Deva Lord and the devas.[54]

[T6:34]

これを、天帝拜畜爲師の因縁、と稱す。あきらかにしりぬ、佛名・法名・
僧名のききがたきこと、天帝の野干を師とせし、その證なるべし。いまわ
れら宿善のたすくるによりて、如來の遺法にあふたてまつり、晝夜に三寶
の寶號をききたてまつること、時とともにして不退なり。これすなはち法
要なるべし。天魔波旬、なほ三寶に歸依したてまつりて、患難をまぬか
る。いかにいはんや餘者の、三寶の功德におきて、積功累德せらん、はか
りしらざらめやは。

This is called the case of "*the Deva Lord bows to a beast and makes
it his teacher.*"[55] It is clear from this how difficult it is to hear the word
"buddha," the word "dharma," the word "saṃgha"; the Deva Lord taking a fox as his teacher is surely evidence for this. Now, aided by the
good karma from our past lives, we encounter the dharma bequeathed by
the Tathāgata and hear the treasured names of the three treasures day and
night, never receding with the passage of time. Surely this is "the essentials of the dharma." Even the Deva Māra-pāpīyān escapes from distress
by taking refuge in the three treasures; how much more others — in their
merit from the three treasures, when they "accumulate merit and amass
virtue," how could we not fail to gauge it?[56]

54　**The fox then extensively preached the essentials of the dharma for the Deva
Lord and the devas** (*yakan, i Tentai kyū shoten kōsetsu hōyō* 野干、爲天帝及諸天廣説
法要): Though given in Chinese as if a continuation of the quotation, this sentence does
not occur in Dōgen's sources here.

55　**"the Deva Lord bows to a beast and makes it his teacher"** (*Tentai hai chiku i shi*
天帝拜畜爲師): E.g., in the *Mohe zhiguan* 摩訶止觀, T.1911.46:45b28-29.

56　**the Deva Māra-pāpīyān** (*Ten Mahajun* 天魔波旬): Perhaps an allusion to the story

T6. Refuge in the Three Treasures *Kie buppōsōbō* 歸依佛法僧寶 189

[T6:35]

おほよそ佛子の行道、かならずまづ十方の三寶を敬禮したてまつり、十方
の三寶を勸請したてまつりて、そのみまへに焼香散華して、まさに諸行を
修するなり、これ、即ち古先の勝躅なり、佛祖の古儀なり。もし歸依三寶
の儀、いまだかつておこなはざるは、これ外道の法なり、としるべし、ま
たは、天魔の法ならんとしるべし。佛佛祖祖の法は、かならずそのはじめ
に歸依三寶の儀軌あるなり。

In sum, when children of the Buddha practice the way, we always first
pay obeisance to the three treasures in the ten directions, inviting the
three treasures of the ten directions, burning incense and scattering flowers before them, and performing the various rites. This is the splendid
example of our old forebears, the ancient rites of the buddhas and ancestors. If the rite of refuge in the three treasures has not been performed,
we should recognize that this is the teaching of an other path; we should
recognize that it is the teaching of the Deva Māra. The teachings of buddha after buddha and ancestor after ancestor always has at its beginning
the rite of refuge in the three treasures.

{2:386}

正法眼藏歸依三寶第六
Treasury of the True Dharma Eye
Refuge in the Three Treasures[57]
Number 6

建長七年乙卯夏安居日、以先師之御草本書寫畢。
未及中書清書等、定御再治之時、有添削歟。於今不可叶其儀。仍御草
如此云

*Completed the copying of my former master's draft, on a day of the
summer retreat, junior wood year of the rabbit, the seventh year of
Kenchō [1255].*[58]

---

of Māra, the Evil One, taking the three refuges under the fourth Chan ancestor, Upagupta
(see *Jingde chuandeng lu* 景德傳燈錄, T.2076.51:207b4-25).

57 **Refuge in the Three Treasures** (*kie sanbō* 歸依三寶): Following the Kawamura
edition, based on a text in which the title in the colophon differs from that at the head.

58 **Completed the copying of my former master's draft** (*i senshi shi gosōhon shosha
hitsu* 以先師之御草本書寫畢): A colophon appearing in some manuscript traditions and
thought to be by Dōgen's disciple Ejō 懷奘 (1198-1280).

day of the summer retreat (*ge ango no hi* 夏安居日): Dates of the summer retreat
vary; a common practice put it from the fifteenth of the fourth lunar month through the
fifteenth of the seventh month; in 1255, this would have corresponded to 22 May through
18 August.

*He had yet to reach an intermediate or clean copy; doubtless, when he
did the revision, he would have made some additions and deletions.
Now, that cannot be done. So, his draft is like this.*

弘安二年己卯夏安居五月廿一日、在越宇中浜新善光寺書寫之。義雲
*Copied this at the new Zenkō Monastery, Nakahama, Etsuu,
Twenty-first day, fifth month, the summer retreat of the junior earth
year of the rabbit, the second year of Kōan [1 August 1279]. Giun*[59]

---

59 **Giun** 義雲: Fifth abbot of Eiheiji (1253–1333).

TREASURY OF THE TRUE DHARMA EYE
THE TWELVE-CHAPTER COMPILATION
NUMBER 7

Deep Faith in Cause and Effect
Jinshin inga
深信因果

Deep Faith in Cause and Effect

Jinshin inga

INTRODUCTION

This text, though undated, is assumed to be one of its author's later works. A colophon by Ejō preserved in the twenty-eight-text *Shōbōgenzō* collection reports that Dōgen had only completed a rough draft of the text at the time of his death. The chapter occurs as number 5 of fascicle 1 in that collection and as number 89 in the Honzan edition.

"Jinshin inga" represents a reflection on the famous story of Baizhang and the fox, in which a monk is turned into a fox for claiming that a person of "great practice" does not fall into cause and effect; he is then freed from his fox body upon hearing that such a person is "not in the dark about cause and effect." In his comments here, Dōgen argues strongly against interpretations of the story that tend to deny the ultimate reality of cause and effect — interpretations, he warns, that represent the false views of non-Buddhists. The tendency, he complains, is strong among Chan Buddhists in Song-dynasty China, among whom, he singles out the famous Linji figures Yuanwu Keqin 圜悟克勤 and his disciple Dahui Zonggao 大慧宗杲, as well as, rather surprisingly, the renowned Caodong master Hongzhi Zhengjue 宏智正覺.

The story of Baizhang and the fox is also the focus of the "Dai shugyō" 大修行 chapter, from early 1244, where Dōgen offers his own interpretations rather less conservative than what we read here. Hence, this chapter has been a focus of attention in discussions over whether Dōgen changed his views toward the end of his life.

正法眼藏第七
Treasury of the True Dharma Eye
Number 7

深信因果
Deep Faith in Cause and Effect

[T7:1] {2:387}

百丈山大智禪師懷海和尚、凡參次、有一老人、常隨衆聽法、衆退老人亦退。忽一日不退。師遂問、面前立者、復是何人。老人曰、某甲是非人也、於過去迦葉佛時、曾住此山、因學人問、大修行底人、還落因果也無。某甲答他云、不落因果、後五百生、墮野狐身。今請和尚代一轉語、貴脱野狐身。遂問曰、大修行底人、還落因果也無。師云、不昧因果。老人於言下大悟、作禮曰、某甲已脱野狐身、住在山後、敢告和尚、乞依亡僧事例。師令維那白槌告衆云、食後送亡僧。大衆言議、一衆皆安、涅槃堂又無病人、何故如是。食後只見師領衆、至山後巖下、以杖指出一死野狐。乃依法火葬。師至晚上堂、舉前因緣。黄檗便問、古人錯對一轉語、墮五百生野狐身、轉轉不錯、合作箇什麼。師云、近前來、與儞道。檗遂近前與師一掌。師拍手笑云、將爲胡鬚赤、更有赤鬚胡。

Whenever Reverend Huaihai, Chan Master Dazhi of Mount Baizhang held a convocation, there was an old man who always joined the assembly to hear the dharma and who also withdrew when the assembly withdrew.[1] One day, unexpectedly, he did not withdraw. Whereupon, the Master asked him, "Just who are you, standing there?"

The old man answered, "I'm not a human. At the time of the past Buddha Kāśyapa, I once lived on this mountain.[2] A student asked me, 'Does the person of great practice fall into cause and effect?' I answered him saying, 'He doesn't fall into cause and effect.' Thereafter,

---

1 **Reverend Huaihai, Chan Master Dazhi of Mount Baizhang** (*Hyakujōzan Daichi zenji Ekai oshō* 百丈山大智禪師懷海和尚): I.e., Baizhang Huaihai 百丈懷海 (749-814). This famous story of Baizhang and the fox occurs in many sources. In the next section, Dōgen cites the *Tiansheng guangdeng lu* 天聖廣燈錄 as a source; but, in fact, that version is rather different from the one given here. Rather, the version here reflects Dōgen's own *shinji Shōbōgenzō* 眞字正法眼藏 (DZZ.5:178-80, case 102), which seems based on the *Zongmen tongyao ji* 宗門統要集, ZTS.1:58b1-c5. Dōgen quotes the same version in his "Shōbōgenzō dai shugyō" 正法眼藏大修行 but offers there a very different interpretation of the story from the one given here.

2 **"At the time of the past Buddha Kāśyapa"** (*o kako Kashō butsu ji* 於過去迦葉佛時): Or "in the past, at the time of Buddha Kāśyapa." Kāśyapa is the sixth in the series of seven buddhas of the past, culminating with Buddha Śākyamuni; see Supplementary Notes, s.v. "Seven buddhas."

194 DŌGEN'S *SHŌBŌGENZŌ* VOLUME VI

for five hundred lives, I have descended into the body of a fox. Now I beg the Reverend to say a turning word in my stead and let me shed this fox body." Whereupon, he asked, "Does the person of great practice fall into cause and effect?"

The Master said, "He's not in the dark about cause and effect."[3]

At these words, the old man had a great awakening. He made a prostration and said, "I've shed the body of the fox, which lived behind this mountain. May I be so bold as to beg the Reverend for rites for a deceased monk?"

The Master had the rector strike the mallet and announce to the assembly, "After the meal, we send off a deceased monk."[4]

The great assembly expressed doubt, [saying] "The assembly is all well, and there is no one ill in the nirvāṇa hall. So, what is this?"[5]

But after the meal, the Master led the assembly beneath a cliff behind the mountain, where he uncovered a dead fox with his staff. They then cremated it in accordance with the dharma.

In a convocation that evening, the Master raised the above incident. Huangbo then asked, "The ancient, with the single turning word of a mistaken response, descended for five hundred lives into the body of a fox.[6] What would happen if he turned and turned without a mistake?"[7]

The Master said, "Come forward and I'll tell you."

Po thereupon came forward and gave the Master a blow.

The Master clapped his hands and laughed, saying, "Here, I thought the foreigner's beard is red, but now here's a red-bearded foreigner."[8]

"I once lived on this mountain" (*sō jū shi san* 曾住此山): The suggestion is that he served as abbot of the monastery on Mount Baizhang; hence, below he will be referred to as "the former Baizhang."

3 **"He's not in the dark about cause and effect"** (*fumai inga* 不昧因果): The predicate *fumai* 不昧 is variously interpreted as "not blind to," "not oblivious to," "not ignorant of (or about)," "not confused by (or about)," etc.

4 **had the rector strike the mallet** (*rei ino byakutsui* 令維那白槌): The rector (*ino* 維那) is the administrator in charge of the assembly of monks, one of the six principle monastic offices (*roku chiji* 六知事). "Strike the mallet" translates *byakutsui* 白槌, the "announcement mallet" with the sound of which the *ino* signals the assembly.

5 **"nirvāṇa hall"** (*nehan dō* 涅槃堂): I.e., the monastic infirmary.

6 **Huangbo** (*Ōbaku* 黄檗): I.e., Huangbo Xiyun 黄檗希運 (dates unknown), famous disciple of Baizhang 百丈.

7 **"turned and turned without a mistake"** (*tenden fushaku* 轉轉不錯): "Turned and turned" (*tenden* 轉轉) here is generally taken to mean "through lifetime after lifetime."

8 **"Here, I thought the foreigner's beard is red, but now here's a red-bearded foreigner"** (*shō i koshu shaku, kō u shakushu ko* 將爲胡鬚赤、更有赤鬚胡): A saying

T7. Deep Faith in Cause and Effect *Jinshin inga* 深信因果

[T7:2] {2:388}

この一段の因縁、天聖廣燈録にあり。しかあるに、參學のともがら、因果の道理を明らめず、いたづらに撥無因果のあやまりあり。あはれむべし、澆風一扇して、祖道陵替せり。不落因果は、まさしくこれ撥無因果なり、これによりて惡趣に堕す。不昧因果は、あきらかにこれ深信因果なり、これによりて、きくもの惡趣を脱す。怪しむべきにあらず、疑ふべきにあらず。近代、參禪學道と稱するともがら、おほく因果を撥無せり。なにによりてか因果を撥無せりとしる。いはゆる、不落と不昧と一等にしてことならず、とおもへり、これによりて、因果を撥無せりとしるなり。

This episode is found in the *Tiansheng guangdeng lu*.[9] Yet those who study it, unclear on the principle of cause and effect, foolishly make the mistake of denying cause and effect. How sad, that *the winds of dissolution blow about, and the way of the ancestors goes into decline*. "*He doesn't fall into cause and effect*" — this is precisely denying cause and effect; and due to this, one falls into an evil destiny. "*He's not in the dark about cause and effect*" — this is clearly deep faith in cause and effect; and due to this, one who hears it is released from the evil destiny. We should not be suspicious of this or have doubts about it. In recent times, many of those who call themselves practitioners of meditation and students of the way have denied cause and effect. How do we know they have denied cause and effect? Because they think that "he doesn't fall" and "he's not in the dark" are equivalent, with no difference. By this, they have denied cause and effect.

[T7:3] {2:389}

第十九祖鳩摩羅多尊者曰、且善惡之報、有三時焉。凡人但見仁夭・暴壽・逆吉・義凶、便謂亡因果虚罪福。殊不知影響相隨、毫釐靡忒。縱經百千劫萬劫、亦不磨滅。

The Nineteenth Ancestor, Venerable Kumāralāta, said,[10]
The recompense for good and evil exists through the three times. The common people seeing only that the benevolent die young, while the

---

subject to various interpretations; perhaps meaning here something like, "while I knew that foreigners had red beards, I didn't expect to encounter such a person." The term *hu* (*ko* 胡), often translated "barbarian," is used to refer to non-Han people to the north and west of the Chinese heartland.

9 *Tiansheng guangdeng lu* (*Tenshō kōtō roku* 天聖廣燈録): A variant version of the story from that given here can be found in this text at ZZ.135:656b13-657a7; but see above, Note 1.

10 **Nineteenth Ancestor, Venerable Kumāralāta** (*dai jūkyū so Kumorata sonja* 第十九祖鳩摩羅多尊者): The passage, which appears in a number of Chan texts (as well as Dōgen's "Shōbōgenzō sanji gō" 正法眼藏三時業), is likely taken here from the *Jingde chuandeng lu* 景德傳燈録 (T.2076.51:212c29-213a2). Like many of the reconstructions of the Sanskrit names of the Indian ancestors of Zen, Kumāralāta is conjecture; it is also reconstructed as Kumāralabdha and Kumārata.

violent live long, the treasonous have good fortune, while the righteous have misfortune, think that cause and effect do not exist, and evils and blessings are void. They are completely ignorant of the fact that the shadow and the echo follow without a hair's breadth of variation.[11] Even over a hundred thousand kalpas, a myriad kalpas, they will not be erased.[12]

[T7:4]

明らかにしりぬ、曩祖、いまだ因果を撥無せずといふことを。いまの晩進、いまだ祖宗の慈誨をあきらめざるは、稽古の、おろそかなるなり。稽古おろそかにして、みだりに人天の善知識と自稱するは、人天の大賊・學者の怨家なり。なむだち前後のともがら、亡因果のおもむきをもて、後學・晩進のためにかたることなかれ。これは邪說なり、さらに佛祖の法にあらず。なむぢらが疏學によりて、この邪見に墮せり。

It is clear here that the Ancient Ancestor never denied cause and effect. That latecomers today remain unclear about the Ancestor's compassionate instruction is their negligence in investigating the ancients. Those who, while negligent in investigating the ancients, call themselves the wise friends to humans and devas are the great thieves of humans and devas, the enemies of those who study. You people in this group, do not talk to latter-day students and latecomers of the absence of cause and effect. It is a false teaching, by no means the dharma of the buddhas and ancestors. You have fallen into this false view because of your neglect of study.

[T7:5] {2:390}

いま震旦國の衲僧等、ままにいはく、われらが人身をうけて佛法にあふ、一生二生の事、なほしらず、前百丈の、野狐となれり、よく五百生をしれり、はかりしりぬ、業報の墜墮にあらじ、金鎖玄關留不住、行於異類且輪廻なるべし。大善知識とあるともがらの見解、かくのごとし。

Nowadays, the patch-robed monks of the Land of Cīnasthāna frequently say, "We have received a human body and encountered the buddha dharma, but we do not know about even one or two of our lives; yet the former Baizhang became a fox and knew about five hundred lives. Clearly, this must not be a case of falling [into the body of fox] from karmic recompense; it must be,

---

11 **the shadow and the echo follow** (*yōgō sōzui* 影響相隨): After the old adage that fortune and misfortune follow deeds just as the shadow follows the object, and the echo, the sound.

12 **a hundred thousand kalpas, a myriad kalpas** (*hyakusen kō man kō* 百千劫萬劫): The "Shōbōgenzō sanji gō" 正法眼藏三時業 version accords with the *Jingde chuandeng lu* 景德傳燈錄 in reading *hyakusenman kō* 百千萬劫 ("a hundred thousand myriad kalpas").

T7. Deep Faith in Cause and Effect *Jinshin inga* 深信因果 197

Unimpeded by the dark barrier with golden chains,
He turns on, moving among different types."[13]

Such is the view of those held to be great wise friends.

[T7:6]

この見解は、佛祖の屋裏におきがたきなり。或いは人、或いは狐、或いは
餘趣のなかに、生得にしばらく宿通をえたるともがらあり。然れども、明
了の種子にあらず、惡業の所感なり。この道理、世尊、ひろく人天のため
に演説しまします、これをしらざるは疏學のいたりなり。憐れむべし、た
とひ一千生、一萬生をしるとも、必ずしも佛法なるべからず。外道、すで
に八萬劫をしる、いまだ佛法とせず。わづかに五百生をしらむ、いくばく
の能にあらず。

This view is difficult to place within the house of the buddhas and ancestors. Among humans or foxes or in other destinies, there are those who
have acquired from birth the power to know a bit of their former lives.
This is not, however, the seed of clear understanding but the result of bad
karma. The World-Honored One has preached this truth extensively to
humans and devas; not to know it is an extreme neglect of study. How
sad. Even knowing one thousand lives, or ten thousand lives, does not
necessarily make it the buddha dharma. Followers of other paths may
know eighty thousand kalpas; that is not taken to be the buddha dharma.[14]
To know a mere five hundred lives is not much of an ability.

[T7:7]

近代宋朝の參禪の輩ら、もともくらき處、ただ不落因果を邪見の説としら
ざるにあり。あはれむべし、如來の正法の流通する處、祖祖正傳せるにあ
ひながら、撥無因果の邪儻とならむ。參學のともがら、まさにいそぎて因
果の道理を明らむべし。今百丈の不昧因果の道理は、因果にくらからずと
なり。然れば、修因感果のむね、明らかなり、佛佛祖祖の道なるべし。お
ほよそ、佛法いまだ明らめざらむとき、みだりに人天のために説法するこ
となかれ。

---

13 **"Unimpeded by the dark barrier with golden chains, He turns on, moving among
different types"** (*kinsa genkan ru fuju gyō o irui sho rinne* 金鎖玄關留不住、行於異
類且輪廻): Quoting a verse from the *Shi xuantan* 十玄談, by Dong'an Changcha 同安
常察 (dates unknown) (*Jingde chuandeng lu* 景德傳燈錄, T.2076.51:455c12-13). "Turn
on" renders *rinne* 輪廻, a term for rebirth in saṃsāra. "Moving among different types"
renders *gyō o irui* 行於異類, a variation on *irui chū gyō* 異類中行, an idiom occurring
frequently in Chan literature (and in Dōgen's writing), suggesting the bodhisattva's salvific activities among all living beings (including foxes); see Supplementary Notes, s.v.
"Move among different types."

14 **Followers of other paths may know eighty thousand kalpas** (*gedō, sude ni hachiman kō o shiru* 外道、すでに八萬劫をしる): See, e.g., the *Mahāvibhāṣā* (*Apidamo da
piposha lun* 阿毘達磨大毘婆沙論, T.1545.27:519c24-27), on three levels of "eternal-
ists"; or the *Zhiguan fuxing zhuan hongjue* 止觀輔行傳弘決 (T.1912.46:434b22), on the
Sāṃkhya founder Kapila.

198 DŌGEN'S *SHŌBŌGENZŌ* VOLUME VI

Where those who study Chan in recent times in the Song dynasty are most in the dark is precisely their failure to recognize that "*not falling into cause and effect*" is the teaching of a false view.[15] How pathetic that, where the true dharma of the Tathāgata has spread, and even while encountering its direct transmission by ancestor after ancestor, they would form a heretical band that denies cause and effect. Students should hasten to clarify the principle of cause and effect. The principle of the present Baizhang's "*not in the dark about cause and effect*" means not being in the dark about cause and effect.[16] So, the point that one *cultivates the cause and experiences the effect* is clear, is the word of buddha after buddha and ancestor after ancestor.[17] In sum, when you have not clarified the buddha dharma, do not recklessly preach the dharma to humans and devas.

[T7:8] {2:391}

龍樹祖師云、如外道人、破世間因果、則無今世・後世。破出世因果、則無三寶・四諦・四沙門果。

The Ancestral Master Nāgārjuna said,[18]

If, like the followers of other paths, one denies cause and effect in the mundane realm, there would be no present and no future lives; if one denies cause and effect in the transmundane, there would be no three treasures, four truths, or four fruits of the śramaṇa.[19]

---

15 **Where those who study Chan in recent times in the Song dynasty are most in the dark** (*kindai Sōchō no sanzen no tomogara, motomo kuraki tokoro* 近代宋朝の參禪の輩ら、もともくらき處): Here and below in this section, Dōgen plays with the terms "darkness" (*mai* 昧; i.e., "ignorance") and "brightness" (*myō* 明; translated "clarify," "clear").

16 **The principle of the present Baizhang's "not in the dark about cause and effect" means not being in the dark about cause and effect** (*kon Hyakujō no fumai inga no dōri wa, inga ni kurakarazu to nari* 今百丈の不昧因果の道理は、因果にくらからずとなり): Dōgen here puts Baizhang's Chinese phrase into Japanese, with the implication that it means, "is not ignorant of cause and effect."

17 **cultivates the cause and experiences the effect** (*shuin kanka* 修因感果): A fixed expression occurring throughout Buddhist literature.

18 **The Ancestral Master Nāgārjuna** (*Ryūju soshi* 龍樹祖師): The source is the *Mohe zhiguan* 摩訶止觀, by Zhiyi 智顗 (538–597) (T.1911.46:31a16-18), which attributes the lines to the *Zhonglun* 中論, Kumārajīva's translation of Nāgārjuna's *Madhyama-ka-kārikā* (though the lines do not, in fact, seem to occur there).

19 **four fruits of the śramaṇa** (*shi shamon ka* 四沙門果): The four stages on the *śrā-vaka* path to nirvāṇa.

T7. Deep Faith in Cause and Effect *Jinshin inga* 深信因果 199

[T7:9]

あきらかにしるべし、世間・出世の因果を破するは、外道なるべし。今世なし、といふは、かたちはこの處にあれども、性はひさしくさとりに歸せり、性すなはち心なり、心は身とひとしからざるゆえに。かくのごとく解する、すなはち外道なり。あるいはいはく、ひと、死するとき、必ず性海に歸す、佛法を修習せざれども、自然に覺海に歸すれば、さらに生死の輪轉なし、このゆえに後世なし、といふ。これ斷見の外道なり。かたち、たとひ比丘にあひにたりとも、かくのごとくの邪解あらむともがら、さらに佛弟子にあらず、まさしくこれ外道なり。おほよそ因果を撥無するより、今世・後世なし、とはあやまるなり。因果を撥無することは、眞善識に參學せざるにより、眞善識に久參するがごときは、撥無因果等の邪解あるべからず。龍樹祖師の慈誨、ふかく信仰したてまつり、頂戴したてまつるべし。

It is clear from this that denial of cause and effect in the mundane world and the transmundane is an other path. To maintain that there is no present life is to say that while one's body exists here, one's nature abides forever in awakening; for the nature is the mind, and the body and mind are not the same. Such an understanding is that of an other path. Or others say that when one dies, one invariably returns to the ocean of the nature. Since, even without studying the buddha dharma, one naturally returns to the ocean of awakening, one does not revolve through birth and death; hence, there is no future life. This is the nihilistic view of an other path. Even though they may resemble bhikṣus in appearance, those who maintain this kind of false understanding are definitely not disciples of the Buddha; truly, they are followers of other paths. In sum, by denying cause and effect, they make the mistake of maintaining that present lives and future lives do not exist. Their denial of cause and effect is a result of their failure to study with a true wise friend; those who have long studied with a true wise friend do not have false understandings like the denial of cause and effect. We should have deep faith in, and accept, the compassionate instructions of the Ancestral Master Nāgārjuna.

[T7:10]

永嘉眞覺大師玄覺和尚は、曹溪の上足なり、もとはこれ天台の法華宗を習學せり、左谿玄朗大師と同室なり。涅槃經を披閲せるところに、金光、その室にみつ、ふかく無生の悟をえたり。すすみて曹溪に詣し、證をもて六祖に告す。六祖、つひに印可す。のちに證道歌をつくるにいはく、豁達空撥因果、莽莽蕩蕩招殃過。

Reverend Xuanjue, Great Master Zhenjue of Yongjia, was a top disciple of Caoxi.[20] Originally, he studied the *Lotus* teachings of Tiantai,

---

20 **Reverend Xuanjue, Great Master Zhenjue of Yongjia** (*Yōka Shinkaku daishi Genkaku oshō* 永嘉眞覺大師玄覺和尚): I.e., Yongjia Xuanjue 永嘉玄覺 (665-713).

Caoxi (*Sōkei* 曹溪): I.e., Caoxi Huineng 曹溪慧能, the Sixth Ancestor.

200 DŌGEN'S *SHŌBŌGENZŌ* VOLUME VI

sharing quarters with Great Master Xuanlang of Zuoxi.[21] While he was reading the *Nirvāṇa Sūtra*, a golden light filled his room, and he attained awakening to the unborn. He went on to visit Caoxi and reported his realization to the Sixth Ancestor. The Sixth Ancestor gave his seal of approval. Later, he composed the *Zhengdao ge*, in which it is said,

A wide-open void, dismissing cause and effect;
An endless vastness, inviting disaster.[22]

[T7:11] {2:392}

明らかにしるべし、撥因果は、招殃過なるべし。往代は、古德ともに因果を明らめたり、近世には、晩進みな因果にまどへり。いまのよなりといふとも、菩提心いさぎよくして、佛法のために佛法を習學せむともがらは、古德のごとく因果を明らむべきなり。因なし、果なし、といふは、即ちこれ外道なり。

We should clearly recognize that "*dismissing cause and effect*" is "*inviting disaster.*" In past times, the ancient worthies all clarified cause and effect; in recent times, the latecomers are all confused about cause and effect. Even in today's world, those who, with a pure mind of bodhi, would study the buddha dharma for the sake of the buddha dharma, should clarify cause and effect just as the ancient worthies did. To say there is no cause and no effect — this is [a view of] other paths.

[T7:12]

宏智古佛、かみの因緣を頌古するに云く、一尺水一丈波、五百生前不奈何、不落不昧商量也、依然撞入葛藤窠。阿呵呵、會也麼。若是儞洒洒落落、不妨我哆哆和和。神歌社舞自成曲、拍手其間唱哩囉。いま、不落不昧商量也、依然撞入葛藤窠、の句、即ち、不落と不昧とおなじかるべし、といふなり。

Old Buddha Hongzhi said in a verse comment on the above episode,[23]

One foot of water; ten feet of wave:
Five hundred lives ago; nothing can be done.[24]
Discussing "not falling" or "not in the dark,"

---

21 **Great Master Xuanlang of Zuoxi** (*Sakei Genrō daishi* 左谿玄朗大師): (673-754) Teacher of the famed Tiantai exegete Zhanran 湛然 (711–782).

22 ***Zhengdao ge*** (*Shōdō ka* 證道歌): Famous early Chan poem traditionally attributed to Yongjia. The line quoted here can be found at T.2014.48:396a27-28.

23 **Old Buddha Hongzhi** (*Wanshi kobutsu* 宏智古佛): I.e., Hongzhi Zhengjue 宏智正覺 (1091–1157). His verse comment (*juko* 頌古) can be found in the *Hongzhi chanshi guanglu* 宏智禪師廣錄 (T.2001.48:29a24-28). Dōgen generally held Hongzhi in high esteem; his criticism here is striking.

24 **One foot of water; ten feet of wave** (*isshaku sui ichijō ha* 一尺水一丈波): An idiom with a sense something like "making a mountain out of a molehill."

T7. Deep Faith in Cause and Effect *Jinshin inga* 深信因果 201

Still pushing into the nest of tangled vines.[25]
Ha! Ha! Ha!
Do you understand?
If you're easygoing and relaxed,
I might as well babble on.
Spirits sing, and gods dance to their own tune;
Clapping my hands, I chant to the beat.

The lines here, "*Discussing 'not falling' or 'not in the dark,' still pushing into the nest of tangled vines*" — this is saying that "not falling" and "not in the dark" must be the same.

[T7:13]

おほよそこの因縁、その理、いまだつくさず。そのゆえいかん、となれば、脱野狐身は、いま現前せりといへども、野狐身をまぬかれてのち、すなはち人間に生ず、といはず、天上に生ず、といはず、および餘趣に生ず、といはず、人の疑ふ處なり。脱野狐身の、すなはち善趣にむまるべくは、天上・人間にうまるべし、惡趣にむまるべくは、四惡趣等にむまるべきなり。脱野狐身ののち、むなしく生處なかるべからず。もし、衆生死して性海に歸し、大我に歸す、といふは、ともにこれ外道の見なり。

More broadly, this episode does not fully make sense. Why is this? While the fox body that he shed appears before [the monks], after he escaped the fox body, it does not say that he was then reborn as a human; it does not say he was born in a heaven; it does not say he was born in some other destiny. This is what people will have doubts about. If, upon shedding the body of the fox, he is to be born in a good destiny, he should be born in a heaven or as a human; if he is to be born in an evil destiny, he should be born in one of the four evil destinies. After he shed the fox body, he cannot be without a place of rebirth. To say that the living being dies and returns to the ocean of the nature or returns to the great self — these are the views of other paths.[26]

---

25 **nest of tangled vines** (*kattō ka* 葛藤窠): I.e., semantic distinctions. See Supplementary Notes, s.v. "Tangled vines."

26 **ocean of the nature** (*shōkai* 性海); **great self** (*daiga* 大我): These expressions, used in some Buddhist literature to describe the ultimate reality of the self, recall Hindu notions of *puruśa* or ātman, respectively.

202   DŌGEN'S *SHŌBŌGENZŌ* VOLUME VI

[T7:14] {2:393}

夾山圜悟禪師克勤和尚、頌古云、魚行水濁、鳥飛毛落。至鑑難逃、太虛寥
廓。一往迢迢五百生、只緣因果大修行、疾雷破山風震海、百煉精金色不
改。

> Reverend Keqin, Chan Master Yuanwu of Jiashan, said in a verse comment,[27]

> When the fish moves, the water gets muddy; when the bird flies, its feathers fall.
> The perfect mirror is hard to escape; the great void is boundless expanse.
> One long, long trip of five hundred lives,
> Just the great practice by means of cause and effect.
> A sudden thunderclap rends the mountain; a wind stirs up the sea.
> Pure gold of a hundred refinements never changes it color.

[T7:15]

この頌、なほ撥無因果のおもむきあり、さらに、常見のおもむきあり。

> This verse also has a tendency to denial of cause and effect; moreover, it has a tendency to eternalism.[28]

[T7:16]

杭州徑山大慧禪師宗杲和尚、頌云、不落不昧、石頭土塊。陌路相逢、銀山
粉碎。拍手呵呵笑一場、明州有箇憨布袋。

> Reverend Zonggao, Chan Master Dahui, of Jingshan in Hangzhou, said in a verse comment,[29]

> "Not falling," "not in the dark": a rock and a clod.
> When they meet on the road, the silver mountain crumbles.
> One scene of clapping and laughing, ha, ha.
> In Mingzhou, there's this halfwit Budai.[30]

---

27 **Reverend Keqin, Chan Master Yuanwu of Jiashan** (*Kassan Engo zenji Kokugon oshō* 夾山圜悟禪師克勤和尚): I.e., Yuanwu Keqin 圜悟克勤 (1063-1135). His verse can be found at *Yuanwu Foguo chanshi yulu* 圓悟佛果禪師語錄 (T.1997.47:804a10-12); or at *Chanzong songgu lianzhu tongji* 禪宗頌古聯珠通集 (ZZ.115:113b13-15).

28 **eternalism** (*jōken* 常見): The view that body and self persist indefinitely; S. *nitya-dṛṣṭi*.

29 **Reverend Zonggao, Chan Master Dahui, of Jingshan in Hangzhou** (*Kōshū Kinzan Daie zenji Sōkō oshō* 杭州徑山大慧禪師宗杲和尚): I.e., Dahui Zonggao 大慧宗杲 (1089-1163). His verse can be found at *Dahui Pujue chanshi yulu* 大慧普覺禪師語錄, T.1998A.47:852b14-15; or at *Chanzong songgu lianzhu tongji* 禪宗頌古聯珠通集 (ZZ.115:114a13-14).

30 **In Mingzhou, there's this halfwit Budai** (*Minshū u ko kan Hotei* 明州有箇憨布袋): Reference to the eccentric tenth-century monk Qici 契此, said to be from Mingzhou; popularly called Budai 布袋 ("cloth sack") after his shoulder bag; he is often identified in popular lore with the future buddha, Maitreya, and/or counted among the seven gods of fortune.

T7. Deep Faith in Cause and Effect *Jinshin inga* 深信因果

[T7:17]

これらを、いまの宋朝の輩、作家の祖師とおもへり。然れども、宗杲が見解、いまだ佛法の施權のむねにおよばず、ややもすれば自然見のおもむきあり。おほよそこの因縁に、頌古・拈古の輩、三十餘人あり。一人としても、不落因果これ撥無因果なり、と疑ふものなし。愍むべし、このともがら、因果を明らめず、いたづらに紛紜のなかに一生を空しくせり。佛法參學には、第一、因果を明らむなり。因果を撥無するがごときは、おそらくは猛利の邪見をおこして、斷善根とならむことを。

People in the Song dynasty today regard these as virtuoso ancestral masters. However, Zonggao's views do not amount to the message of the provisional teachings of the buddha dharma and have a tendency toward the view of spontaneity.[31]

Overall, more than thirty people have verses or comments on this episode; not a single one of them raises doubts that "not falling into cause and effect" is denying cause and effect. What a pity, that these people, never clarifying cause and effect, wasted their entire lives in a state of confusion. In studying the buddha dharma, clarifying cause and effect comes first. Those who deny cause and effect will surely develop radically false views and cut off their good roots.

[T7:18]

おほよそ因果の道理、歷然としてわたくしなし。造惡のものは堕し、修善のものはのぼる、毫釐もたがはざるなり。もし、因果亡じ、むなしからんがごときは、諸佛の出世あるべからず、祖師の西來あるべからず、おほよそ衆生の見佛聞法あるべからざるなり。因果の道理は、孔子、老子等のあきらむるところにあらず、ただ佛佛祖祖、あきらめ、つたへましますところなり。澆季の學者、薄福にして、正師にあはず、正法をきかず、このゆえに、因果をあきらめざるなり。撥無因果すれば、このとがによりて、莽莽蕩蕩として殃過をうくるなり。撥無因果のほかに、餘惡いまだつくらずといへども、まづこの見毒、はなはだしきなり。

In sum, the principle of cause and effect is obvious and not personal: those who commit evil fall; those who practice good rise, without a hair's breadth of deviation.[32] Were cause and effect gone and nonexistent, the buddhas would not have appeared in the world, the Ancestral Master would not have come from the west, and living beings would not have seen the Buddha and heard the dharma. The principle of cause and effect is not something clarified by Confucius, Laozi, and the like; it is

---

31 **view of spontaneity** (*jinen ken* 自然見): The false view that things occur of their own accord, rather than from prior causes. Dōgen is quite critical of Dahui Zonggao elsewhere in the *Shōbōgenzō* as well; see, e.g., "Shōbōgenzō dai shugyō" 正法眼藏大修行.

32 **the principle of cause and effect is obvious** (*innen no dōri, rekinen toshite* 因果の道理、歷然として): From the fixed expression *inga rekinen* 因果歷然 ("cause and effect are obvious").

something clarified and transmitted only by buddha after buddha and ancestor after ancestor. Students in this season of decline, being unfortunate, do not meet true masters nor hear the true dharma; and, therefore, do not clarify cause and effect. When they "dismiss cause and effect," by this error, in "an endless vastness," they incur "disaster."[33] Even though they may commit no other evil beyond dismissing cause and effect, the poison from this view is extremely potent.

[T7:19]
しかあればすなはち、參學のともがら、菩提心をさきとして、佛祖の洪恩を報ずべくは、すみやかに諸因諸果をあきらむべし。

Therefore, those who study, putting the mind of bodhi first and seeking to repay the immense beneficence of the buddhas and ancestors, should quickly clarify the causes and effects.

正法眼藏深信因果第七
Treasury of the True Dharma Eye
Deep Faith in Cause and Effect
Number 7

[*Himitsu* MS:]
彼御本奧書ニ云、
建長七年乙卯夏安居日、以御草案書寫之。
未及中書清、定有可有再治事也、雖然書寫之。懷奘
In the colophon of his text, it is said,[34]
Copied this from his draft,
on a day of the summer retreat, junior wood year of the rabbit, seventh
year of Kenchō [1255].[35]
He had not yet reached an intermediate draft or clean copy, and surely
there would have been revisions; nevertheless, I have copied it. Ejō

---

33   **When they "dismiss cause and effect," by this error, in "an endless vastness," they incur "disaster"** (*hatsumu inga sureba, kono toga ni yorite, mōmō tōtō to toshite ōka o ukuru nari* 撥無因果すれば、このとがによりて、莽莽蕩蕩として殃過をうくるなり): Echoing Yongjia's verse, quoted in section 10, above.

34   **In the colophon of his text** (*hi gohon okusho* 彼御本奧書): Apparently, a note by the copyist of the text in the *Himitsu Shōbōgenzō* collection. "His text" (*hi gohon* 彼御本) presumably refers to Ejō's original copy.

35   **his draft** (*gosōan* 御草案): I.e., Dōgen's draft.

day of the summer retreat (*ge ango no hi* 夏安居日): Dates of the summer retreat vary; a common practice put it from the fifteenth of the fourth lunar month through the fifteenth of the seventh month; in 1255, this would have corresponded to 22 May through 18 August.

TREASURY OF THE TRUE DHARMA EYE
THE TWELVE-CHAPTER COMPILATION
NUMBER 8

Karma of the Three Times
Sanji gō

三時業

Karma of the Three Times

Sanji gō

INTRODUCTION

This chapter occurs as number 8 in the twelve-chapter *Shōbōgenzō*. Like other texts in that compilation, it is undated, though it is assumed to be among Dōgen's later works. What appears to be an earlier version, (translated below as Variant Text 7 in Volume VII), is preserved in the sixty-chapter *Shōbōgenzō*, from which it was included in the Honzan edition as number 83 (or 84 in the Iwanami and Shūmuchō versions).

As its title indicates, "Karma of the Three Times" is concerned with the effects of good and evil deeds, especially the inevitability of eventual recompense for such deeds. The "three times" in the title refers to the three lifetimes in which such recompense can occur: in this life, in the next life, or in some subsequent life.

The work opens with a story from the Chan literature featuring a teaching on karma by the Indian ancestor Kumāralāta, but the bulk of the essay that follows relies almost entirely on the standard scholastic literature of Buddhism. Only near the end of the work does Dōgen return to his Zen tradition to bring up a case featuring the Tang-dynasty Chan Master Changsha Jingcen 長沙景岑. In his comments, Dōgen is scathing in his criticism of Changsha's identification of karmic recompense with fundamental emptiness.

正法眼藏第八
Treasury of the True Dharma Eye
Number 8
三時業
Karma of the Three Times

[T8:1] {2:395}

第十九祖鳩摩羅多尊者、至中天竺國。有大士、名闍夜多。問曰、我家父母、素信三寶。而嘗縈疾瘵、凡所營事、皆不如意。而我隣家、久爲旃陀羅行、而身常勇健、所作和合。彼何幸、而我何辜。尊者曰、何足疑乎、且善惡之報、有三時焉。凡人但見仁夭暴壽、逆吉、義凶、便謂亡因果虛罪福。殊不知、影響相隨、毫釐靡忒、縱經百千萬劫、亦不磨滅。時闍夜多、聞是語已、頓釋所疑。

When the Nineteenth Ancestor, Venerable Kumāralāta, went to a land of Central Sindhu, there was a great one named Jayata who asked him, "In my family, my father and mother always had faith in the three treasures, yet they suffered from sickness, and all their undertakings went amiss.[1] The family next door to us, however, while they had long worked as candāla, *were always strong and fit, and whatever they did went well.[2] Why are they so fortunate, and what is our crime?"*

The Venerable said, "What is there to doubt? The recompense for good and evil exists through the three times. The common people, seeing only that the benevolent die young, while the violent live long, the treasonous have good fortune, while the righteous have misfortune, think that cause and effect do not exist, and evils and blessings are void. They are completely ignorant of the fact that the shadow and the echo follow without a hair's breadth of variation.[3] Even over a hundred thousand myriad kalpas, they will not be erased."

---

1 **the Nineteenth Ancestor, Venerable Kumāralāta** (*dai jūkyū so Kumorata sonja* 第十九祖鳩摩羅多尊者): The passage, which appears in a number of Chan texts (as well as Dōgen's "Shōbōgenzō jinshin inga" 正法眼藏深信因果), is likely taken here from the *Jingde chuandeng lu* 景德傳燈錄 (T.2076.51:212c25-213a3). Like many of the reconstructions of the Sanskrit names of the Indian ancestors of Zen, Kumāralāta is conjecture; it is also reconstructed as Kumāralabdha and Kumārata.

Jayata (*Shayata* 闍夜多): Traditionally identified as the twentieth ancestor.

2 **"candāla"** (*sendara* 旃陀羅): I.e., lowly occupations, such as butcher, etc.

3 **"the shadow and the echo follow"** (*yōgō sōzui* 影響相隨): After the old adage that fortune and misfortune follow deeds just as the shadow follows the object, and the echo, the sound.

208 DŌGEN'S *SHŌBŌGENZŌ* VOLUME VI

After Jayata heard these words, his doubts were immediately resolved.

[T8:2] {2:396}

鳩摩羅多尊者は、如來より第十九代の附法なり。如來、まのあたり名字を
記しまします。ただ釋尊一佛の法を、明らめ、正傳せるのみにあらず、か
ねて三世の諸佛の法をも、曉了せり。

Venerable Kumāralāta was vouchsafed the dharma in the nineteenth
generation after the Tathāgata. The Tathāgata himself prophesied his
name.[4] He not only clarified and directly transmitted the dharma of one
Buddha, Śākyamuni, he also fully comprehended the dharma of the buddhas of the three times.

[T8:3]

闍夜多尊者、いまの問をまうけしよりのち、鳩摩羅多尊者にしたがひて如
來の正法を修習し、つひに第二十代の祖師となれり。これもまた、世尊は
るかに、第二十祖は闍夜多なるべし、と記しましませり。しかあれば即
ち、佛法の批判、もつともかくのごとくの祖師の所判のごとく習學すべき
なり。いまのよに、因果をしらず、業報を明らめず、三世をしらず、善惡
をわきまへざる邪見の輩には、群すべからず。

After Jayata asked this question, he practiced the true dharma of the
Tathāgata under Kumāralāta and eventually became the ancestral master of the twentieth generation. Here, too, the World-Honored One had
prophesied long ago that the twentieth ancestor would be Jayata.[5] Hence,
we should learn that our judgments of the buddha dharma are to be just
like such a decision by the Ancestral Master.[6] We should not associate
with those who, ignorant of cause and effect in the present time, unclear
about actions and their consequences, ignorant of the three times, hold a

---

4 **The Tathāgata himself prophesied his name** (*Nyorai, manoatari myōji o shirushi-
mashimasu* 如來、まのあたり名字を記しまします): Possibly an allusion to a passage
in the biography of Kumāralāta's teacher, the Eighteenth Ancestor, Gayāśata, in the
Jingde chuandeng lu 景德傳燈錄 (T.2076.51:212c11-14). Upon their first meeting, in
Tukhāra, "the Land of the Great Yuezhi" (*dai Gesshi koku* 大月氏國; in the northwest of
India), Gayāśata informed Kumāralāta:

> 昔世尊記日、吾滅後一千年有大士、出現於月氏國、紹隆玄化。今汝值吾應斯嘉
> 運。
>
> "Long ago, the World-Honored One prophesied, saying, 'One thousand years after
> my extinction, there will be a great one, who will appear in the Land of Tukhāra to
> perpetuate the dark teachings.' Your encountering me now must be that auspicious
> event."

5 **the World-Honored One** (*Seson* 世尊): Dōgen's source for the claim that Jayata's
place in the Zen lineage was predicted by the Buddha is unknown.

6 **such a decision by the Ancestral Master** (*kaku no gotoku no soshi no shohan* かく
のごとくの祖師の所判): Presumably, Kumāralāta's decision to recognize Jayata as the
twentieth ancestor. The phrase could be (and often is) read in the plural: "such decisions
by the ancestral masters."

T8. Karma of the Three Times *Sanji gō* 三時業 209

false view that fails to differentiate good from evil.[7]

[T8:4]

いはゆる善悪之報有三時焉、といふは、三時、一者順現法受、二者順次生受、三者順後次受、これを三時といふ。佛祖の道を修習するには、その最初より、この三時の業報の理をならひ、明らむるなり。しかあらざれば、おほくあやまりて邪見に堕するなり。ただ邪見に堕するのみにあらず、惡道におちて、長時の苦をうく。續善根せざるあひだは、おほくの功徳をうしなひ、菩提の道、ひさしくさはりあり、をしからざらめや。この三時の業、善悪にわたるなり。

"The recompense for good and evil exists through the three times," refers to the "three times": [karma] (1) experienced in the present; (2) experienced in the next life; (3) experienced in lives after the next. These are called the "three times." In practicing the way of the buddhas and ancestors, from the outset, we learn and clarify the principle of actions and consequences over these three times. Where this is not the case, many are mistaken and fall into false views. Not only do they fall into false views, but they fall into the evil paths and suffer for a long time.[8] So long as they do not maintain their good roots, they lose much of their merit and long have obstacles on the path to bodhi. How regrettable! The actions of these three times include both good and evil.

* * * * *

[T8:5] {2:397}

第一順現法受業者、謂、若業此生造作増長、即於此生受異熟果、是名順現法受業。

Of the first, "karma experienced in the present," it is said,[9]

When the karma is performed and develops in this life, and its ripened fruit is experienced in this life, it is called "karma experienced in the present."[10]

---

7 **in the present time** (*ima no yo* いまのよ): Treating this phrase in contrast to "the three times" (*sanze* 三世) just below. The sentence could also be parsed, "We should not associate with those nowadays who . . . ."

8 **evil paths** (*akudō* 惡道): I.e., the three lower realms of rebirth: animal, hungry ghost, and hell; see Supplementary Notes, s.v. "Six paths."

9 **"karma experienced in the present"** (*jungen hō jugō* 順現法受業): Quoting the *Mahāvibhāṣā* (*Apidamo da piposha lun* 阿毘達磨大毘婆沙論, T.1545.27:592a23-24).

10 **ripened fruit** (*ijukuka* 異熟果): S. *vipāka-phala*; the consequences of an act, morally distinct from the act itself.

210 DŌGEN'S *SHŌBŌGENZŌ* VOLUME VI

[T8:6]

いはく、人ありて、或は善にもあれ、あるいは悪にもあれ、この生につくりて即ちこの生にその報をうくるを、順現法受業といふ。

That is, when a person performs [an act] in this life, be it good or evil, and receives the recompense in this life, it is called "karma experienced in the present."[11]

[T8:7]

悪をつくりて、この生にうけたる例、

An example of doing evil and receiving [the consequences] in this life:[12]

[T8:8]

曽有採樵者、入山遭雪、迷失途路。時會日暮。雪深寒凍、將死不久。即前入一蒙密林中、即見一羆。先在林内、形色青紺、眼如双炬。其人惶恐、當失命、此實菩薩現受羆身。見其憂恐、尋慰諭言、汝今勿怖、父母於子、或有異心、吾今於汝、終無惡意。即前捧取、將入窟中、温煖其身、令蘇息已、取諸根果、勸隨所食。恐令不消、抱持而臥。如是恩養、經於六日。至第七日、天晴路現。人有歸心、羆既知已、復取甘果、飽而餞之、送至林外、殷懃告別。人跪謝曰、何以報。羆言、我今不須餘報、但如比日我護汝身、汝於我命、亦願如是。其人敬諾。

> There was once a woodcutter who, having entered the mountains and encountering a snowstorm, became disoriented and lost his way. Time passed, and the sun set; the snow was deep, it was bitter cold, and he was on the verge of death. Upon entering a dense grove, he came upon a bear that had long been living in the grove. Its body was a dark blue; its eyes, like twin torches. The man was terrified that he was about to lose his life; but this was in fact a bodhisattva that had manifested in the body of a bear. Seeing his fear, it reassured him, saying, "Do not be afraid. Parents may be disloyal to their child, but I will never think of harming you."

> Then it approached and grasped him, brought him into a cave, and warmed him. After it had revived him, it brought him roots and fruits, urging him to eat all he could. Concerned that his chill was not thawed, it embraced him and lay down.[13] For six days, it cared for him like this. On the seventh day, the weather cleared, and the path appeared.

---

11   **That is** (*iwaku* いはく): Dōgen is here simply explaining the Chinese passage in Japanese.

12   **An example** (*rei* 例): Dōgen here introduces the following two sections, which continue to quote the passage on the three times in the *Apidamo da piposha lun* 阿毘達磨大毘婆沙論 (T.1545.27:592b3-c2).

13   **Concerned that his chill was not thawed** (*kyō rei fushō* 恐令不消): A tentative translation, reading *rei* 冷 ("cold") for *rei* 令 ("to cause"), after the *Apidamo da piposha lun* 阿毘達磨大毘婆沙論 at T.1545.27:592b11. Some readers take *fushō* 不消 (rendered

T8. Karma of the Three Times *Sanji gō* 三時業 211

The man wished to return; and the bear, realizing this, again brought him sweet fruits and fed him as a parting gift. Accompanying him to edge of the grove, it bade him a polite farewell. The man kneeled and thanked it, saying, "How can I repay you?"

The bear said, "I don't need any repayment. I only ask that, just as I have protected your body these last days, you will do the same for my life."

The man politely agreed.

[T8:9]

担樵下山、逢二猟師。問言、山中見何蟲獸。樵人答曰、我亦不見餘獸、唯見一羆。獵師求請、能示我不。樵人答曰、若能與三分之二、吾當示汝。獵師依許。相與俱行、竟害羆命。分肉爲三。樵人兩手欲取羆肉、惡業力故、双臂俱落、如珠縷斷、如截藕根。獵師危忙、驚問所以。樵人恥愧、具述委曲。是二獵師、責樵人曰、他既於汝有此大恩、汝今何忍行斯惡逆、怪哉、汝身何不糜爛。於是獵師共其肉施僧伽藍。時僧上座、得妙願智、即時入定、觀是何肉、即是知與一切衆生作利樂者、大菩薩肉。即時出定、以此事白衆。衆聞驚歎、共取香薪、焚燒其肉。收其餘骨、起窣堵婆、禮拜供養。如是惡業、待相續、或度相續、方受其果。

Bearing his wood and descending the mountain, he met two hunters, who asked him, "What beasts have you seen in the mountains?"[14]

The woodcutter replied, "I haven't seen any beasts except a bear."

The hunters asked him, "Can you show us?"

The woodcutter replied, "If you give me two-thirds, I'll show you."

The hunters agreed, and they went together. Eventually, they took the bear's life and divided its meat into three. When the woodcutter went to take the bear meat with his two hands, by the force of his evil deed, both his arms fell off, like pearls from a severed string, like lotus roots cut off. The hunters were panic-stricken; alarmed, they asked the reason. The woodcutter, ashamed, related in full the details. The two hunters reproached the woodcutter, saying, "It showed you such great kindness; how could you commit such treachery? It's strange that your entire body didn't decompose."

Thereupon, the hunters both donated their meat to a saṃghārāma.[15] At the time, the senior seat of the monastery had attained the wondrous wisdom that knows at will.[16] He immediately entered into meditation

---

here "not thawed") to mean "not digested"; and it has been suggested that the bear is concerned that, being cold, the woodcutter cannot digest the food it has given him.

14 **Bearing his wood and descending the mountain** (*tan shō ge san* 担樵下山): Continuing to quote the *Apidamo da piposha lun* 阿毘達磨大毘婆沙論 (T.1545.27:592b16-c2).

15 **saṃghārāma** (*sōgaran* 僧伽藍): I.e., a Buddhist monastery.

16 **wondrous wisdom that knows at will** (*myōgan chi* 妙願智): I.e., the paranormal

and saw what meat it was, realizing that it was the flesh of a great bodhisattva who offered benefit and joy to all living beings. Immediately emerging from meditation, he reported this to the assembly. Hearing it, the assembly was amazed. Collecting fragrant kindling, they cremated the flesh. Collecting the remaining bones, they erected a stūpa and paid obeisance and made offerings to it.

One who commits an evil deed such as this will surely experience its fruit, whether in the ensuing continuum or a continuum beyond.[17]

[T8:10] {2:399}

かくのごとくなるを、悪業の順現法受業となづく。おほよそ恩をえては、報をこころざすべし。他に恩しては、報を求ることなかれ。いまも、恩ある人を逆害をくはへむとせん、その悪業、必ずうくべきなり。衆生、ながくいまの樵人のこころなかれ。林外にして告別するには、いかがしてこの恩を謝すべき、といふといへども、山のふもとに獵師にあふては、二分の肉をむさぼる。貪欲にひかれて、大恩所を害す。在家・出家、ながくこの不知恩のこころなかれ。悪業力のきるところ、兩手を断ずること、刀劍のきるよりもはやし。

Cases such as this are called "karma experienced in the present" for an evil action. In general, when receiving a kindness, we should aim to repay it; but, in being kind to another, do not seek repayment. As in the present case, one who would betray and harm a person who has shown kindness will inevitably experience the evil karma. May living beings never have the mind of this woodcutter! In bidding farewell at the edge of the grove, he asked how he could thank [the bear] for its kindness; yet, on meeting the hunters at the foot of the mountain, he craved two parts of its meat. Drawn by this craving, he harmed one who had shown him great kindness. May householders and renunciants never have this mind that does not recognize kindness! The cutting of his two arms by the power of his evil karma was faster than cutting by a sword.

[T8:11] {2:400}

此の生に善をつくりて、順現法受に、善報をえたる例、

An example of doing good and receiving good recompense in this life:[18]

---

power to perceive whatever one wishes to see; one in a list of eight wisdoms found in the *Apidamo da piposha lun* 阿毘達磨大毘婆沙論 (T.1545.27:547a4-6).

17 **whether in the ensuing continuum or a continuum beyond** (*tai sōzoku, waku do sōzoku* 待相續、或度相續): I.e., in the next life or a subsequent life.

18 **An example** (*rei* 例): Continuing to quote the passage on the three times in the *Apidamo da piposha lun* 阿毘達磨大毘婆沙論 (T.1545.27:593a15-25).

T8. Karma of the Three Times *Sanji gō* 三時業

[T8:12]

昔健駄羅國迦膩色迦王、有一黃門、恆監內事。暫出城外、見有群牛數盈五百、來入城內。問駆牛者、此是何牛。答言、此牛將去其種。於是黃門即自思惟、我宿惡業受不男身、今應以財救此牛難。遂償其債、悉令得脱。善業力故、令此黃門即復男身。深生慶悦、尋還城內、侍立宮門、附使啓王、請入奉覲。王令喚入、怪問所由。於是黃門具奏上事。王聞驚喜、厚賜珍財、轉授高官、令知外事。如是善業、要待相續、或度相續、方受其果。

Long ago, in the Land of Gandhāra under King Kaniṣka, there was a eunuch who permanently served as overseer of internal affairs.[19] Once, when he was outside the city, he saw a herd of fully five hundred oxen coming into the city. He asked the herdsman, "What are these oxen for?"

He replied, "These oxen are going to be castrated."

At this, the eunuch thought to himself, "Due to my past evil deeds, I have received this non-male body. Now, I should use my wealth to rescue these oxen from their misfortune."

He thereupon redeemed them and had them all released. By the power of this good deed, the eunuch immediately recovered his male body. Overjoyed, he returned to the city. At the palace gate, he dispatched a messenger to the king requesting an audience. The king had him summoned and, thinking [his request] strange, asked him the reason. Thereupon, the eunuch reported the above incident in full. The king was delighted; he lavished him with precious gifts, promoted him to high rank, and put him in charge of external affairs.

One who commits a good deed such as this will surely experience its fruit, whether in the ensuing continuum or a continuum beyond.

[T8:13] {2:401}

明らかにしりぬ、牛畜の身、をしむべきにあらざれどもすくふと、ひと、善果をうく。いはむや恩田をうやまひ、德田をうやまひ、もろもろの善を修せんをや。かくのごとくなるを、善の順現法受業となづく。善により惡によりて、かくのごとく、ことおほかれど、つくしあぐるにいとまあらず。

We see clearly here that, while the body of an ox is not something to prize, the person who comes to its rescue experiences a good fruit.[20] How much more so one who practices various good deeds honoring the

---

19 **Land of Gandhāra under King Kaniṣka** (*Kendara koku Kanishika ō* 健駄羅國迦膩色迦王): I.e., the kingdom, located in modern Pakistan and eastern Afghanistan, during the reign of Kaniṣka, famous third ruler of the Kuṣāṇa empire (ca. 129-162).

20 **the person who comes to its rescue** (*sukuu to hito* すくふとひと): Reading *sukuu hito* すくふひと.

fields of kindness or the fields of merit.[21] Such cases are called good "karma experienced in the present." Although there are many such cases, both of good and of evil, there is no time here to give them all.

* * * * *

[T8:14]
第二順次生受業者、謂、若業此生造作増長、於第二生受異熟果、是名順次生受業。

Of the second, "karma experienced in the next life," it is said,[22]

When the karma is performed and develops in this life, and its ripened fruit is experienced in the next life, it is called "karma experienced in the next life."

[T8:15]
いはく、もし人ありて、この生に五無間業をつくれる、かならず順次生に地獄におつるなり。順次生とは、この生の、つぎの生なり。餘のつみは、順次生に地獄におつるもあり、また順後次受のひくべきあれば、順次生には大地獄におちず、順後業となることもあり。この五無間業は、さだめて順次生受業に地獄におつるなり。順次生、また第二生とも、これをいふなり。

That is, when a person commits the five deeds of the uninterrupted hell, he or she necessarily falls into that hell in the next life.[23] "The next life" refers to the life after this life. There are other offenses for which one falls into hell in the next life; there are also cases in which, when it [is karma that] involves experience in lives after the next, instead of falling into a great hell in the next life, it becomes karma of subsequent lives. These five deeds of the uninterrupted hell are invariably "karma experienced in the next life," for which one falls into the hell. "The next life" is also referred to as "the second life."

[T8:16]
五無間業、一者、殺父。二者、殺母。三者、殺阿羅漢。四者、出佛身血。五者、破和合僧。

---

21 **fields of kindness** (*onden* 恩田); **fields of merit** (*tokuden* 德田): The former term typically refers to one's parents; the latter term, to the Buddhist saṃgha.

22 **"karma experienced in the next life"** (*jun jishō ju gō* 順次生受業): Again quoting the *Apidamo da piposha lun* 阿毘達磨大毘婆沙論 (T.1545.27:593b4-5).

23 **five deeds of the uninterrupted hell** (*go muken gō* 五無間業): I.e., the five offenses of *ānantarya-karma*, acts leading to *avīci*, the hell of uninterrupted suffering, as listed here in the following section.

T8. Karma of the Three Times *Sanji gō* 三時業 215

The five deeds of the uninterrupted hell: (1) killing one's father; (2) killing one's mother; (3) killing an arhat; (4) spilling the blood of a buddha's body; (5) disrupting the harmony of the saṃgha.[24]

[T8:17] {2:402}

この五無間の業のなかに、いづれににても、一無間業をつくれるもの、必ず順次生に地獄に墮するなり。あるいは、つぶさに五無間業ともにつくるものあり、いはゆる、迦葉波佛のときの華上比丘、これなり。あるいは、一無間業をつくるもの、いはゆる釋迦牟尼佛のとき、阿闍世王なり、そのちちをころす。あるいは、三無間業をつくれるものあり、釋迦牟尼佛のときの阿逸多、これなり、ちちをころし、母をころし、阿羅漢をころす。この阿逸多は、在家のときつくる、のちに出家をゆるさる。提婆達多、比丘として三無間業をつくれり、いはゆる、破僧・出血・殺阿羅漢なり。あるいは、提婆達兜といふ、此翻天熱。その破僧といふは、

Among these five deeds of the uninterrupted hell, those committing any single deed of the uninterrupted hell will necessarily fall into hell in the next life. There are those who commit all of the five deeds of the uninterrupted hell — for example, the bhikṣu Padmottara at the time of Buddha Kāśyapa.[25] There are those who commit one deed of the uninterrupted hell — for example, King Ajātaśatru at the time of Buddha Śākyamuni, who killed his father.[26] There are those who commit three deeds of the uninterrupted hell — for example, Ajita, at the time of Buddha Śākyamuni, who killed his father, killed his mother, and killed an arhat.[27] This Ajita committed them when he was a householder; later he was

---

24 **five deeds of the uninterrupted hell** (*go muken gō* 五無間業): A standard list, found throughout the Buddhist literature, the Chinese terminology for which varies somewhat. Dōgen is here using the language found in the *Dasheng yi zhang* 大乘義章, by Huiyuan 慧遠 (523-592) (T.1851.44:608a25-26), a text he will cite below; his other major source in this fasicle, the *Apidamo da piposha lun* 阿毘達磨大毘婆沙論 (T.1545.27:600a25-27), uses slightly different terminology.

25 **the bhikṣu Padmottara at the time of Buddha Kāśyapa** (*Kashōha butsu no toki no Kejō biku* 迦葉波佛のときの華上比丘): An example given in the *Apidamo da piposha lun* 阿毘達磨大毘婆沙論 (T.1545.27:620b29-c3). The reconstructed Sanskrit name Padmottara is conjecture.

26 **King Ajātaśatru** (*Ajase ō* 阿闍世王): Son of Bimbisāra, king of Magadha, and his queen, Vaidehī; held to have usurped the throne after murdering his father and imprisoning his mother. He later became a follower of the Buddha.

27 **Ajita** (*Aitta* 阿逸多): An example found in the *Nirvāṇa Sūtra* (*Da banniepan jing* 大般涅槃經, T.374.12:479a21-b2; T.375.12:722a24-5; also cited in the *Fahua wenju ji* 法華文句記, by Zhanran 湛然 [711–782], T.1719.34:188a24-26). Ajita, the son of a wealthy family of Vārāṇasī, out of lust for his mother, murdered his father and then murdered his mother when she took a lover; finally, out of shame for his deed, he murdered an arhat. Enraged when he was subsequently denied admission into the Buddhist order by the bhikṣus, he burned their dwellings, killing many of them. Ultimately, he was granted permission to leave home by the Buddha and, upon hearing the Buddha's teachings, aroused the aspiration to attain unsurpassed bodhi.

216 DŌGEN'S *SHŌBŌGENZŌ* VOLUME VI

permitted to leave home. Devadatta committed three deeds of the uninterrupted hell as a bhikṣu: disrupting the saṃgha, spilling the blood of a buddha, and killing an arhat.[28] His name is also written "*Daibadatto*" and translated here "Deva-heat."[29] Regarding his disrupting the saṃgha,

[T8:18]

将五百新學愚蒙比丘吉伽耶山、作五邪法、而破法輪僧。身子厭之眠熟、目連擎衆將還。提婆達多眠起發誓、誓報此恩、捧縱三十肘、廣十五肘石、擲佛。山神以手遮石、小石迸傷佛足、血出。

He took five hundred ignorant new bhikṣus to auspicious Mount Gajaśīrṣa, where they engaged in the five false dharmas and disrupted the dharma wheel saṃgha.[30] Śāriputra despised him and put him into a deep sleep; Maudgalyāyana roused the group to return.[31] Devadatta, awaking from sleep, made a vow, swearing to avenge this kindness.[32]

---

28 **Devadatta** (*Daibadatta* 提婆達多): The Buddha Śākyamuni's infamous evil cousin, whose misdeeds are described below.

29 **"*Daibadatto*"** 提婆達兜: The Japanese reading of an alternative Chinese transliteration of the Sanskrit *Devadatta*. This sentence represents Dōgen's Japanese rendering of the introduction to the passage from the *Miaofa lianhua jing wenju* 妙法蓮華經文句 (T.1718:34.115a2-3) that he will quote in the next section.

"Deva-heat" (*Tennetsu* 天熱): The Sanskrit name *Devadatta* is usually interpreted to mean "god-given" (*Tianshou* 天授). It is said that the Chinese rendering *Tianre* 天熱 derives from the fact that the devas all felt heat when Devadatta was born, because they knew he would commit the three evil deeds and seek to destroy the Buddha dharma (see, e.g., *Fahua yishu* 法華義疏, by Jizang 吉藏 [549–623], T.1718.34:591c12-15).

30 **He took five hundred ignorant new bhikṣus to auspicious Mount Gajaśīrṣa** (*shō gohyaku shingaku gumō biku Kitsu Kayasan* 将五百新學愚蒙比丘吉伽耶山): This section is largely taken from the *Miaofa lianhua jing wenju* 妙法蓮華經文句, by Zhiyi 智顗 (538–597) (T.1718.34:115a2-6). The first sentence, however, does not occur there and seems rather to reflect a passage in the *Zhiguan fuxing zhuan hongjue* 止觀輔行傳弘決, by Zhanran 湛然 (T.1912.46:161c5-9). Mount Gajaśīrṣa (*Kayasan* 伽耶山, translated as *Zōzusen* 象頭山, "Elephant Head") is a peak in the vicinity of Mount Gṛdhrakūṭa.

engaged in the five false dharmas (*sa go jahō* 作五邪法): A set of austerities that Devadatta is said to have sought, against the wishes of the Buddha, to make compulsory for all bhikṣus. The members of the set vary slightly according to the source: one version gives abstinence from (1) dairy, (2) meat, (3) and salt; (4) avoidance of tailored garments; and (5) residence in isolation (see, e.g., *Abhidharma-nyāyānusāra-śāstra* [*Apidamo shun zhengli lun* 阿毘達磨順正理論, T.1562.29:588a4-7]); a second version lists (1) wearing castoff rags, (2) eating only food from begging, (3) eating but once a day, (4) dwelling in the open, and (5) avoiding fish, meat, salt, and dairy (see *Apidamo da piposha lun* 阿毘達磨大毘婆沙論, T.1545.27:602c1-4).

disrupted the dharma wheel saṃgha (*ha hōrin sō* 破法輪僧): I.e., sought to establish an order separate from the Buddha's saṃgha; see the following section.

31 **Śāriputra** (*Shinshi* 身子); **Maudgalyāyana** (*Mokuren* 目連): Two of the Buddha's leading disciples.

32 **swearing to avenge this kindness** (*sei hō shi on* 誓報此恩): The *Miaofa lianhua*

T8. Karma of the Three Times *Sanji gō* 三時業 217

Taking up a rock thirty cubits high and fifteen cubits wide, he threw it at the Buddha. The mountain deity blocked the rock with his hand, but fragments of the rock scattered and injured the Buddha's foot, spilling his blood.

[T8:19] {2:403}

もしこの説によらば、破僧さき、出血のち、なり。もし餘説によらば、破僧・出血の先後、いまだ明らめず。また拳をもて、蓮華色比丘尼をうちころす、この比丘尼は阿羅漢なり。これを、三無間業をつくれり、といふなり。破僧罪につきては、破羯摩僧あり、破法輪僧あり。破羯摩僧は、三洲にあるべし、北洲をのぞく。如來在世より、法滅のときにいたるまでこれあり。破法輪僧は、ただ如來在世のみにあり、餘時にはただ南洲にあり、三洲になし。この罪、最大なり。

According to this account, the disruption of the saṃgha came first and the shedding of the blood later. According to other accounts, the sequence of the disruption of the saṃgha and the shedding of the blood is not clear.[33] In addition, he beat the Bhikṣuṇī Utpalavarṇa to death with his fists.[34] This *bhikṣuṇī* was an arhat. It is these [acts], for which it is said he committed three deeds of the uninterrupted hell.

Regarding disruption of the saṃgha, there is disruption of the karma saṃgha and disruption of the dharma wheel saṃgha.[35] Disruption of the karma saṃgha may occur on three continents, excluding the northern continent; it may occur from the time of the Tathāgata to the extinction of his dharma.[36] Disruption of the dharma wheel saṃgha occurs only at the time

---

jing wenju 妙法蓮華經文句 (T.1718.34:115a4) gives the more likely *yuan* 怨 ("grudge") here for *en* 恩 ("kindness") — hence, "swearing to get revenge for this."

33   **According to other accounts** (*moshi yosetsu ni yoraba* もし餘説によらば): Or, perhaps, "according to another account." Dōgen is likely relying here, as he does repeatedly in this chapter, on the *Dasheng yi zhang* 大乗義章 (T.1851.44:610a17-29): noting that the *Dharmaguptaka-vinaya* (*Sifen lü* 四分律) has the injury to the Buddha preceding Devadatta's disruption of the saṃgha, Huiyuan 慧遠 concludes that it is difficult to determine which sequence is correct.

34   **the Bhikṣuṇī Utpalavarṇa** (*Rengeshiki bikuni* 蓮華色比丘尼): Dōgen recounts the story of this *bhikṣuṇī*, as told in the *Dazhidu lun* 大智度論 (T.1509.25:161a28-b12), in his "Shōbōgenzō kesa kudoku" 正法眼藏袈裟功德. Her beating by Devadatta is said to have been in response to her criticizing him for trying to kill the Buddha (see, e.g., *Dazhidu lun* 大智度論, T.1509.25:165a2-5).

35   **disruption of the karma saṃgha and disruption of the dharma wheel saṃgha** (*ha konma sō ari, ha hōrin sō ari* 破羯摩僧あり、破法輪僧あり): The former, known as *karma-bheda*, involves promotion of deviant procedures (*karma*) within a circumscribed Buddhist ritual community (S. *karma-saṃgha*); the latter, *cakra-bheda*, seeks to establish a separate order distinct from the Buddha's community (S. *dharma-cakra-saṃgha*).

36   **Disruption of the karma saṃgha may occur on three continents** (*ha konma sō wa, sanshū ni aru beshi* 破羯摩僧は、三洲にあるべし): I.e., three of the four continents making up a Sumeru world system, excluding the northern continent, on which there

218 DŌGEN'S *SHŌBŌGENZŌ* VOLUME VI

of the Tathāgata; at other times, it occurs only on the southern continent, not on the other three continents.[37] This offense is the most serious.[38]

[T8:20]

この三無間業をつくれるによりて、提婆達多、順次生に阿鼻地獄に堕す。かくのごとく、五逆、つぶさにつくれるものあり、一逆をつくれるものあり、提婆達多がごときは、三逆をつくれり、ともに阿鼻地獄に堕すべし。その一逆をつくれるがごとき、阿鼻地獄一劫の壽報なるべし。具造五逆のひと、一劫のなかに、つぶさに五報をうくとやせむ、また前後にうくとやせむ。

Due to his having committed these three deeds of the uninterrupted hell, Devadatta fell into the *avīci* hell. Thus, there are those who have committed all five of the heinous offenses, those who have committed one of them, and those, like Devadatta, who have committed three of them; all these will fall into the *avīci* hell. For those who have committed one heinous offense, it is recompense of a lifetime of one kalpa in the *avīci* hell.[39] Do those who commit all five heinous offenses suffer all five recompenses in one kalpa, or do they receive them sequentially?

---

is no Buddhist saṃgha; see Supplementary Notes, s.v. "Four Continents." This and the following sentence reflect the discussion of the times and places in which disruption may occur found in the *Dasheng yi zhang* 大乘義章 (T.1851.44:609a22-c1).

37 **at other times, it occurs only on the southern continent** (*yoji ni wa tada nanshū ni ari* 餘時にはただ南洲にあり): I.e., it occurs only in Jambudvīpa, where the Buddha appears. The introductory adverbial phrase seems out of place here, since it conflicts with the previous sentence. The corresponding lines in the *Dasheng yi zhang* 大乘義章 (T.1851.44:609a25-26; 609c1) read:

破法輪僧. . . 唯佛在世不通末代. . . 唯在閻浮不在餘方。

Disruption of the dharma wheel saṃgha occurs only during the lifetime of the Buddha and does not extend to the final age . . . . It occurs only in Jambudvīpa and not in other places.

38 **This offense is the most serious** (*kono tsumi, saidai nari* この罪、最大なり): The antecedent of "this" here is slightly ambiguous. It could be "disruption of the dharma wheel saṃgha," which offense is deemed more serious than disruption of the karma saṃgha (see *Dasheng yi zhang* 大乘義章, T.1851.44:609c28-a1). More likely, it refers to "disruption of the saṃgha" more broadly, which is held to be the most serious of the five deeds of the uninterrupted hell (see *Dasheng yi zhang* 大乘義章, T.1851.44:610a6-7).

39 **For those who have committed one heinous offense** (*sono ichigyaku o tsukureru ga gotoki* その一逆をつくれるがごとき): This and the following sentence are Japanese paraphrases of a passage in the *Dasheng yi zhang* 大乘義章 (T.1851.44:610b12-14):

五逆之罪、若有作者、阿鼻獄中一劫壽報。問曰、有人具造五逆、是人爲當一劫之中具受五報、爲當前後。

One who commits any of the five heinous offenses suffers recompense of a lifetime of one kalpa in the *avīci* hell.

Question: If a person commits all of the five offenses, will this person receive all five recompenses in one kalpa, or sequentially?

T8. Karma of the Three Times *Sanji gō* 三時業　　　219

[T8:21]

先德日、阿含・涅槃、同在一劫、火有厚薄。あるいはいはく、唯在增苦
增。

A prior worthy has said, "In the *āgamas* and *Nirvāṇa*, they all occur in one *kalpa*, with the fires being stronger or weaker."[40] Or it is said, "With an increase, the suffering increases."[41]

[T8:22]

いま提婆達多、かさねて三逆をつくれり、一逆つくれる罪人の苦には、三
陪すべし。しかあれども、すでに臨命終のときは、南無の言をとなへて、
惡心、すこしきまぬかる。うらむらくは、具足して南無佛と稱せざるこ
と。阿鼻にしては、はるかに釋迦牟尼佛、歸命したてまつる、續善ちかき
にあり。

In this case, Devadatta, having committed three heinous offenses, should have had three times the suffering of an offender who committed one offense. However, since, at the end of his life, he recited the word *namas*, he reduced his evil thoughts somewhat.[42] Regrettably, he did not fully recite *namo-buddhāya*. In *avīci*, he took refuge in Buddha Śākyamuni from afar, thus coming close to maintaining good roots.[43]

40　**A prior worthy** (*sentoku* 先德): Reference to Huiyuan 慧遠, author of the *Dasheng yi zhang* 大乘義章, whose answer (at T.1851.44:610b14-16) to the question posed in the previous section Dōgen is citing here:

> 如阿含中、同在一劫、火有厚薄。涅槃亦然。若依毘曇、具五逆者、五劫受報、
> 不在一時。成實亦然。

> According to the *āgamas*, they all occur in one kalpa, with the fires being stronger or weaker. The *Nirvāṇa* is the same. According to the *abhidharma*, those who commit all five of the heinous offenses receive the recompense over five kalpas, not at one time. The *Satyasiddhi* is the same.

41　**Or it is said** (*arui wa iwaku* あるいはいはく): Likely reflecting a line in the *Abhidharma-kośa* (*Epidamo jushelun* 阿毘達磨俱舍論, T.1558:29.93b9):

> 隨罪增苦增。

> With an increase in the offense, the suffering increases.

42　**he recited the word *namas*** (*namu no gon o tonaete* 南無の言をとなへて): Likely reflecting the *Miaofa lianhua jing wenju* 妙法蓮華經文句 (T.1718.34:57b28-29):

> 調達臨終稱南無。未得稱佛便墮地獄。

> At the end of his life, he recited *namas*; but, before he could say *buddhāya*, he fell into hell.

43　**In *avīci*** (*abi ni shite wa* 阿鼻にしては): Based on the legend that the Buddha's disciple Maudgalyāyana visited Devadatta in hell, where the latter made obeisance to Buddha Śākyamuni; see, e.g., *Ekottarāgama* (*Zengyi ahan jing* 增一阿含經, T.125.2:805c21-23).

[T8:23] {2:404}

なほ、阿鼻地獄に四佛の提婆達多あり。瞿伽離比丘は、千釋出家の時、その
なかの一人なり。調達・瞿伽離二人、出城門のとき、二人のれる馬、た
ちまちに仆倒し、二人の、むまよりおち、冠、ぬけておちぬ。ときのみる
人、みないはく、この二人は、佛法におきて益をうべからず。この瞿伽離
比丘、また倶伽離といふ。此生に舍利弗・目犍連を謗するに、無根の波
羅夷をもてす。世尊みづから、ねんごろにいさめましますに、やまず、梵
王、くだりていさむるに、やまず。二尊者を謗するによりて、次生に地獄
に堕しぬ。いまに、續善根の緣にあはず。

In the *avīci* hell, there were Devadattas under the four buddhas.[44] The
Bhikṣu Kokālika was one of the thousand Śākyas who left home.[45] When
Devadatta and Kokālika were leaving the city gate, their horses suddenly stumbled, and the two men fell off, their headgear coming loose and
falling off.[46] The people who witnessed this at the time all said that these
two would receive no benefit from the buddha dharma. [The name of]
this Bhikṣu Kokālika is also given as "*Juqieli*."[47] In this life, he slandered Śāriputra and Maudgalyāyana, groundlessly accusing them of a
pārājika offense.[48] When the World-Honored One kindly admonished
him, he did not stop; when the Brahmā King descended to admonish
him, he did not stop. Due to his slandering the two venerables, he fell
into hell in his next life. He still has not encountered the conditions in
which to maintain his good roots.

---

44 **Devadattas under the four buddhas** (*shibutsu no Daibadatta* 四佛の提婆達多):
I.e., a person named Devadatta living under each of the first four buddhas of our present Bhadra-kalpa: Krakucchanda, Kannikamuni, Kāśyapa, and Śākyamuni; reflecting a
tradition, found in the *Ekottarāgama* (*Zengyi ahan jing* 增一阿含經, T.125.2:805a9-12),
that, when Maudgalyāyana sought after Devadatta in hell, he was told there were Devadattas there from the times of the three buddhas preceding Śākyamuni.

45 **The Bhikṣu Kokālika** (*Kukari biku* 瞿伽離比丘): A follower of Devadatta.

the thousand Śākyas who left home (*sen Shaku shukke* 千釋出家): Reference to the
tradition that the Buddha's father sent a thousand of his subjects to the Buddha, all of
whom "left home" (i.e., joined the order) and became arhats.

46 **When Devadatta and Kokālika were leaving the city gate** (*Chōdatsu Kokari
ninin, shutsu jōmon no toki* 調達・瞿伽離二人、出城門のとき): Likely reflecting an
account of the incident in the *Fahua xuanyi shiqian* 法華玄義釋籤 by Zhanran 湛然
(T.1717.33:841a6-9).

47 **[The name of] this Bhikṣu Kokālika is also given as "*Juqieli*"** (*kono Kukari biku,
mata Kukari to iu* この瞿伽離比丘、また倶伽離といふ): Dōgen is here simply provid-
ing a second common Chinese transliteration for the Sanskrit *Kokālika*.

48 **he slandered Śāriputra and Maudgalyāyana** (*Sharihotsu Mokukenren o bō
suru* 舍利弗・目犍連を謗する): Based on the account in the *Dazhidu lun* 大智度論
(T.1509.25:157b4-c13), in which Kokālika falsely accuses the two monks of sleeping
with a woman at the house of a potter with whom they had sought lodging in a storm. A
pārājika offense (*harai* 波羅夷) requires expulsion from the monastic order.

T8. Karma of the Three Times *Sanji gō* 三時業 221

[T8:24]

四禪比丘、臨命終のとき、謗佛せしによりて、四禪の中陰かくれて、阿鼻
地獄に墮せり。かくのごとくなるを、順次生受業となづく。

Because the bhikṣu of the fourth dhyāna slandered the Buddha as he
approached the end of his life, his intermediate state in the fourth dhyāna
disappeared, and he fell into *avīci* hell.[49] Such a case is called "karma
experienced in the next life."

[T8:25]

この五無間業を、なにによりて無間業となづく。そのゆえ、五あり。

Why are these five deeds of the uninterrupted hell called "uninterrupted" deeds? There are five reasons for this.[50]

[T8:26]

一者、趣果無間故、名無間。捨此身已、次身即受故、名無間。二者、受苦
無間故、名無間。五逆之罪、生阿鼻獄、一劫之中、受苦相續無有樂眠。因
從果稱名無間業。三者、時量無間故、名無間。五逆之罪、生阿鼻獄、決定
一劫時不斷故、故名無間。四者、壽命無間故、名無間。五逆之罪、生阿鼻
獄、一劫之中、壽命無絕。因從果稱、名爲無間。　五者、身形無間故、名
無間。五逆之罪、生阿鼻獄。阿鼻地獄、縱・廣八萬四千由旬、一人入中身
亦遍滿、一切人入身亦遍滿、不相障礙。因從果號、名曰無間。

*1) Because the development of the fruit is without interval, they are
called "uninterrupted": because the next body is received as soon as
this body is cast off, they [i.e., the five heinous offenses] are called
"uninterrupted."*

*2) Because the experience of suffering is incessant, they are called
"uninterrupted": one guilty of the five heinous offenses is born in the
avīci hell, where one experiences suffering continuously, without any
interval of pleasure. Described by their fruit, the causes are called "uninterrupted karma."*

49　**bhikṣu of the fourth dhyāna** (*shizen biku* 四禪比丘): Reference to a story, found
in the *Dazhidu lun* 大智度論 (T.1509.25:189a11-27). A monk mistakenly thinks that his
attainment of the fourth level of dhyāna makes him an arhat, free from rebirth. When
he foresees the intermediate state between his death and his next birth, he accuses the
Buddha of falsely promising that arhats enter nirvāṇa upon death — slander for which
he falls into hell. Dōgen quotes the story in full in his "Shōbōgenzō shizen biku" 正法
眼藏四禪比丘.

50　**There are five reasons for this** (*sono yue, go ari* そのゆえ、五あり): The two sentences in this section reflect the introduction to the passage from the *Dasheng yi zhang*
大乘義章 (T.1851.44:608b3-12), the Chinese of which Dōgen seems to be using in the
following section. The *Dasheng yi zhang*, however, lists only four senses of the term
"uninterrupted" (lacking number 3 below); and, though Dōgen's list of five does occur
in the literature (sometimes attributed to the *Chengshi lun* 成實論), it is unclear where
Dōgen may have found his particular version.

222   DŌGEN'S *SHŌBŌGENZŌ* VOLUME VI

3) Because the amount of time is uninterrupted, they are called "uninterrupted": one guilty of the five heinous offenses is born in the *avīci* hell, where the time spent is fixed at one kalpa and not abbreviated. Therefore, they are called "uninterrupted."

4) Because the lifespan is continuous, they are called "uninterrupted": one guilty of the five heinous offenses is born in the *avīci* hell, where one's lifespan does not end during an entire kalpa. Described by their fruit, the causes are called "uninterrupted karma."

5) Because the body is without interstice, they are called "uninterrupted": one guilty of the five heinous offenses is born in the *avīci* hell. The *avīci* hell is eighty-four thousand yojanas in height and width, and the body of each person in it fills it; the bodies of all the people in it fill it, without obstructing each other.[51] Named for its fruit, the causes are called "uninterrupted karma."

* * * * *

[T8:27] {2:405}

第三順後次受業者、謂、若業此生造作増長、隨第三生、或隨第四生、或復過此、雖百千劫、受異熟果、是名順後次受業。

Of the third, "karma experienced in a life after the next," it is said,[52]

When the karma is produced and developed in this life, and its ripened fruit is experienced in the third life, or in the fourth life, or after these, even after a hundred thousand kalpas, it is called "karma experienced in a life after the next."[53]

[T8:28]

いはく、人ありて、この生に、あるいは善にもあれ、あるいは悪にもあれ、造作しをはれりといへども、あるいは第三生、あるいは第四生、乃至百千生のあひだにも、善悪の業を感ずるを、順後次受業となづく。菩薩の三祇劫の功徳、おほく順後次受業なり。かくのごとくの道理、しらざるがごときは、行者おほく疑心をいだく。いまの闍夜多尊者の、在家のときのごとし。もし鳩摩羅多尊者にあはずば、その疑ひ、とけがたからん。行者

---

51   **eighty-four thousand yojanas** (*hachiman shisen yujun* 八萬四千由旬): "Eighty-four thousand" is a standard term for a great number. A yojana (*yujun* 由旬) is a measure of distance, varying greatly depending on the source, but often said to range from seven to nine miles.

52   **"karma experienced in a life after the next"** (*jun goji ju gō* 順後次受業): Returning to the *Apidamo da piposha lun* 阿毘達磨大毘婆沙論 passage (T.1545.27:593b6-8) last quoted in section 14.

53   **even after a hundred thousand kalpas** (*sui hyakusen kō* 雖百千劫): This phrase does not appear in the source.

T8. Karma of the Three Times *Sanji gō* 三時業　　　　223

も、思惟それ善なれば、悪、すなはち滅す、それ悪思惟すれば、善、すみ
やかに滅するなり。

That is, while a person may complete an act, be it good or evil, in this
life, he or she will experience the good or evil karma in the third life or in
the fourth life or even during as many as a hundred thousand lives — this
is called "karma experienced in a life after the next." The merit of the
bodhisattva's three *asaṃkhyeya* kalpas is mostly karma experienced in a
life after the next.[54] When they do not recognize this truth, practitioners
often harbor doubts. Such was the case here with Venerable Jayata when
he was a householder. Had he not encountered Venerable Kumāralāta,
his doubts would have been difficult to overcome.

When the practitioner's thoughts are good, evil will quickly disappear;
when he or she has evil thoughts, good will quickly disappear.[55]

[T8:29] {2:406}

室羅筏國昔有二人、一恆修善、一常作惡。修善行者、於一身中、恆修善
行、未嘗作惡。作惡行者、於一身中、常作惡行、未嘗修善。修善行、臨命
終時、順後次受惡業力故、歘有地獄中有現前。便作是念、我一身中、恆修
善行、未嘗作惡、應生天趣、何緣有此中有現前。遂起念言、我定應有順後
次受業今熟故、此地獄中有現前。即自憶念一身已來所修善業、深生歡喜。
由勝善思現在前故、地獄中有、即便陰歿、天趣中有、歘爾現前。從此命
終、生於天上。

*Long ago in the Land of Śrāvastī, there were two people, one who al-
ways did good, and one who always did evil.[56] The one who practiced
good deeds throughout his life constantly practiced good deeds and
never did evil; the one who did evil deeds throughout his life always
did evil deeds and never practiced good. When the one who practiced
good deeds was approaching the end of his life, because of the power
of bad karma experienced in a life after the next, there suddenly appeared before him his intermediate state in a hell. Thereupon, he had
this thought, "Throughout this life, I have constantly practiced good
deeds, never doing evil; I should be born in a heaven. Why is this intermediate state appearing before me?" He then gave rise to the thought,*

54　**The merit of the bodhisattva's three *asaṃkhyeya* kalpas** (*bosatsu no san gikō no
kudoku* 菩薩の三祇劫の功德): I.e., the good karma accumulated by bodhisattvas over
the course of their three incalculable æons of practice on the path to buddhahood, most
of which will bear fruit only at the end of their path.

55　**When the practitioner's thoughts are good** (*gyōsha mo, shii sore zen nareba* 行
者も、思惟それ善なれば): This sentence would seem to be an introduction to the story
that follows in the next section.

56　**Long ago in the Land of Śrāvastī** (*Shiraba koku shaku* 室羅筏國昔): Quoting a
story found in the *Apidamo da piposha lun* 阿毘達磨大毘婆沙論 (T.1545.27:359c21-
360a9).

224   DŌGEN'S *SHŌBŌGENZŌ* VOLUME VI

"Surely, it must be because karma experienced in a life after the next has now matured that this intermediate state in hell has appeared before me." He reflected on the good deeds he had done throughout his life and felt profound joy; and, due to the appearance of this excellent good thought, the intermediate state in hell vanished, and an intermediate state in heaven suddenly appeared before him. When his life ended, he was born in a heaven.

[T8:30] {2:407}

この恆修善行のひと、順後次受の、さだめてうくべきがわがみにありける、とおもふのみにあらず、さらにすすみておもはく、一身の修善も、またさだめてのちにうくべし。ふかく歡喜す、とはこれなり。この憶念、まことなるがゆえに、地獄の中有即ちかくれて、天趣の中有、忽ちに現前して、いのちをはりて、天上にむまる。この人、もし惡人ならば、命終のとき、地獄の中有現前せば、おもふべし、われ一身の修善、その功德なし、善惡あらむには、いかでかわれ地獄の中有をみむ。このとき因果を撥無し、三寶を毀謗せん。もしかくのごとくならば、即ち命終し、地獄におつべし。かくのごとくならざるによりて、天上にむまるるなり。この道理、あきらめしるべし。

This person who had constantly done good deeds not only thought that he was surely to experience what is experienced in a life after the next, but went on to think that the good he had practiced throughout his life would also surely be experienced thereafter; his feeling "profound joy" refers to this.[57] Because this reflection was a true one, the intermediate state in hell disappeared, an intermediate state in heaven suddenly appeared before him, and, when his life ended, he was born in a heaven. Had this person been an evil person, when his life ended and an intermediate state in hell appeared before him, he would have thought, "The good I practiced throughout my life produced no merit; if good and evil exist, why do I see an intermediate state in a hell?" At this time, he would be denying cause and effect and disparaging the three treasures. Had this been the case, his life would have ended forthwith, and he would have fallen into a hell. Because this was not the case, he was born in a heaven. We should clearly recognize this truth.

[T8:31]

作惡行者、臨命終時、順後次受善業力故、歘有天趣中有現前。便作是念、我一身中、常作惡行、未嘗修善、應生地獄、何緣有此中有現前。遂起邪見、撥無善惡及異熟果。邪見力故、天趣中有、尋即陰歿、地獄中有、歘爾現前。從此命終、生於地獄。

When the one who had done evil deeds was approaching the end of his life, because of the power of the good karma experienced in a life

---

57 **This person who had constantly done good deeds** (*kono gō shu zengyō no hito* この恆修善行のひと): Dōgen pauses here in his quotation of the story to explain its moral.

T8. Karma of the Three Times *Sanji gō* 三時業

after the next, there suddenly appeared before him his intermediate state in a heaven.[58] *Thereupon, he had this thought, "Throughout this life, I have always done evil, never practicing good; I should be born in a hell. Why is this intermediate state appearing before me?" He then gave rise to a false view that denied good and evil as well as their ripened fruits. By the power of this false view, the intermediate state in heaven immediately died out, and an intermediate state in hell suddenly appeared before him. When his life ended, he was born in a hell.*

[T8:32] {2:408}

この人、いけるほど、つねに惡をつくり、さらに一善を修せざるのみにあらず、命終のとき、天趣の中有の現前せるをみて、順後次受をしらず。われ一生のあひだ、惡をつくれりといへども、天趣にむまれんとす、はかりしりぬ、さらに善惡なかりけり。かくのごとく善惡を撥無するは、邪見力のゆえに、天趣の中有、たちまちに陰殁して、地獄の中有、すみやかに現前し、いのちをはりて、地獄におつ。これは邪見のゆえに、天趣の中有、かくるるなり。しかあれば即ち、行者必ず邪見なることなかれ。いかなるか邪見、いかなるか正見と、かたちをつくすまで學習すべし。

Not only had this person throughout his entire life always committed evil and never performed a single good deed, but, seeing the appearance of his intermediate state in a heaven, he failed to recognize it as [karma] experienced in a life after the next. [Seeing that] although he had committed evil his entire life, he was about to be born in a heaven, he concluded that there was no good or evil. Because of the power of his false view that denied good and evil in this way, the intermediate state of heaven immediately died out, an intermediate state of hell quickly appeared, and, when his life ended, he fell into a hell.[59] Here, the intermediate state of heaven vanished because of a false view. Thus, practitioners must never hold false views. What are false views and what correct views — we should study this for as long as we live.

---

58 **the one who had done evil deeds** (*sa akugyō sha* 作惡行者): Dōgen returns here to the story from the *Apidamo da piposha lun* 阿毘達磨大毘婆沙論 (T.1545.27:360a2-9).

59 **the power of his false view that denied good and evil** (*zen'aku o hatsumu suru wa, jaken riki* 善惡を撥無するは、邪見力): Ignoring the problematic *wa* は after *suru* する in Kawamura's text (which might otherwise be read something like, "Because his denying good and evil in this way had the power of a false view . . . .") Dōgen is here simply paraphrasing his Chinese text.

[T8:33]

まづ因果を撥無し、佛法僧を毀謗し、三世および解脱を撥無する、ともに
これ邪見なり。まさにしるべし、今生のわがみ、ふたつなし、みつなし。
いたづらに邪見におちて、むなしく惡業を感得せむ、をしからざらむや。
惡をつくりながら惡にあらずとおもひ、惡の報あるべからずと邪思惟する
によりて、惡報の、感得せざるにはあらず。惡思惟によりては、きたるべ
き善根も、轉じて惡報のきたることもあるなり。惡思惟は無間によれり。

First of all, denying cause and effect, denigrating buddha, dharma, and
saṃgha, denying the three times and liberation — these are all false
views. We should recognize that we do not have two or three selves in
this life. What a waste, then, foolishly to fall into false views and mean-
inglessly suffer evil karma. By believing while committing evil that it
is not evil and falsely thinking that there will be no evil recompense,
we cannot but suffer the evil recompense. Due to evil thoughts, it also
happens that the [recompense of] good roots that should be coming to us
is transformed, so that an evil recompense comes.[60] Evil thinking leads
to uninterrupted hell.

* * * * *

[T8:34] {2:409}

皓月供奉、問長沙景岑和尚、古德云、了即業障本來空、未了應須償宿債。
只如師子尊者・二祖大師、爲什麼得償債去。長沙云、大德不識本來空。皓
月云、如何是本來空。長沙云、業障是。皓月又問、如何是業障。長沙云、
本來空是。皓月無語。長沙便示一偈云、假有元非有、假滅亦非無。涅槃償
債義、一性更無殊。

The Officiant Haoyue asked Reverend Jingcen of Changsha, "A worthy of old has said,

If you've understood, karmic hindrances are fundamentally empty;
If you haven't understood, you have to repay your outstanding
debts.[61]

---

60 **Due to evil thoughts** (*aku shii ni yorite wa* 惡思惟によりては): This and the following sentence do not occur in the sixty-chapter *Shōbōgenzō* version of this text.

61 **Officiant Haoyue** (*Kōgetsu gubu* 皓月供奉): A conversation found in the *Jingde
chuandeng lu* 景德傳燈錄 (T.2076.51:221a17-19). Haoyue's 皓月 dates are unknown; he
also appears as a student of Changsha 長沙 at *Jingde chuandeng lu*, T.2076.51:274b24;
judging from his title here, he was a monk serving at court.

Reverend Jingcen of Changsha (*Chōsha Keishin oshō* 長沙景岑和尚): Dates unknown;
a disciple of Nanquan Puyuan 南泉普願 (748-835), as Dōgen will note below.

"A worthy of old" (*kotoku* 古德): I.e., Rongjia Xuanjue 永嘉玄覺 (d. 713), in his
Zhengdao ge 證道歌 (T.2014.48:396c12-13).

T8. Karma of the Three Times *Sanji gō* 三時業 227

How then could those like the Worthy Siṃha and the Great Master, the Second Ancestor, have repaid their debts?"[62]

Changsha said, "The Most Virtuous One has not understood 'fundamental emptiness.'"

Haoyue said, "What is 'fundamental emptiness'?"

Changsha said, "It's 'karmic hindrances.'"

Haoyue asked again, "What are 'karmic hindrances'?"

Changsha said, "'They're 'fundamental emptiness.'"

Haoyue said nothing. Changsha then presented a gāthā:

Nominal existence is from the start not existence;
And nominal extinction is also not extinction.
Nirvāṇa and repayment of debts
Are of one nature, without any difference.

[T8:35]
長沙景岑は、南泉の願禪師の上足なり、久しく參學のほまれあり。ままに道得是あれども、いまの因縁は、渾無理會得なり。ちかくは、永嘉の語を會せず、つぎに、鳩摩羅多の慈誨を明らめず、はるかに、世尊の所説、ゆめにもいまだみざるがごとし。佛祖の道處、すべてつたはれずば、たれかなむぢを尊崇せむ。

Jingcen of Changsha was a top disciple of Chan Master Yuan of Nanchuan, with a reputation for his lengthy study. Though he sometimes said it right, in the present episode, he shows a complete lack of understanding.[63] Most proximately, he does not understand the words of Yongjia; next, he has not clarified the kind instructions of Kumāralāta; and most remotely, he seems never even to have dreamt of what the World-Honored One taught.[64] Since you do not transmit anything of what was said by the buddhas and ancestors, who would revere you?[65]

---

62 **the Worthy Siṃha and the Great Master, the Second Ancestor** (*Shishi sonja Niso daishi* 師子尊者・二祖大師): I.e., the twenty-fourth Indian ancestor, Siṃha, and the second Chinese ancestor, Huike 慧可, both of whom were said to have been murdered.

63 **in the present episode, he shows a complete lack of understanding** (*ima no innen wa, kon muri etoku nari* いまの因縁は、渾無理會得なり): Though elsewhere he seems to appreciate certain sayings of Changsha 長沙, Dōgen's strong criticism of his answers here echoes a passage in the *Hōkyō ki* 寶慶記 (DZZ.7:20, record 16), in which Dōgen's teacher, Rujing 如淨, agrees that Changsha does not understand the karma of the three times. The discussion here and below considerably expands on the brief treatment found in the sixty-chapter *Shōbōgenzō* version of this text.

64 **kind instructions of Kumāralāta** (*Kumorata no jike* 鳩摩羅多の慈誨): I.e., the teachings quoted in section 1, above.

65 **who would revere you?** (*tare ka namuji o sonsū semu* たれかなむぢを尊崇せむ): Dōgen here addresses Changsha directly — a device repeated throughout the following

228

DŌGEN'S *SHŌBŌGENZŌ* VOLUME VI

[T8:36]

業障とは、三障のなかの一障なり。いはゆる三障とは、業障・報障・煩悩
障なり。業障とは、五無間業をなづく。皓月が問、このこころなしといふ
とも、先來いひきたること、かくのごとし。皓月が問は、業不亡の道理に
よりて、順後業のきたれるにむかうて、とふ處なり。長沙のあやまりは、
如何是本來空と問するとき、業障是とこたふる、おほきなる僻見なり。業
障、なにとしてか本來空ならむ。つくらずば業障ならじ、つくられば本來
空にあらず。つくるは、これつくらぬなり。業障の當體をうごかさずなが
ら、空なり、といふは、すでにこれ外道の見なり。業障本來空なり、とし
て、放逸に造業せむ衆生、さらに解脱の期、あるべからず、解脱のひ、
なくば、諸佛の出世あるべからず、諸佛の出世なくば、祖師西來すべから
ず、祖師西來せずば、南泉あるべからず、南泉なくば、たれかなむぢが參
學眼を換却せむ。

    "Karmic hindrances" are one of the three hindrances; the three hin-
drances are karmic hindrances, recompensive hindrances, and afflictive hindrances.[66] "Karmic hindrances" is a name for the five deeds of
the uninterrupted hell. While Haoyue's question may not have had this
sense, this is how it has previously been discussed.[67] Haoyue's question
is based on the principle that karma does not vanish and asks about the
occurrence of karma in subsequent lives. Changsha's error — answering
that "*It's karmic hindrances,*" when asked "*What is fundamental emptiness?*" — is a seriously one-sided view. Why are karmic hindrances
fundamentally empty? If we do not produce them, they are not karmic
hindrances; if we produce them, they are not fundamentally empty. To
say that producing them is not producing them, and that karmic hindrances just as they are without being altered are empty, is a view of
other paths. Living beings who, holding that karmic hindrances are fundamental emptiness, commit wanton deeds will never reach the point of
liberation; if there is no day of liberation, the buddhas would not appear
in the world; if the buddhas do not appear in the world, the Ancestral

---

discussion of this case.

66 **"Karmic hindrances" are one of the three hindrances** (*gosshō to wa, sanshō no
naka no isshō nari* 業障とは、三障のなかの一障なり): The "three hindrances" (*sanshō*
三障) are a traditional list of three types of spiritual obstacles (*sanshō* 三障): (1) afflictive
hindrances (*bonnōshō* 煩悩障; S. *kleśāvaraṇa*), caused by one's defiled states of mind;
(2) karmic hindrances (*gosshō* 業障; S. *karmāvaraṇa*), caused by one's past deeds; and
(3) recompensive hindrances (*hōshō* 報障, *ijukushō* 異熟障; S. *vipākāvaraṇa*), caused by
the conditions of one's rebirth. See, e.g., *Abhidharma-kośa* (*Apidamo jushe lun* 阿毘達
磨倶舍論, T.1558.29:92b23-c1).

67 **While Haoyue's question may not have had this sense, this is how it has previously been discussed** (*Kōgetsu ga mon, kono kokoro nashi to iu tomo, senrai iikitaru
koto, kaku no gotoshi* 皓月が問、このこころなしといふとも、先來いひきたること、
かくのごとし): Exactly what Dōgen means here is not certain. Most likely, his point is
that Haoyue's question does not involve the traditional definition of "karmic hindrances"
as the five deeds of the uninterrupted hell.

T8. Karma of the Three Times *Sanji gō* 三時業 229

Master does not come from the west; if the Ancestral Master does not come from the west, there is no Nanquan; if there is no Nanquan, who will replace your eye of study?[68]

[T8:37] {2:410}
また、如何是業障、と問するとき、さらに、本來空是、と答する、ふるくの縛馬答に相似なりといふとも、おもはくは、なむぢ未了得の短才をもて、久學の供奉に相對するがゆえに、かくのごとくの狂言を發するなるべし。

Again, when asked, "*What are karmic hindrances?*" to respond once more with, "*They're fundamental emptiness,*" while it may resemble the old "tethered horse answer," looks to me as if you produce such nonsense because you are responding to the learned officiant with the ineptitude of one who has not yet understood.[69]

[T8:38]
のち、偈にいはく、涅槃償債義、一性更無殊。なむぢがいふ一性は、什麼性なるぞ。三性のなかに、いづれなりとかせむ。おもふらくは、なむぢ、性をしらず、涅槃償債義とは、いかに。なんぢがいふ涅槃は、いづれの涅槃なりとかせむ。聲聞の涅槃なりとやせむ、支佛の涅槃なりとやせむ、諸佛の涅槃なりとやせむ。たとひいづれなりとも、償債義にひとしかるべからず。なむぢが道處、さらに佛祖の道處にあらず、更買草鞋行脚すべし。師子尊者・二祖大師等、惡人のために害せられむ、なむぞうたがふにたらむ。最後身にあらず、無中有の身にあらず、なむぞ順後次受業のうくべきなからむ。すでに後報のうくべきが熟するあらば、いまのうたがふところにあらざらん。あきらかにしりぬ、長沙いまだ三時業をあきらめずといふこと。

Then, you say in your gāthā,

Nirvāṇa and repayment of debts
Are of one nature, without any difference.

What nature is the "one nature" you are talking about? Which of the

---

68 **who will replace your eye of study?** (*tare ka namuji ga sangaku gen o kankyaku semu* たれかなむぢが參學眼を換却せむ): I.e., who will correct your understanding. A question again addressed directly to Changsha 長沙, likely reflecting the familiar idiom used elsewhere in the *Shōbōgenzō*, "to replace one's eye with soapberry seeds [of the Buddhist rosary]" (*shō mokukansu kankyaku ni ganzei* 將木槵子換卻爾眼睛) (see, e.g., *Yunmen yulu* 雲門語錄, T.1988.47:544a12).

69 **old "tethered horse answer"** (*furuku no bakume tō* ふるくの縛馬答): I.e., an answer that merely circles back to the original question; from an example found in the *Abhidharma-kośa* (*Apidamo jushe lun* 阿毘達磨倶舍論, T.1558.29:92b23-c1):

猶如有問縛馬者誰。答言馬主。即彼復問馬主是誰。答言縛者。

Suppose someone asks, "Who tethered that horse?" And the answer is, "The owner of the horse." So, he asks again, "And who is the owner of the horse?" And the answer is, "The one who tethered it."

three natures is it?[70] What I think is that you do not understand "nature." And how about "nirvāṇa and repayment of debts"? Which nirvāṇa is the nirvāṇa you are talking about? Is it the nirvāṇa of the *srāvaka*? The nirvāṇa of the *pratyeka-buddha*? The nirvāṇa of the buddhas? Whichever it is, it is not the same as "repayment of debts." What you say is not at all what the buddhas and ancestors say; you should *buy a pair of straw sandals and go on a pilgrimage again.*[71] How can we doubt that the Worthy Siṃha and the Great Master, the Second Ancestor, were killed by evildoers? They were not in their final bodies; they were not in bodies without an intermediate state: why should they not experience *karma experienced in a life after the next?*[72] If it is the maturation of the later recompense that they were to experience, it does not raise the present doubts. Clearly, Changsha has not yet clarified the karma of the three times.

[T8:39] {2:411}
参學のともがら、この三時業をあきらめむこと、鳩摩羅多尊者のごとくなるべし。すでにこれ祖宗の業なり、廢怠すべからず。このほか不定業等の八種の業あること、ひろく参學すべし。いまだこれをしらざれば、佛祖の正法つたはるべからず。この三時業の道理あきらめざらんともがら、みだりに人天の導師と稱することなかれ。

To clarify this karma of the three times, those who study should be like Venerable Kumāralāta. Since it is the karma of our ancestors, we should not neglect it.[73] In addition, we should study extensively that there are the eight types of karma of indeterminate karma and the rest.[74] If one does

---

70   **three natures** (*sanshō* 三性): Here, undoubtedly referring to the three types of karma: good, evil, and neutral.

71   **buy a pair of straw sandals and go on a pilgrimage again** (*kō mai sōai angya* 更買草鞋行脚): A fixed idiom meaning to go study some more.

72   **They were not in their final bodies; they were not in bodies without an intermediate state** (*saigo shin ni arazu, muchūu no shin ni arazu* 最後身にあらず、無中有の身にあらず): References to those in their last rebirth in saṃsāra, of whom it is said that they cannot die prematurely (*muchūyō* 無中夭). (See, e.g., *Apidamo jushe lun* 阿毘達磨倶舍論, T.1558.29:61c28-a4.) The sixty-chapter *Shōbōgenzō* version of "Sanji gō" includes a list of such types, beginning with the bodhisattva in his final body. It has been suggested that the somewhat anomalous *muchūu* 無中有 ("without an intermediate state") in our text here is an error for *muchūyō* 無中夭 ("without premature death").

73   **karma of our ancestors** (*soshū no gō* 祖宗の業): Or, perhaps, "the karma of our ancestor [Kumāralāta]."

74   **eight types of karma of indeterminate karma and the rest** (*fujō gō tō no hasshu no gō* 不定業等の八種の業): A list consisting of the karma of the three times plus karma experienced at an indeterminate time (*jun fujō ju gō* 順不定受業), each being of two sorts: that in which the recompense is determined (*ijuku ketsujō* 異熟決定) and that in which it is indeterminate (*ijuku fuketsujō* 異熟不決定). (See *Apidamo da piposha lun* 阿毘達磨大毘婆沙論, T.1545.27:593c7-10.)

T8. Karma of the Three Times *Sanji gō* 三時業   231

not know about this, the true dharma of the buddhas and ancestors is not transmitted. Do not rashly name as the teachers of humans and devas those who have not clarified the principle of the karma of the three times.

[T8:40]

世尊言、假令經百千劫、所作業不亡、因緣會遇時、果報還自受。汝等當知、若純黑業、得純黑異熟、若純白業、得純白異熟、若黑白業、得雜異熟。是故汝等、應離純黑及黑白雜業。當勤修學純白之業。時諸大衆、聞佛說已、歡喜信受。

The World-Honored One said,[75]

Though you pass through a hundred thousand kalpas,
The karma you have done will not disappear:
When causes and conditions come together,
You will naturally experience the fruits of your deeds.
You should know that, if your deeds are pure black, you will get pure black ripened fruits; if your deeds are pure white, you will get pure white ripened fruits; if your deeds are black and white, you will get mixed ripened fruits. Therefore, you should avoid pure black, as well as black and white, deeds and should strive to practice pure white deeds.

At that time, the great assembly, having heard the Buddha's speech, rejoiced, believed, and accepted it.

[T8:41] {2:412}

世尊のしめしましますがごときは、善惡の業、つくりをはりぬれば、たとひ百千萬劫をふといふとも、不亡なり。もし因緣にあへば、かならず感得す。しかあれば、惡業は、懺悔すれば滅す、また轉重輕受す。善業は、隨喜すればいよいよ增長するなり、これを不亡といふなり、その報、なきにはあらず。

What the World-Honored One is indicating is that, once we have performed a good or evil deed, it "will not disappear" even over "a hundred thousand myriad kalpas." When we encounter the [relevant] "causes and conditions," we will inevitably experience the effects. Therefore, with bad karma, if we repent, it is extinguished, or it is transformed from serious to minor; and with good karma, if we rejoice in it, it increases.[76] This is what is meant by "it will not disappear": its recompense is not nonexistent.

---

75   **The World-Honored One** (*Seson* 世尊): Quoting, with slight variation, the *Mūla-sarvāstivāda-vinaya-vibhaṅga* (*Genben shuo yiqie youbu pinaiye* 根本説一切有部毘奈耶, T.1442.23:674b9-10, 18-22).

76   **transformed from serious to minor** (*ten jū kyō ju* 轉重輕受): A fixed expression for the transformation of very bad karma (especially that leading to rebirth in hell) to karma of less unpleasant recompense (especially that can be exhausted in this life).

232 DŌGEN'S *SHŌBŌGENZŌ* VOLUME VI

正法眼藏三時業第八
Treasury of the True Dharma Eye
Karma of the Three Times
Number 8

[Tōunji MS:][77]

建長五年癸丑三月九日、在於永平寺之首座寮書寫之。懷奘
Copied this in the Head Seat's Quarters of Eiheiji; the ninth day of the
third month of the junior water year of the ox, the fifth year of Kenchō
[8 April 1253]. Ejō

---

77 The twelve-chapter *Shōbōgenzō* text has no colophon; this colophon belongs to the earlier draft of the chapter preserved in the sixty-chapter compilation.

TREASURY OF THE TRUE DHARMA EYE
THE TWELVE-CHAPTER COMPILATION
NUMBER 9

Four Horses
Shime

四馬

Four Horses

Shime

INTRODUCTION

This short, undated work is found as number 39 in the sixty-chapter *Shōbōgenzō*, from which it was included in the Honzan edition as number 84 (or 85 in the Iwanami and Shūmuchō versions). Like other texts of the twelve-chapter compilation, it was copied by Ejō during the summer retreat of 1255, some three years after its author's death.

The title refers to a teaching of Buddha Śākyamuni, in which he likens the diverse spiritual sensitivities of his audience to four types of horses, according to their responsiveness to the whip. Dōgen quotes two slightly different examples of the teaching — an early version from the *Saṃyuktāgama*, and a second from the *Nirvāṇa Sūtra* — both of which he says should be known and studied by all students of Buddhism.

正法眼藏第九

Treasury of the True Dharma Eye
Number 9

四馬

Four Horses

[T9:1] {2:413}

世尊一日、外道來詣佛所問佛、不問有言、不問無言。世尊據座良久。外道禮拜讚歎云、善哉世尊大慈大悲、開我迷雲、令我得入。乃作禮而去。外道去已、阿難尋白佛言、外道以何所得、而言得入、稱讚而去。世尊云、如世間良馬、見鞭影而行。

One day, the World-Honored One was visited by a member of an other path, who asked the Buddha, "I don't ask about the spoken; I don't ask about the unspoken."[1]

The World-Honored One sat silently for some time. The outsider paid obeisance and praised him, saying, "Excellent, World-Honored One. Your great compassion and great mercy have parted my clouds of delusion and enabled me to enter."

Then he bowed and departed. After the member of an other path had left, Ānanda inquired of the Buddha, saying, "What did that outsider attain, that he said he had entered, praised you, and departed?"

The World-Honored One said, "He is like the good horse in the everyday world that goes upon seeing the shadow of the whip."

[T9:2]

祖師西來よりのち、いまにいたるまで、諸善知識、おほくこの因縁を擧して、參學のともがらに示すに、あるひは年歳をかさね、あるひは日月をかされて、ままに開明し、佛法に信入するものあり。これを外道問佛話と稱す。しるべし、世尊に聖黙・聖説の二種の施設まします。これによりて得入するもの、みな如世間良馬見鞭影而行なり。聖黙・聖説にあらざる施設によりて得入する、またかくのごとし。

From the time the Ancestral Master came from the west down to the present, the wise friends have frequently taken up this episode; and when

---

1 **One day, the World-Honored One** (*Seson ichijitsu* 世尊一日): An episode found in many Chan sources; see especially *Zongmen tongyao ji* 宗門統要集 (ZTS.1:11a1-4); *Jingde chuandeng lu* 景德傳燈錄 (T.2076.51:434c06-10).

member of an other path (*gedō* 外道): Follower of a non-Buddhist religious community; S. *tīrthika*. Also rendered by the more euphonious "outsider" in this dialogue.

they taught it to their students, there were often those who, after taking years or taking days or months, clarified it and had faith in the buddha dharma.[2] It is called "*the tale of the member of an other path questioning the Buddha.*" We should understand that the World-Honored One has two devices, his sacred silence and his sacred speech.[3] Those who "enter" by these are all "*like the good horse in the everyday world that goes upon seeing the shadow of the whip.*" Entering by devices neither sacred silence nor sacred speech is also like this.

[T9:3] {2:414}

龍樹祖師曰、爲人説句、如快馬見鞭影即入正路。

The Ancestral Master Nāgārjuna said, "Teaching the phrases to people is like the swift horse seeing the shadow of the whip and immediately entering the right road."[4]

[T9:4]

あらゆる機縁、あるひは生・不生の法をきき、三乘・一乘の法をきく、しばしば邪路におもむかんとすれども、鞭影しきりにみゆるがごときんば、即ち正路に入るなり。もし師にしたがひ、人にあひぬるごときは、ところとして説句にあらざることなし、ときとして鞭影をみずといふことなきなり。即座に鞭影をみるもの、三阿僧祇をへて鞭影をみるもの、無量劫をへて鞭影をみ、正路に入ることをうるなり。

In all our circumstances, whether hearing the dharma of arising or non-arising, or hearing the dharma of the three vehicles or one vehicle, while we often head toward the wrong road, when we repeatedly see the shadow of the whip, we immediately enter "the right road." For one who has followed a teacher and met a person, there is no place that is not "teaching the phrases," there is no time when one does not see "the

---

2 **From the time the Ancestral Master came from the west** (*soshi seirai yori nochi* 祖師西來よりのち): I.e., following Bodhidharma's arrival in China from India. "Wise friends" (*shozenchishiki* 諸善知識) refers to the masters in the generations following Bodhidharma.

3 **the World-Honored One has two devices, his sacred silence and his sacred speech** (*Seson ni shōmoku shōsetsu no nishu no sesetsu mashimasu* 世尊に聖黙・聖説の二種の施設まします): See, e.g., the *Siyi fantian suowen jing* 思益梵天所問經, T.586.15:50b10-11.

4 **The Ancestral Master Nāgārjuna** (*Ryūju soshi* 龍樹祖師): Based on a statement in the *Miaofa lianhua jing xuanyi* 妙法蓮華經玄義, by Zhiyi 智顗 (538–597) (T.1716.33:687a20-21) that cites Nāgārjuna's *Zhonglun* 中論 for this saying — though the saying does not, in fact, occur in the *Zhonglun*. (Zhiyi may have had in mind a passage in the *Dazhidu lun* 大智度論, traditionally attributed to Nāgārjuna; see T.1509.25:62a6-7.)

"Teaching the phrases to people" (*inin sekku* 爲人説句): The *Miaofa lianhua jing xuanyi* 妙法蓮華經玄義 passage reads "teaching the four phrases to practitioners" (*wei xiang daoren shuo sigou* 爲向道人説四句), a reference to the four propositions (*shiku* 四句; S. *catuṣkoti*) of Buddhist rhetoric: A, not-A, both A and not-A, neither A nor not-A.

T9. Four Horses *Shime* 四馬 237

shadow of the whip."[5] Those who see the shadow of the whip on the spot, or those who see the shadow of the whip after three *asaṃkheya*, see the shadow of the whip after innumerable kalpas and are able to enter the right road.[6]

* * * * *

[T9:5]

雜阿含經曰、佛告比丘、有四種馬。一者、見鞭影即便驚悚、隨御者意。二者、觸毛便驚悚、隨御者意。三者、觸肉然後乃驚。四者、徹骨然後方覺。初馬、如聞他聚落無常、即能生厭。次馬、如聞己聚落無常、即能生厭。三馬、如聞己親無常、即能生厭。四馬、猶如己身病苦、方能生厭。

In the *Saṃyuktāgama*, it is said,[7]

The Buddha addressed the bhikṣus,

There are four kinds of horses: the first, startled and frightened when it sees the shadow of the whip, obeys its handler; the second, startled when [the whip] touches its hair, obeys its handler; the third is startled after it touches its flesh; the fourth notices it only after it penetrates to the bone. The first horse is like those who feel abhorrence upon hearing of [an instance of] impermanence in another village; the next horse is like those who feel abhorrence upon hearing of impermanence in their own village; the third horse is like those who feel abhorrence upon hearing of the impermanence of their own relative; the fourth horse is like those who only feel abhorrence when their own body is suffering from illness.[8]

[T9:6] {2:415}

これ阿含の四馬なり。佛法を參學するとき、必ず學する處なり。眞善知識として人中・天上に出現し、ほとけのつかひとして祖師なるは、必ずこれを參學しきたりて、學者のために傳授するなり。しらざるは人天の善知識にあらず。學者、もし厚殖善根の衆生にして、佛道、ちかきものは、必ずこれをきくこと、うるなり。佛道、とほきものは、きかず、しらず。しか

---

5 **met a person** (*hito ni ainuru* 人にあひぬる): I.e., encountered a real person.

6 **three *asaṃkheya*** (*san asōgi* 三阿僧祇): i.e., three incalculable æons, the traditional length of the bodhisattva path. Some MS witnesses read here, "there are those who see . . ." (*miru mono ari* みるものあり).

7 **Saṃyuktāgama** (*Zō agon kyō* 雜阿含經): Dōgen's source here is the *Zhiguan fuxing chuanhong jue* 止観輔行傳弘決, by Zhanran 湛然 (711-782) (T.1912.46:212a20-26), which gives an abbreviated version of a sūtra in the *Saṃyuktāgama* (*Za ehan jing* 雜阿含經, T.99.2:234a16-b20).

8 **impermanence** (*mujō* 無常): I.e., death. The Āgama passage (e.g., at T.99.2:234b5-6) has "the pain of old age, sickness, and death" (*lao bing si ku* 老病死苦).

238 DŌGEN'S *SHŌBŌGENZŌ* VOLUME VI

あれば即ち、師匠、いそぎとかむことをおもふべし、弟子、いそぎきかん
ことをこひねがふべし。

These are the four horses in the *Āgama*. It is something always studied when we study the buddha dharma. Those who appear as true wise friends among humans and devas, who are ancestral masters as the envoys of the buddhas, have always studied this and transmitted it to students. Those who do not know it are not the wise friends of humans and devas. Students who are living beings with densely planted good roots, close to the buddha way, will surely be able to hear this. Those far from the buddha way do not hear it, do not know it. Therefore, teachers should think of quickly teaching it, and disciples should be eager quickly to hear it.

[T9:7]

いま生厭といふは、佛以一音演説法、衆生隨類各得解脱、或有恐怖、或歡
喜、或生厭離、或斷疑なり。

To "feel abhorrence" here means:

The Buddha expounds the dharma with a single voice;
And beings gain liberation according to type:
They may be afraid; they may feel joy;
They may feel abhorrence; they may sever doubts.[9]

* * * * *

[T9:8]

大經曰、佛言、復次善男子、如調馬者、凡有四種。一者觸毛、二者觸皮、
三者觸肉、四者觸骨。隨其所觸、稱御者意。如來亦而。以四種法、調伏衆
生。一者爲説生、便受佛語。如觸其毛隨御者意。二者説生老、便受佛語。
如觸毛皮隨御者意。三者説生及以老病、便受佛語。如觸毛皮肉隨御者意。
四者説生及老病死、便受佛語。如觸毛皮肉骨隨御者意。善男子、御者調
馬、無有決定。如來世尊、調伏衆生、必定不虚。是故號佛調御丈夫。

In the *Great Sūtra*, it is said that the Buddha said,[10]

Furthermore, good sons, there are, generally speaking, four ways of training a horse: first, by touching the hair; second, by touching the

---

9 **The Buddha expounds the dharma with a single voice** (*butsu i itton enzetsu hō* 佛以一音演説法): Quoting the *Mohe zhiguan* 摩訶止觀 (T.1911.46:2b27-28), which cites the *Vimalakīrti-nirdeśa-sūtra* (*Weimojie suoshuo jing* 維摩詰所説經, T.475.14:538a4-7).

gain liberation (*toku gedatsu* 得解脱): Following Kawamura's text; the source text and other manuscript witnesses of this chapter read the more likely "understand" (*toku ge* 得解).

10 **Great Sūtra** (*Daikyō* 大經): Reference to the *Nirvāṇa Sūtra* (*Da banniepan jing* 大般涅槃經) (T.374.12:469b1-10; T.375.12:712a2-12).

skin; third, by touching the flesh; fourth, by touching the bones. According to where it is touched, it conforms to the will of the driver. The Tathāgata is also like this. He uses four kinds of dharma to tame living beings. First, he speaks of birth, and they accept the word of the Buddha; this is like conforming to the will of the driver when the hair is touched. Second, he speaks of birth and old age, and they accept the word of the Buddha; this is like conforming to the will of the driver when the hair and skin are touched. Third, he speaks of birth, as well as old age and sickness, and they accept the word of the Buddha; this is like conforming to the will of the driver when the hair, skin, and flesh are touched. Fourth, he speaks of birth, as well as old age, sickness, and death, and they accept the word of the Buddha; this is like conforming to the will of the driver when the hair, skin, flesh, and bones are touched. Good sons, when the driver trains the horse, nothing is certain; when the Tathāgata, the World-Honored One, tames living beings, it is definitely not in vain. Therefore, the Buddha is called "Trainer of Persons."[11]

[T9:9] {2:416}

これを涅槃經の四馬となづく。學者、ならはざるなし、諸佛、ときたまはざるおはしまさず。ほとけに隨ひたてまつりて、これをきく。ほとけをみたてまつりて、供養したてまつるごとには、必ず聽聞し、佛法を傳授するごとには、衆生のためにこれをとくこと、歷劫におこたらず。つひに佛果にいたりて、はじめ初發心のときのごとく、菩薩・聲聞・人天大會のためにこれをとく。このゆえに、佛法僧寶種不斷なり。

This is called "the four horses of the *Nirvāṇa Sūtra*." There are no students who have failed to learn it; there are no buddhas who have failed to teach it. When we follow the buddhas, we hear it. Whenever we see the buddhas and make offerings to them, we invariably hear it; whenever they transmit the buddha dharma, across the kalpas, their teaching of it to living beings never flags. When they finally reach the fruit of buddhahood, just as they did when they first brought forth the mind [of bodhi], they teach it to the great assemblies of bodhisattvas, *śrāvakas*, humans, and devas. Therefore, the seeds of the treasures of buddha, dharma, and saṃgha are never cut off.

[T9:10] {2:417}

かくのごとくなるがゆえに、諸佛の所説と菩薩の所説と、はるかにことなり。しるべし、調馬師の法に、おほよそ四種あり。いはゆる、觸毛・觸皮・觸肉・觸骨なり。これなにものを觸毛せしむるとみえざれども、傳法の大士おもはくは、鞭なるべしと解す。しかあれども、必ずしも調馬の法に鞭をもちいるもあり、鞭を用いざるもあり、調馬、かならず鞭のみに

---

11 **"Trainer of Persons"** (*chōgo jōbu* 調御丈夫): S. *puruṣa-damya-sārathi*; one of the ten standard epithets of a buddha.

240 　　DŌGEN'S *SHŌBŌGENZŌ* VOLUME VI

はかぎるべからず。たてるたけ八尺なる、これを龍馬とす。この馬、とと
のふること、人間にすくなし。また千里馬といふむまあり、一日のうちに
千里をゆく。このむま、五百里をゆくあひだ、血汗をながす、五百里すぎ
ぬれば、清涼にして、はやし。このむまにのる人、すくなし、ととのふる
法、しれるものすくなし。このむま、神丹國にはなし、外國にあり。この
むま、おのおのしきりに鞭を加すとみえず。

Thus, what the buddhas teach and what the bodhisattva teaches are
very different.[12] We can see that, overall, the horse trainer has four methods: touching the hair, touching the skin, touching the flesh, and touching the bones. Although we do not read here what it is that is made to
touch the hair, the Great One who transmitted the dharma understood it
as a whip.[13] Be that as it may, in training a horse, one may or may not use
a whip: training a horse is not limited to the whip. One that stands eight
feet is called a "dragon horse"; this horse, few humans would train.[14]
Again, there is a horse called the "thousand-mile horse," which can cover a thousand miles in one day.[15] During the first five hundred miles, it
sweats blood; once it exceeds five hundred miles, it cools down and
picks up speed. This horse, few would ride, and few would know how to
control. This horse does not exist in the Land of Cīnasthāna; it is found
in other countries. We do not read that a whip is frequently used on of
any of these horses.[16]

[T9:11]

しかあれども、古德いはく、調馬必ず鞭を加す。鞭にあらざれば、むま、
ととのほらず、これ調馬の法なり。いま觸毛・皮・肉・骨の四法あり。毛
をのぞきて皮に觸することあるべからず、毛・皮をのぞきて肉・骨に觸す
べからず。かるがゆえにしりぬ、これ鞭を加すべきなり。いまここにとか
ざるは、文の不足なり。諸經かくのごときの處おほし。

Nevertheless, a virtuous one of old has said, "In training a horse, we
always use a whip; without the whip, the horse isn't trained."[17] This is the

---

12　**what the buddhas teach and what the bodhisattva teaches are very different**
(*shobutsu no shosetsu to bosatsu no shosetsu to, haruka ni kotonari* 諸佛の所説と菩
薩の所説と、はるかにことなり): Presumably, "the bodhisattva" here is a reference to
Nāgārjuna, to whom is attributed the saying quoted in section 3.

13　**Great One who transmitted the dharma** (*denbō no daishi* 傳法の大士): Again,
presumably, a reference to Nāgārjuna.

14　**"dragon horse"** (*ryōme* 龍馬): From the classical definition given in the *Rites of Zhou*
(*Zhouli* 周禮, Xiaguan Sima 夏官司馬, KR.1d0002.008.24a).

15　**"thousand-mile horse"** (*senrime* 千里馬): From the famous "divine horses" (*tianma*
天馬) of Ferghana (*Dayuan* 大宛); also known as "blood sweating horses" (*han xue ma*
汗血馬, a name thought to derive from bleeding caused by parasitic worms).

16　**these horses** (*kono muma* このむま): Probably a reference to thousand-mile horses,
though the dragon horse might also be intended.

17　**a virtuous one of old** (*kotoku* 古德): A saying given in Japanese, the source for

T9. Four Horses *Shime* 四馬 241

method for training a horse. Here, we have four methods: touching the hair, skin, flesh, and bones. It is not possible to touch the skin but not the hair; one cannot touch the flesh and bones but not the hair and skin. From this, we know that we should use the whip. That this is not mentioned here is a deficiency of the text.[18] There are many such passages in the sūtras.

[T9:12]

如來世尊・調御丈夫またしかあり。四種の法をもて、一切衆生を調伏して、必定不虚なり。いはゆる生を爲説するに、即ち佛語をうくるあり、生・老を爲説するに、佛語をうくるあり、生・老・病を爲説するに、佛語をうくるあり、生・老・病・死を爲説するに佛語をうくるあり。のちの三をきくもの、いまだはじめの一をはなれず、世間の調馬の、觸毛をはなれて、觸皮・肉・骨あらざるがごとし。生・老・病・死を爲説すといふは、如來世尊の生・老・病・死を爲説しまします。衆生をして生・老・病・死をはなれしめんがためにあらず。生・老・病・死すなはち道、ととかず、生・老・病・死すなはち道なり、と解せしめんがためにとくにあらず。この生・老・病・死を爲説するによりて、一切衆生をして、阿耨多羅三藐三菩提の法をしめさんがためなり。これ、如來世尊、調伏衆生、必定不虚、是故號佛調御丈夫なり。

The Tathāgata, the World-Honored One, the Trainer of Persons, is also like this.[19] Employing his four methods, when he tames all living beings, it is "definitely not in vain." That is, when he speaks to them of birth, there are those that accept the word of the Buddha; when he speaks to them of birth and old age, there are those that accept the word of the Buddha; when he speaks to them of birth, old age, and sickness, there are those that accept the word of the Buddha; and when he speaks to them of birth, old age, sickness, and death, there are those that accept the word of the Buddha. Those who hear the last three are never apart from the first one, just as, in training a horse in the everyday world, there is no touching the skin, flesh, and bone apart from touching the hair. That he speaks to them of birth, old age, sickness, and death means the Tathāgata, the World-Honored One, speaks to them of birth, old age, sickness, and death. This is not in order to free them from birth, old age, sickness, and death. He does not teach that birth, old age, sickness, and death are themselves the way; he does not teach them in order for them to understand that birth, old age, sickness, and death are themselves the way. He does it in order that, by speaking to them of birth, old age, sickness, and

which is unknown; hence, it is possible that the next sentence should be treated as part of the quotation.

18 **That this is not mentioned here** (*ima koko ni tokazaru wa* いまここにとかざるは): I.e., that the necessity of the whip is not mentioned in the *Nirvāṇa Sūtra* passage.

19 **is also like this** (*mata shika ari* またしかあり): Some MSS read here *mata shika nari* またしかなり.

death, he would enable all living beings to gain the dharma of *anuttara-samyak-saṃbodhi*.[20] This is "*when the Tathāgata, the World-Honored One, tames living beings, it is definitely not in vain. Therefore, the Buddha is called 'Trainer of Persons.'*"

{2:418}

正法眼藏四馬第九
Treasury of the True Dharma Eye
Four Horses
Number 9[21]

[Yōkoji MS:]

此四馬永平寺六十巻正法眼藏内第三十九也
永興寺十二巻正法眼藏第九巻也

This "Shime" is number thirty-nine of the Eiheiji sixty-chapter Shōbōgenzō; it is chapter number 9 of the Yōkōji twelve-chapter Shōbōgenzō.[22]

[Tōunji MS:]

建長七年乙卯夏安居日、以御草案書寫之畢。懐奘一校了

Copied this from his draft, on a day of the summer retreat, junior wood year of the rabbit, the seventh year of Kenchō [1255]. Proofed by Ejō[23]

20　**he would enable all living beings to gain the dharma of *anuttara-samyak-saṃbodhi*** (*issai shujō o shite, anokutara sanmyaku sanbodai no hō o shimesan* 一切衆生をして、阿耨多羅三藐三菩提の法をしめさん): The form of the predicate here (translated as "enable to gain") varies according to the manuscript witness; Kawamura's text reads *shimesan* しめさん, while others give *eseshimen* えせしめん, *eshimu* えしむ, or *eshimen* えしめん.

21　**Number 9** (*daiku* 第九): Kawamura's text corrects the chapter number here to "9"; the Yōkōji 永光寺 MS gives "39," the number of this chapter in the sixty-chapter *Shōbōgenzō*.

22　Presumably, an explanation, by an unknown hand, of the discrepancy in the numbering of the chapter explained in the note above. The monastery "Yōkōji" is given here as 永興寺, the name of the monastery in Kyōto of Dōgen's disciple Senne 詮慧, rather than the homophonous 永光寺, the monastery in Ishikawa that owns the MS of the twelve-chapter *Shōbōgenzō*. It is not known whether this is simply a copyist error or indicates that Senne's monastery once owned a copy of this MS.

23　**his draft** (*gosōan* 御草案): I.e., Dōgen's draft.

day of the summer retreat (*ge ango no hi* 夏安居日): Dates of the summer retreat vary; a common practice put it from the fifteenth of the fourth lunar month through the fifteenth of the seventh month; in 1255, this would have corresponded to 22 May through 18 August.

Proofed by Ejō (*Ejō ikkō ryō* 懐奘一校了): The Tōunji 洞雲寺 MS lacks this statement; it is supplied in Kawamura's text from the Rurikōji 瑠璃光寺 MS.

TREASURY OF THE TRUE DHARMA EYE
THE TWELVE-CHAPTER COMPILATION
NUMBER 10

The Bhikṣu of the Fourth Dhyāna
Shizen biku

四禪比丘

The Bhikṣu of the Fourth Dhyāna

Shizen biku

INTRODUCTION

This chapter is not preserved elsewhere in early manuscripts. It is listed as number 2 in fascicle 3 of the twenty-eight-text collection of *Shōbō-genzō* texts, but in fact that manuscript only preserves the title and the first two lines of the text. The work was known during the Edo period and does appear as number 90 in the ninety-five-chapter Honzan *Shōbō-genzō*, though the source of that text is unclear. Like other texts in the twelve-chapter compilation, the "Shizen biku" is undated. The Honzan text bears a colophon, also found on manuscripts of several other chapters in the twelve-chapter *Shōbōgenzō*, stating that the work was copied by Ejō during the summer retreat of 1255.

The title of the chapter refers to the story, quoted at the outset of the work, of a monk who thought that, by achieving the calm concentration of the fourth level of dhyāna, he had attained the fourth and final fruit of the traditional path to nirvāṇa. When he foresaw on his deathbed that he would be reborn rather than enter nirvāṇa, instead of realizing his error, he charged the Buddha with deceiving him by teaching that there was such a thing as nirvāṇa.

This story, which Dōgen also discusses in the "Sanji gō" 三時業 chapter, here serves primarily as an example of a false view about Buddhism; indeed, it occupies only the first third of the text, the remainder of which is taken up with a quite different false view: the belief, popular in China in Dōgen's day, that the three teachings of Buddhism, Daoism, and Confucianism were in basic agreement with each other. Dōgen argues strongly against this view as the opinion of those ignorant of the Buddhist tradition.

正法眼藏第十

Treasury of the True Dharma Eye
Number 10

四禪比丘

The Bhikṣu of the Fourth Dhyāna

[T10:1] {2:419}

第十四祖龍樹祖師言、佛弟子中有一比丘。得第四禪、生增上慢、謂得四
果。初得初禪、謂得於須陀洹果、得第二禪時、謂是斯陀含果、得第三禪
時、謂是阿那含果、得第四禪時、謂是阿羅漢。恃是自高、不復求進。命欲
盡時、見有四禪中陰相來、便生邪見、謂無涅槃、佛爲欺我。惡邪見故、失
四禪中陰、便見阿鼻泥梨中陰相、命終即生阿鼻泥梨中。諸比丘問佛、阿蘭
若比丘、命終生何處。佛言、是人生阿鼻泥梨中。諸比丘大驚、坐禪持戒便
爾耶。佛如前答言、彼皆因增上慢。得四禪時、謂得四果。臨命終時、見四
禪中陰相、便生邪見、謂無涅槃、我是羅漢、今還復生、佛爲虛誑。是時即
見阿鼻泥梨中陰相、命終即生阿鼻泥梨中。是時佛説偈言、多聞・持戒・
禪、未得漏盡法、雖有此功德、此事難可信、墮獄由謗佛、非關第四禪。

The Fourteenth Ancestor, the Ancestral Master Nāgārjuna, said,[1]

*Among the disciples of the Buddha, there was a bhikṣu who, having
attained the fourth dhyāna, gave rise to conceit, thinking he had attained the fourth fruit.*[2] *First, attaining the first dhyāna, he thought he
had attained the fruit of the srotāpanna; when he attained the second
dhyāna, he thought it was the fruit of the sakṛdāgāmin; when he attained the third dhyāna, he thought it was the fruit of the anāgāmin;
and when he attained the fourth dhyāna, he thought he was an arhat.*[3]

---

1 **The Fourteenth Ancestor, the Ancestral Master Nāgārjuna** (*daijūshi so Ryūju soshi* 第十四祖龍樹祖師): Introducing a passage from the *Dazhidu lun* 大智度論
(T.1509.25:189a11-27), traditionally attributed to Nāgārjuna. Dōgen's version reflects a
retelling of the story in the *Zhiguan fuxing zhuan hongjue* 止觀輔行傳弘決, by Zhanran
湛然 (711–782) (T.1912.46:257b16-26), a work on which he will often draw in this
chapter. The last line here does not appear in the *Dazhidu lun* but is taken from Zhanran's
text at T.1912.46:257b25-26.

2 **fourth dhyāna** (*daishizen* 第四禪); **fourth fruit** (*shika* 四果): I.e., (a) the deepest of
the four levels of meditation, characterized by extreme concentration and perfect equanimity; and (b) the highest of the four stages (the Sanskrit names of which follow in the
text) on the traditional Buddhist path, the status of the arhat, who will enter final nirvāṇa
upon death, without further rebirth in saṃsāra.

3 *srotāpanna* (*shudaon* 須陀洹); *sakṛdāgāmin* (*shidagon* 斯陀含); *anāgāmin* (*anagon*
阿那含); **arhat** (*arakan* 阿羅漢): The four fruits (*shika* 四果), or stages on the *śrāvaka*

246 DŌGEN'S *SHŌBŌGENZŌ* VOLUME VI

Based on this, he became haughty and did not seek to make further progress.

When his life was about to expire, he saw approaching an image of his intermediate state in the fourth dhyāna; thereupon, he conceived a false view, thinking, "There is no nirvāṇa; the Buddha has deceived me."[4] Because of this evil false view, the intermediate state in the fourth dhyāna disappeared, and he saw instead an image of his intermediate state in the avīci-niraya; and, when his life came to an end, he was born in the avīci-niraya.[5]

The bhikṣus asked the Buddha, "When the āraṇyaka bhikṣu died, where was he reborn?"[6]

The Buddha said, "This person was born in the avīci-niraya."

The bhikṣus were very surprised. "Can this be so for one who practiced seated meditation and kept the precepts?"

The Buddha answered as before, saying,

> *It was all caused by his conceit. When he attained the fourth dhyāna, he thought he had attained the fourth fruit. When he approached the end of his life, he saw an image of his intermediate state in the fourth dhyāna; thereupon, he conceived a false view, thinking, "There is no nirvāṇa: I am an arhat, but now I'm to be reborn. The Buddha has deceived us." At this point, he saw the form of his intermediate state in the avīci-niraya; and, when his life came to an end, he was born in the avīci-niraya.*

At this time, the Buddha recited a gāthā, saying,

> *He was learned, kept the precepts, and practiced dhyāna,*
> *But he hadn't attained the exhaustion of the contaminants.[7]*

---

path to nirvāṇa, given here in transliterations of the Sanskrit: (1) "stream-entrant" (*yoru* 預流): one who has attained the path of vision (*kendō* 見道; S. *darśana-mārga*) and entered the path of practice (*shudō* 修道; S. *bhavanā-mārga*); (2) "once-returner" (*ichirai* 一來): one on the path of practice who has but one rebirth in the desire realm (*yokkai* 欲界) remaining; (3) "nonreturner" (*fugen* 不還): one who will no longer be born in the desire realm but will enter nirvāṇa directly from one of heavens of the form realm (*shikikai* 色界) or formless realm (*mushikikai* 無色界); and (4) "worthy" (*arakan* 阿羅漢): one who has achieved nirvāṇa in this body and will not be reborn.

4 **intermediate state** (*chūin* 中陰): I.e., the state, often reckoned as 49 days, between death and rebirth; S. *antarābhava*.

5 *avīci-niraya* (*abinairi* 阿鼻泥梨): I.e., the *avīci* ("uninterrupted") hell, deepest of the eight hot hells.

6 **"āraṇyaka bhikṣu"** (*arannya biku* 阿蘭若比丘): I.e., a monk of the *araṇya* ("forest"), a term that could refer simply to a monk of the monastery, though Dōgen takes it, in his comments below, to mean a monk living apart from the community.

7 **exhaustion of the contaminants** (*rojin* 漏盡): S. *āsrava-kṣaya*; elimination of the

T10. The Bhikṣu of the Fourth Dhyāna *Shizen biku* 四禪比丘　　　247

Even though he had these virtues,
It was hard for him to believe this fact.

He fell into hell for slandering the Buddha; it had nothing to do with
the fourth dhyāna.

[T10:2] {2:420}

この比丘を稱して四禪比丘といふ、または無聞比丘と稱す。四禪をえたる
を四果と僻計せることをいましめ、また謗佛の邪見をいましむ。人天大會
みなしれり。如來在世より今日にいたるまで、西天・東地、ともに是にあ
らざるを是と執せるをいましむとして、四禪をえて四果とおもふがごと
し、とあざける。

This bhikṣu is known as "the bhikṣu of the fourth dhyāna," also called
the "unlearned bhikṣu."[8] [His tale] warns us against biased reckonings
that take attainment of the fourth dhyāna for the fourth fruit, and also
warns us against false views that slander the Buddha. The great assemblies of humans and devas have all known this. Since the time the
Tathāgata was in the world till today, in Sindh in the West and the Land
of the East, as a warning against clinging to what is not right as right, all
have dismissed it as "like thinking that attaining the fourth dhyāna is the
fourth fruit."

[T10:3] {2:421}

この比丘の不是、しばらく略して擧するに三種あり。第一には、みづから
四禪と四果とを分別するにおよばざる無聞の身ながら、いたづらに師をは
なれて、むなしく阿蘭若に獨處す。さいはひにこれ如來在世なり、つねに
佛所に詣して、常恆に見佛聞法せば、かくのごとくのあやまりあるべから
ず。しかあるに、阿蘭若に獨處して、佛所に詣せず、つねに見佛聞法せざ
るによりてかくのごとし。たとひ佛所に詣せずといふとも、諸大阿羅漢の
處にいたりて、教訓を請すべし。いたづらに獨處する、増上慢のあやまり
なり。第二には、初禪をえて初果とおもひ、二禪をえて第二果とおもひ、
三禪をえて第三果とおもひ、四禪をえて第四果とおもふ、第二のあやまり
なり。初・二・三・四禪の相と、初・二・三・四果の相と、比類におよばず、た
とふることあらむや。これ、無聞のとがによれり。師につかへず、くらき
によれるとがあり。

Briefly stated, the error of this bhikṣu is threefold. First, while an unlearned person who could not himself distinguish between the fourth
dhyāna and the fourth fruit, he foolishly left his teacher and pointlessly
lived in solitude in the *araṇya*. Fortunately, this was when the Tathāgata
was in the world; if he had always visited the Buddha and continually
met the Buddha and listened to the dharma, he would not have made

---

defilements (*bonnō* 煩惱; S. *kleśa*), a necessary condition for nirvāṇa.

8　**"unlearned bhikṣu"** (*mumon biku* 無聞比丘): Perhaps reflecting his characteriza-
tion as such in the *Shoulengyan jing* 首楞嚴經 (T.945.19:147a28).

248 DŌGEN'S *SHŌBŌGENZŌ* VOLUME VI

such a mistake. Instead, since he lived in solitude in the *araṇya*, did not visit the Buddha, and did not continually meet the Buddha and listen to the dharma, he was like this. Even if he did not visit the Buddha, he should have gone to the great arhats and requested their instruction. Pointlessly living in solitude was a mistake born of pride.

Second, he thought that attaining the first dhyāna was the first fruit; he thought that attaining the second dhyāna was the second fruit; he thought that attaining the third dhyāna was the third fruit; he thought that attaining the fourth dhyāna was the fourth fruit. This was his second mistake. The attributes of the first, second, third, and fourth dhyānas and the attributes of the first, second, third, and fourth fruits are not comparable; how could they be likened to each other? This is a fault due to his being unlearned, a fault due to his failing to serve a master and being ignorant.

[T10:4]

優婆毱多弟子中、有一比丘。信心出家、獲得四禪、謂爲四果。毱多方便令往他處。於路化作群賊、復化作五百賈客。賊劫賈客、殺害狼藉。比丘見生怖、即便自念、我非羅漢、應是第三果。賈客亡後、有長者女、語比丘言、唯願大德、與我共去。比丘答言、佛不許我與女人行。女言、我大德而随其後。比丘憐愍相望而行。尊者次復變作大河。女人言、大德、可共我度。比丘在下、女在上流。女便墮水、白言、大德濟我。爾時比丘、手接而出、生細滑想、起愛欲心、即便自知非阿那含。於此女人、極生愛著、將向屏處、欲共交通、方見是師、生大慚愧、低頭而立。尊者語言、汝昔自謂是阿羅漢、云何欲爲如此惡事。將至僧中、教其懺悔、爲説法要、得阿羅漢。

Among the disciples of Upagupta, there was a bhikṣu who, having faith, had left home and had attained the fourth dhyāna, which he thought was the fourth fruit.[9] As an expedient, Upagupta sent him off somewhere. On the road, he magically produced a band of thieves, and magically produced five hundred merchants. The thieves robbed the merchants and slaughtered them indiscriminately. Seeing this, the bhikṣu was terrified and immediately thought to himself, "I am not an arhat. I must be at the third fruit."

After the death of the merchants, a daughter of one of the wealthy merchants said to the bhikṣu, "Please, Virtuous One, take me with you."

The bhikṣu replied, "The Buddha does not permit me to travel with a woman."

---

9   **Among the disciples of Upagupta** (*Ubakikuta deshi chū* 優婆毱多弟子中): Another story found in Zhanran's *Zhiguan fuxing zhuan hongjue* 止觀輔行傳弘決 (T.1912.46:302c22-303a8). Upagupta was a monk at the time of King Aśoka, reckoned as the fourth ancestor in the Indian lineage of Zen.

T10. The Bhikṣu of the Fourth Dhyāna *Shizen biku* 四禪比丘 249

The woman said, "I shall [watch] the Virtuous One and follow be-hind."[10]

The bhikṣu took pity on her, and they walked on, watching each other. The Venerable [Upagupta] then manifested a great river. The woman said, "Virtuous One, cross over with me."

The bhikṣu was downstream and the woman was upstream. Then, the woman fell into the water, crying out, "Virtuous One, save me!"

Thereupon, the bhikṣu grabbed her and pulled her out. Sensing her fine, smooth skin, he gave rise to lust and immediately realized he was not an anāgāmin. Feeling extreme attachment to this woman, he took her to an enclosed place. Only as he went to have intercourse with her did he see that she was his teacher. In great shame, he stood with head bowed. The Venerable said, "You used to think yourself an arhat. How could you do such an evil deed as this?"

He took him to the saṃgha and had him repent. He taught him the essentials of the dharma, and he became an arhat.

[T10:5] {2:422}

この比丘、はじめ生見のあやまりあれど、殺害の狼藉をみるにおそりを生ず。ときに、われ羅漢にあらず、とおもふ、なほ、第三果なるべし、とおもふあやまりあり。のちに、細滑の想によりて、愛欲心を生ずるに、阿那含にあらず、としる。さらに、謗佛のおもひを生ぜず、謗法のおもひなし、聖教にそむくおもひあらず、四禪比丘にはひとしからず。この比丘は、聖教を習學せるちからあるによりて、みづから阿羅漢にあらず、阿那含にあらず、としるなり。いまの無聞の輩は、阿羅漢はいかなりともしらず、佛はいかなりともしらざるがゆえに、みづから阿羅漢にあらず、佛にあらずともしらず、みだりに、われは佛なり、とのみおもひいふは、おほきなるあやまりなり、ふかきとがあるべし。學者まづすべからく、佛はいかなるべし、とならふべきなり。

Initially, this bhikṣu was mistaken in his personal view, but when he saw the indiscriminate slaughter, he became terrified; and thereupon, he thought, "I am not an arhat."[11] But he was still mistaken in thinking he had the third fruit. Later, when he gave rise to lust from the sensation of the fine, smooth skin, he realized he was not an *anāgāmin*. He did not further produce thoughts that would slander the Buddha; without thoughts of disparaging the dharma, or thoughts opposing the sacred

---

10 **"I shall [watch] the Virtuous One"** (*ga taitoku* 我大德): Supplying the predicate *mō* 望, missing in the MS.

11 **personal view** (*shōken* 生見): A tentative translation of a somewhat unusual term repeated several times in this chapter but not elsewhere in the *Shōbōgenzō*. In its context here, it seems to suggest "a view arbitrarily produced by oneself"; but some interpret it as an abbreviation of *shujō ken* 衆生見, either in the sense of "the view of the reality of the self of living beings," or simply "the view held by ordinary living beings."

teachings, he was not the same as the bhikṣu in the fourth dhyāna.[12] This bhikṣu, through the power of his having studied the sacred teachings, recognized himself that he was not an arhat and not an *anāgāmin*. The unlearned today, because they do not know what an arhat is, or what a buddha is, do not recognize they are not arhats, are not buddhas; their arbitrarily thinking, "I am a buddha," is a huge mistake and a grave failing. What students need to do first is learn what a buddha is.

[T10:6] {2:423}

古德云、習聖教者、薄知次位、縱生逾濫、亦易開解。

A virtuous one of old has said,[13]

Those who have studied the sacred teachings have some knowledge of their stage; even if they exceed it, they easily understand it.[14]

[T10:7]

まことなるかな、古德の言。たとひ生見のあやまりありとも、すこしきも佛法を習學せらむ輩は、みづからに欺誑せられじ、他人にも欺誑せられじ。

How true, the words of the virtuous one of old. One may be mistaken in one's personal view, but those who have studied the buddha dharma even a little will not be deceived by themselves and will not be deceived by others.

[T10:8]

曾聞、有人自謂成佛。待天不曉、謂爲魔障。曉已、不見梵王請説。自知非佛、自謂是阿羅漢。又被他人罵之、心生異念、自知非是阿羅漢、仍謂是第三果也。又見女人起欲想、知非聖人。此亦良由知教相故、乃如是也。

---

12 **he was not the same as the bhikṣu in the fourth dhyāna** (*shizen biku ni wa hito-shikarazu* 四禪比丘にはひとしからず): I.e., he differs from the bhikṣu in the story told in section 1, above.

13 **virtuous one of old** (*kotoku* 古德): I.e., Zhanran, in the lines immediately following his telling of the story of Upagupta's disciple, above, section 4 (*Zhiguan fuxing zhuan hongjue* 止觀輔行傳弘決, T.1912.46:303a8-9).

14 **even if they exceed it** (*jū shō yūran* 縱生逾濫): A tentative translation of a phrase subject to two readings. The phrase might be rendered, "even if they commit a *sthūlātyaya*," taking 逾濫 as *chūran* 偸濫, understood as a transliteration of Sanskrit *sthūlātyaya* (more often rendered *chūran* 偸蘭), a transgression of the vinaya through intent to commit a serious offense — in this case, presumably, the monk's intention to have intercourse. The reading here takes *yūran* 逾濫 in its common meaning of "excessive" — in this case, presumably in reference to the monk's mistaken sense of his spiritual status — as is suggested by Dōgen's comment, in the following section, that the learned can easily resolve a mistaken view.

T10. The Bhikṣu of the Fourth Dhyāna *Shizen biku* 四禪比丘 251

Once I heard that there was a person who thought he had attained bud-dhahood.[15] When dawn did not break as he expected, he thought it was due to the obstruction of Māra.[16] When dawn did break, and he failed to see King Brahmā requesting him to preach, he realized he was not a buddha but thought he was an arhat. When he was criticized for this by others and felt resentment, he realized he was not an arhat but thought he was at the third fruit. When he saw a woman and gave rise to lust, he knew he was not a sage. Again, it was very much because he knew the teachings that this was so.[17]

[T10:9] {2:424}

それ、佛法をしれるは、かくのごとくみづからが非を覺知し、はやくその
あやまりをなげすつ。しらざるともがらは、一生むなしく愚蒙のなかにあ
り。生より生を受くるも、またかくのごとくなるべし。この優婆毱多の弟
子は、四禪をえて四果とおもふといへども、さらに我非羅漢の智あり。無
聞比丘も、臨命終のとき、四禪の中陰みゆることあらむに、我非羅漢とし
らば、謗佛の罪あるべからず。況や四禪をえてのちひさし、なむぞ四果に
あらざるとかへりみしざらむ。すでに四果にあらずとしらば、なむぞ改め
ざらむ。いたづらに僻計にとどこほり、空しく邪見にしづめり。

Those who know the buddha dharma, recognize their own errors like this and quickly cast aside their mistakes. Those who do not know spend their entire lives in pointless ignorance. Even receiving one life after another, they will still be like this. This disciple of Upagupta, though he may have thought that attaining the fourth dhyāna was the fourth fruit, had the wisdom to recognize he was not an arhat. When, at the end of his life, the unlearned bhikṣu saw his intermediate state in the fourth dhyā-na, had he recognized he was not an arhat, he would not have committed the offense of slandering the Buddha. Not to mention that it had been a long time since he attained the fourth dhyāna; why, then, had he never reflected that it was not the fourth fruit? If he knew that it was not the fourth fruit, why did he never correct himself? He is fruitlessly stuck in his biased reckonings, pointlessly sunk in his false view.

---

15 **Once I heard** (*sō mon* 曾聞): Continuing to quote Zhanran at *Zhiguan fuxing zhuan hongjue* 止觀輔行傳弘決, T.1912.46:303a9-14.

16 **When dawn did not break as he expected** (*tai ten fugyō* 待天不曉): Presumably, a reference to the tradition that the Buddha's awakening occurred as the dawn star arose in the east. Similarly, the failure to see King Brahmā reflects the tradition that, following his awakening, the Buddha was encouraged to preach by the deva Brahmā.

17 **this was so** (*nai nyoze ya* 乃如是也): These four glyphs, appearing at the end of the passage, do not occur in the source.

[T10:10]

第三には、命終の時、おほきなる誤りあり。そのとが、ふかくして、つひに阿鼻地獄におちぬるなり。たとひなむち一生のあひだ、四果とおもひきたれりとも、臨命終の時、四禪の中陰みゆることあらば、一生の誤りを懺悔して、四果にはあらざりとおもふべし。いかでか、佛、われを欺誑して、涅槃なきに涅槃ありと施設せさせたまふとおもふべき。これ、無聞のとがなり、このつみすでに謗佛なり。これによりて、阿鼻の中陰現じて、命終して阿鼻地獄におちぬ。たとひ四果の聖者なりとも、いかでか如來におよばむ。

Third, at the end of his life, he committed a grave mistake.[18] His fault was profound and eventually led to his falling into the *avīci* hell. Even had you thought throughout your entire life that [the fourth dhyāna] was the fourth fruit, if, when facing the end of life, the intermediate state in the fourth dhyāna appeared, you should repent your lifelong mistake and admit that it was not the fourth fruit. How could you think that the Buddha deceives you by proposing nirvāṇa when there is no nirvāṇa? That is the error of the unlearned; this offense is clearly slandering the Buddha. As a result, his intermediate state in *avīci* appeared, and when his life ended, he fell into the *avīci* hell.

Even if one is a sage of the fourth fruit, how could one equal a tathāgata?[19]

[T10:11] {2:425}

舍利弗は、久しくこれ四果の聖者なり。三千大千世界の所有の智慧をあつめて、如來をのぞきたてまつりて、ほかを一分とし、舍利弗の智慧を十六分にせる一分と、三千大千所有の智慧とを格量するに、舍利弗の十六分之一分に及ばざるなり。しかあれど、如來未曾説の法をときましますをききて、前後の佛説、ことにして、われを欺誑しましますと、おもはず、波旬無此事と、ほめたてまつる。如來は福増をわたし、舍利弗は福増をわたさず、四果と佛果と、はるかにことなることかくのごとし。たとひ舍利弗及びもろもろの弟子のごとくならむ、十方界にみちみてたらむ、ともに佛智を測量せんこと、うべからず。孔・老にかくのごとくの功徳、いまだなし。佛法を習學せむもの、たれか、孔子・老子測度せざらむ。孔・老を習學するもの、佛法を測量することいまだなし。いま宋國の輩、おほく孔・老と佛道と一致の道理をたつ、僻見、もともふかきものなり。しもにまさに廣説すべし。

Śāriputra was long a sage of the fourth fruit. If we were to collect all the wisdom existing in the trichiliocosm, excluding that of the tathāgatas, as a single sum, and measure the single sum of one sixteenth of the wisdom of Śāriputra against that wisdom of the trichiliocosm, the latter

---

18 **Third** (*daisan ni wa* 第三には): Turning to the last of the three errors proposed in section 3, above.

19 **Even if one is a sage of the fourth fruit** (*tatoi shika no shōja nari tomo* たとひ四果の聖者なりとも): Dōgen here introduces his topic of the next section.

T10. The Bhikṣu of the Fourth Dhyāna *Shizen biku* 四禪比丘 253

would not equal the single sum of one sixteenth of that of Śāriputra.[20] However, when he heard a dharma never previously preached by the Tathāgata, instead of thinking, "The Buddha's earlier and later teachings are different; he has deceived me," he praised it, saying, "*Pāpīyān has no such thing.*"[21] The Tathāgata delivered Śrīvaddhi; Śāriputra did not deliver Śrīvaddhi.[22]

The vast difference between the fourth fruit and the buddha fruit is like this.[23] Even if Śāriputra and the likes of all the disciples filled the worlds in the ten directions, all together they could not fathom the wisdom of the Buddha. Confucius and Laozi never had such virtue. Among those who

---

20 **If we were to collect all the wisdom existing in the trichiliocosm** (*sanzen daisen sekai no shou no chie o atsumete* 三千大千世界の所有の智慧をあつめて): A convoluted way of expressing the claim that (not counting the wisdom of the buddhas) all the wisdom in the universe does not equal a sixteenth of Śāriputra's wisdom. Dōgen is rephrasing here a verse, quoted in Zhanran's *Zhiguan fuxing zhuan hongjue* 止觀輔行傳弘決 (T.1912.46:334c5-7), from the *Dazhidu lun* 大智度論 (T.1509.25:136a11-13):

一切衆生智、唯除佛世尊、欲比舍利弗、智慧及多聞、於十六分中、猶尚不及一。

The wisdom of all living beings,
Only excepting the buddhas, the world-honored ones —
Were we to compare it with
The wisdom and learning of Śāriputra,
Of sixteen parts,
It would not amount to one.

21 **"Pāpīyān has no such thing"** (*Hajun mu shi ji* 波旬無此事): A reference to Māra, the Evil One (*Mahajun* 魔波旬; S. Māra-pāpīyān), quoting a verse in the *Lotus Sūtra*, in which Śāriputra expresses his conviction that the apparent inconsistencies in Śākyamuni's teaching are merely a reflection of his skillful means and not the deception of Māra appearing as the Buddha (*Miaofa lianhua jing* 妙法蓮華經, T.262.9:11b1-2):

世尊説實道、波旬無此事。以是我定知、非是魔作佛。

The World-Honored One teaches the real path;
Pāpīyān has no such thing.
Therefore, I definitely know
This is not Māra becoming the Buddha.

22 **The Tathāgata delivered Śrīvaddhi** (*Nyorai wa Fukuzō o watashi* 如來は福増をわたし): Reference to a story in which Śāriputra declines to accept a 120-year-old man, Śrīvaddhi, into the order of bhikṣus, but the Buddha does accept him. The story, which Dōgen quotes at length in his *Eihei kōroku* 永平廣錄 (DZZ.3:246-252, no. 381), is found in the *Damamūka-nidāna-sūtra* (*Xianyu jing* 賢愚經, T.202.4:376c13ff).

23 **The vast difference between the fourth fruit and the buddha fruit is like this** (*shika to bukka to, haruka ni kotonaru koto kaku no gotoshi* 四果と佛果と、はるかにことなることかくのごとし): The traditional distinction between the two fruits is that, while the arhat has fully mastered the four sacred truths and eliminated the defilements, the buddha is omniscient and in command of salvific expedient devices. The reader may wish to compare Dōgen's remarks here with his treatment of the arhat in "Shōbōgenzō arakan" 正法眼藏阿羅漢.

254 DŌGEN'S *SHŌBŌGENZŌ* VOLUME VI

study the buddha dharma, who could not fathom Confucius and Laozi?
Among those who study Confucius and Laozi, there has never been one
who fathomed the buddha dharma. Nowadays many in the Land of the
Song have established the principle of the unity of Confucius, Laozi, and
the way of the buddhas — a deeply biased view, on which we shall have
more to say below.

[T10:12]
四禪比丘、みづからが僻見をまこととして、如來の、欺誑しましますと思
ふ、ながく佛を違背したてまつるなり。愚癡の甚だしき、六師等にひとし
かるべし。

The bhikṣu in the fourth dhyāna, taking his own biased view as the
truth, thinks the Tathāgata has deceived him and forever turns his back
on the Buddha. His stupidity is as extreme as that of the six teachers.[24]

[T10:13]
古德云、大師在世、尚有僻計生見之人、況滅後、無師不得禪者。

A virtuous one of old has said,[25]

Even when the Great Master was in the world, there were people with
biased reckonings and personal views; how much more so after his
extinction, among those without a teacher, who have not attained the
dhyānas.

[T10:14] {2:426}
いま大師とは、佛世尊なり。まことに世尊在世、出家受具せる、なほ無聞
によりては、僻計生見の誤り、のがれがたし。況や如來滅後、後五百歳、
邊地下賤の時處、誤りなからむや。四禪を發せるもの、なほかくのごと
し。況や四禪を發するに及ばず、徒に貪名愛利にしづめらむもの、官途世
路を貪る輩、不足言なるべし。いま大宋國に寡聞愚鈍の輩多し。かれらが
いはく、佛法と老子・孔子の法と、一致にして異轍あらず。

"The Great Master" here means the Buddha, the World-Honored One.
Indeed, even for those who left home and received the full precepts when
the World-Honored One was in the world, it was hard to escape the mistakes of "*biased reckonings and personal views.*" How much less, then,
could there be no mistakes in remote places and debased times in *the lat-*
ter five hundred years following the extinction of the Tathāgata.[26] Even

---

24 **six teachers** (*rokushi tō* 六師等): I.e., six major non-Buddhist religious leaders at
the time of Buddha Śākyamuni.

25 **A virtuous one of old** (*kotoku* 古德): Zhanran, again, in lines following the passage Dōgen quoted in section 1, above (*Zhiguan fuxing zhuan hongjue* 止觀輔行傳弘決,
T.1912.46:257b27-28).

26 **latter five hundred years following the extinction of the Tathāgata** (*nyorai metsu*
go, go gohyaku sai 如來滅後、後五百歳): A fixed expression for the final, degenerate

T10. The Bhikṣu of the Fourth Dhyāna *Shizen biku* 四禪比丘 255

those who have produced the fourth dhyāna are like this; how much more is this the case with those unable to produce the fourth dhyāna, those who would drown in vain in their lust for fame and love of profit, those who covet official posts and worldly advancement — they are not worth mentioning.

Nowadays, in the Land of the Great Song, there are many people who are ignorant and dimwitted.[27] They say that the buddha dharma and the teachings of Laozi and Confucius are a unity, without different tracks.

[T10:15]

大宋嘉泰中、有僧正受、撰進普燈錄三十卷。云、臣聞孤山智圓之言曰、吾道如鼎也。三教如足也。足一虧而鼎覆。臣嘗慕其人稽其説。乃知、儒之爲教、其要在誠意、道之爲教、其要在虚心。釋之爲教、其要在見性。誠意也、虚心也、見性也、異名體同。究厥攸歸、無適而不與此道會。云云。

During the Jiatai of the Great Song, there was a monk, Zhengshou, who composed and presented the Pudeng lu in thirty scrolls.[28] He said,

Your servant has heard that Gushan Zhiyuan said, "My way is like a three-legged cauldron: the three teachings are like the feet. If one foot is missing, the cauldron topples over."[29]

Your servant has long admired this man and reflected on what he said. I have come to understand that, in what the Confucians teach, the essence is in sincere intention; in what the Daoists teach, the essence is in an empty mind; and in what Śākyamuni teaches, the essence is in seeing one's nature. Sincere intention, empty mind, and seeing one's nature — the terms are different, but the substance is the same. When we fully study their convergence, there is nothing that does not accord with this way. . . .

---

age of the dharma of Buddha Śākyamuni. (See, e.g., the *Lotus Sūtra* (*Miaofa lianhua jing* 妙法蓮華經, T.262.9:54b29.)

27　**Nowadays, in the Land of the Great Song** (*ima Daisō koku ni* いま大宋國に): Dōgen here begins his critique of the doctrine of the unity of the three teachings.

28　**During the Jiatai of the Great Song** (*Dai Sō Katai chū* 大宋嘉泰中): The Song-dynasty era spanning 1201-1204.

Zhengshou (*Shōju* 正受): I.e., Leian Zhengshou 雷庵正受 (1146-1209?), author of the Chan history *Jiatai Pudeng lu* 嘉泰普燈錄. The work was completed in 1204 and presented to the Song Emperor Ningzong 寧宗 (r. 1194-1224). Dōgen's quotation here comes from the text accompanying the presentation ("Jinshang shu" 進上書, ZZ.137:2a5-9).

29　**Gushan Zhiyuan** (*Kozan Chien* 孤山智圓): 976-1022; a prominent figure in the "Off Mountain" (Shanwai 山外) branch of the Tiantai 天台 tradition.

[T10:16]

かくのごとく、僻計生見の輩のみ多し、ただ智圓・正受のみにはあらず。この輩は、四禪を得て四果と思はむよりも、その誤りふかし。謗佛・謗法・謗僧なるべし。すでに撥無解脱なり、撥無三世なり、撥無因果なり、莽莽蕩蕩招殃禍、疑がひなし。三寶・四諦・四沙門なし、とおもふし輩にひとし。佛法、いまだその要、見性にあらず。西天二十八祖・七佛、いづれの處にか佛法の、ただ見性のみなりとある。六祖壇經に、見性の言あり、かの書、これ僞書なり、附法藏の書にあらず、曹溪の言句にあらず、佛祖の兒孫、またく依用せざる書なり。正受・智圓、いまだ佛法の一隅をしらざるによりて、一鼎三足の邪計をなす。

Those of biased reckonings and arbitrary views like this are many; it is not just Zhiyuan and Zhengshou. The mistakes of this lot are graver even than believing that attaining the fourth dhyāna is the fourth fruit. They disparage the buddha, disparage the dharma, disparage the saṃgha: it is the complete denial of liberation, the denial of the three times, the denial of cause and effect; without any doubt it is "an endless vastness, inviting disaster."[30] They are equivalent to those who have thought there were no three treasures, four truths, or four śramaṇa.[31] In the buddha dharma, the essence has never been "seeing one's nature." Where have the twenty-eight ancestors of Sindh in the West or the seven buddhas said that the buddha dharma was just "seeing one's nature"? The words "seeing one's nature" are found in the *Platform Sūtra of the Sixth Ancestor*, but that book is a spurious text — not a text of the transmitted dharma treasury, not the words of Caoxi, a book absolutely not relied on by the descendants of the buddhas and ancestors.[32] Because Zhengshou and Zhiyuan never understood a single corner of the buddha dharma, they maintain their biased reckoning of a single cauldron with three legs.

[T10:17] {2:427}

古德云、老子・莊子、尚自未識小乘能著所著・能破所破、況大乘中若著若破。是故不與佛法少同。然世愚者迷於名相、濫禪者惑於正理、欲將道德・逍遙之名齊於佛法解脱之説。豈可得乎。

30　**"an endless vastness, inviting disaster"** (*mōmō tōtō shō ōka* 莽莽蕩蕩招殃禍): From a line in the *Zhengdao ge* 證道歌, attributed to Yongjia Zhenjue 永嘉眞覺 (665–713) (T.2014.48:396a27-28); also quoted in "Shōbōgenzō sanji gō" 正法眼藏三時業):

豁達空撥因果、莽莽蕩蕩招殃禍。
A wide-open void, dismissing cause and effect;
An endless vastness, inviting disaster.

31　**four śramaṇa** (*shi shamon* 四沙門): Alternate term for the four fruits (*shika* 四果).

32　***Platform Sūtra of the Sixth Ancestor*** (*Rokuso dan kyō* 六祖壇經): The famous *Liuzu tan jing* 六祖壇經 (T.2007, T.2008), in which the expression "seeing one's nature" (*jianxing* 見性) appears many times. "Caoxi" 曹溪 refers to the Sixth Ancestor, Huineng of Caoxi 曹溪慧能.

T10. The Bhikṣu of the Fourth Dhyāna *Shizen biku* 四禪比丘 257

A virtuous one of old has said,[33]

Even Laozi and Zhuangzi themselves never recognized what grasps and is grasped, rejects and is rejected, according to the Small Vehicle, much less grasping and rejecting according to the Great Vehicle. Therefore, [their teachings] are not even slightly similar to the buddha dharma. Yet worldly fools, deluded about names and forms, and excessive meditators, confused about correct principles, seek to equate the words of the Way and Its Virtue and Free and Easy with the teachings of liberation in the buddha dharma.[34] *How could this be?*

[T10:18]

むかしより、名相にまどふもの、正理をしらざるともがら、佛法、莊子・老子にひとしむるなり。いささかも佛法の稽古あるともがら、むかしより、莊子・老子をおもくする一人なし。

Since long ago, those lost in "names and forms" and those ignorant of the "correct principles" have equated the buddha dharma with Zhuangzi and Laozi. Of those with even the slightest investigation of the ancients in the buddha dharma, since long ago there has not been a single person who took Zhuangzi and Laozi seriously.

[T10:19]

清淨法行經云、月光菩薩、彼稱顏回、光淨菩薩、彼稱仲尼、迦葉菩薩、彼稱老子。云云。

In the Sūtra of Pure Dharma Conduct, it is said,[35]

Bodhisattva Candraprabha is there called Yan Hui; Bodhisattva Prabhāsvara is there called Zhongni; Bodhisattva Kāśyapa is there called Laozi.[36]

33　**A virtuous one of old** (*kotoku* 古德): Again, a quotation from the *Zhiguan fuxing zhuan hongjue* 止觀輔行傳弘決 (T.1912.46:247a11-15).

34　**worldly fools** (*se gusha* 世愚者): Zhanran's original reads *shi jiangzhe* 世講者, "worldly lecturers" — i.e., scholars, in contrast to the following meditators. The compound "names and forms" (*myōsō* 名相) is generally interpreted here as "doctrines" or "doctrinal concepts."

Way and Its Virtue **and** *Free and Easy* (*Dōtoku Shōyō* 道德・逍遙): I.e., The *Daode jing* 道德經 of Laozi 老師 and the opening chapter of the *Zhuangzi* 莊子, entitled "Free and Easy Wandering" (Xiaoyao you 逍遙遊).

35　*Sūtra of Pure Dharma Conduct* (*Shōjō hōgyō kyō* 清淨法行經): An indigenous Chinese scripture, probably composed in the fifth century, only a fragment of which is extant today. The quotation here is again from Zhanran's *Zhiguan fuxing zhuan hongjue* 止觀輔行傳弘決 (T.1912.46:343c18-20), quoting the *Qingjing faxing jing* 清淨法行經.

36　**Bodhisattva Candraprabha is there called Yan Hui** (*Gakkō bosatsu, hi shō Gankai* 月光菩薩、彼稱顏回): Bodhisattva "Moonlight," in iconography often associated with Buddha Bhaiṣajyaguru, is "there" (i.e., in China) Confucius's favorite disciple, Yan Hui 顏回 (521-481 BCE). Bodhisattva Prabhāsvara (*Kōjō bosatsu* 光淨菩薩) has not been

258 DŌGEN'S *SHŌBŌGENZŌ* VOLUME VI

[T10:20] {2:428}

むかしより、この經の説を擧して、孔子・老子等も菩薩なれば、その説、ひそかに佛説に同じかるべし、といひ、また、佛のつかひならむ、その説、おのづから佛説ならむ、といふ。この説、みな非なり。

Citing the teachings of this sūtra, it has long been said that, since Confucius, Laozi, and the like, were bodhisattvas, the intent of their teachings must have been the same as the teachings of the Buddha, or that they were the emissaries of the Buddha, whose teachings were inherently the teachings of the Buddha. These explanations are all false.

[T10:21]

古德云、準諸目錄、皆推此經、以爲疑僞。云云。

A virtuous one of old has said, "Judging from the catalogs, they all consider this sūtra to be spurious."[37]

[T10:22]

いまこの説によらば、いよいよ佛法と孔・老とことなるべし。すでにこれ菩薩なり、佛果にひとしかるべからず。また和光應迹の功德は、ひとり三世諸佛菩薩の法なり、俗塵の凡夫の所能にあらず、實業凡夫、いかでか應迹に自在あらむ。孔・老いまだ應迹の説なし、況や孔・老は先因をしらず、當果をとかず、纔かに一世の忠孝をもて、君につかへ、家ををさむる術をむねとせり、さらに後世の説なし、すでにこれ斷見の流類なるべし。莊・老をきらふに、小乘なほしらず、況や大乘をや、といふは、上古の明師なり。三敎一致といふは、智圓・正受なり、後代澆季愚闇の凡夫なり。汝、なんの勝出あればか、上古の先德の所説をさみして、みだりに孔老と佛法とひとしかるべしといふ、なんぢたちが所見、すべて佛法の通塞を論ずるにたらず、負笈して明師に參學すべし。智圓・正受、汝ら、大・小兩乘すべていまだしらざるなり、四禪をえて四果と思ひしよりも、くらし。悲しむべし、澆風のあほぐ處、かくのごとくの魔子おほかることを。

Based on this claim here, the buddha dharma and Confucius and Laozi are even more different: since they are bodhisattvas, they cannot be equal to the buddha fruit.[38] Furthermore, the virtue of *softening the radiance and responding in traces* is a dharma only of the buddhas and bodhisattvas of the three times, not something that can be done by the common people in the dust of the world.[39] How could common people with their

---

identified in Indian sources; Zhongni (*Chūji* 仲尼) is the style name of Confucius. Bodhisattva Kāśyapa may be the figure who converses with the Buddha in the eponymous chapter of the *Nirvāṇa Sūtra* (e.g., *Da banniepan jing* 大般涅槃經, T.374.12:560b9ff).

37 **A virtuous one of old** (*kotoku* 古德): Zhanran, in a comment following his quotation of the sūtra (*Zhiguan fuxing zhuan hongjue* 止觀輔行傳弘決, T.1912.46:343c20-21). For an example in the catalogs, see *Kaiyuan lu* 開元祿, T.2154.55:485a20.

38 **Based on this claim here** (*ima kono setsu ni yoraba* いまこの説によらば): I.e., based on the claim that Confucius and Laozi were bodhisattvas.

39 **softening the radiance and responding in traces** (*wakō ōjaku* 和光應迹): A variant

T10. The Bhikṣu of the Fourth Dhyāna *Shizen biku* 四禪比丘   259

actualized karma have the freedom to respond in traces?[40] There are no claims that Confucius and Laozi ever responded in traces; much less do Confucius and Laozi know of prior causes or talk of future effects. Their message is the arts of serving the lord and ordering the family, through the loyalty and filial piety of merely one lifetime; since they have no talk of later lifetimes, they are surely followers of annihilationist views.[41] Those who detested Zhuangzi and Laozi and said that they did not understand even the Small Vehicle, much less the Great Vehicle — they were wise masters of high antiquity; those who declare the unity of the three teachings are Zhiyuan and Zhengshou — ignorant common people of the later generations in our season of decline. What makes you so superior, that you would show contempt for the prior worthies of high antiquity and recklessly assert that Confucius and Laozi are equal to the buddha dharma? Your view is completely inadequate to consider how the buddha dharma is advanced or obstructed.[42] You should shoulder your trunk and go to study under a wise master. Zhiyuan and Zhengshou, you do not know anything about either the Great or the Small Vehicle; you are even more in the dark than the one who attained the fourth dhyāna and thought it was the fourth fruit. How sad, that where the winds of decline are stirring, such children of Māra are numerous.

[T10:23] {2:429}

古德云、如孔丘・姬旦之語、三皇・五帝之書、孝以治家、忠以治國、輔國利民、只是一世之内、不濟過未。齊佛法之益於三世、不謬乎。

A virtuous one of old has said,[43]

---

of the more common expression *wakō dōjin* 和光同塵 ("softening the radiance and sharing the dust"), used in Buddhism in reference to the ability of buddhas and advanced bodhisattvas to manifest themselves in diverse "transformation bodies" (*ōjin* 應身; S. *nirmāṇa-kāya*) in response to the needs of beings.

40   **common people with their actualized karma** (*jitsugō bonbu* 實業凡夫): I.e., ordinary people subject to the consequences of their prior deeds (and, thus, not free to manifest themselves at will).

41   **followers of annihilationist views** (*danken no rurui* 斷見の流類): Or "followers of annihilationism" (S. *uccheda-dṛṣṭi*); i.e., believers in the view that living beings simply disappear at death and are not reborn based on their karma.

42   **how the buddha dharma is advanced or obstructed** (*buppō no tsūsoku* 佛法の通塞): More literally, "the passage and blockage of the buddha dharma." The term *tsūsoku* 通塞 is a common expression indicating that a road or way is "open or blocked"; often carrying the idiomatic sense of affairs "going smoothly or not."

43   **A virtuous one of old** (*kotoku* 古德): The first sentence here is taken from Zhanran (*Zhiguan fuxing zhuan hongjue* 止觀輔行傳弘決, T.1912.46:440b22-23); the remainder, though resembling a continuation of the Chinese passage, does not in fact occur in the source and seems to have been composed by Dōgen.

260 DŌGEN'S *SHŌBŌGENZŌ* VOLUME VI

In the words of Kong Qiu and Ji Dan, and the writings of the Three Sovereigns and Five Lords, through regulating the family by filial piety and regulating the state by loyalty, the state is assisted, and the people benefited.[44]

But this is only in the present time and is no help in past and future. [To say] that it is the equal of the benefits of the buddha dharma in the three times — how is this not a mistake?

[T10:24]

まことなるかなや、古德の語、よく佛法の至理に達せり、世俗の道理にあきらかなり。三皇・五帝の語、いまだ轉輪聖王の教へに及ぶべからず、梵王・帝釋の説にならべ論ずべからず。統領する處、所得の果報、はるかに劣なるべし。輪王・梵王・帝釋、なほ出家・受具の比丘に及ばず、何に況や如來にひとしからむや。孔丘・姫旦の書、また天竺の十八大經に及ぶべからず、四韋陀の典籍にならべがたし。西天婆羅門教、いまだ佛教に齊しからざるなり、なほ小乘聲聞教にひとしからず。あはれむべし、振旦小國邊方にして、三教一致の邪説あり。

How true, the words of the virtuous one of old: they reach the ultimate principle of the buddha dharma and are clear about the principles of the secular world. The words of the Three Sovereigns and Five Lords do not equal the teachings of the wheel-turning sage kings and should not be compared with the teachings of the Brahmā King or Lord Śakra.[45] What they rule over, their recompense, is far less.[46] And the wheel-turning sage kings, the Brahmā King, and Lord Śakra do not equal the bhikṣu who has left home and received the precepts; how much less are they equivalent to the tathāgatas. The books of Kong Qiu and Ji Dan do not equal the eighteen great scriptures of Sindhu and cannot stand alongside the books of the four *Vedas*.[47] The Brahmanical teachings of Sindh in the West are not equivalent to the teachings of the buddhas, not equivalent

---

44   **Kong Qiu and Ji Dan** (*Kōkyū Kitan* 孔丘・姫旦): I.e., Confucius and the Duke of Zhou (Zhou Gong 周公). "The Three Sovereigns and Five Lords" (*sankō gotei* 三皇・五帝) refers to the set of eight mythological rulers of ancient China.

45   **wheel-turning sage kings** (*tenrin shōō* 轉輪聖王); **Brahmā King** (*Bonnō* 梵王); **Lord Śakra** (*Taishaku* 帝釋): I.e., respectively, the *cakravartin*, mythical kings of the four continents; the deva king of the heaven of Brahmā; and the mighty Indra, lord of the devas.

46   **What they rule over, their recompense** (*tōryō suru tokoro, shotoku no kahō* 統領する處、所得の果報): A tentative translation, taking the territory over which the ancient Chinese emperors ruled to be in apposition to their karmic recompense.

47   **eighteen great scriptures of Sindhu** (*Tenjiku no jūhachi daikyō* 天竺の十八大經): Eighteen texts of the Brahmanical tradition in India, comprised of the four *Vedas*; the traditional six *vedāṅgas*, or "limbs of the *Vedas*," that supplement the *Vedas*; and eight śāstras, or treatises, on diverse subjects. A description is given in the *Bailun shu* 百論疏, by Jizang 吉藏 (549-623) (T.1827.42:251a20-b8).

T10. The Bhikṣu of the Fourth Dhyāna *Shizen biku* 四禪比丘　　　261

even to the *śrāvaka* teachings of the Small Vehicle. How pitiful that in the small, marginal country of Cīnasthāna, there is the false theory of the unity of the three teachings.[48]

[T10:25]

第十四祖龍樹菩薩云、大阿羅漢辟支佛、知八萬大劫、諸大菩薩及佛、知無量劫。

The Fourteenth Ancestor, Bodhisattva Nāgārjuna, has said, "The arhats and pratyeka-buddhas know eighty thousand great kalpas; the great bodhisattvas and buddhas know innumerable kalpas."[49]

[T10:26] {2:430}

孔老等、いまだ一世中の前後をしらず、一生・二生の宿通あらむ。何に況や一劫をしらむや、何に況や百劫・千劫をしらむや、何に況や八萬大劫をしらんむや、何に況や無量劫をしらむむや。この無量劫を明らかにてらし、しれること、たなごころをみるよりも明らかなる諸佛・菩薩を、孔・老等に比類せむ、愚闇といふにもたらざるなり。耳を掩て、三教一致の言をきくことなかれ、邪説中、最邪説なり。

Confucius, Laozi, and the like, do not know the past and future of a single life; would they have the power of [recollection of] one or two past lives? How much less could they know a whole kalpa; how much less could they know a hundred or a thousand kalpas; how much less could they know eighty great kalpas; how much less could they know innumerable kalpas. To compare Confucius, Laozi, and the like, to the buddhas and bodhisattvas, who clearly illumine innumerable kalpas, knowing them more clearly than they see the palm of their own hand — "stupidity" is not even the word for it. Cover your ears and do not listen to the words the *"unity of the three teachings"*; among false teachings, this is the worst.

[T10:27]

莊子云、貴賤苦樂、是非得失、皆是自然。

In the Zhuangzi, it is said that noble and base, pain and pleasure, right and wrong, gain and loss — all occur of their own accord.[50]

48　**Cīnasthāna** (*Shintan* 振旦): A transliteration of a Sanskrit name for China.

49　**The Fourteenth Ancestor, the Bodhisattva Nāgārjuna** (*dai jūshi so Ryūju bosatsu* 第十四祖龍樹菩薩): Quoting a line from the *Dajidu lun* 大智度論, traditionally attributed to Nāgārjuna (T.1509.25:98b5-6), defining the paranormal power of remembrance of former lives (*shukumyō tsū* 宿命通).

50　**the Zhuangzi** (*Sōshi* 莊子): Quoting the *Mohe zhiguan* 摩訶止觀 by Zhiyi 智顗 (538-597) (T.1911.46:135a19). The words do not occur in the *Zhuangzi* itself.

262 DŌGEN'S *SHŌBŌGENZŌ* VOLUME VI

[T10:28]

この見、すでに西國の自然見の外道の流類なり。貴賤・苦樂・是非・得失、みなこれ善惡業の感ずる處なり。満業・引業をしらず、過世・未世を明らめざるがゆえに、現在にくらし、いかでか佛法に齊しからむ。

This view is just that of followers in the Western Land of the other path that holds the view of spontaneity.[51] "*Noble and base, pain and pleasure, right and wrong, gain and loss*" — all these are the responses to good and evil karma. Because he does not know about fulfilling karma and directive karma, and is unclear about past and future lives, he is ignorant of the present; how could this be the equivalent of the buddha dharma?[52]

[T10:29]

あるが云く、諸佛如來、ひろく法界を證するゆえに、微塵法界、みな諸佛の所證なり、しかあれば、依正二報ともに如來の所證となりぬるがゆえに、山河大地・日月星辰・四倒三毒、みな如來の所證なり、山河をみるは如來をみるなり、三毒四倒、佛法にあらずといふことなし、微塵をみるは、法界をみるにひとし、造次顛沛、みな三菩提なり、これを大解脱といふ、これを單傳直指の祖道となづく。かくのごとくいふ輩が、大宋國に稲麻竹葦のごとく、朝野に遍満せり。しかあれども、この輩、たれ人の兒孫といふことあきらかならず、おほよそ佛祖の道をしらざるなり。たとひ諸佛の所證となるとも、山河大地忽ちに凡夫の所見なかるべきにあらず、諸佛の所證となる道理をならはず、きかざるなり。汝、微塵をみるは法界をみるに齊し、といふ、民の、王に齊しといはむがごとし。またなむぞ法界をみて微塵に齊しといはざる。もし、この輩の所見を佛祖の大道とせば、諸佛、出世すべからず、祖師、出現すべからず、衆生、得道すべからざるなり。たとひ生即無生と體達すとも、この道理にあらず。

Some say,

Since the buddhas, the tathāgatas, have widely verified the dharma realms, the infinitesimal dust motes and the dharma realms are all verified by the buddhas. Therefore, since the secondary and primary recompenses have both been verified by the tathāgatas, mountains, rivers, and the whole earth, the sun, moon, and stars, the four inversions and three poisons are all verified by the tathāgatas.[53] To see the mountains

---

51 **Western Land** (*Saigoku* 西國): I.e., India.

view of spontaneity (*jinen ken* 自然見): I.e., the view that phenomena occur of their own accord, rather than through cause and effect.

52 **fulfilling karma and directive karma** (*mangō ingō* 満業・引業): Types of karma distinguished by the nature of the effect: the latter determines the realm (deva, human, animal, etc.) into which one is reborn; the former determines one's better or worse status within that realm.

53 **secondary and primary recompenses** (*eshō nihō* 依正二報): A standard Buddhist term for two types of karmic retribution that one experiences in one's present birth; see Supplementary Notes, s.v. "Secondary and primary recompense."

four inversions and three poisons (*shitō sandoku* 四倒三毒): The former, known as the

T10. The Bhikṣu of the Fourth Dhyāna *Shizen biku* 四禪比丘   263

and rivers is to see the tathāgatas. It is not that the three poisons and four inversions are not the buddha dharma. To see an infinitesimal dust mote is the equivalent of seeing the dharma realms. Our *hasty acts when at risk* are all *saṃbodhi*.[54] This is called "the great liberation"; this is named, "the ancestral way of unique transmission and direct pointing."

Those who talk this way are like "*rice, hemp, bamboo, and reeds*" in the Land of the Great Song, filling court and countryside.[55] It is unclear, however, just whose descendants these people are, for they know nothing about the way of the buddhas and ancestors. Even though they have become verified by the buddhas, it is not the case that the mountains, rivers, and whole earth are suddenly not what is seen by common people. They have not learned, have not heard, the principle of [what it means] to become verified by the buddhas. Your saying that to see an infinitesimal dust mote is the equivalent of seeing the dharma realms is like saying that the subjects are equivalent to the king. And why do you not say that to see the dharma realms is equivalent to seeing an infinitesimal dust mote? If we regard the views of these people as the great way of the buddhas and ancestors, the buddhas would not have appeared in the world, the ancestral masters would not have appeared, living beings would not have gained the way. Even if they have personally realized that *arising is not arising*, that is not this principle.[56]

---

viparyāsa (*tendō* 顛倒), refers to the standard set of false views regarding permanence (*jō* 常; S. *nitya*), pleasure (*raku* 樂; S. *sukha*), self (*ga* 我; S. *ātman*), and purity (*jō* 淨; S. *śubha*); the latter refers to a standard list of the basic defilements: greed (*ton* 貪; S. *rāga*), anger (*shin* 瞋; S. *dveṣa*), and delusion (*chi* 癡; S. *moha*).

54 **hasty acts when at risk** (*zōji tenpai* 造次顛沛): A fixed idiom for fleeting experience, from a saying in the *Lunyu* 論語 4 (KR.1h0005.002.11b):

君子無終食之間違仁，造次必於是，顛沛必於是。

The gentleman does not violate humaneness even for the space of a meal: even when in haste, he keeps to it; even when at risk, he keeps to it.

55 **"rice, hemp, bamboo, and reeds"** (*tō ma chiku i* 稻麻竹葦): I.e., dense and profuse; a simile from Kumārajīva's translation of the *Lotus Sūtra*; see Supplementary Notes.

56 **arising is not arising** (*shō soku mushō* 生即無生): A common fixed phrase expressing the doctrine that the phenomena that arise in this world are ultimately empty and, therefore, do not really occur. The grammatical subject is unexpressed here and could be taken as "we." The antecedent of "this principle" (*kono dōri* この道理) here is not entirely obvious; most likely, it refers to "the principle of [what it means] to become verified by the buddhas" (*shobutsu no shoshō to naru dōri* 諸佛の所證となる道理).

264 DŌGEN'S *SHŌBŌGENZŌ* VOLUME VI

[T10:30] {2:431}

眞諦三藏云、振旦有二福、一無羅刹、二無外道。

The Tripiṭaka Master Paramārtha said, "Cīnasthāna has two blessings: first, there are no *rākṣasas*; second, there are no followers of other paths."[57]

[T10:31]

この言、まことに西國の外道婆羅門の傳來せるなり。得道の外道なしといふとも、外道の見、おこす輩なかるべきにあらず。羅刹はいまだみえず、外道の流類はなきにあらず。小國邊地のゆえに、中印度のごとくにあらざることは、佛法を纔かに修習すといへども、印度のごとくに證をとれるなし。

These words are [in reference to] Brāhmans of other paths actually having arrived from the Western Land.[58] There may be no followers of other paths who have gained the way, but it is not the case that there should not be those who produce the views of other paths.[59] Rakṣasas are not found, but it is not the case that there are no followers of other paths. Because it is a small country and a marginal place, [China] differs

---

57 **Tripiṭaka Master Paramārtha** (*Shintai sanzō* 眞諦三藏): Seeming to combine two separate passages: from (a) *Mohe zhiguan* 摩訶止觀, T.1911.46:134b10-11:

眞諦三藏云、震旦國有二種福云云。

The Tripiṭaka Master Paramārtha said, "Cīnasthāna has two blessings, etc."

And (b) *Zhiguan fuxing zhuan hongjue* 止觀輔行傳弘決, T.1912.46:440a11-12:

震旦有二福者、一無羅刹、二無外道。

Cīnasthāna has two blessings: first, there are no *rākṣasas*; second, there are no followers of other paths.

58 **These words are [in reference to] Brāhmans of other paths actually having arrived from the Western Land** (*kono kotoba, makoto ni Saigoku no gedō baramon no denrai seru nari* この言、まことに西國の外道婆羅門の傳來せるなり): I.e., in denying that there are non-Buddhist religious figures in China, Pāramārtha is referring only to those from India (not indigenous types). Some texts read here *denrai seru naku* 傳來せるなく — a version that would yield the less awkward, "Although these words say that non-Buddhist Brāhmans did not actually arrive from the Western Land, and there are no followers of other paths who have attained the way, still it is not the case . . . ."

59 **followers of other paths who have gained the way** (*tokudō no gedō* 得道の外道): The sense is uncertain: "non-Buddhist religious who converted to Buddhism," or "non-Buddhist religious who attained awakening"? Some texts read here *tokutsū no gedō* 得通の外道 ("followers of other paths who have attained [spiritual] powers"), perhaps reflecting the line immediately following Pāramārtha's saying in the *Zhiguan fuxing zhuan hongjue* 止觀輔行傳弘決 (T.1912.46:440a11-13):

震旦有二福者。一無羅刹二無外道。儻使此土有得通外道、此方道俗誰不歸之。

Cīnasthāna has two blessings: first, there are no *rākṣasas*; second, there are no followers of other paths. While this land may have had followers of other paths who have attained powers, none of the religious or laity here has taken refuge with them.

T10. The Bhikṣu of the Fourth Dhyāna *Shizen biku* 四禪比丘 265

from a place like central India in that, while the buddha dharma may be practiced somewhat, there are none who have got verification as there are in India.

[T10:32]
古德云、今時多有還俗之者、畏憚王役、入外道中。偸佛法義、竊解莊老、遂成混雜、迷惑初心執正執邪。是爲發得韋陀法之見也。

A virtuous one of old has said,[60]

Recently, there are many laicized monks who, fearing they might be drafted into imperial service, have joined other paths. They steal the doctrines of the buddha dharma and surreptitiously interpret Zhuangzi and Laozi. In the end, they create a mixture, confusing beginners about what is true and what is false and claiming that this is a view developed from the teachings of the Vedas.

[T10:33] {2:432}
しるべし、佛法と莊・老と、いづれか正、いづれか邪、をしらず、混雜するは、初心の輩なり。いまの智圓・正受等これなり。ただ愚昧の甚だしきのみにあらず、稽古なきいたり、顯然なり、炳焉なり。近日宋朝の僧徒、ひとりとしても、孔・老は佛法に及ばず、としれる輩なし。名を佛祖の兒孫にあれる輩、稻麻竹葦のごとく、九州の山野にみてりといふとも、孔・老のほかに佛法すぐれいでたりと曉了せる一人・半人あるべからず。ひとり先師天童古佛のみ、佛法と孔・老とひとつにあらず、と曉了せり、晝夜に施設せり。經論師、また講者の名あれども、佛法はるかに孔・老の邊を勝出せりと曉了せるなし。近代一百年來の講者、おほく參禪學道の輩の儀をまなび、その解會をぬすまぬとす、尤もあやまれりといふべし。

We should recognize that those who mix together the buddha dharma with Zhuangzi and Laozi, not knowing which is true and which is false — they are the "beginners"; Zhiyuan and Zhengshou and their ilk here are this type.[61] Not only is it the height of stupidity, it completely lacks any investigation of the ancients. This is evident; this is clear. Among the monks of the Song dynasty in recent days, there are none who recognize that Confucius and Laozi are not the equal of the buddha dharma. Although those who in name are descendants of the buddhas and ancestors fill the mountains and fields of the nine provinces like "rice, hemp, bamboo, and reeds," not a single person or half a person has

---

60 **A virtuous one of old** (*kotoku* 古德): Quoting Zhiyi 智顗 in the *Mohe zhiguan* 摩訶止觀 (T.1911.46:134b14-17).

61 **they are the "beginners"** (*shoshin no tomogara nari* 初心の輩なり): The Honzan edition reads here "they confuse the beginners" (*shoshin no tomogara o meiwaku suru* 初心の輩を迷惑する). While such a reading reflects the wording of Zhiyi's passage in section 32, it loses the sarcasm in Dōgen's remark — that those like Zhiyuan and Zhengshou who mix together Buddhism with the teachings of Zhuanzi and Laozi are themselves the confused beginners. See Supplementary Notes, s.v. "Beginner's mind."

266 DŌGEN'S *SHŌBŌGENZŌ* VOLUME VI

clearly comprehended that the buddha dharma is superior to Confucius and Laozi.[62] Only my former master, the Old Buddha of Tiantong, clearly comprehended, and preached day and night, that the buddha dharma and Confucius and Laozi are not the same.[63] Even among those with names as sūtra or treatise masters, or as lecturers, there are none who have clearly comprehended that the buddha dharma far surpasses the confines of Confucius and Laozi. Recently, during the last one hundred years, many lecturers have learned the deportment of those who practice meditation and study the way, hoping to appropriate their understanding; we have to say they are seriously mistaken.

[T10:34]

孔子の書、有生知、佛教、無生知、佛法有舍利之説、孔老不知舍利之有無。ひとつにして混雑せんと思ふとも、廣説の通塞、つひに不得ならむ。

In the writings of Confucius, *there is knowledge at birth; in the teachings of the buddhas, there is knowledge of non-birth.*[64] *In the buddha dharma, there are accounts of* śarira; *Confucius and Laozi do not know of the existence of* śarira. Even though one thinks to combine them into one, in the end working out a detailed account will be impossible.[65]

[T10:35]

論語云、生而知之上、學而知之者次、困而學之又其次也。困而不學、民斯爲下矣。

In the *Lunyu, it is said,*[66]

62　**nine provinces** (*kyūshū* 九州): I.e., the whole of China, from the nine states of ancient China.

63　**my former master, the Old Buddha of Tiantong** (*senshi Tendō kobutsu* 先師天童古佛): I.e., Dōgen's teacher, Tiantong Rujing 天童如淨 (1162–1227).

64　**there is knowledge at birth** (*ushōchi* 有生知); **knowledge of non-birth** (*mushōchi* 無生知): For some reason, Dōgen here shifts into Chinese, though there is no known source for these two sentences. The parallel play here with two quite different terms also occurs in "Shōbōgenzō hosshō" 正法眼藏法性. The expression "knowledge at birth," or "innate knowledge" (*shōchi* 生知), derives from the saying of Confucius quoted just below, in section 35; see Supplementary Notes, s.v. "Knowledge at birth." The Buddhist expression *mushōchi* 無生知 is typically understood here as "knowledge of non-arising" (i.e., recognition that dharmas are empty and do not arise (*mushō hō nin* 無生法忍; S. *anutpattika-dharma-kṣānti*); alternatively, it could be taken as equivalent to the common *mushō chi* 無生智 (S. *anutpāda-jñāna*), knowledge that one has achieved nirvāṇa and will not experience future rebirths.

65　**working out a detailed account** (*kōsetsu no tsūsoku* 廣説の通塞): More literally, "the passages and obstructions of an extended explanation," presumably referring to the difficulties of reconciling the particulars of Buddhism with Confucianism and Daoism.

66　*Lunyu* (*Rongo* 論語): A slightly variant version of *Lunyu* 論語 16 (KR.1h0005.008.16b–17a). The first two types here are also invoked in "Shōbōgenzō daigo" 正法眼藏大悟.

Those who know at birth are the highest; those who know through study are next; those who are wanting but study are next; those who are wanting and do not study — of the people, these are the lowest.

[T10:36] {2:433}

もし生知あらば、無因のとがあり、佛法には無因の説なし。四禪比丘は、臨命終の時、忽ちに謗佛の罪に堕す。佛法をもて孔・老の教に齊しとおもはむ、一生中より謗佛の罪ふかかるべし。學者、はやく孔老と佛法と一致なりと邪計する解をなげすつべし。この見、たくはへてすてずば、遂に惡趣におつべし。學者明らかにしるべし、孔・老は、三世の法をしらず、因果の道理をしらず、一洲の安立をしらず、況や四洲の安立をしらんや、六天のこと、なほしらず、況や三界九地の法をしらんや、小千界、しらず、中千界、しるべからず、三千大千世界をみることあらんや、しることあらんや。振旦一國、なほ小臣にして帝位にのぼらず、三千大千世界に王たる如來に比すべからず。如來は、梵王・帝釋・轉輪聖王等、晝夜に恭敬侍衞し、恆時に説法を請したてまつる。孔・老、かくのごとくの徳なし、ただこれ流轉の凡夫なり、いまだ出離解脱のみちをしらず、いかでか如來のごとく、諸法實相を究盡することあらん、もしいまだ究盡せずは、なにによりてか世尊にひとしとせん。孔・老、内徳なし、外用なし、世尊におよぶべからず、三教一致の邪説をはかむや。孔・老、世界の有邊際・無邊際を通達すべからず、廣をしらず、みず、大をしらず、みざるのみにあらず、極微色をみず、刹那量をしるべからず、世尊、明らかに極微色をみ、刹那量をしらせたまふ、いかにしてか孔・老にひとしめたてまつらむ。孔・老・莊子・惠子等は、ただこれ凡夫なり、なほ小乘の須陀洹に及ぶべからず、いかに況や第二・第三・第四の阿羅漢に及ばむや。

If you posit innate knowledge, you commit the error of denying causality; in the buddha dharma, there is no teaching that denies causality. The bhikṣu at the fourth dhyāna, when he faced the end of his life, suddenly fell into committing the offense of slandering the Buddha; to think that the buddha dharma is equivalent to the teachings of Confucius and Laozi is the grievous offense of slandering the Buddha for an entire lifetime. Students should quickly cast aside the understanding that falsely reckons Confucius and Laozi and the buddha dharma to be one. If we retain this view without discarding it, we shall eventually fall into an evil destiny. Students should clearly recognize that Confucius and Laozi do not know of the teachings on the three times; they do not know the principles of cause and effect; they do not know of the establishment of a single continent, how much less could they know of the establishment of the four continents; they do not know even of the six heavens, how much less could they know of the three realms and nine levels.[67] Not knowing of a small chiliocosm, they could not know of the medium chiliocosm;

67　**four continents** (*shishū* 四洲): I.e., the four continents surrounding Mount Sumeru in the Buddhist world system; see Supplementary Notes, s.v. "Four Continents."

six heavens (*rokuten* 六天): I.e, the six heavens of the desire realm, atop and above Mount Sumeru.

268 DŌGEN'S *SHŌBŌGENZŌ* VOLUME VI

could they then see, could they know of, the three-thousandfold great chiliocosm?[68] They are petty officials in the single Land of Cīnasthāna, who do not rise to the rank of emperor; they are not to be compared to a tathāgata, king of a three-thousandfold great chiliocosm. King Brahmā, Lord Śakra, the wheel-turning sage kings, and the like, venerate, serve, and protect the tathāgata day and night, constantly requesting him to preach the dharma. Confucius and Laozi have no such virtue; they are merely common people adrift, still ignorant of the path to escape and liberation. How could they exhaustively investigate the real marks of the dharmas, as does the Tathāgata?[69] And, if they have not exhaustively investigated it, on what basis should we take them as equal to the World-Honored One? Confucius and Laozi, lacking internal virtue and external function, do not reach the level of the World-Honored One; are we then to profess the false claim of the unity of the three teachings? Confucius and Laozi cannot penetrate the question of whether the world is limited or limitless; not only do they fail to know or to see how wide it is, and fail to know or to see how large it is, they cannot see the atoms of matter, nor know the duration of a *kṣaṇa*. The World-Honored One clearly sees the atoms of matter and knows the duration of a *kṣaṇa*. How could he be equaled by Confucius and Laozi? Confucius, Laozi, Zhuangzi, Huizi, and the like — they are just common people, who do not reach even the *srotāpanna* of the Small Vehicle, much less the second or third [stages], or the arhat on the fourth [stage].[70]

[T10:37] {2:434}

しかあるを、學者くらきによりて、諸佛に齊しむる、迷中深迷なり。孔老は三世をしらず、多劫をしらざるのみにあらず、一念しるべからず、一心しるべからず。なほ日月天に比すべからず、四大王・衆天に及ぶべからざるなり。世尊に比するは、世間・出世間に迷惑せるなり。

---

three realms and nine levels (*sangai kuji* 三界九地): See Supplementary Notes, s.v. "Three realms."

68　**small chiliocosm** (*shō senkai* 小千界); **medium chiliocosm** (*chū senkai* 中千界); **three-thousandfold great chiliocosm** (*sanzen daisen sekai* 三千大千世界): The first represents 1000 Mount Sumeru world systems; the second represents 1000 of the first; the third represents 1000 of the second, or one billion world systems, the extent of a buddha's domain.

69　**exhaustively investigate the real marks of the dharmas** (*shohō jissō o gūjin suru* 諸法實相を究盡する): Invoking a line in the *Lotus Sūtra*; see Supplementary Notes, s.v. "Only buddhas with buddhas can exhaustively investigate the real marks of the dharmas."

70　**Huizi** (*Keishi* 惠子): I.e. Hui Shi 惠施 (c. 370-310 BCE), philosopher friend of Zhuangzi, appearing often in the latter's writing.

srotāpanna **of the Small Vehicle** (*shōjō no shudaon* 小乘の須陀洹): See above, section 1.

T10. The Bhikṣu of the Fourth Dhyāna *Shizen biku* 四禪比丘   269

Nevertheless, that students, in their ignorance, make them the equal of the buddhas, is *deeper delusion within delusion*.[71] Not only are Confucius and Laozi ignorant of the three times and ignorant of the many kalpas; they do not know a single moment of thought or a single mental state. They should not be compared even to the devas of sun and moon; they do not reach the level of the devas of the four great kings.[72] To compare them with the World-Honored One is to be deluded about both the mundane and transmundane realms.[73]

[T10:38]

列傳云、喜、爲周大夫善星象。因見異氣、而東迎之、果得老子。請著書五千有言。喜亦自著書九篇、名關令子。準化胡經。老過關西、喜、欲從聃求去。聃云、若欲志心求去、當將父母等七人頭來、乃可得去。喜乃從教、七頭皆變豬頭。古德云、然俗典孝儒尚尊木像、老聃設化、令喜害親。如來教門、大慈爲本、如何老氏逆爲化原。

In the biographies, it is said that Xi was a grand master in the Zhou who excelled in astrology.[74] On one occasion, sensing a strange aura, he traveled east to greet it and, as he expected, it was Laozi. He asked him to write some five thousand words.[75] Xi himself also composed a book in nine chapters entitled Commander of the Barrier, a standard for the Sūtra on the Conversion of the Northern Foreigners.[76] When

---

71   **deeper delusion within delusion** (*meichū shin mei* 迷中深迷): Variant of the more common "further delusion within delusion" (*meichū u mei* 迷中又迷) that occurs several times in Dōgen's writing; perhaps reflecting the *Dahui Pujue chanshi yulu* 大慧普覺禪師語錄 at T.1998A.47:893a21.

72   **devas of the four great kings** (*shidaiō shuten* 四大王衆天): Although sometimes parsed as "the four great kings and the multitude of devas," this common expression is probably better understood as a reference to the devas of the heaven of the four kings, the lowest of the heavens in the realm of desire.

73   **mundane and transmundane realms** (*seken shusseken* 世間・出世間): A distinction variously defined but typically indicating, respectively, the defiled (*uro* 有漏; S. *sāsrava*) world of the spiritual commoner (*bonbu* 凡夫; S. *pṛthagjana*) and the undefiled (*muro* 無漏; S. *anāsrava*) world of the sage, or noble (*shō* 聖; S. *ārya*) on the advanced stages of the spiritual path.

74   **biographies** (*retsuden* 列傳): Dōgen is here quoting Zhanran's *Zhiguan fuxing zhuan hongjue* 止觀輔行傳弘決 (T.1912.46:325b21-28). The term *liezhuan* 列傳 refers to the biographical sections of traditional histories. It is typically taken here as the biographical section of the *Hanshu* 漢書 (KR.2a.0007ff; or, sometimes, the *Lie xian zhuan* 列仙傳, KR.5a0306), though Zhanran's text does not appear to be a direct quotation from any one source.

Xi (*Ki* 喜): I.e., Yin Xi 尹喜, official of the Zhou court, commander of the Hangu Barrier (*Kankoku kan* 函谷關).

75   **some five thousand words** (*gosen u gon* 五千有言): I.e., the roughly five thousand words of Laozi's *Daode jing* 道德經.

76   ***Commander of the Barrier*** (*Kanreishi* 關令子): A work, named after Yin Xi's title,

Laozi went west through the barrier, Xi wished to accompany Dan.[77]
*Dan said, "If you are determined to accompany me, bring the heads
of seven people including your father and mother; then you can go."
When Xi did as he was told, the seven heads all turned to boars' heads.*

A virtuous one of old has said,[78]

*However, filial Confucians in the secular texts revere even wooden images [of their parents], while Lao Dan's instructions cause Xi to harm
his parents. The teaching of the Tathāgata has great compassion as its
base; how could Lao Shih's heinous deed be the source of teaching?*

[T10:39] {2:435}

むかしは、老聃をもて世尊にひとしむる邪儻あり、いまは、孔・老ともに
世尊にひとししといふ愚侶あり、あはれまざらめやは。孔・老、なほ轉輪
聖王の、十善をもて世間を化するに及ぶべからず。三皇・五帝、いかでか
金・銀・銅・鐵諸輪王の、七寶・千子具足して、或は四天下を化して、或
は三千界を領せるに及ばん。孔子はまたこれにも比すべからず。過・現・
當來の諸佛諸祖、ともに孝順父母・師僧・三寶・病人等を供養するを化原
とせり。害親を化原とせる、いまだむかしよりあらざる處なり。

Long ago, there was a nefarious bunch that equated Lao Dan with
the World-Honored One; and now there are stupid monks who say both
Confucius and Laozi are equal to the World-Honored One.[79] Is this not
pathetic? Confucius and Laozi do not reach the level of the wheel-turning sage king's teaching the world with the ten virtues.[80] How could the
Three Sovereigns and Five Lords acquire the seven treasures and thousand children possessed by the gold, silver, copper, and iron wheel-turning kings, or teach the four continents under heaven, or rule over the
threefold chiliocosm?[81] And Confucius cannot be compared even to

---

Guanlingzi, apparently lost after the Han dynasty; the extant text purporting to be the
original is regarded as a creation of the Tang or Song dynasties.

Sūtra of the Conversion of the Northern Foreigners (*Keko kyō* 化胡經): I.e., the *Laozi
huahu jing* 老子化胡經 (not extant) attributed to the Daoist figure Wang Fu 王浮 (fl. 300
CE), which famously claimed that Laozi taught in India.

77 **Dan** (*Tan* 聃): I.e., Laozi, posthumously also known as Li Dan 李聃.

78 **virtuous one of old** (*kotoku* 古德): I.e., Zhanran. Dōgen has here inserted a warning
to the reader that what follows is Zhanran's comment on the story he has related.

79 **stupid monks** (*guryo* 愚侶): Taking *ryo* 侶 ("confederate") here as *sōryo* 僧侶
("monk"). A somewhat unusual term, not occurring elsewhere in the *Shōbōgenzō*.

80 **ten virtues** (*jūzen* 十善): I.e., the way of ten virtuous deeds (*jūzengōdō* 十善業道),
or the ten virtuous precepts (*jūzenkai* 十善戒) to be followed by the laity.

81 **Three Sovereigns and Five Lords** (*sankō gotei* 三皇・五帝): See above, section 23.

seven treasures and thousand children (*shippō senshi* 七寶・千子): Standard possessions of the *cakravartin*.

gold, silver, copper, and iron wheel-turning kings (*kon gon dō tetsu shorinnō* 金・

T10. The Bhikṣu of the Fourth Dhyāna *Shizen biku* 四禪比丘 　271

them.[82] The buddhas and the ancestors of past, present, and future all regard as the source of teaching "*filial obedience toward father and mother, teachers, and the three treasures,*" and making offerings to the sick, and so on; to make killing one's parents the source of teaching is something they have never done throughout their history.[83]

[T10:40]

しかあれば即ち、老聃と佛法と、ひとつにあらず。父母を殺害するは、必ず順次生業にして、泥犂に堕すること必定なり。たとひ老聃みだりに虚無を談ずとも、父母を害せむもの、生報まぬかれざらむ。

Thus, Lao Dan and the buddha dharma are not one. Killing one's father or mother is invariably karma [to be experienced] in the next life, and descent into *niraya* is certain.[84] Lao Dan may talk wildly about the void, but those who kill their father or mother will not escape the recompense in the next life.[85]

[T10:41]

傳燈錄云、二祖每歎云、孔老之教、禮術風規、莊易之書、未盡妙理。近聞達磨大士、住止少林。至人不遠、當造玄境。

In the Record of the Transmission of the Flame, it is said,[86]

The Second Ancestor always lamented, saying,[87]

銀・銅・鐵諸輪王): The four types of *cakravartin*, ranked by the extent of their territories: The gold king rules over all of the four continents surrounding Mount Sumeru; the silver king, over the eastern, western, and southern continents; the copper king, over the eastern and southern; the iron king, over our southern continent of Jambudvīpa.

82　**And Confucius cannot be compared even to them** (*Kōshi wa mata kore ni mo hisu bekarazu* 孔子はまたこれにも比すべからず): The antecedent of "them" (*kore* これ) here is undoubtedly "the Three Sovereigns and Five Emperors."

83　**"filial obedience toward father and mother, teachers, and the three treasures"** (*kōjun bumo shisō sanbō* 孝順父母・師僧・三寶): A phrase from the *Fanwang jing* 梵網經 (T.1484.24:1007b27-28). In the same text (T.1484.24:10005c8-9), making offerings to the sick is also recommended as the first among the eight fields of merit (*hachi fukuden* 八福田).

source of teaching (*kegen* 化原): Borrowing the expression from the last sentence of the quote from Zhanran in section 38, above.

84　**karma [to be experienced] in the next life** (*junji shō gō* 順次生業): Variant of *junji shō ju gō* 順次生受業. Patricide and matricide are two of the "five uninterrupted deeds" (*go muken gō* 五無間業) that lead to birth in the *avīci* hell in the life immediately following. The term *nairi* 泥犂 is a transliteration of Sanskrit *niraya* ("hell").

85　**Lao Dan may talk wildly about the void** (*tatoi Rōtan midari ni kyomu o danzutomo* たとひ老聃みだりに虚無を談ずとも): The compound term *xuwu* 虚無 does not actually occur in the *Daode jing*, though of course its two elements do.

86　***Record of the Transmission of the Flame*** (*Dentō roku* 傳燈錄): *Jingde chuandeng lu* 景德傳燈錄 (T.2076.51:219b6-8).

87　**The Second Ancestor** (*niso* 二祖): I.e., Huike 慧可 (487–593), on his decision to

272 DŌGEN'S *SHŌBŌGENZŌ* VOLUME VI

The teachings of Kong and Lao are techniques of rites and guides for manners; the writings of Zhuang and Yi have not fully expressed the wondrous truth.[88] *Recently, I heard that Bodhidharma, the Great One, is staying at Shaolin. Since a perfected person is not far off, I should visit his mysterious realm.*

[T10:42]

いまの輩、明らかに信ずべし、佛法の、振旦に正傳せることは、ただ偏へに二祖の參學の力なり。初祖たとひ西來せりとも、二祖をえずば、佛法つたはれざらむ。二祖もし佛法をつたへずば、東地いまに佛法なからん。おほよそ二祖は、餘輩に群すべからず。

Clearly, people today should believe that the direct transmission of the buddha dharma in Cīnasthāna is solely due to the power of the study of the Second Ancestor. Even though the First Ancestor came from the west, if he had not got the Second Ancestor, the buddha dharma would not have been transmitted. And, if the Second Ancestor had not received the transmission, there would not now be the buddha dharma in the Land of the East. In sum, the Second Ancestor should not be grouped with other people.

[T10:43] {2:436}

傳燈錄云、僧神光者、曠達之士也。久居伊洛、博覽群書、善談玄理。

In the *Record of the Transmission of the Flame*, it is said,[89]

The monk Shenguang was a widely accomplished gentleman.[90] *Residing for a long time in Yiluo, he read widely and skillfully discussed the profound principles.*[91]

[T10:44]

むかし二祖の、群書を博覽すると、いまの人の書卷をみると、はるかにことなるべし。得法・傳衣ののちも、むかしわれ孔・老教、禮術風規とおもふしは誤りなり、としめすことばなし。しるべし、二祖すでに孔老は佛法

---

abandon the study of the Chinese classics and seek instruction from Bodhidharma.

88　**teachings of Kong and Lao** (*Kō Rō shi kyō* 孔老之教): I.e., the teachings of Confucius and Laozi.

writings of *Zhuang* and *Yi* (*Sō Eki shi sho* 莊易之書): I.e., the work of the late-fourth-century BCE Daoist philosopher Zhuangzi 莊子 and the *Zhou i* 周易, or *I jing* 易經 (*Book of Changes*).

89　*Record of the Transmission of the Flame* (*Dentō roku* 傳燈錄): *Jingde chuandeng lu* 景德傳燈錄 (T.2076.51:219b5-6), the lines just preceding those quoted in section 41, above.

90　**Shenguang** (*Shinkō* 神光): I.e., Huike; his name before he was renamed by Bodhidharma.

91　**Yiluo** (*Iraku* 伊洛): I.e., the area of the capital at Luoyang 洛陽, the confluence of the Yi 伊 and Luo 洛 Rivers.

T10. The Bhikṣu of the Fourth Dhyāna *Shizen biku* 四禪比丘

にあらずと通達せり、いまの遠孫、なにとしてか祖父に違背して、佛法と一致なりといふや。まさにしるべし、これ邪説なり。二祖の遠孫にあらずば、正受等が説、誰か用いむ。二祖の兒孫たるべくは、三教一致といふことなかれ。

There is a huge difference between the wide reading of the Second Ancestor long ago and the reading of people today. Even after he attained the dharma and received transmission of the robe, he has no words indicating that he was mistaken earlier in thinking that *"the teachings of Confucius and Laozi are techniques of rites and guides for manners."*[92] We should recognize that the Second Ancestor fully penetrated the fact that Confucius and Laozi were not the buddha dharma; how, then, could his distant descendants turn their backs on their progenitor and say that they form a unity with the buddha dharma? We should recognize that this is a false teaching. Unless one is not a distant descendant of the Second Ancestor, who would use the teachings of Zhengshou and his ilk?[93] Those who would be a scion of the Second Ancestor, do not speak of "the unity of the three teachings."

[T10:45]

如來在世有外道、名論力。自謂、論議無與等者、其力最大。故曰論力。受五百梨昌募、撰五百明難、來難世尊、來至佛所、而問佛云、爲一究竟道、爲衆多究竟道。[佛言、唯一究竟道。論力云、我等諸師、各説有究竟道。]以外道中、各各自謂是、毀訾他人法、互相是非故、有多道。世尊其時、已化鹿頭成無學果、在佛邊立。佛問論力、衆多道中、誰爲第一。論力云、鹿頭第一。佛言、其若第一、云何捨其道、爲我弟子、入我道中。論力見已、慚愧低頭、歸依入道。是時、佛説義品偈言、

各各謂究竟、而各自愛著、各自是非彼、是皆非究竟、
是人入論衆、辯明義涅槃、各各相是非、勝負懷憂苦、
勝者墮慢坑、負者墮憂獄、是故有智者、不墮此二法、
論力汝當知、我諸弟子法、無虛亦無實、汝欲何處求、
汝欲壞我論、終已無此處、一切知難明、還是自毀壞。

When the Tathāgata was in the world,[94]

---

92 **Even after he attained the dharma and received transmission of the robe** (*tokuhō den'e no nochi mo* 得法・傳衣ののちも): Reference to Huike's recognition as Bodhidharma's successor. The point here is that (unlike those Buddhists today who see wisdom in the writings of Confucius and Laozi) Huike seems never to have changed his earlier opinion that they were merely mundane teachings.

93 **Unless one is not a distant descendant of the Second Ancestor** (*niso no enson ni arazuba* 二祖の遠孫にあらずば): Tentative interpretation of a problematic reading. Other versions read here *nite araba* にてあらば or *ni araba* にあらば ("if one is . . ."), as well as *ni arazu wa* にあらずは or *nite arazuba* にてあらずば.

94 **When the Tathāgata was in the world** (*nyorai zaise* 如來在世): Introducing a sto-

274   DŌGEN'S *SHŌBŌGENZŌ* VOLUME VI

There was a follower of an other path called Vivādabala.[95] *He thought himself to be unequaled in debate and supremely strong; hence, he was called "Strong in Debate." Recruited by five hundred Licchavis, he compiled five hundred difficulties to be explained and came to challenge the World-Honored One.*[96] *Arriving where the Buddha was, he questioned the Buddha, saying, "Is there one ultimate path, or many ultimate paths?"*

[The Buddha said, "There is only one ultimate path."[97]

Vivādabala said, "Our teachers each say they have the ultimate path.] Among the non-Buddhists, each claims to be right and disparages the teaching of others. Since they are mutually right and wrong, there are many paths."

At the time, the World-Honored One had already converted Mṛgaśīrṣa, who had attained the fruit of the non-student, and who was standing by the Buddha.[98] *The Buddha asked Vivādabala, "Among the many paths, whose is first?"*

Vivādabala said, "That of Mṛgaśīrṣa is first."

The Buddha said, "If his is first, why has he abandoned that path, become my disciple, and entered my path?

When Vivādabala saw him, he was ashamed, bowed, took refuge, and entered the path. At this time, the Buddha recited a gāthā expressing his meaning: [99]

---

ry in Zhanran's *Zhiguan fuxing zhuan hongjue* 止觀輔行傳弘決 (T.1912.46:440b5-15), which is based on a passage in the *Dazhidu lun* 大智度論 (T.1509.25:193b8-29). While Dōgen's version follows Zhanran's text fairly closely, the concluding verse here, lacking in the latter, is supplied from the *Dazhidu lun* account.

95   **Vivādabala** (*Ronriki* 論力): Tentative reconstruction of a name, not attested in Sanskrit, meaning "strong in debate."

96   **Licchavis** (*Rishō* 梨昌): The clan inhabiting Vaiśālī.

97   **[The Buddha said, "There is only one ultimate path"]** (*Butsu gon, yui ichi kukyō dō* 佛言、唯一究竟道): The Chinese for this and the following words in square brackets here is missing in the MS and has been interpolated from the *Zhiguan fuxing zhuan hongjue* 止觀輔行傳弘決 (T.1912.46:440b9-10).

98   **Mṛgaśīrṣa** (*Rokutō* 鹿頭): A disciple of the Buddha who had formerly been a member of a non-Buddhist religious community.

fruit of the non-student (*mugaku ka* 無學果): I.e., the status of arhat.

99   **gāthā expressing his meaning** (*gibon ge* 義品偈): Tentative translation of an obscure expression. The term *gibon* 義品 is sometimes used to render the Sanskrit *artha-vargīya*, in reference to a collection of early teachings corresponding to the Pali *Aṭṭhaka-vagga* — in which case, our expression might be rendered "a verse of the *Artha-vargīya*"; but the verse that follows here is not found in the extant Chinese translation, the *Yizu jing* 義足經 (T.198).

T10. The Bhikṣu of the Fourth Dhyāna *Shizen biku* 四禪比丘

Each claims to have the ultimate,
So, each is attached to his own.
One's own is right and the other wrong —
None of them is ultimate.
These people enter into debates,
To elucidate nirvāṇa as a doctrine.
They argue over right and wrong,
But their wins and losses are but sorrow and pain.
The winners fall into the pit of pride;
The losers, into the hell of sorrow.
Therefore, those possessed of wisdom
Do not fall into these two things.
Vivādabala, you should know,
The dharma taught by my disciples,
Is neither false nor yet true.
What is it, then, that you seek?
You wish to refute my position,
But, in the end, you have no grounds.
Omniscience is difficult to explain;
Instead, your own views fall apart.

[T10:46] {2:438}

いま世尊の金言、かくのごとし。東土愚闇の衆生、みだりに佛教に違背して、佛道とひとしきみちありいふことなかれ。即ち謗佛・謗法となるべきなり。西天の鹿頭、ならびに論力、乃至長爪梵志・先尼梵志等は、博學の人たり、東土にむかしよりいまだなし。孔・老さらに及ぶべからざるなり。これらみなみづからが道をすてて、佛道に歸依す。いま孔・老の、俗人をもて佛法に比類せむは、きかぬものもつみあるべし。　況や阿羅漢・辟支佛も、みなつひに菩薩となる、一人としても小乘にしてをはるものなし。いかでかいまだ佛道にいらざる孔・老を、諸佛にひとしとし、いはむ。大邪見なるべし。

Such are the golden words of the World-Honored One. Ignorant beings of the Land of the East must not rashly turn their backs on the teachings of the buddhas and say that there is a way equal to the way of the buddhas. To do so amounts to slandering the buddhas and denigrating their dharma. Mṛgaśīrṣa, along with Vivādabala, and including the brahman Dīrghanakha, the brahman Śreṇika, and the like in Sindh in the West, were persons of extensive learning, such as never existed in the Land of the East.[100] Confucius and Laozi surely could never equal them. They

---

100 **the brahman Dīrghanakha, the brahman Śreṇika, and the like** (*Chōsō bonshi Senni bonshi tō* 長爪梵志・先尼梵志等): No doubt reflecting a list of learned men converted to Buddhism that appears in the *Dazhidu lun* 大智度論 (T.1509.25:61b20-22). Dīrghanakha ("Long Nails") is said to have converted to Buddhism under Śāriputra after

276 DŌGEN'S *SHŌBŌGENZŌ* VOLUME VI

all abandoned their own ways and took refuge in the way of the buddhas. Those who compare the laymen Confucius and Laozi to the buddha dharma — even those who listen to them would be guilty of an offense. Moreover, the arhats and *pratyeka-buddhas* all eventually become bodhisattvas; not a single one will end up in the Small Vehicle.[101] How can we say that Confucius and Laozi, who have not even entered the way of the buddhas, are equal to the buddhas? This is a major false view.

[T10:47]

おほよそ如來世尊、はるかに一切を超越しましますこと、即ち諸佛如來・諸大菩薩・梵天帝釋、みなともにほめたてまつり、しりたてまつる處なり。西天二十八祖・唐土六祖、ともにしれる處なり。おほよそ參學力あるもの、みなともにしれり。いま澆運の輩、宋朝の愚闇の輩、三教の狂言、用いるべからず、不學のいたりなり。

In sum, the fact that the Tathāgata, the World-Honored One, far transcends all is something known and celebrated by the buddhas, the tathāgatas, the great bodhisattvas, the Deva Brahmā, and the Lord Śakra; it is something known by the twenty-eight ancestors of Sindh in the West and the six ancestors in the Land of the Tang. In sum, all those with the power of study know it. Those now in a time of declining fortune should not use the crazy words on the three teachings of the stupid bunch in the Song dynasty. It is the height of ignorance.

正法眼藏四禪比丘第十

Treasury of the True Dharma Eye
The Bhikṣu of the Fourth Dhyāna
Number 10

[Honzan edition:]

建長七年乙卯夏安居日、以御草案本書寫畢。懷弉

Finished copying from his draft, on a day of the summer retreat, in the junior wood year of the rabbit, the seventh year of Kenchō [1255]. Ejō[102]

---

studying the eighteen classics of Hinduism; Śreṇika Vatsagotra is said to have achieved wisdom through faith.

101   **the arhats and *pratyeka-buddhas* all eventually become bodhisattvas** (*arakan byakushibutsu mo, mina tsui ni bosatsu to naru* 阿羅漢・辟支佛も、みなつひに菩薩となる): Invoking the doctrine of the *Lotus Sūtra* that there is ultimately only one vehicle, which leads all Buddhists to buddhahood.

102   The source for this colophon in the Honzan edition is uncertain; identical (or very similar) colophons are found in four other texts of the twelve-chapter *Shōbōgenzō*.

his draft (*gosōan* 御草案): I.e., Dōgen's draft.

day of the summer retreat (*ge ango no hi* 夏安居日): Dates of the summer retreat vary; a common practice put it from the fifteenth of the fourth lunar month through the fifteenth of the seventh month; in 1255, this would have corresponded to 22 May through 18 August.

TREASURY OF THE TRUE DHARMA EYE
THE TWELVE-CHAPTER COMPILATION
NUMBER 11

One Hundred Eight Gateways to the Illumination of the Dharma

Ippyakuhachi hōmyō mon

一百八法明門

One Hundred Eight Gateways
to the Illumination of the Dharma

Ippyakuhachi hōmyō mon

INTRODUCTION

This undated work is unusual among the *Shōbōgenzō* texts in that it is found only in the twelve-chapter compilation and, therefore, was long unknown before that compilation's discovery in the twentieth century. It is also unusual in that it consists almost entirely of a quotation from a single scripture, simply listing, without comment, the items in the venerable Buddhist teaching of the one hundred eight gateways to the dharma, as given in the *Abhiniṣkramaṇa-sūtra* (*Fo benxing ji jing* 佛本行集經; *Sūtra of the Collection of the Past Acts of the Buddha*). Only at the very end of the text does Dōgen add his own note, complaining that the teaching has been much neglected and recommending that those who would become teachers should make themselves familiar with it. In this literary character, the work is quite similar to the last text of the twelve-chapter compilation, "Hachi dainin gaku" 八大人覺.

279

正法眼藏第十一

Treasury of the True Dharma Eye
Number 11

一百八法明門

One Hundred Eight Gateways
to the Illumination of the Dharma

[T11:1] {2:439}

爾時護明菩薩、觀生家已。時兜率陀有一天宮、名曰高幢。縱廣正等、六十
由旬。菩薩時時上彼宮中、爲兜率天説於法要。是時菩薩、上於彼宮、安坐
訖已、告於兜率諸天子言、汝等諸天、應來聚集、我身不久、下於人間。我
今欲説一法明門、名入諸法相方便門、留教化汝最後。汝等憶念我故、汝等
若聞此法門者、應生歡喜。時兜率陀諸天大衆、聞於菩薩如此語已、及天玉
女、一切眷属、皆來聚會畢已。欲爲説法、即時更化作一天宮、在彼高幢本
天宮上。高大廣闊、覆四天下、可喜微妙端正少雙、威德巍巍、衆寶莊飾。
一切欲界天宮殿中、無匹喩者。色界諸天、見彼化殿、於自宮殿、生如是
心、如塚墓相。

*At that time, Bodhisattva Jyotipala completed his contemplation of the
family into which he would be reborn.[1] At the time, there was in Tuṣita
a heavenly palace named Uccadhvaja, in height and breadth exactly
sixty yojanas.[2] From time to time, the Bodhisattva would ascend to*

---

1 **One Hundred Eight Gateways to the Illumination of the Dharma** (*ippyakuhachi
hōmyō mon* 一百八法明門): I.e., one hundred eight teachings providing access to the
buddha dharma. The expression *hōmyō mon* 法明門 translates the Sanskrit *dharmāloka-mukha* ("gateway to the light of the dharma"), but *myō* 明 is often read here as a verbal noun, "to illumine," and *hōmyō* 法明 parsed as an object-predicate compound with
the sense "clarification of the dharma."

the Bodhisattva Jyotipala (*Gomyō bosatsu* 護明菩薩): Here and in the following sections
(through section 21), Dōgen is quoting the *Abhiniṣkramaṇa-sūtra* (*Fo benxing ji jing* 佛
本行集經, T.190.3:680b20-682b9). A parallel text occurs in the *Lalitavistara* translated
by Divākara (*Vaipulya-mahāvyūha-sūtra*; *Fangguang da zhuangyan jing* 方廣大莊嚴經,
T.187). Jyotipala is the name of the bodhisattva, dwelling in Tuṣita Heaven, who is to be
born in his next life as Prince Siddhārtha and become Buddha Śākyamuni. At this point in
the sūtra, Jyotipala has realized that he is about to be born among humans on the continent
of Jambudvīpa and prepares to give his obligatory final teachings to the devas in heaven.

2 **Tuṣita** (*Tosotsuda* 兜率陀): Fourth of the six heavens of the realm of desire (*yokukai*
欲界), from which the bodhisattva descends to the human realm in his last incarnation.

Uccadhvaja (*Kōdō* 高幢): "High Banner," famed palace of the devas, occurring often
in the literature.

280   DŌGEN'S *SHŌBŌGENZŌ* VOLUME VI

that palace and preach the essentials of the dharma for the devas of Tuṣita. At that time, the Bodhisattva ascended to that palace and, after sitting peacefully, addressed the devas of Tuṣita, saying:

> *Devas, come and gather round. This body of mine will before long descend among humans. So now, I wish to speak of a gateway for the illumination of the dharma, called the "gateway of expedience for entering into the marks of the dharmas," that I shall leave as my final teaching to you.[3] Since you will remember me, when you hear this dharma gate, you will feel joy.*

At the time, having heard the Bodhisattva speak thus, the great throng of devas in Tuṣita, including the heavenly jewel maidens and all their retinue, all came and gathered.[4] After they had assembled, wishing to preach the dharma, he thereupon magically produced a heavenly palace atop his original Uccadhvaja heavenly palace. Lofty and vast, covering the four continents under heaven; pleasing, exquisite, of proportions rarely matched; majestic and towering, adorned with many jewels. Among all the palaces in the heavens of the desire realm, none could compare with it. Upon seeing this magical palace, the devas of the form realm thought of their own palaces as looking like tombs.

[T11:2] {2:440}

護明菩薩、已於過去、行於寶行、種諸善根、成就福聚、功德具足。所成莊嚴、師子高座、昇上而座。護明菩薩、在彼師子高座之上、無量諸寶、莊嚴間錯、無量無邊。種種天衣、而敷彼座、種種妙香、以薫彼座。無量無邊寶爐燒香、出於種種微妙香華、散其地上。高座周帀、有諸珍寶、百千萬億、莊嚴放光、顯耀彼宮。彼宮上下、寶網羅覆、於彼羅網、多懸金鈴。彼諸金鈴、出聲微妙。彼大寶宮、復出無量種種光明。彼寶宮殿、千萬幡蓋、種種妙色、映覆於上。彼大宮殿、垂諸流蘇、無量無邊、百千萬億諸天玉女、各持種種七寶、音聲作樂讚歎、説於菩薩往昔無量無邊功德。護世四王、百千萬億、在於左右、守護彼宮。千萬帝釋、禮拜彼宮。千萬梵天、恭敬彼宮。又諸菩薩、百千萬億那由他衆、護持彼宮、十方諸佛、有於萬億那由他數、護念彼宮。百千萬億那由他劫、前修行行、諸波羅蜜、福報成就、因緣具足、日夜增長、無量功德、悉皆莊嚴、如是如是、難説難説。彼大微妙、師

---

yojana (*yujun* 由旬): A measure of distance, varying greatly depending on the source, but often said to range from seven to nine miles.

3   **"gateway of expedience for entering into the marks of the dharmas"** (*nisshohō sō hōben mon* 入諸法相方便門): Presumably meaning something like, "a teaching providing aids to the understanding of the characteristics of the dharmas"; a title that does not seem to occur elsewhere in the canon.

4   **all came and gathered** (*kai rai shu* 皆來聚): Kawamura's text omits hereafter 14 glyphs from the sūtra (at *Fo benxing ji jing* 佛本行集經, T.190.3:680b28-29):

> 集、上於彼宮。護明菩薩見彼天衆聚
>
> [. . . all came and gathered] together and ascended to his palace. Bodhisattva Jyotipala, seeing that the throng of devas had assembled, [wishing to preach the dharma . . . .]

T11. One Hundred Eight Gateways *Ippyakuhachi hōmyō mon* 一百八法明門 281

子高座、菩薩座上、告於一切諸天衆言、汝等諸天、今此一百八法明門、一
生補處菩薩大士、在兜率宮、欲下託生於人間者、於天衆前、要須宣暢説此
一百八法明門、留與諸天、以作憶念、然後下生。汝等諸天、今可至心諦聽
諦受、我今説之。

Bodhisattva Jyotipala had in the past already performed precious practices, planted good roots, achieved an accumulation of blessings, and
was fully possessed of merit, with which he had adorned the high lion
seat to which he had mounted and on which he now sat.[5] On the high
lion seat where Bodhisattva Jyotipala sat were incalculable jewels
and inlaid adornments, incalculable and limitless. Various heavenly
garments were draped over his seat, and various marvelous scents
perfumed his seat. Incense burned in incalculable, limitless jeweled
censers, from which came forth all manner of delicate and wondrous
fragrant flowers that scattered on the ground. Surrounding the high
seat were rare jewels, numbering in the hundreds of thousands of myriads of *koṭis*, the light emitted from these adornments illuminating the
palace. The palace from top to bottom was covered by jeweled nets,
from which hung golden bells that rang with a marvelous subtle sound.
That great jeweled palace emitted incalculable lights of all sorts, the
thousand myriad banners and canopies of the palace covered it with
marvelous colors of all sorts, and tassels hung from the great palace.
Incalculable, limitless hundreds of thousands of myriads of *koṭis* of
heavenly jewel maidens, each holding various of the seven treasures,
their voices melodious, praised the bodhisattva, telling of the incalculable, limitless merit of his past. The four kings who protect the world,
a hundred thousand myriad million of them, guarded the palace on the
left and right; a thousand myriad Lord Śakras paid obeisance at the
palace; and a thousand myriad Deva Brahmās venerated the palace.
In addition, a multitude of bodhisattvas, a hundred thousand myriad
koṭis of *nayutas* of them, protected the palace; and the buddhas of the
ten directions, numbering a myriad *koṭis* of *nayutas*, bore the palace
in mind.[6] All the adornments of his incalculable merit increased day
and night, from a hundred thousand myriad *koṭis* of *nayutas* of kalpas
of past practices, in which he practiced the *pāramitās*, fulfilled the
blessed recompense, and fully equipped himself with the causes and
conditions — what they were like is impossible to describe.

---

5 **Bodhisattva Jyotipala** (*Gomyō bosatsu* 護明菩薩): Continuing the quotation of
the *Fo benxing ji jing* 佛本行集經 (T.190.3:680c5-681a1). Though not given in verse
format, this entire passage in the sūtra is composed of four-glyph lines.

6 **myriad *koṭis* of *nayutas*** (*man'oku nayuta* 萬億那由他): Countless numbers; S. *koṭi*
was used for a crore (ten million), while *nayuta* indicates an indefinite "multitude."

282 DŌGEN'S *SHŌBŌGENZŌ* VOLUME VI

On that huge, finely-crafted high seat of the lion, the Bodhisattva sat and announced to all the heavenly host, "You devas, regarding the present one hundred eight gateways to the illumination of the dharma, when a successor bodhisattva, a great being, residing in his Tuṣita palace, is about to descend to incarnation among humans, he must proclaim these one hundred eight gateways to the illumination of the dharma before the devas, leaving them with the devas to remember; after which, he descends to his rebirth.[7] You devas, listen intently and accept, as I now explain them."

[T11:3] {2:442}

一百八法明門者何、

What are the one hundred eight gateways to the illumination of the dharma?[8]

[T11:4]

正信是法明門、不破堅牢心故。淨心是法明門、無濁穢故。歡喜是法明門、安穩心故。愛樂是法明門、令心清淨故。

Correct faith is a gateway to the illumination of the dharma, for a steadfast mind is imperturbable.[9]

A pure mind is a gateway to the illumination of the dharma, for it is without impurities.[10]

Delight is a gateway to the illumination of the dharma, for it is a mind at ease.[11]

Enjoyment is a gateway to the illumination of the dharma, for it purifies the mind.[12]

---

7 **successor bodhisattva** (*isshō fusho bosatsu* 一生補處菩薩): I.e., a bodhisattva who will become a buddha in his next life.

8 **What are the one hundred eight gateways to the illumination of the dharma?** (*ippyakuhachi hōmyō mon sha ka* 一百八法明門者何): *Fo benxing ji jing* 佛本行集經, T.190.3:681a1. The following list, through section 20, below, is found at *Fo benxing ji jing* 佛本行集經, T.190.3:681a2-682b6; and at *Da zhuangyan jing* 大莊嚴經, T.187.3:544b02-545a26.

9 **Correct faith** (*shōshin* 正信): S. *śraddhā*.

10 **pure mind** (*jōshin* 淨心): S. *prasāda* ("purity").

11 **Delight** (*kanki* 歡喜): S. *prāmodya*.

12 **Enjoyment** (*airaku* 愛樂): S. *prīti*.

T11. One Hundred Eight Gateways *Ippyakuhachi hōmyō mon* 一百八法明門 283

[T11:5]

身行正行是法明門、三業淨故。口行淨行是法明門、斷四惡故。意行淨行是法明門、斷三毒故。

> *Correct practice of physical behavior is a gateway to the illumination of the dharma, for the three acts are purified.*[13]

> *Pure practice of verbal behavior is a gateway to the illumination of the dharma, for it eliminates the four evils.*[14]

> *Pure practice of mental behavior is a gateway to the illumination of the dharma, for it eliminates the three poisons.*[15]

[T11:6]

念佛是法明門、觀佛清淨故。念法是法明門、觀法清淨故。念僧是法明門、得道堅牢故。

> *Recollecting the Buddha is a gateway to the illumination of the dharma, for one's view of the Buddha is pure.*[16]

> *Recollecting the dharma is a gateway to the illumination of the dharma, for one's view of the dharma is pure.*[17]

> *Recollecting the saṃgha is a gateway to the illumination of the dharma, for one's gaining of the way is steadfast.*[18]

---

13 **Correct practice of physical behavior** (*shingyō shōgyō* 身行正行): S. *kāya-saṃvara* ("physical restraint"; *shinkai* 身戒). This and the following two items cover the three types of karma (*sangō* 三業): body, speech, and mind. The reference here to the purification of "the three acts" is not to the three types of karma but to the three physical acts — killing (*sesshō* 殺生), stealing (*chūtō* 偷盗), and illicit sex (*jain* 邪淫) — in the standard list of the ten evil deeds (*jū aku* 十惡), the remainder of which will be covered in the following two items. The *Da zhuangyan jing* 大莊嚴經 (T.187.3:544b5) has here:

除三惡故。

For one eliminates the three evils.

14 **Pure practice of verbal behavior** (*kugyō jōgyō* 口行淨行): S. *vāk-saṃvara* ("verbal restraint"; *gokai* 語戒). "The four evils" (*shi aku* 四惡) refers to the four verbal acts — lying (*mōgo* 妄言), flowery speech (*kigo* 綺語), abusive speech (*akuku* 惡口), and treachery (*ryōzetsu* 兩舌) — in the list of ten evil deeds.

15 **Pure practice of mental behavior** (*igyō jōgyō* 意行淨行): S. *manaḥ-saṃvara* ("mental restraint"; *ikai* 意戒). "The three poisons" (*san'aku* 三惡) are greed (*tonyoku* 貪欲), anger (*shin'i* 瞋恚), and delusion (*guchi* 愚癡), the three mental acts in the list of ten evil deeds.

16 **Recollecting the Buddha** (*nenbutsu* 念佛): S. *buddhānusmṛti*. The three items in this section cover the three refuges (*san kie* 三歸依; S. *triśaraṇa*) of Buddha, dharma, and saṃgha; together with the three items in the following section, they form a traditional set known as "the six recollections" (*rokunen* 六念; S. *ṣaḍ anusmṛtayaḥ*).

17 **Recollecting the dharma** (*nenpō* 念法): S. *dharmānusmṛti*.

18 **Recollecting the saṃgha** (*nensō* 念僧): S. *saṃghānusmṛti*.

[T11:7]

念施是法明門、不望果報故。念戒是法明門、一切願具足故。念天是法明門、發廣大心故。

> Recollecting giving is a gateway to the illumination of the dharma, for one anticipates no reward.[19]

> Recollecting the discipline is a gateway to the illumination of the dharma, for all one's aspirations are fulfilled.[20]

> Recollecting the heavens is a gateway to the illumination of the dharma, for one develops a broad mind.[21]

[T11:8]

慈是法明門、一切生處善根攝勝故。悲是法明門、不殺害衆生故。喜是法明門、捨一切不喜事故。捨是法明門、厭離五欲故。

> Kindness is a gateway to the illumination of the dharma, for it surpasses all good roots wherever they arise.[22]

> Compassion is a gateway to the illumination of the dharma, for one does not kill living beings.[23]

> Joy is a gateway to the illumination of the dharma, for it removes all unpleasantness.[24]

> Equanimity is a gateway to the illumination of the dharma, for one loaths the five desires.[25]

---

19 **Recollecting giving** (*nense* 念施): S. *tyāgānusmṛti*. The *Da zhuangyan jing* 大莊嚴經 (T.187.3:544b8) gives the reason here as:

棄一切事故。
For one abandons everything.

20 **Recollecting the discipline** (*nenkai* 念戒): S. *śīlānusmṛti*.

21 **Recollecting the heavens** (*nenten* 念天): S. *devānusmṛti*. The "broad mind" (*kōdai shin* 廣大心; S. *udāra-citta*) typically refers to a liberal, or lenient, mind, though here it may well indicate the "great" mind of the four immeasurable states of mind that are covered in the following section.

22 **Kindness** (*ji* 慈): S. *maitrī*. The translation of the reason here is tentative. The four items in this section cover the four "immeasurables" (*shi muryō shin* 四無量心; S. *apramāṇa*), practiced in the meditations of the four *brahma-vihāras* (*shi bonju* 四梵住).

23 **Compassion** (*hi* 悲): S. *karuṇā*.

24 **Joy** (*ki* 喜): S. *muditā*.

25 **Equanimity** (*sha* 捨): S. *upekṣa*. The "five desires" (*goyoku* 五欲) are the desires associated with the five senses.

T11. One Hundred Eight Gateways *Ippyakuhachi hōmyō mon* 一百八法明門 285

[T11:9] {2:443}

無常觀是法明門、觀三界欲故。苦觀是法明門、斷一切願故。無我觀是法明
門、不染著我故。寂定觀是法明門、不擾亂心意故。

Examination of impermanence is a gateway to the illumination of the dharma, for one observes the desires of the three realms.[26]

Examination of suffering is a gateway to the illumination of the dharma, for it cuts off all our longings.[27]

Examination of lack of self is a gateway to the illumination of the dharma, for one is undefiled by attachment to self.[28]

Examination of quiescence is a gateway to the illumination of the dharma, for one's mind is not agitated.[29]

[T11:10]

慚愧是法明門、內心寂定故。羞恥是法明門、外惡滅故。

Shame is a gateway to the illumination of the dharma, for internally the mind is calm.[30]

Modesty is a gateway to the illumination of the dharma, for externally evil ceases.[31]

[T11:11]

實是法明門、不誑天人故。眞是法明門、不誑自身故。法行是法明門、隨順
法行故。三歸是法明門、淨三惡道故。知恩是法明門、不捨善根故。報恩是
法明門、不欺負他故。不自欺是法明門、不自譽故。爲衆生是法明門、不毀
呰他故。爲法是法明門、如法而行故。知時是法明門、不輕言説故。攝我慢
是法明門、智慧滿足故。不生惡心是法明門、自護護他故。無障導是法明
門、心無疑惑故。信解是法明門、決了第一義故。不淨觀是法明門、捨欲染
心故。不諍鬪是法明門、斷瞋訟故。不癡是法明門、斷殺生故。樂法義是法
明門、求法義故。愛法明是法明門、得法明故。求多聞是法明門、正覺法相
故。正方便是法明門、具正行故。知名色是法明門、除諸障導故。除因見是

---

26 **Examination of impermanence** (*mujō kan* 無常觀): S. *anitya-pratyavekṣā*. The phrase *sangai yoku* 三界欲, rendered here "desires of the three realms," might also be read "desire for [existence in] the three realms (of desire, form, and formlessness)." See Supplementary Notes, s.v. "Three realms." The *Da zhuangyan jing* 大莊嚴經 (T.187.3:544b13) gives simply:

息諸貪愛故。

For one ceases desires.

The four items in this section cover "the four seals of the dharma" (*shi hōin* 四法印): impermanence, suffering, lack of self, and nirvāṇa.

27 **Examination of suffering** (*ku kan* 苦觀): S. *duḥkha-pratyavekṣa*.

28 **Examination of lack of self** (*muga kan* 無我觀): S. *anātma-pratyavekṣā*.

29 **Examination of quiescence** (*jakujō kan* 寂定觀): S. *śānta-pratyavekṣā*.

30 **Shame** (*zangi* 慚愧): S. *hrī*.

31 **Modesty** (*shūchi* 羞恥): S. *apatrāpya*.

法明門、得解脱故。無怨親心是法明門、於怨親中生平等故。陰方便是法明
門、知諸苦故。諸大平等是法明門、斷於一切和合法故。諸入是法明門、修
正道故。無生忍是法明門、證滅諦故。

Truth is a gateway to the illumination of the dharma, for one does not deceive devas and humans.[32]

Genuineness is a gateway to the illumination of the dharma, for one does not deceive oneself.[33]

Dharma practice is a gateway to the illumination of the dharma, for it accords with the dharma.[34]

The three refuges are a gateway to the illumination of the dharma, for they purify the three evil paths.[35]

Gratitude is a gateway to the illumination of the dharma, for one does not forsake one's good roots.[36]

Obligation is a gateway to the illumination of the dharma, for one does not mistreat others.[37]

Not deceiving oneself is a gateway to the illumination of the dharma, for one does not praise oneself.[38]

Taking living beings into account is a gateway to the illumination of the dharma, for one does not disparage others.[39]

Taking the dharma into account is a gateway to the illumination of the dharma, for one practices according to the dharma.[40]

---

32 **Truth** (*jitsu* 實): S. *satya*.

33 **Genuineness** (*shin* 眞): S. *bhūta*.

34 **Dharma practice** (*hōgyō* 法行): S. *dharma-caraṇa*.

35 **three refuges** (*sanki* 三歸): S. *triśaraṇagamana*. I.e., taking refuge in the three treasures of Buddha, dharma, and saṃgha. The three evil paths (*san akudō* 三惡道) are the lower realms of rebirth: animal, *preta*, and hell. The *Da zhuangyan jing* 大莊嚴經 (T.187.3:544b18) gives as the reason here the more expected,

超三惡趣故。

For one transcends the three evil destinies.

36 **Gratitude** (*chion* 知恩): S. *kṛtajñatā*.

37 **Obligation** (*hōon* 報恩): S. *kṛtaveditā*.

38 **Not deceiving oneself** (*fujigi* 不自欺): S. *ātmajñatā* ("self-knowledge"). The set, beginning here, of four types of knowledge — self, others, dharma, and time — is obscured by the *Fo benxing ji jing* 佛本行集經 translation that Dōgen is using; the *Da zhuangyan jing* 大莊嚴經 (T.187.3:544b20) has "knowing oneself" (*jichi* 自知).

39 **Taking living beings into account** (*i shujō* 爲衆生): Or "[doing] for the sake of living beings." S. *sattvajñatā* ("knowledge of beings").

40 **Taking the dharma into account** (*i hō* 爲法). Or "[doing] for the sake of the dharma." S. *dharmajñatā* ("knowledge of dharma").

T11. One Hundred Eight Gateways *Ippyakuhachi hōmyō mon* 一百八法明門 287

Knowing the time is a gateway to the illumination of the dharma, for one does not take words lightly.[41]

Controlling pride is a gateway to the illumination of the dharma, for one's wisdom is perfected.[42]

Not giving rise to hostile thoughts is a gateway to the illumination of the dharma, for it protects both self and other.[43]

Absence of obstacles is a gateway to the illumination of the dharma, for the mind is without doubts.[44]

Confidence is a gateway to the illumination of the dharma, for one decisively comprehends the prime meaning.[45]

Examination of impurity is a gateway to the illumination of the dharma, for one abandons thoughts of desire.[46]

Non-dissension is a gateway to the illumination of the dharma, for it eliminates anger and litigiousness.[47]

Nondelusion is a gateway to the illumination of the dharma, for it eliminates the taking of life.[48]

Delighting in the meaning of the dharma is a gateway to the illumination of the dharma, for one pursues the meaning of the dharma.[49]

---

41 **Knowing the time** (*chi ji* 知時): S. *kālajñatā*. Divākara (*Da zhuangyan jing* 大莊嚴經, T.187.3:544b22) gives as the reason here,

無癡暗見故。

For one's views are not worthless.

42 **Controlling pride** (*setsu gaman* 攝我慢): S. *nihata-mānatā*.

43 **Not giving rise to hostile thoughts** (*fushō akushin* 不生惡心): S. *apratihata-cittatā*.

44 **Absence of obstacles** (*mu shōge* 無障礙): S. *anupanāha* ("non-hostility"). Divākara (*Da zhuangyan jing* 大莊嚴經, T.187.3:544b24) gives:

不恨是法門由不悔故。

Non-hostility is a dharma gate, for one does not regret.

45 **Confidence** (*shinge* 信解): S. *adhimukti*. Divākara (*Da zhuangyan jing* 大莊嚴經, T.187.3:544b25) gives as the reason here:

無疑滯故。

For one will have no impediment of doubt.

46 **Examination of impurity** (*fujō kan* 不淨觀): S. *aśubha-pratyavekṣa*.

47 **Non-dissension** (*fujōtō* 不諍鬪): S. *avyāpāda*.

48 **Nondelusion** (*fuchi* 不癡): S. *amoha*. Again, Divākara (*Da zhuangyan jing* 大莊嚴經, T.187.3:544b27) gives the more likely reason here:

破壞無智故。

For it destroys ignorance.

49 **Delighting in the meaning of the dharma** (*rakuhō* 樂法): S. *dharmārthikatā* ("wanting dharma"). Divākara (*Da zhuangyan jing* 大莊嚴經, T.187.3:544b27) reads:

288 DŌGEN'S *SHŌBŌGENZŌ* VOLUME VI

Love of the illumination of dharma is a gateway to the illumination of the dharma, for one gains the gateways to the illumination of the dharma.[50]

Seeking learning is a gateway to the illumination of the dharma, for one correctly perceives the marks of the dharma.[51]

Correct application is a gateway to the illumination of the dharma, for one is possessed of correct practice.[52]

Knowledge of names and forms is a gateway to the illumination of the dharma, for it removes obstacles.[53]

Removal of views of causality is a gateway to the illumination of the dharma, for one attains liberation.[54]

Absence of anger and affection is a gateway to the illumination of the dharma, for it produces impartiality of anger and affection.[55]

Skill with the aggregates is a gateway to the illumination of the dharma, for one knows sufferings.[56]

Equality of the elements is a gateway to the illumination of the dharma, for it eliminates all causes.[57]

The sense fields are a gateway to the illumination of the dharma, for one practices the correct path.[58]

Acceptance of non-arising is a gateway to the illumination of the dharma, for one realizes the truth of extinction.[59]

求法是法門依止於義故。
Seeking the dharma is a dharma gate, for one relies on the meaning.

50 **Love of the illumination of dharma** (*ai hōmyō* 愛法明): S. *dharmakāmatā*.

51 **Seeking learning** (*kyū tamon* 求多聞): S. *śruta-paryeṣṭi*.

52 **Correct application** (*shō hōben* 正方便): S. *samyakprayoga*.

53 **Knowledge of names and forms** (*chi myōshiki* 知名色): S. *nāmarūpaparijñā*.

54 **Removal of views of causality** (*jo inken* 除因見): S. *hetudṛṣṭisamuddhāta*.

55 **Absence of anger and affection** (*mu onshin shin* 無怨親心): S. *anunaya-pratigha-prahāṇa*.

56 **Skill with the aggregates** (*on hōben* 陰方便): S. *skandhakauśalya*. The reasons for this and the following three items cover the four sacred truths: suffering, cause, path, and cessation.

57   **Equality of the elements** (*shodai byōdō* 諸大平等): S. *dhātusamatā*. "Causes" here loosely translates *wagō hō* 和合法, used for *samudaya* ("aggregation"), the second sacred truth.

58 **sense fields** (*shonyū* 諸入): S. *āyatanāpakarṣaṇa* ("withdrawal of the sense fields"). The *Da zhuangyan jing* 大莊嚴經 (T.1087.3:544c4) reads "not grasping" (*fushu* 不取).

59 **Acceptance of non-arising** (*mushōnin* 無生忍): S. *anutpāda-kṣānti*. I.e., acceptance of the fact that all dharmas are empty and do not really occur.

T11. One Hundred Eight Gateways *Ippyakuhachi hōmyō mon* 一百八法明門　289

[T11:12]

身念處是法明門、諸法寂靜故。受念處是法明門、斷一切諸受故。心念處是法明門、觀心如幻化故。法念處是法明門、智慧無礙故。

Mindfulness of the body is a gateway to the illumination of the dharma, for the dharmas are quiescent.[60]

Mindfulness of sensations is a gateway to the illumination of the dharma, for one eliminates all sensations.[61]

Mindfulness of the mind is a gateway to the illumination of the dharma, for one examines the mind as an illusion.[62]

Mindfulness of the dharmas is a gateway to the illumination of the dharma, for one's wisdom is unclouded.[63]

[T11:13] {2:444}

四正懃是法明門、斷一切惡成諸善故。四如意足是法明門、身心輕故。

The four right efforts are a gateway to the illumination of the dharma, for they eliminate all vices and perfect the virtues.[64]

The four wish-fulfilling bases are a gateway to the illumination of the dharma, for one's body and mind are light.[65]

---

60 **Mindfulness of the body** (*shin nenjo* 身念處): S. *kāyagatānusmṛti*. Divākara (*Da zhuangyan jing* 大莊嚴經, T.187.3:544c6) gives as the reason here:

分析觀身故。

For one observes the body analytically.

The four items in this section cover the four foundations of mindfulness (*shi nenjo* 四念處; S. *catvāri-smṛty-upasthānāni*): body, sensations, mind, and dharmas. This set is the first of the thirty-seven factors of bodhi (*sanjūshichi hon bodai bunpō* 三十七品菩提分法; S. *saptatriṃśad-bodhi-pakṣikā-dharmāḥ*), which will be covered in the items listed through section 17, below; Dōgen discusses them in his "Shōbōgenzō sanjūshichi hon bodai bunpō" 正法眼藏三十七品菩提分法.

61 **Mindfulness of sensations** (*ju nenjo* 受念處): S. *vedanāgatānusmṛti*.

62 **Mindfulness of the mind** (*shin nenjo* 心念處): S. *cittagatānusmṛti*.

63 **Mindfulness of the dharmas** (*hō nenju* 法念處): S. *dharmagatānusmṛti*. This item is missing in the *Da zhuangyan jing* 大莊嚴經.

64 **The four right efforts** (*shi shōgon* 四正懃): S. *catvāri samyakprahāṇāni*. The second set of the thirty-seven factors of bodhi; also known as "the four right abandonments" (*shi shōdan* 四正斷): eliminating evils already arisen; avoiding evils not yet arisen; producing good not yet arisen; and continuing good already arisen.

65 **The four wish-fulfilling bases** (*shi nyoi soku* 四如意足): S. *catvāra ṛddhipādā*; i.e., the bases for developing paranormal powers. The third set of the thirty-seven factors of bodhi; also known as "spiritual bases" (*jinsoku* 神足): desire (*yoku* 欲), effort (*gon* 勤), thought (*shin* 心), and examination (*kan* 觀).

[T11:14]

信根是法明門、不隨他語故。精進根是法明門、善得諸智故。念根是法明門、善作諸業故。定根是法明門、心清淨故。慧根是法明門、現見諸法故。

The faculty of faith is a gateway to the illumination of the dharma, for one does not follow the words of others.[66]

The faculty of effort is a gateway to the illumination of the dharma, for one's wisdom is well acquired.[67]

The faculty of mindfulness is a gateway to the illumination of the dharma, for one's deeds are well done.[68]

The faculty of concentration is a gateway to the illumination of the dharma, for the mind is pure.[69]

The faculty of wisdom is a gateway to the illumination of the dharma, for one directly perceives the dharmas.[70]

[T11:15]

信力是法明門、過諸魔力故。精進力是法明門、不退轉故。念力是法明門、不共他故。定力是法明門、斷一切念故。慧力是法明門、離二邊故。

The power of faith is a gateway to the illumination of the dharma, for it surpasses the powers of Māra.[71]

The power of effort is a gateway to the illumination of the dharma, for one does not regress.[72]

The power of mindfulness is a gateway to the illumination of the dharma, for one does not associate with others.[73]

---

66 **faculty of faith** (*shinkon* 信根): S. *śraddhendriya*. Here begins the list of the five faculties (*gokon* 五根), the fourth set of the thirty-seven factors of bodhi.

67 **faculty of effort** (*shōjin kon* 精進根): S. *vīryendriya*.

68 **faculty of mindfulness** (*nenkon* 念根): S. *smṛtīndriya*.

69 **faculty of concentration** (*jōkon* 定根): S. *samādhīnriya*. The *Da zhuangyan jing* 大莊嚴經 (T.187.3:544c11) gives as the reason here:

由心解脱故。

For the mind is thereby liberated.

70 **faculty of wisdom** (*ekon* 慧根): S. *prajñendriya*.

71 **power of faith** (*shinriki* 信力): S. *śraddhābala*. Here begins the list of the five powers (*goriki* 五力), the fifth set of the thirty-seven factors of bodhi.

72 **power of effort** (*shōjin riki* 精進力): S. *vīryabala*.

73 **power of mindfulness** (*nenriki* 念力): S. *smṛtibala*. The *Da zhuangyan jing* 大莊嚴經 (T.187.3:544c13-14) gives as the reason here:

不遺忘故。

For one does not forget.

T11. One Hundred Eight Gateways *Ippyakuhachi hōmyō mon* 一百八法明門 291

The power of concentration is a gateway to the illumination of the dharma, for one eliminates all thoughts.[74]

The power of wisdom is a gateway to the illumination of the dharma, for one is free from the two extremes.[75]

[T11:16]

念覺分是法明門、如諸法智故。法覺分是法明門、照明一切諸法故。精進覺分是法明門、善知覺故。喜覺分是法明門、得諸定故。除覺分是法明門、所作已辨故。定覺分是法明門、知一切法平等故。捨覺分是法明門、厭離一切生故。

The factor of awakening of mindfulness is a gateway to the illumination of the dharma, for it is knowledge of the dharmas as they are.[76]

The factor of awakening of dharma [analysis] is a gateway to the illumination of the dharma, for it illumines all dharmas.[77]

The factor of awakening of effort is a gateway to the illumination of the dharma, for one perceives correctly.[78]

The factor of awakening of joy is a gateway to the illumination of the dharma, for one attains the concentrations.[79]

The factor of awakening of alleviation is a gateway to the illumination of the dharma, for what is done is taken care of.[80]

The factor of awakening of concentration is a gateway to the illumination of the dharma, for one knows the equality of all dharmas.[81]

---

74 **power of concentration** (*jōriki* 定力): S. *samādhibala*.

75 **power of wisdom** (*eriki* 慧力): S. *prajñābala*. The *Da zhuangyan jing* 大莊嚴經 (T.187.3:544c15) gives as the reason here:

無能損壞故。

For one cannot be injured.

76 **factor of awakening of mindfulness** (*nen kakubun* 念覺分): S. *smṛti-saṃbodhyaṅga*. Here begins the list of the seven factors of awakening (or "limbs of awakening" [*kakushi* 覺支; S. *bodhyaṅga*]), the sixth set of the thirty-seven factors of bodhi.

77 **factor of awakening of dharma [analysis]** (*chakuhō kakubun* 擇法覺分): Supplying *chaku* 擇, missing in Kawamura's text. S. *dharma-pravicaya-saṃbodhyaṅga*. The *Da zhuangyan jing* 大莊嚴經 (T.187.3:544c16) gives as the reason here:

圓滿一切法故。

For it perfects all dharmas.

78 **factor of awakening of effort** (*shōjin kakubun* 精進覺分): S. *vīrya-saṃbodhyaṅga*.

79 **factor of awakening of joy** (*ki kakubun* 喜覺分): S. *prīti-saṃbodhyaṅga*.

80 **factor of awakening of alleviation** (*jo kakubun* 除覺分): S. *praśrabdhisaṃbodhyaṅga*. The *Da zhuangyan jing* 大莊嚴經 (T.187.3:544c18) translates this as "serenity" (*kyōan* 輕安).

81 **factor of awakening of concentration** (*jō kakubun* 定覺分): S. *samādhisaṃbodhyaṅga*.

The factor of awakening of equanimity is a gateway to the illumination of the dharma, for one loaths all births.[82]

[T11:17]

正見是法明門、得漏盡聖道故。正分別是法明門、斷一切分別・無分別故。正語是法明門、一切名字・音聲・語言、知如響故。正命是法明門、除滅一切惡道故。正行是法明門、至彼岸故。正念是法明門、不思念一切法故。正定是法明門、得無散亂三昧故。

Correct views are a gateway to the illumination of the dharma, for one attains the noble path on which the contaminants are exhausted.[83]

Correct discrimination is a gateway to the illumination of the dharma, for one eliminates all discrimination and nondiscrimination.[84]

Correct speech is a gateway to the illumination of the dharma, for one knows that all words, sounds, and language are like echoes.[85]

Correct livelihood is a gateway to the illumination of the dharma, for it does away with all evil paths.[86]

Correct exertion is a gateway to the illumination of the dharma, for it leads to the other shore.[87]

Correct mindfulness is a gateway to the illumination of the dharma, for one does not think of any dharmas.[88]

Correct concentration is a gateway to the illumination of the dharma, for one attains samādhi, free from distraction.[89]

---

82 **factor of awakening of equanimity** (*sha kakubun* 捨覺分): S. *upekṣāsaṃbodhyaṅga*.

83 **Correct views** (*shōken* 正見); S. *samyagdṛṣṭi*. Here begin the items of the noble eightfold path, the seventh and final set of the thirty-seven factors of bodhi.

84 **Correct discrimination** (*shō funbetsu* 正分別): S. *samyaksaṃkalpa*.

85 **Correct speech** (*shō go* 正吾): S. *samyagvāg*. Dōgen's text is missing the fourth item of the eightfold path, "correct action" (*shōgō* 正業; S. *samyakkarmānta*), which occurs at *Fo benxing ji jing* 佛本行集經, T.190.3:681c22:

正業是法明門、無業無報故。

Correct action is a gateway to the illumination of the dharma, for it is without acts and without recompense.

86 **Correct livelihood** (*shōmyō* 正命): S. *samyagājīva*. The *Da zhuangyan jing* 大莊嚴經 (T.187.3:544c23) gives as the reason here:

離一切希求故。

For one is free from all seeking.

87 **Correct exertion** (*shōgyō* 正行): S. *samyagvyāyāma*.

88 **Correct mindfulness** (*shōnen* 正念): S. *samyaksmṛti*.

89 **Correct concentration** (*shōjō* 正定): S. *samyaksamādhi*.

T11. One Hundred Eight Gateways *Ippyakuhachi hōmyō mon* 一百八法明門 293

[T11:18]
菩提心是法明門、不斷三寶故。依倚是法明門、不樂小乘故。正信是法明門、得最勝佛法故。增進是法明門、成就一切諸善根法故。

> The thought of bodhi is a gateway to the illumination of the dharma, for it does not cut off the three treasures.[90]

> Reliance is a gateway to the illumination of the dharma, for one does not desire the Small Vehicle.[91]

> Correct faith is a gateway to the illumination of the dharma, for one attains the supreme buddha dharma.[92]

> Advancement is a gateway to the illumination of the dharma, for one achieves all good roots.[93]

[T11:19]
檀度是法明門、念念成就相好、莊嚴佛土、教化慳貪諸衆生故。戒度是法明門、遠離惡道諸難、教化破戒諸衆生故。忍度是法明門、捨一切瞋恚・我慢・諂曲・調戲、教化如是諸惡衆生故。精進度是法明門、悉得一切諸善法、教化懈怠諸衆生故。禪度是法明門、成就一切禪定及諸神通、教化散亂諸衆生故。智度是法明門、斷無明黑暗及著諸見、教化愚癡諸衆生故。

> Perfection of *dāna* is a gateway to the illumination of the dharma, for, moment by moment, one achieves the marks and signs, adorns a buddha land, and instructs living beings who are greedy.[94]

> Perfection of morality is a gateway to the illumination of the dharma, for one is distant from the troubles of the evil paths and instructs living beings who have broken the precepts.[95]

> Perfection of patience is a gateway to the illumination of the dharma, for one abandons all malice, arrogance, deceit, and frivolousness, and instructs living beings who are [afflicted by] such evils.[96]

---

90 **thought of bodhi** (*bodai shin* 菩提心): S. *bodhicitta*.

91 **Reliance** (*ei* 依椅): S. *āsaya*. The *Da zhuangyan jing* 大莊嚴經 (T.187.3:544c2) takes this as "great intention" (*dai igyō* 大意樂).

92 **Correct faith** (*shōshin* 正信): S. *adhyāśaya* ("higher intention"); compare *shōshin* 正信 for śraddhā, section 4, above.

93 **Advancement** (*zōshin* 增進): S. *prayoga* ("application").

94 **Perfection of *dāna*** (*dan do* 檀度): S. *dāna-pāramitā*. "Marks and signs" (*sōkō* 相好) refers to the major marks and minor auspicious signs on the body of a buddha. Here begins the list of the six perfections (*rokudo* 六度; S. *ṣaṭ-pāramitā*).

95 **Perfection of morality** (*kai do* 戒度): S. *śīla-pāramitā*.

96 **Perfection of patience** (*nin do* 忍度): S. *kṣānti-pāramitā*.

294 DŌGEN'S *SHŌBŌGENZŌ* VOLUME VI

Perfection of vigor is a gateway to the illumination of the dharma, for one acquires all good dharmas and instructs living beings who are lazy.[97]

Perfection of dhyāna is a gateway to the illumination of the dharma, for one achieves all the meditations and spiritual powers, and instructs living beings who are distracted.[98]

Perfection of wisdom is a gateway to the illumination of the dharma, for one eliminates the darkness of ignorance and attachment to views, and instructs living beings who are ignorant.[99]

[T11:20]

方便是法明門、隨衆生所見威儀、而示現教化、成就一切諸佛法故。四攝法是法明門、攝受一切衆生、得菩提已、施一切衆生法故。教化衆生是法明門、自不受樂、不癡勸故。攝受正法是法明門、斷一切衆生諸煩惱故。福聚是法明門、利益一切諸衆生故。修禪定是法明門、滿足十力故。寂定是法明門、成就如來三昧具足故。慧見是法明門、智慧成就滿足故。入無尋辯是法明門、得法眼成就故。入一切行是法明門、得佛眼成就故。成就陀羅尼是法明門、聞一切諸佛法、能受持故。得無尋辯是法明門、令一切衆生皆歡喜故。順忍是法明門、順一切諸佛法故。得無生法忍是法明門、得受記故。不退轉地是法明門、具足往昔諸佛法故。從一地至一地智是法明門、灌頂成就一切智故。灌頂地是法明門、從生出家、乃至得成阿耨多羅三藐三菩提故。

Expedient means is a gateway to the illumination of the dharma, for one displays instructions according to the views and behaviors of living beings, and one achieves the dharma of all the buddhas.[100]

The four methods of attraction are a gateway to the illumination of the dharma, for one gathers in all living beings and, after attaining bodhi, offers the dharma to all of them.[101]

Instructing living beings is a gateway to the illumination of the dharma, for one does not enjoy pleasure for oneself and does not become exhausted.[102]

---

97 **Perfection of vigor** (*shōjin do* 精進度): S. *vīrya-pāramitā*.

98 **Perfection of dhyāna** (*zen do* 禪度). S. *dhyāna-pāramitā*.

99 **Perfection of wisdom** (*chi do* 知度): S. *prajñā-pāramitā*.

100 **Expedient means** (*hōben* 方便): S. *upāyakauśala*.

101 **four methods of attraction** (*shi shōbō* 四攝法): S. *catvāri-saṃgrahavastūni*. Four ways in which the bodhisattva can attract people to the buddha dharma: giving (*fuse* 布施; S. *dāna*), kind words (*aigo* 愛語; S. *priyavacana*), helpful deeds (*rigyō* 利行; S. *arthakṛtya*), and participation (*dōji* 同事; S. *samānārtha*). The *Da zhuangyan jing* 大莊嚴經 (T.1873:545a11-12) gives as the reason here:

攝諸群生令求趣證大菩提法故。

For one gathers in living beings and causes them to seek verification of the dharma of great bodhi.

102 **Instructing living beings** (*kyōke shujō* 教化衆生): S. *sattva-paripāka*. "Become

T11. One Hundred Eight Gateways *Ippyakuhachi hōmyō mon* 一百八法明門   295

Embracing the true dharma is a gateway to the illumination of the dharma, for one eliminates the afflictions of all living beings.[103]

Accumulation of merit is a gateway to the illumination of the dharma, for it benefits all living beings.[104]

Practice of meditation is a gateway to the illumination of the dharma, for one perfects the ten powers.[105]

Calm concentration is a gateway to the illumination of the dharma, for one achieves the fulfillment of the samādhi of the tathāgatas.[106]

Insight is a gateway to the illumination of the dharma, for wisdom is achieved and perfected.[107]

Entrance into unimpeded analysis is a gateway to the illumination of the dharma, for one gains achievement of the dharma eye.[108]

Entrance into all things is a gateway to the illumination of the dharma, for one gains achievement of the buddha eye.[109]

Acquiring dhāraṇīs is a gateway to the illumination of the dharma, for one can receive and keep all the dharmas of the Buddha.[110]

---

exhausted" (*hiken* 疲勌): reading *hi* 疲 ("to tire") for *chi* 癡 ("ignorance"), after the sūtra text.

103   **Embracing the true dharma** (*shōju shōbō* 攝受正法): S. *saddharma-parigraha*.

104   **Accumulation of merit** (*fukuju* 福聚): S. *puṇya-sambhāra*.

105   **Practice of meditation** (*shu zenjō* 修禪定): S. *jñāna-sambhāra* ("accumulation of knowledge"). Lists of the ten powers (*jūriki* 十力) of a buddha vary, but a common version gives: (1) knowledge of what is appropriate (*sho riki* 處力), (2) knowledge of karma (*gō riki* 業力), (3) knowlege of concentrations (*jō riki* 定力), (4) knowledge of faculties (*kon riki* 根力), (5) knowledge of desires (*yoku riki* 欲力), (6) knowledge of natures (*shō riki* 性力), (7) knowledge of destinies (*shisho riki* 至處力), (8) knowledge of former lives (*shukumyō riki* 宿命力), (9) the deva eye (*tengen* 天眼), (10) knowledge of the exhaustion of the contaminants (*rojin riki* 漏盡力). (See, e.g., *Lüzong xinxue mingju* 律宗新學名句, ZZ.105:661a5-7.)

106   **Calm concentration** (*jakujō* 寂定): S. *śamatha-sambhāra*.

107   **Insight** (*eken* 慧見): S. *vidarśanā-sambhāra* ("accumulation of insight"). The *Da zhuangyan jing* 大莊嚴經 (T.187.3:545a17) gives as the reason here:

獲得慧眼故。

For one attains the wisdom eye.

This and the following two items, then, cover the attainment of the three spiritual eyes in the list of the five eyes (*gogen* 五眼): physical, deva, wisdom, dharma, and buddha.

108   **Entrance into unimpeded analysis** (*nyū mugeben* 入無导辯): S. *prati-samvid-avatāra*.

109   **Entrance into all things** (*nyū issai gyō* 入一切行): S. *pratiśaraṇāvatāra* ("entrance into the reliable"?). The *Da zhuangyan jing* 大莊嚴經 (T.187.3:545a18) translates as *jueze* 決擇 ("discrimination," "selection," etc.).

110   **Acquiring *dhāraṇīs*** (*jōju darani* 成就陀羅尼): S. *dhāraṇī-pratilambha*.

Attaining unimpeded eloquence is a gateway to the illumination of the dharma, for it causes all living beings to rejoice.[111]

Patience in accordance is a gateway to the illumination of the dharma, for one accords with all the dharmas of the Buddha.[112]

Attaining patience in the non-arising of dharmas is a gateway to the illumination of the dharma, for one receives a prediction.[113]

The stage of non-regression is a gateway to the illumination of the dharma, for one is fully endowed with the dharma of the buddhas of the past.[114]

The wisdom that progresses from stage to stage is a gateway to the illumination of the dharma, for one is consecrated in the achievement of omniscience.[115]

The stage of consecration is a gateway to the illumination of the dharma, for one goes from birth and leaving home up to attaining anuttara-samyak-sambodhi.[116]

---

111 **Attaining unimpeded eloquence** (*toku muge ben* 得無礙辯): S. *pratibhāna-pra-tilambha*.

112 **Patience in accordance** (*junnin* 順忍): S. *ānulomika-dharma-kṣānti* ("patience in accordance with the dharma"). One of the three (or five) types of patience, variously defined; beginning here, the final members of the list represent the bodhisattva's progress through the stages (S. *bhūmi*) of the path to buddhahood — this member representing the stages before the seventh *bhūmi*.

113 **Attaining patience in the non-arising of dharmas** (*toku mushōbō nin* 得無生法忍): S. *anutpattika-dharma-kṣānti*, commonly held to occur at the seventh *bhūmi*. "Prediction" (*juki* 受記; S. *vyākaraṇa*) refers to the prediction of eventual buddhahood.

114 **stage of non-regression** (*fu taiten ji* 不退轉地): S. *avaivartika-bhūmi*; typically located at the seventh *bhūmi* of the bodhisattva path.

115 **wisdom that progresses from stage to stage** (*jū ichiji shi ichiji chi* 從一地至一地智): S. *bhūmerbhūmi-saṃkrānti-jñāna*; i.e., on (the higher stages of) the bodhisattva path.

116 **stage of consecration** (*kanjō ji* 灌頂地): S. *abhiṣeka-bhūmi*; i.e., the final, buddha stage of the bodhisattva path. The *Da zhuangyan jing* 大莊嚴經 (T.187.3:545a24-26) gives as the reason here the full career of the bodhisatta:

從兜率天下生。入胎初生出家苦行。詣菩提場降魔成佛。轉正法輪起大神通。從忉利天下現入涅槃故。

For one goes from the descent from the Tuṣita heaven, entrance into the womb, birth, leaving home, painful practice, reaching the place of bodhi, defeating Māra, becoming a buddha, turning the great dharma wheel, displaying the great spiritual powers, descending from the Trāyastriṃśa heaven, and entering nirvāṇa.

T11. One Hundred Eight Gateways *Ippyakuhachi hōmyō mon* 一百八法明門 297

[T11:21]

爾時護明菩薩、説是語已、告彼一切諸天衆言、諸天當知、此是一百八法門、留與諸天。汝等受持、心常憶念、勿令忘失。

At that time, Bodhisattva Jyotipala, having finished speaking these words, addressed all the devas, saying, "Devas, you should know these are the one hundred eight dharma gates. I leave them for the devas. Receive and keep them, always remembering them, without ever letting them be forgotten."[117]

[T11:22] {2:450}

これ、即ち一百八法門なり。一切の一生所繋の菩薩、都史多天より閻浮提に下生せむとする時、必ずこの一百八法明門を、都史多天衆のために敷揚して、諸天を化するは、諸佛の常法なり。

These are the one hundred eight dharma gates. It is the constant norm of the buddhas that, whenever bodhisattvas bound to a single life are about to descend from the Tuṣita heaven to rebirth in Jambudvīpa, they always instruct the devas by expounding these one hundred eight gateways to illumination of the dharma for the throngs in the Tuṣita heaven.[118]

[T11:23]

護明菩薩とは、釋迦牟尼佛、一生補處として、第四天にましますときの名なり。李駙馬、天聖廣燈録を撰するに、この一百八法門の名字をのせたり。參學の輩、明らめ、しれるはすくなく、しらざるは稲麻竹葦のごとし。いま初心・晩學の輩のために、これを撰す。師子の座にのぼり、人天の師となれらん輩、審細參學すべし。この都史多天に一生所繋として住せざれば、さらに諸佛にあらざるなり。行者、みだりに我慢することなかれ。一生所繋の菩薩は、中有なし。

Bodhisatta Jyotipala was the name of Buddha Śākyamuni when he was in the fourth heaven as the successor. When Escort Li composed the *Tiansheng guangdeng lu*, he included the term "one hundred eight dharma gates."[119] Yet few who study have clarified or known them; and those who are ignorant of them are like "rice, hemp, bamboo, and reeds."[120] Now, I have composed this for beginners and latecomers. Those who

---

117 **At that time** (*niji* 爾時): *Fo benxing ji jing* 佛本行集經, T.190.3:682b7-9.

118 **bodhisattvas bound to a single life** (*isshō shoke no bosatsu* 一生所繋の菩薩): I.e., bodhisattvas with one final life, during which they will attain buddhahood.

119 **Escort Li** (*Ri Fuba* 李駙馬): I.e., Li Zunxu 李遵勗 (988-1038). His *Tiansheng guangdeng lu* 天聖廣燈録 was completed in 1036. Mention of the bodhisattva's teaching of the hundred eight gateways occurs at ZZ.135:609a14.

120 **"rice, hemp, bamboo, and reeds"** (*tō ma chiku i* 稲麻竹葦): I.e., dense and profuse; a simile from Kumārajīva's translation of the *Lotus Sūtra*; see Supplementary Notes.

would ascend the seat of the lion and become the teachers of humans and devas should study it in detail. Those who have not resided in the Tuṣita heaven as one bound to a single life are definitely not buddhas. Practitioners, do not foolishly be proud of yourselves. Bodhisattvas bound to a single life have no intermediate state.[121]

正法眼藏一百八法明門第十一

Treasury of the True Dharma Eye
One Hundred Eight Gateways to the Illumination of the Dharma
Number 11

121　**have no intermediate state** (*chūu nashi* 中有なし): I.e. no state between rebirths (S. *antarā-bhava*). Perhaps, an error for the more likely *chūyō* 中夭 (S. *antarā-mṛthu*; "premature death"), said of the bodhisattva in Tuṣita.

TREASURY OF THE TRUE DHARMA EYE
THE TWELVE-CHAPTER COMPILATION
NUMBER 12

The Eight Understandings
of the Great Person
Hachi dainin gaku

八大人覺

The Eight Understandings
of the Great Person

Hachi dainin gaku

INTRODUCTION

According to its colophon, this chapter, written at the start of 1253, just months before its author's death, was the last work Dōgen composed for the *Shōbōgenzō*. The same colophon, by Dōgen's disciple Ejō 懷奘, famously reports that the work represents the twelfth of a planned hundred-chapter *Shōbōgenzō* collection, left unfinished due to Dōgen's final illness. In addition to the twelve-chapter compilation, the work is found as number 12 in the twenty-eight-text *Shōbōgenzō* collection (in fascicle 2, number 9), as well as number 95 in the vernacular edition.

As its title indicates, the text is devoted to a standard list of eight spiritual desiderata found in a number of early sūtras. Dōgen draws on two sources here, introducing each of the eight topics according to the list in the *Dasheng yi zhang* 大乘義章 (*Compendium of Meanings of the Great Vehicle*), by the sixth-century scholar Jingying Huiyuan 淨影慧遠, and then explaining each as defined in the *Fo yijiao jing* 佛遺教經 (*Sūtra of the Bequeathed Teachings of the Buddha*), a popular sūtra, translated by Kumārajīva, that purports to be the final teaching of the Buddha. As is the case with the preceding chapter, "Ippyakuhachi hōmyō mon" 一百八法明門, this material is merely quoted verbatim, with almost no comment. Only at the end of the text does Dōgen offer brief remarks lamenting his contemporaries' neglect of the teaching and urging his audience to study it.

正法眼藏第十二

Treasury of the True Dharma Eye
Number 12

八大人覺

The Eight Understandings
of the Great Person

[T12:1] {2:451}

諸佛是大人、大人之所覺知、所以稱八大人覺也。覺知此法、爲涅槃因。我
釋迦牟尼佛、入涅槃夜、最後之所説也。

The buddhas are great persons.[1] *What the great person understands is
called the "eight understandings of the great person."*[2] *Understanding of
these dharmas is the cause of nirvāṇa. They are the final teaching of our
Buddha Śākyamuni, on the night he entered nirvāṇa.*[3]

---

1   **The buddhas are great persons** (*shobutsu ze dainin* 諸佛是大人): "Great person" (*dainin* 大人; S. *mahāpuruṣa*) is a standard epithet of a buddha. The first three
sentences here are a paraphrase of lines introducing the entry on the eight understandings in the *Dasheng yi zhang* 大乘義章, by Jingying Huiyuan 淨影慧遠 (523-592)
(T.1851.44:735a13-14):

> 八大人覺者、佛是大人。諸佛大人覺知此法爲涅槃因、名大人覺。所覺不同、一
> 門説八。

> "The eight understandings of the great person": A buddha is a great person. The under-
> standing by the buddhas, the great persons, of these dharmas is the cause of their nir-
> vāṇa. What they understand is not the same; so, the one teaching is spoken of as eight.

2   **"eight understandings of the great person"** (*hachi dainin gaku* 八大人覺): I.e.,
eight desiderata recognized by a buddha. The term *kaku* 覺 ("to be aware," "to recognize," etc.) here probably renders the Sanskrit *vitarka* ("to consider," etc.).

3   **They are the final teaching** (*saigo shi shosetsu ya* 最後之所説也): Dōgen's
comment, in Chinese, perhaps reflecting the opening of the *Fo yijiao jing* 佛遺教經
(T.389.12:1110c17-20), the sūtra to which Huiyuan directs his reader for details on the
eight understandings, and from which Dōgen will quote repeatedly below.

[T12:2]

一者少欲。於彼未得五欲法中、不廣追求、名爲少欲。

1) Few desires.[4] Among the objects of the five desires, not widely pursuing those not yet acquired is called "few desires."[5]

[T12:3]

佛言、汝等比丘、當知、多欲之人、多求名利故、苦惱亦多。少欲之人、無求・無欲、則無此患。直爾少欲尚應修習、何況少欲能生諸功德。少欲之人、則無諂曲以求人意、亦復不爲諸根所牽。行少欲者、心則坦然、無所憂畏、觸事有餘、常無不足。有少欲者、則有涅槃。是名少欲。

The Buddha said,[6]

Bhikṣus, you should know that those with many desires, because they seek much fame and profit, also have much suffering. Those of few desires, being without seeking and without desiring, are without these troubles. Having few desires should be practiced in its own right; how much more, then, when having few desires can produce merits. Those of few desires are not obsequious in order to please others, nor are they led about by their senses. In those who practice few desires, the mind is at ease, without anxiety or fear; they have plenty in all matters, never feeling unsatisfied. For those with few desires, there is nirvāṇa. This is called "few desires."

[T12:4] {2:452}

二者知足。已得法中、受取以限、稱曰知足。

2) Knowing contentment.[7] Among those already acquired, setting limits on what is taken is called "knowing contentment."

[T12:5]

佛言、汝等比丘、若欲脫諸苦惱、當觀知足。知足之法、即是富樂安穩之處。知足之人、　雖臥地上、猶爲安樂、不知足者、雖處天堂、亦不稱意。不知足者、雖富而貧、知足之人、雖貧而富。不知足者、常爲五欲所牽、爲知足之者之所憐愍。是名知足。

4　**Few desires** (*shōyoku* 少欲): The virtue known as having "few wants" (S. *alpeccha*). Quoting the *Dasheng yi zhang* 大乘義章 (T.1851.44:735a15, 17-18).

5　**five desires** (*goyoku* 五欲): S. *pañca-kāma*; the desires associated with the five senses.

6　**The Buddha said** (*butsu gon* 佛言): Quoting the *Fo yijiao jing* 佛遺教經 (T.389.12:1111b28-c4).

7　**Knowing contentment** (*chisoku* 知足): The virtue of being satisfied with what one has (S. *saṃtuṣṭi*). Quoting the *Dasheng yi zhang* 大乘義章 (T.1851.44:735a15, 18).

T12. The 8 Understandings of the Great Person *Hachi dainin gaku* 八大人覺 303

The Buddha said,[8]

Bhikṣus, if you wish to be liberated from sufferings, you should contemplate knowing contentment. The dharma of knowing contentment — this is a place of wealth and joy, peace and tranquility. Those who know contentment are happy even when sleeping on the ground; those who do not know contentment are still dissatisfied even when staying in a heavenly mansion. Those not knowing contentment are poor even when rich; those knowing contentment are rich even when poor. Those who do not know contentment are always led about by the five desires and are pitied by those who know contentment. This is called "knowing contentment."

[T12:6]

三者樂寂靜。離諸憒鬧、獨處空閒、名樂寂靜。

3) Enjoying quietude.[9] *Living alone in a vacant space, apart from hustle and bustle, is called "enjoying quietude."*

[T12:7] {2:453}

佛言、汝等比丘、欲求寂靜無爲安樂、當離憒鬧獨處閑居。靜處之人、帝釋諸天、所共敬重。是故、當捨己衆他衆、空閒獨處、思滅苦本。若樂衆者、則受衆惱。譬如大樹衆鳥集之、則有枯折之患。世間縛著没於衆苦、譬如老象溺泥、不能自出。是名遠離。

The Buddha said,[10]

If you bhikṣus wish to seek the unconditioned joy of quietude, you should live alone in a quiet abode, apart from hustle and bustle. Those who live in quiet places are all respected by Lord Śakra and the other devas. Therefore, abandoning your own group and other groups, you should live alone in a vacant space, thinking on eradicating the root of suffering. Those who enjoy groups suffer multiple afflictions. They are like a great tree troubled by withering and breaking when birds gather in it. When we are bound to the world, we drown in sufferings, like an old elephant sinking in mud, unable to extricate itself. This is called "isolation."

---

8 **The Buddha said** (*butsu gon* 佛言): Quoting the *Fo yijiao jing* 佛遺教經 (T.389.12:1111c5-10).

9 **Enjoying quietude** (*gyō jakujō* 樂寂靜): The virtue of liking isolation (S. *viveka-kāma*). Quoting the *Dasheng yi zhang* 大乘義章 (T.1851.44:735a15, 18-19).

10 **The Buddha said** (*butsu gon* 佛言): Quoting the *Fo yijiao jing* 佛遺教經 (T.389.12:1111c11-16).

304 DŌGEN'S *SHŌBŌGENZŌ* VOLUME VI

[T12:8]

四者勤精進。於諸善法、勤修無間故、云精進。精而不雜、進而不退。

4) *Diligent exertion.*[11] *Diligently practicing good deeds without interruption is called "exertion."*

Concentrated, without adulteration; advancing, without regressing.[12]

[T12:9]

佛言、汝等比丘、若勤精進、則事無難者。是故汝等、當勤精進。譬如少水常流、則能穿石。若行者之心、數數懈廢、譬如鑽火、未熱而息、雖欲得火、火難可得。是名精進。

The Buddha said,[13]

If you bhikṣus diligently exert yourselves, things will not be difficult for you. Therefore, you should diligently exert yourselves, just as even a small amount of water constantly running can penetrate stone. If the mind of the practitioner repeatedly neglects and abandons the practice, it is just as if one, boring wood to make a fire, were to stop before it got hot: one may want the fire, but the fire will be hard to get. This is called "exertion."

[T12:10] {2:454}

五者不忘念。亦名守正念。守法不失、名爲正念、亦名不忘念。

5) *Not neglecting mindfulness, also called "maintaining right mindfulness."*[14] *Maintaining the dharma without losing it is called "right mindfulness," also called "not neglecting mindfulness."*

[T12:11]

佛言、汝等比丘、求善知識、求善護助、無如不忘念。若有不忘念者、諸煩惱賊、則不能入。是故汝等、常當攝念在心。若失念者、則失諸功德。若念力堅強、雖入五欲賊中、不爲所害。譬如著鎧入陣、則無所畏。是名不忘念。

---

11 **Diligent exertion** (*gon shōjin* 勤精進): The virtue of "vigor" (S. *vīrya*). Quoting the *Dasheng yi zhang* 大乘義章 (T.1851.44:735a15-16, 19-20).

12 **Concentrated, without adulteration; advancing, without regressing** (*shō ni fuzō, shin ni futai* 精而不雜、進而不退): A definition of the two elements in the term *shōjin* 精進 (S. *vīrya*), not given in the *Dasheng yi zhang* passage but found in a number of texts of the Chinese Buddhist canon (see, e.g., *Miaofa lianhua jing jujia* 妙法蓮華經句解, ZZ.47.861a7).

13 **The Buddha said** (*butsu gon* 佛言): Quoting the *Fo yijiao jing* 佛遺教經 (T.389.12:1111c17-20).

14 **Not neglecting mindfulness** (*fumōnen* 不忘念): The virtue of mindfulness (S. *smṛti*). Dōgen here uses the term found in the *Fo yijiao jing* 佛遺教經 (T.389.12:1111c21-25); the alternative term, "maintaining right mindfulness" (*shu shōnen* 守正念), represents the preference of the *Dasheng yi zhang* 大乘義章 (T.1851.44:735a16).

T12. The 8 Understandings of the Great Person *Hachi dainin gaku* 八大人覺 305

The Buddha said,[15]

If you bhikṣus seek a wise friend, if you seek good protection and support, there is nothing like not neglecting mindfulness. In those who do not neglect mindfulness, the bandits of the afflictions cannot enter. Therefore, you should always concentrate your thoughts and be mindful. Those who lose mindfulness lose merit. If one's mindfulness is firm and strong, one will not be harmed even amidst the bandits of the five desires. It is like entering enemy ranks while wearing armor: one feels no fear. This is called "not neglecting mindfulness."

[T12:12]
六者修禪定。住法不亂、名曰禪定。

6) Practicing meditation.[16] *Abiding in the dharma without distraction is called "meditation."*

[T12:13]
佛言、汝等比丘、若攝心者、心則在定。心在定故、能知世間生滅法相。是故汝等、常當精勤、修習諸定。若得定者、心則不散。譬如防水之家、善治堤塘。行者亦爾。爲智慧水故、善修禪定、令不漏失。是名爲定。

The Buddha said,[17]

Bhikṣus, if you gather the mind, it will be in concentration. Because it is in concentration, it can know the marks of the dharmas of the arising and ceasing of the world. Therefore, you should diligently practice the concentrations. If you attain concentration, the mind will not be scattered. It is like a household protecting its water supply by properly maintaining its banks. Practitioners are like this: for the sake of the water of wisdom, they properly practice meditation, so that none will leak out. This is called "concentration."

15　**The Buddha said** (*butsu gon* 佛言): Quoting the *Fo yijiao jing* 佛遺教經 (T.389.12:1111c21-25).

16　**Practicing meditation** (*shu zenjō* 修禪定): The virtue of "meditation" or "concentration" (S. *dhyāna, samādhi*). Quoting the *Dasheng yi zhang* 大乘義章 (T.1851.44:735a16, 20-21).

17　**The Buddha said** (*butsu gon* 佛言): Quoting the *Fo yijiao jing* 佛遺教經 (T.389.12:1111c26-1112a1).

[T12:14] {2:455}

七者修智慧。起聞思修證、爲智慧。

7) Cultivating wisdom.[18] The arousing of hearing, considering, practicing, and verifying is wisdom.

[T12:15]

佛言、汝等比丘、若有智慧、則無貪著。常自省察、不令有失。是則於我法中、能得解脱。若不爾者、既非道人、又非白衣、無所名也。實智慧者、則是度老病死海堅牢舩也、亦是無明黒闇大明燈也、一切病者之良薬也、伐煩惱樹之利斧也。是故汝等、當以聞思修慧、而自增益。若人有智慧之照、雖是肉眼、而是明見人也。是名智慧。

The Buddha said,[19]

Bhikṣus, if you have wisdom, you will have no craving or attachment. By constant self-reflection, you will prevent it from being lost. Thus, you can attain liberation in my dharma. Otherwise, you are neither a wayfarer nor white-robed, one for whom there is no name.[20] True wisdom is a sturdy boat that ferries one across the sea of old age, sickness, and death; it is a bright lamp in the darkness of ignorance; the good medicine for all who are ill; a sharp axe to cut down the tree of the afflictions. Therefore, you should enhance your benefits through the wisdoms of hearing, considering, and practicing. A person with the illumination of wisdom is a person that sees clearly, even with the physical eyes.[21] This is called "wisdom."

---

18 **Cultivating wisdom** (*shu chie* 修智慧): The virtue of "wisdom" (S. *prajñā*). Quoting the *Dasheng yi zhang* 大乘義章 (T.1851.44:735a16, 21). Our text here obscures the definition in the original, which gives the traditional formula of three types of *prajñā*: hearing (*mon* 聞; S. *śruta*), considering (*shi* 思; S. *cintā*), and practicing (*shu* 修; S. *bhāvanā*):

起聞思修説爲智慧。

To arouse hearing, considering, and practicing is called "wisdom."

19 **The Buddha said** (*butsu gon* 佛言): Quoting the *Fo yijiao jing* 佛遺教經 (T.389.12:1112a2-9), with slight variation.

20 **wayfarer** (*dōnin* 道人); **white-robed** (*byakue* 白衣): I.e., Buddhist practitioner and layperson, respectively.

21 **even with the physical eyes** (*nikugen* 肉眼): The sūtra has here "even without the deva eye" (*tengen* 天眼; S. *divya-cakṣus*; i.e., paranormal vision). See Supplementary Notes, s.v. "Eye."

T12. The 8 Understandings of the Great Person *Hachi dainin gaku* 八大人覺　307

[T12:16] {2:456}

八者不戲論。證離分別、名不戲論。究盡實相、乃不戲論。

8) Not engaging in frivolous discourse.[22] *Realizing freedom from discrimination is called "not engaging in frivolous discourse."*

Exhaustively investigating the real marks is not engaging in frivolous discourse.[23]

[T12:17]

佛言、汝等比丘、若種種戲論、其心則亂。雖復出家、猶未得脱。是故比丘、當急捨離亂心・戲論。汝等若欲得寂滅樂者、唯當善滅戲論之患。是名不戲論。

The Buddha said,[24]

Bhikṣus, if you engage in all sorts of frivolous discourse, your minds will be confused. Even if you have left home, you will still not attain liberation. Therefore, bhikṣus, you should quickly abandon the confused mind and frivolous discourse. If you wish to attain the bliss of extinction, you should fully extinguish the troubles of frivolous discourse. This is called "not engaging in frivolous discourse."

* * * * *

[T12:18]

これ八大人覺なり。＜一一各具八、すなはち六十四あるべし。ひろくするときは無量なるべし、略すれば六十四なり。＞大師釋尊、最後之説、大乘之所教誨之至極、二月十五日夜半の極唱。これよりのち、さらに説法しまさず、ついに般涅槃しまします。

These are the eight understandings of the great person. (Each one of these includes the other eight, which would make sixty-four. Fully expanded, they would be incalculable; abbreviated, they are sixty-four.)[25] *They are the last words of Great Master Śākya, the Honored One, the ultimate teaching of the Great Vehicle,* his ultimate song in the middle

---

22　**Not engaging in frivolous discourse** (*fukeron* 不戲論): The virtue of avoidance of prolixity (S. *prapañca*, etc.). Quoting the *Dasheng yi zhang* 大乘義章 (T.1851.44:735a16-17, 21-22).

23　**Exhaustively investigating the real marks** (*gūjin jissō* 究盡實相): A comment in Chinese added by Dōgen, reflecting a line in the *Lotus Sūtra*; see Supplementary Notes, s.v. "Only buddhas with buddhas can exhaustively investigate the real marks of the dharmas."

24　**The Buddha said** (*butsu gon* 佛言): Quoting the *Fo yijiao jing* 佛遺教經 (T.389.12:1112a10-13).

25　**Each one of these includes the other eight** (*ichiichi kaku gu hachi* 一一各具八): The two sentences in parentheses here represent an interlinear note in the MS.

308 DŌGEN'S *SHŌBŌGENZŌ* VOLUME VI

of the night on the fifteenth of the second month.[26] Thereafter, he did not preach the dharma again and finally entered *parinirvāṇa*.

[T12:19]

佛言、汝等比丘、常當一心勤求出離道。一切世間動・不動法、皆是敗壞不安之相。　汝且止、而勿得復語。時欲將過、我欲滅度。是我最後之所教誨。

The Buddha said,[27]

Bhikṣus, you should always single-mindedly strive diligently to seek the way out of here. The dharmas of all worlds, whether changing or unchanging, are all marked by decomposition and instability.[28]

But stop now, do not speak further. The time has come for me to pass into extinction. These are my final instructions.

[T12:20] {2:457}

このゆえに、如來の弟子は、必ずこれを習學したてまつる、これを修習せず、しらざらんは、佛弟子にあらず。これ如來の正法眼藏涅槃妙心なり。

Therefore, the disciples of the Tathāgata invariably study this. Those who do not study it, who do not know it, are not disciples of the Buddha. This is "the treasury of the true dharma eye, the wondrous mind of nirvāṇa" of the Tathāgata.[29]

[T12:21]

しかあるに、いましらざるものはおほく、見聞せることあるものはすくなきは、魔嬈によりてしらざるなり。また宿殖善根すくなきもの、きかず、みず。むかし正法・像法のあひだは、佛弟子みな、これをしれり、修學し參學しき。いまは千比丘のなかに、一・兩、この八大人覺しれるものなし。あはれむべし、澆季の陵夷、たとふるにものなし。如來の正法、いま

26　**last words of Great Master Śākya, the Honored One** (*Daishi Shakuson saigo shi setsu* 大師釋尊最後之説): Dōgen here switches to Chinese to expand on the final sentence of the *Fo yijiao jing* 佛遺教經 (T.389.12:1112b20-21) that he will quote in the next section.

his ultimate song in the middle of the night on the fifteenth of the second month (*nigatsu jūgonichi yahan no gokushō* 二月十五日夜半の極唱): I.e., the Buddha's ultimate teaching on the night traditionally given for his death, in the year 949 BC.

27　**The Buddha said** (*butsu gon* 佛言): Quoting the final lines of the *Fo yijiao jing* 佛遺教經 (T.389.12:1112b18-21).

28　**dharmas of all worlds, whether changing or unchanging** (*issai seken dō fudō hō* 一切世間動・不動法): I.e., dharmas of the fluctuating realm of desire (*yokkai* 欲界; S. *kāma-dhātu*) and the stable realms of form (*shikikai* 色界; S. *rūpa-dhātu*) and formlessness (*mushikikai* 無色界; S. *ārūpya-dhātu*).

29　**"the treasury of the true dharma eye, the wondrous mind of nirvāṇa"** (*shōbōgenzō nehan myōshin* 正法眼藏涅槃妙心): I.e., the teaching handed down by the buddhas and ancestors, as described by the Buddha Śākyamuni in the first transmission of Zen on Vulture Peak.

T12. The 8 Understandings of the Great Person *Hachi dainin gaku* 八大人覺 309

大千に流布して、白法、いまだ滅せざらんとき、いそぎ習學すべきなり、
緩怠なることなかれ。

Nowadays, however, there are many who do not know it, few who have seen or heard it; charmed by demons, they do not know it. Again, those with sparse good roots planted in past lives do not hear it or see it. Long ago, during the true dharma and semblance dharma, the Buddha's disciples all knew it, practiced it, and studied it.[30] Nowadays, among a thousand bhikṣus, there are not even one or two who know the eight understandings of the great person. How pitiful — the deterioration in this season of decline is beyond compare.[31] Now, when the true dharma of the Tathāgata has spread throughout the chiliocosm, and the white dharma has not yet disappeared, we should hasten to study it.[32] Do not be lax or lazy.

[T12:22]

佛法にあふたてまつること、無量劫にかたし。人身をうること、またかたし。たとひ人身をうくるといへども、三洲の人身よし。そのなかに、南洲の人身すぐれたり、見佛・聞法・出家・得道するゆえなり。如來の般涅槃よりさきに涅槃にいり、さきだちて死せるともがらは、この八大人覺をきかず、ならはず。いまわれら、見聞したてまつり、習學したてまつる、宿殖善根のちからなり。いま習學して生生に増長し、かならず無上菩提にいたり、衆生のためにこれをとかむこと、釋迦牟尼佛にひとしくして、ことなることなからむ。

To encounter the buddha dharma is difficult, even in innumerable kalpas. To receive a human body is likewise difficult. And even while having received a human body, it is good to have a human body of the three continents; and, among them, the human body of the southern continent is best, for we can see the Buddha and hear his dharma, leave home and gain the way.[33] Those who entered nirvāṇa before the Buddha's *parinirvāṇa*, who

---

30 **true dharma and semblance dharma** (*shōbō zōhō* 正法・像法): The first two of the three stages in a common reckoning of the degeneration of the dharma: true, semblance, and final dharma (*shō zō mappō* 正像末法). The period of the "true dharma" (*shōbō* 正法) was most often taken as the first thousand years following the *parinirvāṇa* of the Buddha; the "semblance dharma" (*zōhō* 像法), during which there was practice but no longer attainment of awakening, was said to last an additional one thousand years; during the "final dharma" (*mappō* 末法), lasting ten thousand years, there was neither authentic practice nor awakening. Based on the traditional East Asian Buddhist reckoning of the date of Śākyamuni's *parinirvāṇa* as 949 BCE, the final dharma was thought to have begun in 1052 CE.

31 **season of decline** (*gyōki* 澆季): Reference to the final, decadent age of the dharma, following the periods of the true and semblance dharma.

32 **white dharma** (*byakuhō* 白法): I.e., the good, buddha dharma (S. *śukla-dharma*), as opposed to dark, evil teachings.

33 **three continents** (*sanshū* 三洲): Three of the four continents surrounding Mount Sumeru that make up a Buddhist world system, excluding the northern continent of Uttarakuru (*Kurushū* 倶盧洲), where life is so long and easy that its denizens have little ex-

died before him, did not hear, did not learn these eight understandings of the great person; that we now see and hear them, learn and study them is due to the power of good roots planted in past lives. Learning and studying them now, we enhance them in life after life; we shall surely reach unsurpassed bodhi and teach them to living beings. In this, we shall be the same as Buddha Śākyamuni, without any difference from him.

正法眼藏八大人覺第十二

Treasury of the True Dharma Eye
The Eight Understandings of the Great Person
Number 12

[Yōkōji MS:]

彼本奥書曰、建長五年正月六日、書于永平寺

*The colophon of the manuscript says, "Written at Eiheiji; sixth day,
first month, fifth year of Kenchō [5 February 1253]"*[34]

今應永廿七稔孟夏上旬日、於永安精舍衣鉢閣下拜書之

*Respectfully copied this in the Robe and Bowl Hall of Eian Vihāra; first
third, early summer [4th month], twenty-seventh year of Ōei [May 1420]*[35]

于時文安三年三月八日、能州藏見保於藥師堂書之。之意趣者、以此良
結緣、生生世世、見佛聞法、出家得道、供養三寶、濟度衆生、成等正
覺。永平末流小新戒比丘

*Copied this in the Yakushi Hall, Kurumi Estate, Noshū; eighth day,
third month, third year of Bun'an [4 April 1446]. My aspiration is that,
by these favorable karmic conditions, birth after birth and lifetime after lifetime, I will see a buddha and hear the dharma, leave home and
attain the way, make offerings to the three treasures, deliver living beings, and attain perfect awakening. A newly ordained bhikṣu, humble
descendant of Eihei*[36]

[*Himitsu* MS:]

彼本奥書曰、建長五年正月六日書永平寺
如今建長七年乙卯解制之前日、令義演書記書寫畢。同一挍之

---

perience of the first sacred truth of suffering (and, hence, no aptitude for Buddhism). The southern continent of Jambudvīpa (*Enbudai* 閻浮提) is considered especially auspicious, since it is there that buddhas appear. See Supplementary Notes, s.v. "Four Continents."

34 Presumed to be written by Ejō in reference to a colophon by Dōgen. The referent of "the manuscript" (*tahon* 彼本) is uncertain: if a reference to a MS by Dōgen, one would expect the honorific *gohon* 御本, and it may be that 彼 here is an error for 御.

35 Copyist unknown.

36 Copyist unknown.

T12. The 8 Understandings of the Great Person *Hachi dainin gaku* 八大人覺   311

右本、先師最後御病中之御草也。仰以前所撰假名正法眼藏等皆書改、
並新草具都廬一百卷、可撰之云云

The colophon of the manuscript says, "Written at Eiheiji; sixth day, first month, fifth year of Kenchō [5 February 1253]."
Now, on the day prior to the unbinding of the rule, in the junior wood year of the rabbit, the seventh year of Kenchō [17 August 1255], I had the Secretary Gien make a copy and collated them together.[37]
The preceding text is his draft composed during my former master's final illness.[38] *He said that he would rewrite all the kana Shōbōgenzō texts he had previously composed and combine them with new drafts to compose altogether one hundred chapters.*[39]

既始草之御此卷、當第十二卷也。此之後、御病漸漸重增。仍御草案等
事即止也。所以此御草等、先師最後教敕也。我等不幸不拜見一百卷之
御草、尤所恨也。若奉恋慕先師之人、必書此十二卷、而可護持之。此
釋尊最後之教敕、且先師最後之遺教也。懷奘記之。

This chapter, which he had already drafted, corresponds to the twelfth chapter. Thereafter, his illness gradually worsened, and his work on the drafts came to an end. Therefore, these drafts were my former master's final instructions.[40] *It is most regrettable that unfortunately we cannot see the drafts of the one hundred chapters. Those who cherish and admire my former master should copy this twelfth chapter and preserve it.*[41] *It is the final instruction of Buddha Śākyamuni, as well as the bequeathed teaching of my former master.*[42] *Written by Ejō*

---

37   **unbinding of the rule** (*kaisei* 解制): The last day of the summer retreat (*ango* 安居), most often occurring on the fifteenth of the seventh month.

Secretary Gien (*Gien shoki* 義演書記): D. 1314. A student of Dōgen, he became a disciple of Ejō following Dōgen's death and, in 1287, was appointed abbot of Eiheiji. The secretary (*shoki* 書記) is one of the six major monastic offices.

collated them together (*dō ikkō shi* 同一挍之): Presumably, meaning that Ejō collated Dōgen's draft with Gien's copy.

38   **his draft** (*gosō* 御草): I.e., Dōgen's draft.

39   ***kana Shōbōgenzō*** 假名正法眼藏: I.e., the *Shōbōgenzō* texts written in Japanese (presumably, as opposed to the *shinji Shōbōgenzō* 眞字正法眼藏 collection of three hundred cases in Chinese).

40   **these drafts** (*shi gosō tō* 此御草等): The reference is uncertain; usually, taken to be the twelve chapters referred to above but might also be Gien's draft and Ejō's collated draft.

41   **this twelfth chapter** (*shi jūni kan* 此十二卷): Might also be read, "these twelve chapters," though the following sentence suggests otherwise.

42   **bequeathed teaching** (*yuikyō* 遺教): Allusion to the *Fo yijiao jing* 佛遺教經 (*Sūtra of the Bequeathed Teaching of the Buddha*) quoted in this chapter.

The Sōtō Zen Text Project *Shōbōgenzō*

Volume I
The Seventy-five-Chapter Compilation, Part 1

1. The Realized Kōan *Genjō kōan* 現成公案
2. Mahā-prajñā-pāramitā *Maka hannya haramitsu* 摩訶般若波羅蜜
3. Buddha Nature *Busshō* 佛性
4. Studying the Way with Body and Mind *Shinjin gakudō* 身心學道
5. This Mind Itself Is the Buddha *Soku shin ze butsu* 即心是佛
6. Deportment of the Practicing Buddha *Gyōbutsu iigi* 行佛威儀
7. One Bright Pearl *Ikka myōju* 一顆明珠
8. The Mind Cannot Be Got *Shin fukatoku* 心不可得
9. The Old Buddha Mind *Kobutsushin* 古佛心
10. Great Awakening *Daigo* 大悟
11. Principles of Seated Meditation *Zazen gi* 坐禪儀
12. Needle of Seated Meditation *Zazen shin* 坐禪箴
13. Ocean Seal Samādhi *Kaiin zanmai* 海印三昧
14. Sky Flowers *Kūge* 空華
15. Radiance *Kōmyō* 光明

Volume II
The Seventy-five-Chapter Compilation, Part 2

16A. Sustained Practice, Part 1 *Gyōji jō* 行持上
16B. Sustained Practice, Part 2 *Gyōji ge* 行持下
17. Such *Inmo* 恁麼
18. Avalokiteśvara *Kannon* 觀音
19. The Old Mirror *Kokyō* 古鏡
20. Sometimes *Uji* 有時
21. Prediction *Juki* 授記
22. Full Function *Zenki* 全機
23. The Moon *Tsuki* 都機
24. Painted Cake *Gabyō* 畫餅
25. Sound of the Stream, Form of the Mountain *Keisei sanshoku* 谿聲山色
26. Beyond the Buddha *Butsu kōjō ji* 佛向上事
27. Talking of a Dream within a Dream *Muchū setsumu* 夢中説夢
28. Making a Bow and Getting the Marrow *Raihai tokuzui* 禮拜得髓
29. The Mountains and Waters Sūtra *Sansui kyō* 山水經
30. Sūtra Reading *Kankin* 看經

Volume III
The Seventy-five-Chapter Compilation, Part 3

31. Do No Evil *Shoaku makusa* 諸惡莫作
32. Transmitting the Robe *Den'e* 傳衣
33. Sayings *Dōtoku* 道得
34. The Teachings of the Buddhas *Bukkyō* 佛教
35. Spiritual Powers *Jinzū* 神通
36. The Arhat *Arakan* 阿羅漢

37. Spring and Autumn *Shunjū* 春秋
38. Tangled Vines *Kattō* 葛藤
39. The Inheritance Certificate *Shisho* 嗣書
40. The Cypress Tree *Hakujushi* 柏樹子
41. The Three Realms Are Only Mind *Sangai yui shin* 三界唯心
42. Talking of the Mind, Talking of the Nature *Sesshin sesshō* 説心説性
43. The Real Marks of the Dharmas *Shohō jissō* 諸法實相
44. The Way of the Buddhas *Butsudō* 佛道
45. Secret Words *Mitsugo* 密語

Volume IV
The Seventy-five-Chapter Compilation, Part 4

46. The Insentient Preach the Dharma *Mujō seppō* 無情説法
47. Sūtras of the Buddhas *Bukkyō* 佛經
48. Dharma Nature *Hosshō* 法性
49. Dhāraṇī *Darani* 陀羅尼
50. Washing the Face *Senmen* 洗面
51. Face-to-Face Conferral *Menju* 面授
52. Buddhas and Ancestors *Busso* 佛祖
53. Plum Blossoms *Baika* 梅華
54. Washing and Purifying *Senjō* 洗淨
55. The Ten Directions *Jippō* 十方
56. Seeing Buddha *Kenbutsu* 見佛
57. Extensive Study *Henzan* 遍參
58. The Eye *Ganzei* 眼睛
59. Everyday Matters *Kajō* 家常
60. The Thirty-seven Factors of Bodhi *Sanjūshichi hon bodai bunpō* 三十七品菩提分法

Volume V
The Seventy-five-Chapter Compilation, Part 5

61. Song of the Dragon *Ryūgin* 龍吟
62. The Intention of the Ancestral Master's Coming from the West
    Soshi seirai i 祖師西來意
63. Bringing Forth the Mind of Bodhi *Hotsu bodai shin* 發菩提心
64. The Udumbara Blossom *Udonge* 優曇華
65. The Entire Body of the Tathāgata *Nyorai zenshin* 如來全身
66. The King of Samādhis Samādhi *Zanmai ō zanmai* 三昧王三昧
67. Turning the Dharma Wheel *Ten hōrin* 轉法輪
68. Great Practice *Dai shugyō* 大修行
69. The Samādhi of Self Verification *Jishō zanmai* 自證三昧
70. Empty Space *Kokū* 虛空
71. The Pātra Bowl *Hou* 鉢盂
72. The Retreat *Ango* 安居
73. Reading Other Minds *Tashin tsū* 他心通
74. The King Requests Saindhava *Ō saku sendaba* 王索仙陀婆
75. Leaving Home *Shukke* 出家

Volume VI
The Twelve-Chapter Compilation

T1. The Merit of Leaving Home *Shukke kudoku* 出家功徳
T2. Receiving the Precepts *Jukai* 受戒
T3. The Merit of the Kāṣāya *Kesa kudoku* 袈裟功徳
T4. Bringing Forth the Mind of Bodhi *Hotsu bodai shin* 發菩提心
T5. Offerings to the Buddhas *Kuyō shobutsu* 供養諸佛
T6. Refuge in the Treasures of Buddha, Dharma, and Saṃgha
  Kie buppōsōbō 歸依佛法僧寶
T7. Deep Faith in Cause and Effect *Jinshin inga* 深信因果
T8. Karma of the Three Times *Sanjigō* 三時業
T9. Four Horses *Shime* 四馬
T10. The Bhikṣu of the Fourth Dhyāna *Shizen biku* 四禪比丘
T11. One Hundred Eight Gateways to the Illumination of the Dharma
  Ippyakuhachi hōmyōmon 一百八法明門
T12. The Eight Understandings of the Great Person *Hachi dainin gaku* 八大人覺

Volume VII
Supplementary Chapters, Variant Texts

Supplementary Chapters

S1. Talk on Pursuing the Way *Bendōwa* 辦道話
S2. Procedures for the Hall of Gathered Clouds *Jūundō shiki* 重雲堂式
S3. The *Lotus* Turns the *Lotus Hokke ten Hokke* 法華轉法華
S4. The Mind Cannot Be Got *Shin fukatoku* 心不可得
S5. The Four Attractions of the Bodhisattva *Bodaisatta shishōbō* 菩提薩埵四攝法
S6. Instructions to the Administration Cloister *Ji kuin mon* 示庫院文
S7. Only Buddhas with Buddhas *Yui butsu yo butsu* 唯佛與佛
S8. Birth and Death *Shōji* 生死
S9. The Way of the Buddhas *Butsudō* 佛道 (*Dōshin* 道心)

Variant Texts

V1. Talk on Pursuing the Way *Bendōwa* 辦道話
V2. The Inheritance Certificate *Shisho* 嗣書
V3. Beyond the Buddha *Butsu kōjō ji* 佛向上事
V4. Washing the Face *Senmen* 洗面
V5. Extensive Study *Henzan* 遍參
V6. Great Awakening *Daigo* 大悟
V7. Karma of the Three Times *Sanji gō* 三時業

Volume VIII

Introduction
Appendices
Supplementary Notes
Works Cited